FISKE
WORD
POWER

2ND EDITION

THE MOST EFFECTIVE SYSTEM
FOR BUILDING A VOCABULARY
THAT GETS RESULTS FAST

EDWARD B. FISKE
FORMER EDUCATION EDITOR OF THE *NEW YORK TIMES*
JANE MALLISON AND MARGERY MANDELL

sourcebooks

Published by Sourcebooks, Inc.
P.O. Box 4410, Naperville, Illinois 60567-4410
(630) 961-3900
Fax: (630) 961-2168
sourcebooks.com

Library of Congress Cataloging-in-Publication Data

Names: Fiske, Edward B., author. | Mallison, Jane, author. | Mandell, Margery, author.
Title: Fiske Wordpower : the most effective system for building a vocabulary that gets results fast / Edward B. Fiske, Jane Mallison and Margery Mandell.
Other titles: Fiske word power
Description: Second edition. | Naperville, Illinois : Sourcebooks, [2018]
Identifiers: LCCN 2018007724 | ISBN 9781492650744 (Trade paperback)
Subjects: LCSH: Vocabulary. | Vocabulary--Problems, exercises, etc.
Classification: LCC PE1449 .F553 2018 | DDC 428.1--dc23 LC record available at https://lccn.loc.gov/2018007724

Printed and bound in the United States of America.
VP 10 9 8 7 6 5 4 3 2 1

CONTENTS

Acknowledgments

We both thank Grace Freedson for leading us to this project. Margery would also like to thank Mark, Jacob, Alix, and Katie Sugarman for their shared love of language and their invaluable knowledge of contemporary culture, and Charlie Pope for his wit and verbal expertise. Jane offers her gratitude to Carole France, a brilliant teacher, and gives her more-than-thanks to Kenneth Silverman, magic man with words and without.

Introduction

One's vocabulary needs constant fertilizing or it will die," wrote English novelist Evelyn Waugh. The following pages, we hope, will be the fertilizer for all those with an interest in enriching their ability to express themselves eloquently. The fact that you're reading this introduction shows that you are already motivated to improve your vocabulary. So let's take a look at how this book can help you.

We chose the one thousand and fifty-one words here from a variety of sources, including standardized tests such as the SAT, the ACT, and the GRE; the best-written newspapers and magazines in the country; and classic literature. Our goal was to create a collection of over one thousand words that will be useful for learners who may fall into one (or more) of these categories:

Short-range

You might be a student preparing for a standardized test such as the SAT, the ACT, or the GRE. If this describes you, we're here to help. If you're getting ready for the SAT, you may have heard through the grapevine that the latest revision of the test has eliminated any testing of vocabulary. Not so! Here's the fuller truth: the SAT has changed the way it tests vocabulary. Many questions will ask you about the meaning of words *in context*. Here are two examples:

1. Bartram is entertaining the idea of hiking in the Himalayas next fall.

In context, "entertaining" most nearly means which of the following?

(a) considering　(b) performing　(c) amusing　(d) providing hospitality for

The word "entertaining" can mean (a), (b), (c), or (d), but in context, it means (a). Bartram is considering the idea.

2. Studying for my physics exam required intense concentration.

In context, "intense" most nearly means which of the following?

(a) brilliant　(b) focused　(c) emotional　(d) determined

The word "intense" can mean (a), (b), (c), or (d), but in context, it means (b). Studying for the exam required focused concentration.

Working with the Practice, Practice, Practice sections of this book will increase your sensitivity to the ways in which meaning depends on context. No work you do on your vocabulary is ever wasted.

The reading comprehension sections of the SAT are more important than ever before. A strong vocabulary is your key to good performance there.

If you're contemplating the ACT or the GRE, *Fiske WordPower* is here to help. Both the overt vocabulary sections and the analogies and antonyms on the GRE will be more manageable.

Medium-range

You're primarily interested in improving your vocabulary in order to speak and write more expressively. Again, we're here to help. The wide range of subject matter covered in the 105 sections, and the fact that you're always looking at words in full context, will stock your brain with both the words you need to know to talk about many topics and with the knowledge of how to fit those words seamlessly into your sentences.

Does the conversation turn toward finance? Well, you've mastered section 80, so you're at ease. Is your rivalrous colleague slipping Gallic phrases into his dialogue with you? You're fine because section 92 is under your belt.

Long-range

You're not sure why, but you just love words and language. Maybe it was that inspiring seventh-grade teacher who taught you mnemonic devices (memory hooks) for remembering how to spell "rhythm" or "cemetery." Or maybe your parents slipped a dictionary in your crib.

Well, we're here for you too. As we'll state again later in the introduction, we're *logophiles* (lovers of words) and we're thrilled that you are too. In addition to the practical help with words in these sections, we'll be slipping you some fascinating bits of etymology and some intriguing words. For now, we'll offer you *callipygian*: we assure you it will never be on a standardized test, but you may enjoy knowing that there's a word that means "having beautiful buttocks," as in "That statue of Venus is extraordinarily callipygian." And amaze your friends with your knowledge of the etymology of *vanilla* and of *orchid*. Look it up!

Fiske WordPower does not ask you to memorize lists. In fact, it offers you a chance not to *memorize* new words but to *learn* them.

What's the difference? Memorization of words and definitions is the kind of learning satirized in Aldous Huxley's novel *Brave New World*, a dark vision of a futurist society. There, children are taught facts by listening to a recording as they sleep (the fancy term is "hypnagogia"). Thus, if they hear "The Nile is the longest river in the world" on Tuesday night, they can on Wednesday morning tell you that "the Nile is the longest river in the world." But the knowledge is purely rote—it hasn't been integrated with the other knowledge in the child's brain. If you ask them "What is the longest river in the world?" they are at a loss.

We've sometimes encountered well-meaning people with a similar approach to building their vocabulary. They acquire a list of words, often alphabetical with a brief defining phrase, and set about memorizing the list (few get past "H"). At best, they're acquiring what Garrison Keillor, in another context, calls "shallow knowingness." If you ask them to use the words in context, they are at a loss.

We will show you a better way. Using the unique method in this book, you will not just memorize the words, but truly understand them. The result is that you will learn words more effectively and remember them longer. So let's take a look at how this system works.

PATTERNS

First, we take a new approach to how and when you discover these new words. Most vocabulary builders are alphabetical, asking you to learn from A to Z. Here, however, most of the sections are organized using varying types of themes, so that learning any of the words aids you in learning the others. Various sorts of linked patterns will help you connect and remember your new words. The patterns in this book include the following:

- **Words with nearly synonymous meanings.** There are few languages as rich as English in words that have the same—well, nearly the same—meaning. By learning these words together, you will better understand how different words fit best in different contexts, and their different nuances of meaning (see sections 12 or 29 for typical examples).

- **Words on the same topic.** Other sections take a topic such as religion or theater or color and give you words used within that area. Learning them together is easier than learning them separately (see sections 42 or 61 for typical examples).

- **Words that are built the same.** A few sections have words with similar characteristics such as three-letter words or words that end with "o"; the quirkiness of their similarity will help you remember them (see section 70 for an example).

- **Words of similar origin.** Still other sections have origins in common; their ancestors were all in Greek myths or were Germans or French (see section 92 for an example).

The four sections that are exceptions to this principle of grouping are spaced at rough intervals in the book (sections 25, 52, 76, and 99), and what *they* have in common is that their titles—"Farrago," "Hodgepodge," "Gallimaufry," and "Potpourri"—are all useful variations on "assortment."

DEEPER MEANING, MORE EXAMPLES

The next step in the system is to provide more, and more useful, information about each word. We teach you each word in context, giving you two examples—often a fairly simple use paired with a more abstract example—of how the word actually works in sentences. This approach, as contrasted with the "list of words," might be compared with seeing a living animal in its natural habitat as opposed to seeing the creature isolated in a cage. It is one thing to know the definition of a word; it's another to see its subtle meanings come to life in different sentences.

We also frequently give you a nugget of information about the origin and the possibly changing meaning of the word over time. Some of you may wish to ignore those facts. But may we offer two examples here to try to encourage you to get intrigued? You may find that you remember the word *ursine* ("bear-like") because you think of the constellation of "ursa major" (the Big Bear, a.k.a. the Big Dipper). The word *accolade* (roughly, "praise" or "honor") comes from the same root as *collar*—the Latin word for "neck." The connection? Form the mental image of an Olympic athlete having a medal on a ribbon, a visible *accolade*, placed around her neck. Will you be likely to remember *accolade* when you see it again? We think so. These words are creeping into your long-term memory because you're learning them; they're becoming part of you.

ACTIVITIES

The last part of the system uses frequent activities for sizing up what you've learned so far. Not to worry, you'll be the only one to see the score.

Philosophers who specialize in studying how we know what we know (the very fancy term for this study is *epistemology*) disagree on many points about how we acquire knowledge. But everyone who works with the practical aspect of learning agrees that you'll be more likely to remember what you learn if you have early and repeated reinforcement of it. So in addition to jogging your memory through association, as described above, we have included a series of review activities.

Our plan for learning does not let you go more than three sections before you get a check-up about what you're learning. These trios are often grouped to have weightier sections matched with slightly lighter matter, so that admitting thirty new words into your brain is a less difficult process.

After every third section a Make a Match activity asks you to match fifteen to twenty of your newly acquired words with their appropriate meanings. After every ninth section, we provide you with sentences that ask you to use twenty of the words you have acquired in those sections. A "final exam" at the end of the book tests your skill in remembering and using a random sampling of one hundred of the one thousand and fifty-one words in the book. This activity involves word matching, sentence usage exercises, and a series of fun questions that test your ability to use your new vocabulary creatively and effectively within new contexts. We've included a "postscript" section of this kind of question for those who want some extra practice in critical thinking with your new words.

So that is the method we've designed to give your word power an effective and permanent boost. Let's move on now to some very specific suggestions for the *optimum* (best) way to complement your use of this book.

USING THIS BOOK EFFECTIVELY

Have you ever learned a new word and then immediately seen or heard it again? Let's say you just learned *exotic* ("out of the ordinary") and within a week you see an ad for "exotic tropical fruit drinks," hear someone talk about "traveling to exotic places," and find a reference in a history text to the fact that in the eighteenth century the English considered Italian opera "exotic entertainment." Spooky? Mystical? Weird? Not really.

The universe didn't suddenly thrust those words in your path to reward you for your new knowledge. No, it's the other way around—you noticed the word because you'd just learned it. (The same phenomenon occurs when people plan to buy, say, a used car or an engagement ring. Suddenly their worldview becomes newly aware that some cars have two doors and some have four, that Aunt Tilda has a huge pear-shaped diamond.) In short, you're developing what we call strong verbal antennae, an ability to sense what you earlier ignored. These antennae will be your new best friends. If writers are, as novelist Henry James suggested, people "on whom nothing is lost," then alpha students of vocabulary are people on whom no word is lost. If you see it, learn it. If you hear it, learn it. If you learn it, use it.

The system in this book is designed to help you fully learn the one thousand and fifty-one words inside. However, there are many things you can, and should, do to make the process easier as well as to learn new words that aren't even in this book.

Rule #1: Get the proper tools.

No wordsmith worthy of the name will be without a good dictionary—or maybe even dictionaries. If it's possible, have several—one at home, one at school or in your workplace, and maybe even a portable dictionary to carry with you so you can check a meaning whenever you come across a word that pleases you.

Rule #2: Don't be shy.

If someone uses a word you don't know, ask what it means. When the father of your best friend says he's tired of hearing people *pontificate*, you can quickly learn that it means "speaking in a preachy manner." No, people won't think you're stupid for asking; they'll feel good about teaching you something.

Rule #3: Find a way to capture those exotic new words.

Maybe you'll carry a small notebook with you and jot them down quickly. If you prefer an electronic device, that's fine too. Just don't let them get away. Then, be sure to follow through with the next step—learning the meaning of your new words. (See the box on pages 8 to 10 for some suggestions to make this process easier.)

Rule #4: Consider the possibility of a study buddy.

If you know someone who's also motivated to build his or her vocabulary, ask that person to study with you. The same principle that has made Weight Watchers successful for dieters can build your word power. Studying with another person can keep you motivated and make practicing the recommended techniques more fun. For example, your fellow Word Watcher may know some of the words on your list (see Rule #2), saving you the effort of looking them up; similarly, your partner can share his or her list of new words with you.

Rule #5: Employ *interstitial* learning.

This fancy adjective refers to "space between cracks," in this case, small spaces of time. Study whenever you have a small bit of time. You'll be amazed how studying whenever you have a little bit of time can add up. A successful book for students in graduate school is called *Writing Your Dissertation in Fifteen Minutes a Day*. If someone a little older than you can write a long scholarly treatise using such a method, you can build your vocabulary in even smaller units of time. So however silly it may initially feel, get out that list, those cards (see Rule #6 below), while you're waiting for the bus or sitting in the dentist's waiting room. Your new bits of knowledge will add up quickly.

Rule #6: Different techniques.

Try several techniques for getting newly noticed words into your memory, into your vocabulary. Learning styles differ from person to person, and you'll be able to determine fairly quickly what works best for you.

Flash Cards. A system of flash cards (3" x 5") with one word per card, definition on the back of the card, offers little in novelty, but its familiarity doesn't cancel out its effectiveness. Your ever-growing pack can fit in your bookbag or your pocket, readily available at a moment's notice.

Silly Sentences. Make up sentences using your new words, the sillier the better. These are even more fun if you're learning words in a partnership. You'll both remember the day you asked Max if he had done any *ancillary* reading, and after only a brief pause, he slyly replied, "Oh, yes, an *egregious* amount" (*ancillary* = extra, *egregious* = outstandingly bad).

Story Time. Think about expanding the sentence idea into the writing of a little story. You don't have to write it down. You can just run it through your head while you're brushing your teeth. Take twenty words you're trying to master and see how many you can use in retelling, say, an old fairy tale or the plot of a movie you just saw. Little Red Riding Hood will find herself in an *umbrageous* (shaded) area with a *nefarious* (wicked) wolf waiting to *accost* (suddenly speak to) her. Or, the *virile* (manly) actor will be planning to *avenge* (get revenge for) the wrong done to his *pulchritudinous* (beautiful) sister. What happens next in each of these scenarios? What new words can you use to build the plot?

Mnemonic Devices. Employ *mnemonic* devices (memory tricks) whenever they come to you. If you fix *ravenous* (very hungry) in your head by thinking of some really hungry black birds, no representative of the Word Police is going to come arrest you for ignoring the fact that the adjective doesn't come from the name of the bird. Don't censor your silly associations; if they walk into your mind, they'll help you remember. Watch that *saturnine* (gloomy) man get into his Saturn and be unhappy that he's out of gas!

Root Words. While your mnemonic devices can float free of the root meanings of words, do help yourself another way by building some knowledge in this area. For example, if you learn that "pli" is a root referring to bending or folding (think "two-ply" tissues), then you've smoothed the road to learning *implicate, explicate, implicit, explicit, complicate, supplication, pliant,* and some other "pli" cousins. If you're lucky enough to have experience with a foreign language such as Latin, Spanish, or French in your present or your past, you can make strong connections with words you've learned in that area.

Prefixes and Suffixes. Similarly, mastering some basic prefixes and suffixes can help. If you know that "a" at the start of many words means "absence of" (think of *amoral*—absence of morals—or *apathy*—absence of feelings), you'll be ready to make some informed guesses. (If I approach the world in an *ahistorical* manner, am I a dedicated student of the past?) Likewise, if I think how insecticide kills insects, I'm set up to conquer *homicide, fratricide, genocide,* and *regicide* (killing of a person, a brother, a group of people related in some way, a king).

Read. Read. Read. Read. We can't say it too many times. (Read.) Just as runners training for a marathon fare better if they start their training early, those who've been dedicated readers for several years have automatically deposited lots of words and their contexts into their personal memory banks. Those lucky people may not need to do any formal vocabulary study at all. But it's never too late to start. Read in a mindful way, trying to guess at the meaning of the unfamiliar words you see. If you read "The exhausted parent yelled at the *fractious* child," you know that "fractious" doesn't mean "cute" or "sweet" or "smart"! Some readers like to look up words they can't guess at as they go along in their reading. Others find that process disruptive and choose to jot down the words and look them all up later. See which is best for you.

Rule #7: Use this book.

Use it on its own. Use it in connection with your dictionary. Use it to practice many of the rules and techniques described above. We hope this book will expand your verbal worldview. You may already know many of the words in this book well; others you may find familiar but be uncertain of their meanings; still others may sound completely, well, exotic. By providing you with one thousand and fifty-one useful words, we hope to help you develop world-class antennae for words. You'll pay more attention to them when you come across them in books or magazines or newspapers or when you hear them in conversations. Learning the history of many of these words and seeing them all displayed in sentences will help you not only to remember them but to use them as well.

You're lifting words off the *arid* (dry) page and planting them in your own private garden plot of words. In short, you're claiming these words, marking them as your own through the techniques that help you learn them. You're ready to plunge into the first of the three major divisions of the book: Consciousness, Competence, and Mastery.

So, congratulate yourself on beginning your learning, whatever your motives may be. As an ideal we hope to nudge you toward being thrilled to learn, say, that "nice" originally meant "ignorant" or that a "bonfire" was once "a fire of bones" or that "struthious" means "pertaining to ostriches." But we're English teachers and lifelong *logophiles* (lovers of words). For now we're content that you're becoming a student of words, that you've taken the first step toward nurturing a thriving vocabulary.

Okay, enough *pontificating*. On the next page you'll see an impromptu activity, one where you can test yourself on the words you learned almost accidentally while reading this section of the book. We used more than twenty-five words that, by our guess, you may not have already known. If you were waving those antennae about as you read, we're betting you learned a few, maybe several. Did you? If so, think about what made these words stick in your mind. If you can do a little analysis of this sort, you're beginning to understand how *you* learn words, and that understanding gives you a head start at continuing to build your word power.

Remember you're strongly interested here in how you learned these words, however many or few that may be. Consider learning in a separate study session all those you didn't learn the first time around. Answers for all activities in this book can be found in the back of the book.

1. **accolade**
   (a) a refreshing drink (b) closeness (c) an honor (d) assistance

2. **ahistorical**
   (a) lacking a sense of the past (b) relating to time (c) pertaining to a diary (d) relating to the marketplace

3. **amoral**
   (a) romantic (b) lacking a sense of ethics (c) superior (d) longing for food

4. **ancillary**
   (a) shaded (b) extra (c) hopeful (d) related to business

5. **apathy**
   (a) disturbance (b) most direct route (c) absence of feeling (d) ability to learn quickly

6. **arid**
   (a) loss (b) cow-like (c) superior (d) dry

7. **avenge**
   (a) to return home (b) to come when called (c) to speak loudly (d) to get back at

8. **egregious**
   (a) half-hearted (b) talkative (c) outstandingly bad (d) sociable

9. **exotic**
   (a) hard of hearing (b) former (c) out of the ordinary (d) clumsy

10. **fractious**
    (a) badly behaved (b) mathematically talented (c) broken (d) high-achieving

11. **fratricide**
    (a) killing of a brother (b) great hunger (c) absence of feeling (d) excessive partying

12. **genocide**
    (a) DNA experimentation (b) lack of specific information (c) murder of a related group (d) intense dislike

13. **impromptu**
   (a) lacking an appetite (b) devilish (c) lacking money (d) without preparation

14. **interstitial**
   (a) disapproving (b) between the cracks (c) confidential (d) lacking adequate evidence

15. **mnemonic**
   (a) extra (b) relating to memory (c) disobedient (d) like a devil

16. **nefarious**
   (a) closely related (b) outstanding (c) manly (d) wicked

17. **pliant**
   (a) unhappy (b) not rigid (c) not transparent (d) roaming at night

18. **pontificate**
   (a) to pray (b) to argue (c) to adopt a preachy tone (d) to delight in hardship of others

19. **pulchritudinous**
   (a) having a good memory (b) related to mass murder (c) beautiful (d) tiny

20. **ravenous**
   (a) very hungry (b) shallow (c) rude (d) poetic

21. **regicide**
   (a) gloominess (b) killing of a king (c) wickedness (d) extravagant spending

22. **saturnine**
   (a) gloomy (b) astronomical (c) alternative (d) inactive

23. **umbrageous**
   (a) boastful (b) slimy (c) cooperative (d) shaded

24. **virile**
   (a) sick (b) manly (c) speaking well (d) disturbed

Short Words

W e often think of new additions to our vocabulary as likely to be polysyllabic, but these one-syllable words can do the job of refreshing your word hoard.

1. **blanch** (rhymes with ranch) This verb describes the process of becoming pale or white, often from fear. From the French adjective meaning "the soaking of almonds to remove their outer layer of tan," it keeps one specialized kitchen sense: it's used in recipes that require the process of boiling a food briefly.

- Jerome's face **blanched** when the principal's secretary stopped him in the hall and told him to report to the office immediately.

- The chef leeched the bitterness out of the kale by **blanching** it before cooling it and pairing it with bacon.

2. **cull** (rhymes with dull) This verb is used to describe the process of selecting a variety of examples from many sources. Its roots go back to the Latin word for "collect." In the mid-twentieth century, the word took on a specific use describing the reduction of the number of animals in a group in order to ensure the survival of the others.

- Louis **culled** his favorite poems from anthologies in English, Latin, and Spanish.

- The state officials received emails of both praise and horror for their new policy allowing one day a year for hunters to shoot Canada geese in order to **cull** the flock.

3. **doff** (rhymes with off) This old word with the simple meaning of removal of clothing—"do off"—is often associated with its partner word **don**—"do on" or "put on." Scholars of the English language say that both verbs were limited to the speech of the uneducated until the nineteenth century novels of Sir Walter Scott returned them to respectability. (They both retain a "literary feel.")

- The man with impeccable manners **doffed** his hat when he met his landlady on the stairway.

- Can you name the Christmas carol containing the line "**Don** we now our gay apparel"?

4. **flout** (rhymes with out) This verb describes the action of ignoring a law or rule (or something similar) with no sense of embarrassment. Don't confuse this word with **flaunt**—"to show off."

- Despite the arrogant politician's **flouting** of the custom of showing respect to one's opponent, he triumphed in the election.
- The lottery winner **flaunted** his winnings with the purchase of a bright-red sports car.

5. **fraught** (rhymes with ought) The appearance of this word suggests the fact that it's a relative of the word "freight." Literally meaning "loaded" or "supplied with," the word is now used in the figurative sense of "full of stated or implied danger or awkwardness."

- When the *Mayflower* set out on its journey from the Netherlands to the New World, the situation was **fraught** with peril.
- When Agamemnon asked for volunteers to fight hand-to-hand with Hector, there was a **fraught** silence before burly Ajax stepped forward.

6. **limn** (rhymes with trim) Originally, this verb referred to illuminating a manuscript with drawings and designs. Now, it has the blander meaning of representing something in images or in words.

- Speaking to the families of students hoping to enter a summer program in Tahiti, the enthusiastic lecturer **limned** a summer experience full of learning, deepening friendships, and water sports.
- The moon, shining through the branches of the sycamore tree, **limned** a pattern that was both beautiful and ominous.

7. **mete** (rhymes with eat) This verb is virtually always used with "out." "Mete out" means "to dole out, or to give, in a carefully measured way." Pleasant things are seldom dealt with in so stingy a manner.

- In the underworld depicted by the poet Dante, Minos **metes** out to sinners their precise punishment; he indicates the circle where they should go by wrapping his tail around himself a certain number of times.
- As a Sunday afternoon treat, the stern father **meted** out to each child exactly four cashew nuts.

8. **riff** (rhymes with if) This word can be a noun or a verb. Its original meaning comes from the world of jazz; as a noun, it refers to a variation on a previously known musical phrase. As a verb, "to riff" has flexible meanings ranging from doing a variation, to playing with a concept, to talking nonstop on a subject.

- The playwright Tom Stoppard's **riff** on *Hamlet* involves making two minor characters into the protagonists.

- One of James Baldwin's novels depicts musicians sitting around trading memories of **riffs** they've played.

9. **roil** (rhymes with oil) This verb bears the meaning "to stir up," "to upset." The meaning can be literal or figurative. In American usage you'll also hear the dialect verb "to **rile**," (usually paired with "up") offering the same meaning but in a figurative sense.

- Theodore Roosevelt may have been our most athletic president: he once dived over and over again into a **roiling** river, seemingly without fear.

- Mary Jo gets **riled** up whenever anyone refers to the existence of her ex-husband.

10. **sap** (rhymes with tap) Slang offers this word as a noun meaning "an idiot," "a dope." More formally, this noun refers to the fluid in a plant. More interesting is the formal English verb "to sap." Its basic meaning is "to weaken or destroy." The roots of the word come from the practice in warfare of digging a trench toward an enemy's position using a spade (Latin: *sappa*).

- Encouragement can build your confidence, but constant negative comments can **sap** it.

- Jorge is a very robust man, but being the sole caretaker of his invalid wife has **sapped** his energy.

Even Shorter Words

I f you thought the words in the previous section were short, see if you know these three-letter words!

1. ape (rhymes with tape) No, not the animal, but the verb "to ape." It describes the action of attempting an overly exact imitation and ending up with negative or laughable results. Memory hint: think of the animal ape attempting to, say, tango.

- Find your own style of playing tennis; don't try to **ape** Venus or Serena.
- Max, a junior high student, was **aping** his college student sister when he used many long words in his paper, but the result made his classmates snicker.

2. dun (rhymes with sun) Usually used as a verb meaning to insist on the payment of a debt.

- His creditors have been **dunning** Mr. Gooch for weeks. If he doesn't pay, he faces the threat of legal action.
- The **dunning** letter was so harshly worded that it was insulting to Mr. Beason.

("Dun" can also be used to refer to a brownish gray color, as in "a dun horse," but you're not going to see that much these days.)

3. fop (rhymes with mop) It's a noun, always critical and always reserved for males. (Don't worry about discrimination, guys; there are even more negative words reserved for females.) It's used for a man who, in a mainstream opinion, is too concerned with his looks and his clothes.

- While Frank has great taste in clothes and a closet full of cool clothing, no one would ever call him a **fop**.
- In eighteenth-century England many men with money wore patterned silk vests, velvet jackets, and shirts with cuffs of lace. Anyone dressing like that today would be laughed at and deemed a **fop**.

4. gad (rhymes with sad) As a verb, it means to move about, travel, usually in a kind of aimless way. Usually mildly critical but not related to the old-fashioned expression "Ye gads!"

- Ashley has been **gadding** all over the country, trying to decide what colleges she wants to apply to.
- **Gadding** about to different malls to compare sneaker prices can waste a lot of time and gas money.

5. **hex** (rhymes with flex) You don't want to tangle with it because it means "an evil spell" when it's used as a noun or "to put an evil spell on someone" when it's used as a verb. (Maybe you've heard of "hex signs" on barns in some areas of the country. They're designed to ward off your enemy's attempt to hurt you.)

- Did the three witches put a **hex** on Macbeth and cause his downfall, or was everything his own fault?
- Taylor laughingly said that she would **hex** her winning volleyball serve if she didn't wear a purple heart Band-Aid on her arm.

(Extra knowledge: a "hexagon" is not an accursed geometrical figure. It's just a coincidence that classical Greek "hexa" means "six.")

6. **ken** (rhymes with hen) Yes, it's Barbie's boyfriend, but also much more. Usually a noun, "ken" refers to your understanding, the limits of your knowledge.

- When my Latin teacher was asked his opinion of Coldplay, he replied, "I'm afraid that question is beyond my **ken**."
- The poet John Keats describes the sense of delight and wonder of an astronomer when some new planet "swims into his **ken**."

7. **pox** (rhymes with socks) A rather old-fashioned noun meaning bad luck. You'll still hear the phrase "A pox on you" as a kind of humorous curse. You'll also hear it used as a part of a word for a viral disease like smallpox, chickenpox, or a new variety called monkeypox. Such a disease is certainly bad luck because it can put "pocks" or pockmarks on your body. (Before our time, "pox" was often used as a "polite term" for a sexually transmitted disease.)

- When Margot was reminded of last year's boyfriend, who treated her shabbily, she elegantly responded, "A **pox** on him! I've moved on."
- Harry was waiting anxiously for the results of tests to learn if he had contracted **monkeypox**.

8. **sow** As a verb, this is an agricultural term pronounced to rhyme with row and meaning to plant a seed, literally or figuratively. (Did you sow in the row?) As a noun, it rhymes with cow, but refers to a different creature, the female pig. (Did you feed the cow after you fed the sow?) It can't be a coincidence that the traditional call for a pig is "Soo-eeeee!"

- Scott hasn't heard the committee's response to his proposal yet, but he thinks he **sowed** the seed of the idea on fertile ground.

- Sylvia Plath writes of a **sow** in the north of England voracious enough to consume the whole earth. (As you can guess, "voracious" means "hungry.")

9. **vex** (rhymes with flex) To annoy or perplex. It's more often used for small matters than serious concerns. (Would you be vexed if someone hexed you with a variety of pox?)

- The noise of the dripping faucet was a **vexation** to Will as he tried to finish the daily crossword puzzle.

- Will was **vexed** by the clue for six down. He felt sure he knew a unit of Indian currency beginning with "R" but he just couldn't remember it.

10. **vie** (rhymes with cry) A verb meaning compete, contend.

- Many years the New York Yankees and the Boston Red Sox **vie** for the right to represent the American League in the World Series.

- Tyrone and Brianna were **vying** for the title of "Master of Geographical Trivia," but Brianna triumphed when she named Canberra as the capital of Australia.

Down from Mount Olympus

3

The gods and goddesses of Greek and Roman mythology are no longer worshiped, but they live in fossil form in words like these.

1. aphrodisiac (afro DEE zee ak) The Greek goddess Aphrodite was the goddess of erotic love. She has appropriately left her mark in this word. It refers to food or drugs that allegedly make men and women feel more amorous. It can be used as a noun or an adjective.

- Mr. Parbst doesn't really believe oysters are an **aphrodisiac**, but he does give away bumper stickers saying "Oyster eaters are better lovers" at his store—a seafood market.

- For many people, poetry and music in the right setting can have more of an **aphrodisiac** effect than something like powdered rhinoceros horn.

2. chthonic (THON ik) This adjective, describing something related to forces from the underworld, won't often come out of your mouth. (But if it does, remember the "ch" is silent.) Still, you'll impress people with your knowledge of a word that begins with four consonants, and you'll be ready for the wise guy (or the textbook) that pulls the related word "autochthonous" on you. (Don't ask why, but the "c" IS pronounced in this word— say aTOKthonous.) It means, roughly, "on native ground, originating where found," as in autochthonous folktales.

- Linnell had had such a run of bad luck that she quipped, "Could **chthonic** forces be unhappy with me?"

- The doctors were not sure whether the blood clot on Henry's lung was **autochthonous** or whether it had traveled through the bloodstream and lodged there.

3. hector (HEK ter) This verb means "to bully or to try to force someone to do something." Too bad for the original Hector, the greatest warrior for Troy during the Trojan War, and really a very decent guy. The negative sense of the word came in with a mid-seventeenth-century street gang named The Hectors; others perceived them not as valiant but bullying.

- I'll be more likely to get this physics project done if you don't **hector** me about it all the time.

- The supervisor, Mr. Logan, consistently spoke in such a **hectoring** tone that his employees shuddered when he approached the office watercooler.

4. hermetic (her MET ik) Here we have an interesting adjective. It can describe something very literal, a jar so completely sealed that no air can get in. Or in past ages it was used to describe a kind of pseudo-science such as alchemy, that was "sealed off" to those who had not been given the supposed secrets. Its name came from a namesake of the Greek god Hermes, whom we know better by his Latin name Mercury. See #6.

- Ms. Fulton struggled patiently with the childproof medicine bottle before sighing and saying, "I think it is **hermetically** sealed. I'll never get it open."
- Movies such as *Young Frankenstein* give us a humorous depiction of mad scientists roaming the graveyards for body parts or hunkered over steaming lab equipment, practicing their **hermetic** art.

5. junoesque (joo no ESK) This adjective, reserved for women, is a compliment that comes via the Roman goddess Juno. It describes a woman who is unusually tall and stately and so beautiful as to seem divine. Since Juno was the wife of the head honcho Jupiter, she deserves to give her name to this word (as well as to the month of June, even today associated with weddings).

- Members of the Springfield High Film Club, who watched the 1960s film *La Dolce Vita*, enjoyed seeing the **junoesque** Anita Ekberg frolicking in a Roman fountain.
- While one of the finalists for the title of Miss America was cute and petite, the two others were positively **junoesque**.

6. mercurial (mer KYUR ee ul) The Roman god Mercury was the messenger of the gods and as such had to be very swift. Thus, his name gets given to the chemical element mercury, which can travel very fast, and to the adjective mercurial, used to describe someone whose moods change very rapidly. (If you've read *Romeo and Juliet*, think of Mercutio, who is certainly mercurial.) Two for one: a synonym would be "volatile," which comes from a root meaning "flying."

- Shakespeare's character Hamlet is very **mercurial**: one minute he's very gloomy and the next he's wisecracking with old chums.
- George's **mercurial** nature can make him fun to be around for a while, but sometimes you want him to be a little more laid back.

7. mnemonic (neh MON ik) This adjective refers to memory or relating to memory. (And do remember the "m" is silent.) You'll most often see or hear this word in the phrase "mnemonic device." The noun mnemonics refers to memory in general. If you remember your fifth grade teacher giving you the word HOMES to help you remember the Great Lakes, then you've used a mnemonic device. Mnemosyne was the Greek goddess of memory—and here's a mnemonic device to remember that fact. She was the mother of nine daughters, many of whom had four syllable names such as Terpsichore, and so she had to be the goddess of memory to remember them all.

- I find **mnemonics** fascinating: Why can I sometimes remember a person's name starts with an "S," but I can't remember the name?

- Ms. Bevilacqua loves **mnemonic** devices: she taught her seventh graders to spell "rhythm" correctly by having them chant "Ride Hard, You Thick-Headed Monster."

8. **muse, bemuse** (MYOOZ, beh MYOOZ) Maybe you already know the noun "muse," a traditional female figure of artistic inspiration. In Greek mythology there were nine such women, all daughters of Mnemosyne (see #7 above). The verb "to muse" means to lose yourself in your thoughts, perhaps awaiting inspiration. If you are "bemused," you have passively gotten to a state of unfocused thinking, again possibly to allow yourself to receive inspiration. (In short, you muse, but you are bemused.)

- Nyelle **mused** over the curriculum offerings for her senior year. Should she continue with Spanish or drop it and take psychology?

- When the music teacher put on a disk by Elgar, Sean tried to focus but soon became **bemused** and started wondering if chicken nuggets would be on the menu for lunch.

9. **odyssey** (ODD ih see) This useful noun for a long trip comes straight from that great traveler Odysseus, hero of Homer's *Odyssey*. Today it can describe a literal journey or a journey of the intellect or spirit.

- My grandparents took a world cruise to celebrate their golden wedding anniversary. What an **odyssey**! They sailed all the way around the world with stops in ports on every continent.

- Lex felt he had undergone quite an **odyssey** in his first two years of college, for he had changed his career goals as well as his philosophical outlook on life.

10. **saturnine** (SAT er nine) This adjective means gloomy or even bitterly sarcastic and mocking. The Roman god Saturn doesn't deserve such a melancholy or cynical term. Today many people happily bear his name on their cars, and in ancient times he presided over a very jolly festival (Saturnalia, late December). So think, Saturn was NOT saturnine. (This fate hit Hector as well. See #3 above.)

- The judge's **saturnine** countenance increased the nervousness of the first-year lawyer.

• Many people think of *Gulliver's Travels* as a children's book, but careful readers will easily detect the **saturnine** temperament of its author, Jonathan Swift.

MAKE A MATCH #1

Sections 1–3

Match each word in the left-hand column with the phrase on the right that best suggests its meaning. (Don't worry about the part of speech; you're just looking for a suggested meaning, not a formal definition.)

A. ape
B. blanch
C. cull
D. dun
E. fop
F. gad
G. hector
H. hermetic
I. hex
J. junoesque
K. ken
L. limn
M. mercurial
N. mnemonic
O. muse
P. odyssey
Q. sap
R. saturnine
S. vex
T. vie

1. _____ insist on payment
2. _____ imitate
3. _____ turn pale
4. _____ gloomy or sarcastic
5. _____ relate to memory
6. _____ annoy or perplex
7. _____ not a lumberjack kind of guy
8. _____ the given limits of knowledge
9. _____ a trip with many adventures
10. _____ put a spell on someone
11. _____ lose yourself in your thoughts
12. _____ remove inferior examples
13. _____ to drain of energy
14. _____ compete
15. _____ sealed very tightly
16. _____ changing mood very often
17. _____ move about aimlessly
18. _____ stately, beautiful
19. _____ bully others into action
20. _____ shape an outline of

Give and Take

4

Whether you are a "philanthropist" (someone who gives charitable assistance) or a "miser" (someone who hoards money), you'll find a word to describe yourself here.

1. magnanimous (mag NAN im us) From the Latin word meaning "great soul," this adjective means "extremely generous and forgiving" and, more generally, "courageously noble in mind and heart." The noun form, a bit of a tongue twister, is "magnanimity."

- The **magnanimous** World Series losers congratulated and sent sandwiches to their opponents.

- "It was very **magnanimous** of you to lend us your home for the party," said the leader of the prom committee. "Not many people would be comfortable with three hundred teenagers in their living room."

2. parsimonious (par sih MOAN ee us) This adjective comes from the Latin word that means "to spare" and it is the opposite of magnanimous. Someone who is parsimonious is excessively stingy. The noun form is "parsimony" (PAR sih moan ee).

- In order to save money, the **parsimonious** director of the orphanage refused to serve meat to the children more than once a week.

- Knowing her boss's **parsimony**, Nina did not ask for a raise, despite weeks of overtime work during the holidays.

3. prodigal (PROD ih gul) From the Latin word meaning "to squander," this adjective means "extremely wasteful" or "extravagant." It can also be used to mean "lavishly abundant." The noun form is "prodigality."

- The **prodigal** student spent all of his hard-earned money on extravagant gifts and parties with his friends; he had nothing left for paying the rent.

- **Prodigal** praise was heaped upon Filomena for dancing so beautifully in *Swan Lake*.

4. penurious (pen YOOR ee us) From the Latin meaning "want," this adjective means both "stingy, unwilling to spend money" and "poverty-stricken or destitute" (another good word for poor). The noun form is "penury."

- During the Great Depression, millions of Americans were reduced to a **penurious** lifestyle.

- Suffering disease, hunger, and **penury**, the homeless man sought help in a shelter; he didn't have enough money to buy himself a meal.

5. **eleemosynary** (ell ee MOS in air ee) This adjective means both "contributing to charity" and "dependent upon charity." It comes from the Latin word for "alms."

- The congressional commission doubted the proclaimed **eleemosynary** motives of the corrupt corporation.

- "This is an **eleemosynary** institution," said the director of the nursing home. "We take care of our residents and depend upon donations from social service agencies for support."

6. **frugal** (FROO gul) A good synonym for this word is "thrifty." Someone who is frugal is extremely economical.

- My **frugal** wife Betty will only use half a paper towel to wipe up a spill in the kitchen.

- Carlton was so **frugal** that he rationed his weekly earnings between food and rent, and hid all the rest under his mattress.

7. **munificent** (myoon IF ih sent) From the Latin word for "gift," this word means "very generous in giving." The noun form is "munificence."

- The knights were eager to help the generous king, famous for granting **munificent** rewards.

- Thanks to the **munificence** of the Parent Association, our school will be able to build a new library next year.

8. **avaricious** (av ar ISH iss) This adjective means "greedy" or "desirous of gain." A nice synonym is "cupidity," which also means "to want something too much." The noun form is "avarice."

- "Don't be so **avaricious**!" Nick shouted at his brother. "You've kept all of the books, video games, and toys in your room, and you've left nothing for me. Why do you think everything our parents have given to us belongs to you?"

- Known for his **avarice**, the store manager only offered his salespeople a nominal commission and kept the rest as personal profit.

9. **mean** (MEEN) Though we all know this adjective to mean (connote) "nasty and disagreeable," it also belongs in this section because another meaning is "miserly and stingy" or "low in value."

- *Gangs of New York* depicts the **mean** circumstances of Irish immigrants living in the Five Points section of New York City.

- By Mr. Fagin's **mean** calculations, the company didn't have enough money to pay anything but minimum wage, but the company's high stock value suggested otherwise.

10. **indulgent** (in DULL jent) Although the word indulgence has several meanings (including "the remission of punishment for a sin," according to the Roman Catholic Church), the adjective mostly means "lenient" or "willing to gratify."

- "Sure I will buy you a pony," said the **indulgent** grandfather. "And you can have everything else you ask for because I love you so much."

- "Please **indulge** me for a few minutes," said the angry mother, "and tell me why you came home so late last night."

The Menagerie

5

Most of us already know "feline" for cats and "canine" for dogs. Here's an expanded list for the menagerie (a collection of animals on display).

1. **equine** (EE kwine) This adjective describes anything bearing the characteristics of horses, asses, or zebras. Equestrian, on the other hand, is an adjective that describes anything having to do with horseback riding. (An equestrian is also a man who rides horses while an equestrienne is a woman horseback rider.)

    • **Equine** studies is a branch of the veterinary field that involves the care and treatment of horses and horse-related illnesses.

    • This store specializes in **equestrian** products such as saddles, reins, bits, and blankets.

2. **bovine** (BO vine) This adjective means "of or relating to the characteristics of cows, oxen, or buffaloes." It also means "sluggish and dull"—like the behavior of most cows.

    • The veterinarian specialized in **bovine** diseases because most of the families in the area were dairy farmers.

    • With a **bovine** expression on his face, the child stared blankly at the television screen and munched on a cookie.

3. **lupine** (LOO pine) This adjective means ravenous (extremely hungry) or rapacious (greedily taking by force), that is, having the characteristics of a wolf.

    • The **lupine** crowd attacked the platters of cheeses and hors d'oeuvres as if they hadn't eaten in weeks.

4. **ursine** (ER sine) Here's the adjective that means "bear-like," usually a physical description.

    • The rather **ursine** man was tall and husky. He had a bushy beard and a thick head of dark curls.

5. **porcine** (POR sine) The adjective means "resembling a swine or a pig, either physically or behaviorally." The sentence below reveals both meanings.

- Stuffing an assortment of meats and cheeses into his **porcine** face, the obese man smiled contentedly at the buffet table and contemplated going back for more.

6. **simian** (SIM ee an) Anyone who resembles an ape or a monkey might be described by the adjective "simian."

- With **simian** intensity, the mother sat before her child and carefully picked the leaves and sticks from his hair.

7. **serpentine** (SUR pen tine) This adjective means "snake-like in behavior (sly and tempting) or physically resembling a snake."

- The coastal road down to Sorrento **serpentined** along the rocky cliffs in a series of hairpin turns.
- The **serpentine** witch offered Sleeping Beauty a bright-red apple, knowing that one bite would put her to sleep for years and years.

8. **pachyderm** (PAK ah durm) This noun comes from the Greek adjective meaning "thick-skinned" and refers to the group of large, thick-skinned, hoofed animals that includes the elephant, the rhinoceros, and the hippopotamus.

- The best part of the circus is the parade of costumed **pachyderms** bearing the acrobats on their trunks.
- "You have the hands of a **pachyderm**!" exclaimed Jennifer, grasping the rough fingers of her husband, who had spent the morning gardening.

9. **avian** (AY vee an) This adjective means "having the characteristics of birds." An aviary, on the other hand, is a large structure for holding birds in confinement.

- The **avian** Michael Jordan took off from the foul line, flying to the basket for a dunk.
- There is an **aviary** at the zoo that contains brilliantly colored parrots, toucans, and peacocks.

10. **herpetology** (her pet OL oh gee) From the Greek word for "reptile," this noun denotes the study of reptiles and amphibians.

- In the **herpetology** lab at the zoo, there was quite a collection of snakes, lizards, and turtles that were used for a variety of scientific experiments.

ot surprisingly, the English language contains many words about the use of words, whether in talking or writing.

1. **laconic** (luh KON ik) Although this adjective is sometimes used to describe a writing style, it's more often used for those who say little. It derives from a Greek place name, Lakon, better known to us as Sparta. Spartans were famed for fighting, not talking.

- President Calvin Coolidge's **laconic** way of talking earned him the nickname "Silent Cal."

- Since Mrs. VanderVeen had hoped to extract details from her son about the spring break trip to Mexico, she was disappointed with his **laconic** repetition of "It was fine."

2. **taciturn** (TAS it ern) Roughly a synonym for "laconic," this adjective has a history implying an even more grudging conversational style. It derives from the Latin word meaning "silent."

- It is ironic that a Roman historian who wrote a good deal about the early Roman Empire has the name of Tacitus, for he was far from **taciturn**.

- Is there any truth to the gender stereotype that males tend to be more **taciturn** than females?

3. **lapidary** (LAP ih dare ee) The adjective characterizes precision of wording. It more often applies to writing than to speaking since a writer has more time to think of jewel-like phrasing. And, indeed, "lapidary" derives from the Latin word for "stone."

- The **lapidary** style of Abraham Lincoln's Gettysburg Address is easily contrasted with the unremembered two-hour speech by the little-remembered Edward Everett.

- Lines that are quoted often have a **lapidary** quality; for example, "To be or not to be" is more memorable than "I can't decide whether to go on living a harsh life or to remove myself from existence."

4. **pithy** (PITH ee) This is another word of compliment for a style of word use that is both brief and forceful; it can be regarding a writer or a speaker. It derives from the less-used noun "pith," which means "essence."

- Although Shakespeare's character Polonius tells us that "Brevity is the soul of wit," his own style of speaking is far from **pithy**.
- Robert Frost's poems often feature a rural speaker given to **pithy** utterances such as, "Good fences make good neighbors."

5. **succinct** (suk SINKT) This adjective describes concise speaking or writing. Literally, the word suggests your flow of words is "belted" very tightly, since it comes from a word meaning encircled, as with a sash or belt.

- Despite his subject's prolonged entreaty for aid, the cruel king responded with a **succinct** "No."
- When asked why he refused to give the requested aid, the cruel king replied equally **succinctly**, "Because."

6. **terse** (rhymes with purse) Brief, to the point. Like its five predecessors, this adjective for speaking (or writing) minimally also comes from the classics. Although it has a less Latinate sound, it comes from a Latin verb meaning "cleansed." In other words, you have "washed away" all unnecessary words.

- When the general was asked what the army would do if peace negotiations failed, he replied **tersely**, "Fight."
- This verse
  Is **terse**.

7. **garrulous** (GARR uh lus or GARR yuh lus) This adjective moves us from the stingy with words category to the other end of the spectrum, for it means talking a great deal, talking too much, going on and on. You get the idea.

- I like what Paul has to say in class, but he's just too **garrulous**; he'd be more effective if he could make his point more succinctly.
- Eliza's topics of conversation are seldom engaging in themselves, so her **garrulousness** has no redeeming qualities.

8. **prattling** (PRAT ling) This adjective comes from "to prattle," which itself comes from the verb "to prate." If you prattle, you chatter meaninglessly.

- If you **prate** at length about, say, what the weather was like each day of your vacation, you may find your friends dozing off.
- The **prattling** of a three-year-old child may please its parents because it shows the child is becoming able to communicate, but the **prattling** of a twenty-year-old pleases no one.

9. **glib** (rhymes with crib) If you speak or write in a glib manner, your words come easily—but this adjective is never a compliment. A person who is glib is always seen as, at best, speaking without enough thought and, at worst, as being insincere.

- The **glib** promises of the unscrupulous politician pleased for a short period, but ultimately the voters saw through the empty words.

- "Was I," Ramona wondered later, "under some spell when I fell for Prince Mandrake's **glib** declarations of love?"

10. **prolix** (pro LIX *or* PRO lix) More often used of writing than of speaking, "prolix" describes a wordiness of manner, a pouring forth of too many words, too many phrases. Unlike "glib," however, this adjective carries no suggestion of insincerity.

- A professional editor was hired to boil down the **prolix** manuscript to a reasonable length and thus make it more appealing to publishers.

- "I am fascinated by the decline and fall of the Roman empire," said Adam, "but I wish Edward Gibbon were not quite so **prolix**."

11. **maundering** (MAWN der ing) This adjective comes from the verb "to maunder." If you maunder on about something, you just keep going when you could have won praise for being more concise. The word comes from "meander," which can be a pleasant kind of rambling—the word originally denoted a winding river—but "maundering" is always negative.

- Although Norman shared the religious faith of the speaker, he found himself impatient with the **maundering** pieties.

- "Why doesn't the committee chairman get to his point?" thought Basil. "How long will he **maunder** on about the process the group observed?"

MAKE A MATCH #2

Sections 4–6

Match each word in the left-hand column with the phrase on the right that best suggests its meaning.

A. avaricious	1. _____ related to elephants
B. avian	2. _____ greedy for money
C. eleemosynary	3. _____ like a wolf
D. frugal	4. _____ writing that is wordy
E. garrulous	5. _____ willing to gratify
F. herpetology	6. _____ not talking much
G. indulgent	7. _____ relating to monkeys
H. lapidary	8. _____ wasting money
I. lupine	9. _____ talking a lot
J. maunder	10. _____ talk a lot in a rambling way
K. pachyderm	11. _____ related to charity
L. prodigal	12. _____ study of snakes
M. prolix	13. _____ jewel-like prose
N. simian	14. _____ relating to birds
O. taciturn	15. _____ thrifty

What's In? Who's Out?

7

I s she popular? Is it trendy? Are you here? Do you want to participate in the office Super Bowl pool? Did he make the throw in time?
The concepts of "in" and "out" have manifold uses in English. The
ten words below give the flavor of some of the possibilities.

1. indigenous (in DIJ en us) This adjective describes people or things that are
native to a region. Immigrants and transplants don't qualify.

- When Barbara completes her research on plants that are **indigenous** to the
  Smoky Mountain region, she will publish a monograph on the topic.
- The island that is the setting for Shakespeare's play *The Tempest* is populated
  by a father and daughter who came there in a small boat, and by a spirit
  named Ariel and the ill-tempered Caliban, both **indigenous**.

2. interloper (IN ter LOW per) Interlopers intrude where they aren't wanted,
whether they are meddlers in the affairs of others or merely nonindigenous
species of plants (see #1). The word came into English from the Dutch in
the late sixteenth century, a period when England and the Netherlands were
great commercial rivals. The term originally applied to a trading company
attempting business in an area where another company had a monopoly.

- Although the Collinses had lived in Fancy Gap for over twenty years, the
  community was so tight-knit that they sometimes still felt like **interlopers**.
- "I don't need some **interloper** telling me how to raise my children," said
  Mrs. Grundy when her neighbor suggested that Rupert and Rosie shouldn't
  be tossing around a jar of kerosene.

3. extraneous (ek STRAIN ee us) This adjective can mean simply "coming
from the outside," but it is more likely to have the strong sense of irrelevant or unimportant.

- The studio was soundproofed because **extraneous** noises would interfere
  with the quality of the recordings made there.
- Learning how to eliminate **extraneous** details from their intra-office memos
  and their letters to clients made the Rock Creek Public Relations employees
  much better at communication.

4. **inherent** (in HERR ent *or* in HAIR ent) If it's inherent it's literally "stuck into" the nature of the thing (or the person), integral to its being. While "inherit" isn't a root word, it might serve as a memory device, since something "inherent" is a part of the figurative DNA.

- A little investigation showed Carl he had an **inherent** flaw in the design of the computer program; he had to scrap it and start over.

- When Molly admired Enoch's orderly office space, he commented, "Neatness isn't an **inherent** virtue for me; I have to work hard at it."

5. **germane** (jer MAIN) Nothing to do with Germany, this adjective means "relevant" or "suitable" or "closely connected." Literally, the root word means "having the same parents," so if you know Spanish, think "hermano" (brother).

- While that detail about how little Thomas A. Edison slept may be interesting, it's hardly **germane** to your study of elementary electronics.

- "I try to consider your feelings," said Sandra to J. B., "but it's equally **germane** that you try to consider mine."

6. **pariah** (puh RYE uh) This noun refers to a social outcast, someone not accepted in his or her society. The word comes into English from Tamil, a language of southern India, where it refers more specifically to an "Untouchable," a member of the lowest caste.

- Mark Twain calls Huckleberry Finn the "juvenile **pariah** of the village."

- After Aaron reported Matt's misdoings to a teacher, he was treated like a **pariah** by classmates who felt "ratting someone out" was the worst possible offense.

7. **endemic** (en DEM ik) From the Greek words for "in" and "people," this adjective means "native or common to or peculiar to a specific region or abstract area." Perhaps because of the fact it sounds similar to "epidemic," it's often (though not always) used for negative phenomena.

- When the first year teacher felt overwhelmed with work, she consulted her experienced colleague who said consolingly, "Feeling absolutely swamped is **endemic** to being a new teacher. You'll never have the time you need, but you'll learn to accept that and live with the feeling."

- "If you're planning to travel in an equatorial region," said Dr. Abernethy, "you must get shots for diseases that are **endemic** to that region."

8. **intrinsic** (in TRINZ ik) From the Latin word for "inward," this adjective is a rough synonym for "inherent" (#4), though careful stylists will find shades of difference. "Innate" (literally, "in-born") is another synonym.

- Gold, a metal like many others, has no **intrinsic** value, but its comparative rarity and its attractive gleam have bestowed value on it in virtually every society.

- **Intrinsic** in every major religion is the concept of valuing others and treating them well.

9. **ostracize** (OS truh size) If you ostracize someone, you make him or her a pariah (see #6). This verb has the meaning of "expelling a person from a community," either literally or figuratively. Like many words and practices, this one came from ancient Greece where a citizen could be forced to leave a city by vote of his peers. Not yet having paper, the citizens voted with shards of pottery—*ostraka*, forerunners of the modern "blackball."

- Although the charges of sexual harassment against Mr. Larrabee have been dropped, he continues to be **ostracized** by a number of people in his workplace.

- To help her psychology students understand the power of social **ostracism**, Ms. Ewalt had her class participate in an experiment: on a regularly scheduled basis, each member of the class spent two days being shunned by others—no communication, no sharing of a lunchroom table.

10. **tangential** (tan JEN chul) This adjective describes neither "in" nor "out," but something "slightly touching" or "barely connected." This adjective derives from the world of geometry, where a "tangent" is a line or curve touching another at a single point. So if a person "goes off on a tangent," he or she is getting away from the main concern.

- The leader instructed the teachers scoring the essay that would determine a student's placement in a composition class that a **tangential** approach to the given topic was fine: "Think of the topic as merely an 'invitation to write,'" he said.

- Mr. Holland asked all his group leaders to focus on the major points of the task that confronted them on this day, to save all **tangential** considerations for the next meeting.

Something's Coming

8

S ometimes pleasant things are on the way, but the language seems to have more words suggesting the looming disaster. Some of the ten below are neutral, but most are not. Something's coming, something bad.

1. **ominous** (OM in us) A good illustration of the statement above: this adjective, which comes from the Latin word "omen," a foreshadowing of the future, always describes the threatening, the menacing.

- The turnip-shaped cloud on the horizon seemed **ominous** and caused McFarland to drive his truck quickly to the refuge of an exit.
- The skull and crossbones on the label added an **ominous** touch to the jar of rat poison.

2. **portentous** (por TENT us) As with #1, this word describes something carrying a sign, a portent, of the threats of the future. A second meaning laps over into the pretentiously weighty, the pompous.

- Sandy's mid-term grades were passing but hardly **portentous** of a great year: she had three Cs and two Ds.
- When Mr. Jaggers speaks, his words bear a **portentous** air, as if what he had to say was highly meaningful to us all.

3. **inauspicious** (IN aw SPISH us) With the "in" prefix, it forecasts negatively, but make it **auspicious** and it predicts or suggests something favorable. This adjective comes from the Latin *auspex,* a man with the job of predicting the future by watching the actions of birds. Beats the daily horoscope!

- Despite Darryl's **inauspicious** debut as a novelist—his first book, *Tough Is the Night*, received terrible reviews and sold badly—he has moved on to a thriving and respectable writing career.
- When the politician, returning to his hometown from a campaigning trip, stumbled while alighting from the steps of the plane, he turned the misstep into an **auspicious** moment: kissing the earth, he proclaimed, "There's no place like home."

4. **imminent** (IM in ent) This adjective describes something about to occur. Its root word—meaning "jutting out or overhanging"—allows it to be positive or negative. Don't confuse it with the sound-alike **eminent**, which describes people who "jut out" of the common mass, in short, the famous or well-known.

- Odysseus escaped **imminent** disaster from the sea monster Charybdis by swinging up onto the one tree protruding from the rocky cliff.
- The **eminence** of Victorian biographer Lytton Strachey is based heavily on his book *Eminent Victorians.*

5. **impending** (im PEND ing) It can refer to something threatening or not. At any rate, the near arrival of the event hangs over you, and "hangs" (as in "pendulum" or "pendant") is the root word.

- LaForge felt a sense of **impending** doom as he rounded the landing of the squeaking stairs and caught a glimpse of a giant bat just as the power failed.
- When Dr. Grayson was asked if she looked forward to her **impending** retirement, she answered with a smile, "Do you enjoy vacation?"

6. **minatory** (MIN a tore ee) This adjective always means "threatening." While the sound is only a coincidence, if you're a mythology buff you can think of the threatening Minotaur, the bull-monster who demanded human victims.

- The **minatory** howl of the air raid siren was all it took for the hardy Londoners to head for the Underground shelter.
- While tenth-graders were known to fear the **minatory** tones of Ms. Velma Cloyd, a really stern math teacher, graduating seniors flocked around her to thank her for her "tough love."

7. **presage** (pres AGE) This verb refers to a forewarning, an ominous feeling, a prediction.

- The stormy early quarrel between Hortense, the Duchess, and Arcite, the Duke, over the combining of their coats of arms **presaged** their later years of estrangement.
- **Presaging** Clem's difficulties with calculus was the fact of overreliance on his tutor during the Algebra II course.

8. **bode** and **forebode** (for BODE) The one-syllable word is a verb referring to an omen, and the two-syllable repeats or intensifies that presentiment.

- Losing their best pitcher to injuries so early in the season doesn't **bode** well for the Durham Bulls's chance at the championship this year.
- A sense of **foreboding** pervaded Willard's work on his graduate school applications; somehow down deep he may have known it was time to leave the haven of school, at least for a while.

9. **propitiate** (pro PISH ee ate) Sometimes, the forces of good or evil may be modified. This verb describes actions to appease or calm forces that might oppose a favorable outcome.

- Ian hoped to avoid detention and **propitiate** the principal's anger by leaving a box of doughnuts on his desk.

- Before Achates set out on the hazardous journey, he **propitiated** the gods with the sacrifice of a fine plump lamb.

10. **harbinger** (HAR bin jer) This noun refers to a forerunner, an early warning or messenger of what's to come. Its interesting origin derives from a person sent ahead to provide lodging for one to come. (If you've traveled in Francophone Canada or France, you may hear a hint of the word "auberge" or inn.)

- The robin is famous as a **harbinger** of spring, no matter what the calendar might say.

- Getting an A on his first paper in anthropology class was a **harbinger** of the fact that he would win the Margaret Mead Prize at the end of the year.

The Art of Losing

9

In a wonderful short poem, the poet Elizabeth Bishop tells us "the art of losing isn't hard to master." And it's even easier when you have several words for different types of loss.

1. **squander** (SKWAN der) If you spend extravagantly, you're squandering money. If you don't take an interesting summer internship, you're squandering a chance to pick up new skills. Either way, this verb expresses the idea of "wasting." The root word, thus far, baffles linguists.

   - Although Shakespeare's Polonius doesn't use the word, he counsels his son against **squandering** when he says, "Neither a borrower nor a lender be, for loan oft loses both itself and friend."

   - Mr. Fleetwood, my neighbor, was given to quoting the Roman poet Horace, who orders us to "seize the day" and further urging his son and me not to **squander** our youth. "It will pass quickly enough anyway," he'd add, knowingly.

2. **dissipation** (dis uh PAY shun) Two kinds of loss can be expressed by this noun: (a) a literal scattering or dispersing, and (b) a specialized sense of scattering one's energy through immoderate pursuit of trivial pleasures, especially activities such as gambling, intemperate drinking, and sexual activity.

   - The smell of burned marshmallows lingered in the air until the campfire was put out and the odor completely **dissipated** by the wind.

   - Polonius feared that his son Laertes would lead a **dissipated** life in Paris, and this fact caused him, first, to give the young man lots of advice, (see #1) and, second, to send a spy to watch him.

3. **disenfranchise** (dis en FRAN chize) To be disenfranchised is, primarily, to lose the right to vote. The root word is "frank" as in "free."

   - Those convicted of felonies suffer the additional penalty of being **disenfranchised**.

   - The threat of **disenfranchisement** means nothing to those who never exercise their hard-won right to vote.

4. **forfeiture** (FOR fit ure) This noun, from the verb "forfeit," expresses the idea of a penalty, a giving up of something in one's possession. It may be used trivially, as in a game, or extremely seriously.

- "If you lose this game of whist to me, Miss Arabella, you must make **forfeiture** of one of your gloves," said Sir Kenelm. "It can then be redeemed only by a kiss."

- The **forfeiture** of one of his estates was a grievous loss to the young Squire Moulton, and he rued the day he had signed the bond for his feckless friend Bounderby.

5. **denude** (de NEWD) Primarily used of trees that lose their leaves or loss of other vegetation, this verb means "to make bare" (as in "nude").

- Although the lush summer foliage had been wonderful, the **denuded** landscape had a severe beauty all its own.

- Who knew that use of RILLEE-STRAWNG bug killer would also cause **denuding** of the yard within a diameter of three feet? The warning was printed in flyspeck type on the bottom of the spray can!

6. **privation** (pry VAY shun) As the sound makes clear, this noun is related to the verb "deprive." When you're deprived of basic necessities or comforts, you're experiencing privation.

- "I wouldn't call not having cable television in your room the equivalent of living in a state of **privation**," said Jon's mom.

- The recruits at Fort Hard Knox lived in comparative **privation** the first weeks they were in boot camp, but the discipline served its purpose: they quickly became efficient and obedient soldiers.

7. **divest** (de VEST or die VEST) Literal meaning: to undress (just as "invest" has the literal meaning of "clothing," as in "vest" or "vestments"). But you won't hear that today; instead, you'll hear this verb used to mean a more general "getting rid of." The noun form "divestiture" carries a specific financial meaning.

- When Cheryl asked David, a fellow booklover, to come to the bookstore with her, he replied, "Don't tempt me. I'm trying to **divest** myself of surplus books, not add more."

- When Mr. Taterface, Inc. announced the **divestiture** of its Tiniest Taters division, even the sharpest of Wall Street analysts were surprised.

8. **renounce** (re NOWNS) If you renounce something, you give it up. It's a rather formal verb, so, unless you want to be amusing, don't use it for giving up chocolate. (Don't confuse this word with its near twin **denounce**, which now means "to condemn openly" but which, confusingly, can be found in the Declaration of Independence with its older meaning of "giving a formal announcement of an ending" when the colonists "denounce their separation" from Great Britain.)

- "And for this child, I **renounce** the Devil and all his works," said the godfather of the baby at the christening ceremony.
- Prince Handsum made a formal **renunciation** of his right to the throne of Bigland in order to follow a career in circuitry wiring, his deepest passion.
- The mayor **denounced** the perpetrators of the heinous crime and promised they would soon be brought to justice.

9. elegiac (el uh JYE ik) This word is not only the adjective form for elegy, a poem lamenting a death (see #5 in Speech Therapy); in addition, it describes a feeling of sadness at many types of losses—of friends, of love, of youth.

- W. D. Snodgrass's poem "Packing Up the Lute" is beautifully **elegiac**: the reader comprehends not only the loss of the ability to play the instrument but a sense of the generalized lessening of abilities inflicted by age.
- Revisiting the site of her honeymoon forty years later gave Katrina an **elegiac** chill: the mountain town was little changed, but the marriage had long been over.

10. bereave (be REEV) As an active verb, this word means "to leave desolate, usually by death." You'll almost always hear it in its passive form, referring to surviving relatives or close friends of a person who has died. And the related form **bereft** is often used for a sense of abandonment or loss stemming from any cause.

- The announcement at the funeral services stated that the **bereaved** family would receive calls of condolence in their home any night of the following week.
- Though the Bohannons had lost a great deal of their money through unwise investments, they were not **bereft** of their ability to cope and quickly adapted to a modified way of living.

MAKE A MATCH #3

Sections 7–9

Match each word in the left-hand column with the phrase on the right that best suggests its meaning.

A.	bereft	1. _____	an outcast
B.	bode	2. _____	threatening
C.	denounce	3. _____	a forerunner

D.	denude	4.	_____ forsaken
E.	disenfranchised	5.	_____ expressive of sadness
F.	dissipation	6.	_____ give an early omen
G.	elegiac	7.	_____ situation with bad omens
H.	eminent	8.	_____ an unaccepted latecomer to a group
I.	extraneous	9.	_____ famous
J.	germane	10.	_____ give up
K.	harbinger	11.	_____ lose vegetation
L.	impending	12.	_____ a sense of wasting life with no serious purpose
M.	inauspicious	13.	_____ banish from a social group
N.	interloper	14.	_____ not relevant
O.	minatory	15.	_____ self-important
P.	ostracize	16.	_____ lacking the right to vote
Q.	pariah	17.	_____ going to happen soon
R.	portentous	18.	_____ closely connected
S.	renounce	19.	_____ indirectly related
T.	tangential	20.	_____ express strong disapproval

PRACTICE, PRACTICE, PRACTICE #1

Sections 1–9

Directions: Select a word from the list below that best fits the blank in one of the sentences and place the letter in the blank.

A.	aphrodisiac	K.	odyssey
B.	avaricious	L.	ominous
C.	blanched	M.	ostracize
D.	disenfranchised	N.	presage
E.	flout	O.	prodigal
F.	frugal	P.	serpentine
G.	hermetic	Q.	sow
H.	indigenous	R.	succinct
I.	ken	S.	terse
J.	mnemonic	T.	vex

1. Knowing how to repair a computer is just not within Ray's _____.

2. Did Helen of Troy offer men some kind of _____ or was her own beauty enough to ensnare them?

3. It will _____ me until I can think of her name because I certainly know it.

4. Kudzu was not _____ to the South, but once planted there it spread enormously fast.

5. I am trying hard to be _____ this month because I need money to buy my sister a birthday present next month.

6. The _____ road gave us beautiful scenery, but all those curves were a little scary.

7. The medicine bottle had a _____ closing device because air could quickly weaken the power of the medicine inside.

8. Marie's face _____ as she realized she'd left her purse on the train.

9. Winston liked to _____ the rule against smoking by lighting up as he stood beneath the "No Smoking" sign.

10. His _____ manner of speaking made it possible for him to communicate much in a brief period of time.

11. Because the printing company charged by the word, the copy for the marshmallow advertisement was especially _____.

12. The puddle of water on the floor was an _____ sign that the new roof had sprung a leak.

13. Our summer _____ took us to Uruguay, Patagonia, and the Falkland Islands and provided many adventures.

14. Moralists tell us that what we _____ we will reap; the concept of karma has the same idea of our acts affecting our future.

15. Do you know a _____ device that will help me remember the value of pi to eight decimal places?

16. He is rather _____ with his talent, not cherishing it enough to value its further development.

17. We generally esteem those who are thrifty, but those who go to the extreme of becoming _____ are usually condemned.

18. I like this political candidate because she emphasizes that she tries to speak for the _____, who are often forgotten by society.

19. Farmers around here hope this dry spell does not _____ a season of real drought.

20. It is true that societies sometimes _____ a genius when he or she is alive, and only later generations recognize that person's worth.

H ere's a group of words that have to do with food—not the appetizers and entrees but the general category of words dealing with eating.

1. **culinary** (CUL in air ee) This adjective describes anything relating to cooking or the kitchen. There is no noun form.

- Margot decided to go to **culinary** school so that she could learn how to make *béarnaise* sauce to spice up her otherwise bland flank steak.

- Kitchen Magic is a store that specializes in **culinary** equipment, including chopping knives, whisks, sifters, and measuring spoons.

2. **gourmet** (goor MAY) This word, which can be used as an adjective or noun, means "an expert (or "connoisseur") of fine food and drink." It comes from the Old French word *groumet*, which means "servant in charge of wine." It should not be confused with the word gourmand (goor MOND), which comes from the same root. This noun also means "someone with discriminating taste in food and wine," but a gourmand likes food a bit too much. The word means glutton.

- A **gourmet**, James favors Asian-fusion cuisine, a blend of French culinary techniques and Japanese and Thai ingredients.

- Andrea is a real **gourmand**. Even in the most expensive restaurants he orders several appetizers and several entrees because he doesn't want to miss out on any of the chef's specialties.

3. **epicurean** (epp ik yoor EE an) Like a gourmet, an epicure (noun) or someone with epicurean tastes has a very discriminating taste in food and wine, perhaps even a bit too devoted or overly refined. Interestingly, Epicurean philosophy, which burgeoned in Greece between 340 and 270 BC, professed that pleasure was the highest form of good but was not overly concerned with food or drink.

- Catering to the **epicure**, *Les Trois Cochons* is a French restaurant, which has all of its ingredients flown in from the south of France daily. Even their bread is baked in Parisian bakeries because French water is necessary for creating the ideal dough.

- Harcourt is a man of **epicurean** tastes. He has an extensive wine cellar and a staff of chefs from all around the world.

4. **gluttony** (GLUTT un ee) You may know this noun as one of the seven deadly sins. It means "excessive eating or drinking." A person who stuffs himself and drinks too much is a glutton. The word can also be used figuratively to describe someone who overdoes it on anything.

- A **glutton** for punishment, Wilbur always forgot to water the garden, even though he knew this would infuriate his wife Blanche.
- After indulging her natural propensity for **gluttony**, Jill went on a diet. She had eaten almost an entire cheesecake as well as a quart of ice cream and had gained three pounds in one afternoon.

5. **voracious** (vor AYSH us) From the Latin word that means "to swallow or devour," this adjective means "ravenous (see 'Weighty Words' section) or excessively hungry." It can also be used more figuratively to connote excessively greedy or insatiably hungry for things other than food.

- A **voracious** reader, Jody read as many as two books a day.
- "I could eat a horse!" Frank announced, **voracious** after running the marathon. "I feel as if I haven't eaten in a week."

6. **savory** (SAY ver ee) As an adjective, this word means "appetizing to taste or smell." It generally means "a salty or piquant (a word which comes from the French word for 'to prick,' meaning sharply pungent) flavor," not a sweet one. As a noun, the word means a piquant or salty appetizer, such as olives. The verb form, "to savor," means "to taste or smell with enthusiasm or relish."

- The chef began the meal with a platter of **savories**, including chopped anchovies, pickled tomatoes, and salted crackers with a white bean paste.
- The man **savored** the taste of the *madeleine*; the flavor of the soft cookie brought back a rush of childhood memories.

7. **omnivorous** (om NIV er us) This adjective literally means "eating both animal and vegetable foods," but it has come to be used to mean taking in or devouring anything available.

- An **omnivorous** culture addict, Dierdre attended the theater, opera, or ballet at least five nights a week. When she was home, she read the newest books on the bestseller list.
- Jacques indulged his **omnivorous** appetites by attending the Gourmet Club dinner, savoring everything from the roasted pork to the eggplant casserole to the chicken in curried spinach sauce. No main course was too spicy, no dessert too sweet.

8. **gastronomy** (gas TRON oh mee) This noun has two equally common meanings. It refers to the art or science of good eating. It also means "any particular, regional style of cooking." The adjective form is "gastronomical."

- The **gastronomy** in southern France features small, savory olives, rosemary-flavored breads, and wild game.

- Indulging his **gastronomical** interests, Maurice decided to attend the Culinary Institute for the summer in order to learn as much as he could about the preparation of chicken, fish, and red meat.

9. **palatable** (PAL at able) This adjective means "acceptable to taste or sufficiently favorable to be eaten—pleasing to the palate." "Potable," on the other hand, means fit to be drunk.

- It is possible to survive in the forest by eating what is available in nature. Nuts and berries are **palatable**; rocks and pebbles are not.

- "This beef is not **palatable**!" cried the temperamental chef. "It is neither tender nor tasty. In fact, it resembles cardboard."

10. **succulent** (SUK yoo lent) From the Latin word for juice, this adjective means "juicy," either literally or figuratively. A well-cooked piece of roast pig is succulent; so is a good piece of gossip.

- The lavish dinner was highlighted by a **succulent** whole sea bass, served on a bed of Moroccan cous cous.

- Sharing a **succulent** hunk of wild boar, the cavemen gathered around the fire and ate until they were sated.

Fortune's Fool

11

For better or worse, the situations we find ourselves in—whether by luck or by plotting—have plenty of words to characterize them.

1. propitious (pro PISH ess) This adjective means "presenting favorable circumstances or a positive outcome."

- "This is not a **propitious** time for investing," said the astrologer, examining Mr. Pierpont's charts. "Your planets are all out of alignment, and you'll surely lose money."
- With Mike Piazza behind the plate, the runner on first base knew that this was a **propitious** time to steal second.

2. auspicious (aw SPISH ess) Like "propitious," this adjective means "marked by success or producing favorable circumstances." The two words are just about interchangeable.

- "Dolly MacGuire's **auspicious** debut at the Grand Ole Opry wowed audiences," read the review in *The Post Dispatch*. "This girl will go far."
- The loyalty and affection between Irving and Sun Lee was an **auspicious** sign for their upcoming nuptials.

3. boon (BOON) This noun comes from the Middle English word *bon*, which means "prayer." It has lost any religious connotations and just means a "timely benefit" or "stroke of good luck."

- Odysseus received a **boon** when the winds changed; the ship's sails caught the breeze, hastening his escape from the Sirens.
- It was a great **boon** for the tenant farmers to have discovered oil on their land.

4. adverse (ad VURS) Although this adjective comes from the Latin for "turn toward," it actually means "turned against" or "opposing." Circumstances that are "adverse" are unfavorable or opposing one's interests or well-being. A good synonym would be "antagonistic." An "adversary," on the other hand, is the noun form for an "opponent" or "enemy."

- Calpurnia tried to convince her husband that her dream indicated **adverse** circumstances for his going forth in public to greet the Romans. Unfortunately, he ignored her and was assassinated that same day.

- The Germans and the British were **adversaries** during World War II and fought bitterly, resulting in many deaths on both sides.

5. **detrimental** (det rim ENT al *or* DET rim ent al) This adjective comes from the Latin word that means "to wear down" or "rub" and means "causing damage, harm, or loss." The noun form is "detriment."

- The surgeon general says that smoking may be **detrimental** to one's health because it can lead to lung cancer.

- "Daydreaming in class," said Mrs. Grundy, "may be a **detriment** to your understanding the course material. Pay attention or you will surely fail."

6. **travesty** (TRAV ess tee) This noun originally meant "an exaggerated imitation of something, usually of a literary work." It has come to mean any "grotesque parody" of something or a disastrous mockery. It comes from the French word for "disguise" or "parody."

- "Allowing the murderer to go free is a **travesty** of justice," said the lawyer. "It is a gross misinterpretation of the law."

- The soccer game was a **travesty**; the Boston team, usually far superior to their opponents, was careless, clumsy, and thoughtless. It's no wonder they lost by two goals.

7. **debacle** (de BAHK ul *or* de BAK ul) This noun is slightly different from "travesty" although the consequences are the same. There is no element of mockery here; it means "a sudden, disastrous downfall" or "defeat."

- After the **debacle** at Gettysburg, the Confederate army never again crossed the Mason-Dixon line.

- In 1943, the German army in Russia was trapped in a hopeless **debacle** of their own making.

8. **fiasco** (fee ASS ko) Interestingly, this noun may come from the Italian *fare fiasco*. It was used by the French for linguistic errors committed by Italian actors on the eighteenth-century French stage. It means "a complete failure."

- Jonathan's piano recital was a **fiasco** because he never practiced and couldn't read music particularly well.

- All investors hope that there will never be another **fiasco** like the one experienced by Enron.

9. **rout** (rhymes with doubt) Originally spelled "root," this noun once meant only to dig or force out as when a pig "roots" for truffles in the forest. The noun has come to connote an "overwhelming defeat" (see #7, *debacle*) or a "disorderly retreat after battle."

- The battle was a complete **rout** by the Austrians. The Italians were forced to withdraw their fortifications and return home.

- The Dobyns-Bennett Indians **routed** the Hilltoppers in the final basketball game of the season.

10. **enormity** (ee NORM it ee) Originally this noun meant only a "monstrous evil or outrage." Over the years, however, it has been so misused to mean "large size" (as in "enormousness") that "immensity" has gradually come to be another accepted meaning. Excessive evil is still the preferred definition.

- The **enormity** of John F. Kennedy's assassination shocked and saddened the country for many years.

- The **enormity** of the concentration camps is detailed in Elie Wiesel's book *Night*.

Stubborn as a Mule

12

The next time you argue with someone for being too stuck in their ways, this series of adjectives will give you the verbal edge in your quarrel.

1. **recalcitrant** (ree KAL se trant) Speaking of stubborn mules, this word comes from the Latin *calcitrare*, which means "to kick." Someone who is recalcitrant is "stubbornly resistant to authority." The noun form is "recalcitrance" or "recalcitrancy."

   - The **recalcitrant** child sat firmly on the couch with his arms crossed, refusing to go to bed.

   - Ted's **recalcitrance** was obvious when he continued chatting with his classmates, even after the teacher had called for silence.

2. **obdurate** (OB door it) The Latin root of this word means "to harden," and it therefore connotes hardened against feeling or hardhearted.

   - At trial, the **obdurate** thief showed no remorse, even though his victim was a poor widow.

   - Kathleen's **obduracy** surprised her colleagues when she insisted that her secretary be fired for a minor infraction.

3. **fractious** (FRAK shus) Although someone who is fractious is considered unruly or a trouble maker, the adjective also means "peevish" or "cranky." It doesn't quite mean stubborn, but the word does suggest an unwillingness to respect authority.

   - The **fractious** child refused to finish her roast beef and spinach even though her father insisted.

   - "Your **fractiousness** is another explanation for your lack of team spirit," said the coach, referring to Ian's refusal to sit on the bench for the ninth inning.

4. **refractory** (ref RAK tor ee) Just like recalcitrant and fractious, this adjective means "stubbornly resistant to authority." Its noun form is "refractoriness," not "refraction," which has to do with the bending of a sound or light wave.

   - Knowing her son could be **refractory**, Mrs. Silverman brought along several books and magic tricks to keep him occupied during the lecture on parenting techniques.

- The students were particularly **refractory**, knowing they could take advantage of the inexperienced substitute teacher.

5. **intractable** (in TRAK tuh bul) Someone who is intractable is "difficult to manage or govern." The Latin root *tract* means "pull" (think of a tractor pulling a plow). So someone who is intractable figuratively can't be pulled to where you want them to go.

- Michael was **intractable**, refusing to return his new convertible Jaguar when his wife insisted that they couldn't afford the monthly payments.
- The **intractable** boy hid under the piano when his mother called out, "Time for your bath!"

6. **obstreperous** (ob STREP er us) From the Latin word that means "to make a noise against," this adjective means "aggressively and noisily defiant." People who are obstreperous make no bones about their obduracy.

- **Obstreperous** by nature, Arthur threw a tantrum when his mother insisted that he put his pet ferret in the cage before joining the family for dinner.
- "I will not stand for your childish **obstreperousness**, Tom," Aunt Polly said firmly. "I asked you to help me paint the fence and if you continue to ignore me you'll have to paint the neighbor's fence too."

7. **intransigent** (in TRAN sih jent *or* in TRAN zih jent) This adjective comes from the Latin meaning "not to come to an agreement," and it means just that. Someone who is intransigent is "stubbornly uncompromising." The noun form is "intransigency."

- The senator remained **intransigent** after hearing the president's views on Social Security and refused to even consider his ideas about privatization.
- Maude's i**ntransigency** on the subject of allowing gay marriage was shocking, considering that both her sister and her father were homosexual.

8. **incorrigible** (in KOR ij uh bul) Someone who is incorrigible is unable to be reformed or corrected. Its use is usually reserved for unruly children or adults with uncontrollable vices. The noun form is either "incorrigibility" or "incorrigibleness," but both are rarely used.

- "You are an **incorrigible** sugar addict!" exclaimed Harriet. "You always find the cookies, no matter where I hide them."
- No matter how many times the dog trainer came to the house, Otis remained **incorrigible**, pawing food off the counters whenever his owner turned his back.

9. **dogged** (DOG gid) Speaking of dogs, this adjective alludes to the personality of certain breeds of dog and means "stubbornly persevering" (see "tenacious" in section 16), often against all odds.

- Mr. Smythe **doggedly** continued to shovel the walkway in the blizzard.

- Jimmy continued to read *Le Petit Prince* with **dogged** determination even though he barely knew any French.

10. **dogmatic** (dog MAT ik) Though it comes from the Greek word that means "opinion," this word has a more negative connotation. Someone who is dogmatic stubbornly asserts an opinion that is unproved or unprovable. Those beliefs are called "dogma," and the person asserting them is a "dogmatist."

- Spouting religious **dogma**, the zealot called the college students "immoral sinners" and told them they would "never enter the Kingdom of Heaven."

- A **dogmatic** conservative, the president refused to raise taxes even though key social service programs were woefully underfunded.

MAKE A MATCH #4

Sections 10–12

Match each word in the left-hand column with the phrase on the right that best suggests its meaning.

A. adversary	1. _____ really stubborn
B. boon	2. _____ really hungry
C. culinary	3. _____ really delicious
D. debacle	4. _____ the art and science of eating well
E. detrimental	5. _____ grotesque mockery
F. dogged	6. _____ relating to cooking
G. dogmatic	7. _____ holding stubbornly to one belief
H. enormity	8. _____ a timely benefit
I. epicurean	9. _____ sophisticated taste in food and drink
J. gastronomy	10. _____ monstrous offense or evil
K. incorrigible	11. _____ having a negative effect
L. omnivorous	12. _____ unable to be reformed
M. recalcitrant	13. _____ an enemy
N. rout	14. _____ a terrible downfall
O. succulent	15. _____ overwhelming defeat
P. travesty	16. _____ eating everything
Q. voracious	17. _____ persistent, not giving up

13

I n addition to "thank you" and "please," the language gives us lots of words concerning proper—or improper—behavior.

1. **decorum** (de CORE um) This noun for behavior appropriate to a prevailing social code comes straight into English from the Latin for "appropriateness." It suggests a pleasing set of manners and awareness of what is considered proper within any one social group.

- Alexander's well-polished sense of **decorum** hid from the eyes of many his tarnished sense of morality: he could lie with the air of a nobleman.

- The headmistress lectured the new student about her attire: "Perhaps a camisole top and shorts were acceptable in your old school, but they are most **indecorous** here at St. Sniffens."

2. **finesse** (fih NESS) This noun, straight from France, denotes refinements and subtlety in a given situation. It suggests situations less superficial than those dealt with by decorum (#1).

- His **finesse** in dealing with his in-laws made many a tricky situation go more smoothly.

- An ambassador needs both intelligence and **finesse**: you can't be intelligent and graceless nor polished and dumb.

3. **seemly** (SEEM lee) Even grammar experts could be tripped up by this word that looks like many adverbs but is an adjective. It describes behavior that is appropriate, fitting the accepted rules of conduct.

- This adjective enters English from Old Norse, language of the not particularly **seemly** Vikings, who plundered the shores of England for many years.

- It is **seemly** to pay tribute to the memory of an admired elder colleague; Mr. Casson's memorial service will be held on Friday afternoon.

4. **protocol** (PRO tuh call) This noun, in its social sense, names the codes of expected behavior in any given situation. (Although the root word of protocol derives from the Greek word for "glue," a linguist wouldn't agree with a layman's guess that manners hold a society together.)

- Julie, uninstructed in matters of **protocol**, worried about the invitation to lunch with the queen: should she call her "Your Majesty" or just go for a democratic "Elizabeth"?
- Anyone doing business in a foreign country needs help in understanding the unwritten rules, the **protocol** of that land; for example, are gifts to a prospective business party expected, or might they be forbidden?

5. **gaffe** (GAFF) A gaffe is a blunder, an awkward social moment. One who makes a gaffe does not behave in a seemly fashion, does not possess finesse. (Like many words relating to manners, this noun comes from the French; in fact, the French phrase faux pas [*foe pah*—false step] would be a synonym.) It is now coming to be a rough synonym for an embarrassing error or mistake.

- Tex's acquaintance with fingerbowls and pickle forks is limited; he hopes not to commit some **gaffe** when he attends the fancy wedding dinner.
- Jeanette's **gaffe** in sending her negative email message to all members of the department may damage her career.

6. **propriety** (pro PRY it ee) Like decorum (#1), this noun concerns itself with the observation of existing social norms; it's no surprise that it is linguistically related to the word "proper."

- Standards of **propriety** alter radically with time: no one is aghast today if a young woman enters a young man's apartment without a chaperone, but in the early twentieth century this situation was still a shocker.
- The heroine of Jane Austen's *Pride and Prejudice* was independent in her thinking, but she was horrified when her sister offended the **propriety** of her social circle.

7. **boor** (rhymes with door) This noun denotes a person with no social sense, one with rude or nonexistent manners. (It enters English from the Dutch, possibly from an era when England regarded the Netherlands as an enemy.)

- "I would not allow such a **boor** to enter my drawing room, not even as a servant," exclaimed Lady Snoot.
- If you eat all of the cucumber sandwiches provided by your hostess and slurp your tea, you may rightly be accused of **boorishness**.

8. **churl** (rhymes with curl) This noun is a first cousin in sense to the unmannerly "boor" (#7); it has been in the English family even longer, deriving from Anglo Saxon. The shade of difference is this: "boorishness" emphasizes social cluelessness while "churlishness" moves toward a bad disposition or its near-rhyming surliness.

- Would it be **churlish** not to ask my Finnish first cousins to dinner? Not one of them speaks a word of English.

- Stephen is a brilliant man, a highly skilled chemist, but in the workplace he's a bit of a **churl**, not hesitant to let you know you're slowing him down.

9. **nuance** (NOO onss) This noun refers to subtle or slight variation and to sensitivity to those variations. An awareness of nuance is important on the social scene as well as in areas of greater import. (Nuance is derived from the Latin word for that changeable phenomenon, the cloud.)

- Mrs. Ramsay's awareness of the finely layered **nuances** in her guests' interactions was comparable to an orchestra conductor's awareness of the balance among the instruments.

- Prof. Duffy is so sensitive to **nuances** in poetic style that he can often guess the author of a poem he has not previously read.

10. **savoir faire** (sav wahr FARE) Another manners lesson from the French— the phrase literally means "to know what to do." Those with savoir faire not only know what fork to use at a fancy dinner, they also have the grace and tact to put others at ease.

- When I was embarrassed to realize I'd mispronounced my host's name, he had the **savoir faire** to say laughingly, "Oh, that's the other branch of the family," and put me at ease.

- Emile's **savoir faire** makes him a good colleague and a pleasant guest; you know he will behave equally well behind the desk or at a restaurant table.

Be Bloody, Bold, and Resolute

14

B eing daring can run the gamut from heroic courage to foolish boldness. Have the mettle (a nice word for "courage") to use them.

1. resolute (REZ oh loot) From the Latin meaning "relaxed," this adjective actually means the opposite—"bold and determined, unwavering in purpose." The noun is "resoluteness" or "resolution," though the latter form has several other meanings.

- Demanding that he be undaunted in his battle with Macduff, the apparitions tell Macbeth, "Be bloody, bold, and **resolute**; laugh to scorn the power of man."
- **Resolute** of purpose, the cavalry surged onto the field brandishing their swords.

2. undaunted (un DAWN ted) This adjective means "not discouraged or disheartened." Another form of the word is "dauntless." Someone who is undaunted is willing to forge ahead, whatever the odds.

- General Patton's **undaunted** courage during battle earned him the nickname "Blood and Guts."
- **Undaunted** by her learning disabilities, Gillian hired a tutor and signed up for an advanced precalculus class.

3. intrepid (in TREP id) This adjective is a synonym for resolute. Someone who is intrepid is fearlessly brave. Though there are two noun forms— "intrepidity" and "intrepidness"—neither of them is much used.

- The *Intrepid* was a fitting name for the aircraft carrier that was manned by the fearless soldiers who fought in World War II.
- The small boy **intrepidly** resisted the jeers of the bullies and continued to walk to school unaccompanied by his mother.

4. audacity (aw DASS it ee) From the Latin word for "to dare," this noun has a slightly different intent. Someone who has audacity is fearlessly, often recklessly, daring. An audacious act is often committed without regard for prudence or convention.

- The editor **audaciously** translated *The Odyssey* into prose, heedless of the poetic rhyme and meter evident in earlier translations.
- "The **audacity** of that girl!" shouted Mrs. Sloan-Hawkins. "How dare she wear sneakers to the debutante ball?"

5. **restive** (RESS tiv) Though it sounds like "restless," this adjective means something slightly different. It comes from the Old French *rester*, meaning "to remain," and it means to resist control or be impatient under restriction. It's not quite audacity but it does suggest a bold resistance to control.

- The students grew **restive** under the watchful eyes of the principal and began thinking of ways to avoid detention.
- The government did nothing to reduce casualties during the war, and the rebellious students grew more and more **restive** during their demonstrations.

6. **fortitude** (FORT it ood) This is one of several words (fortify, fortification) that takes its meaning from the Latin word for "strong." This noun means "the strength of mind to endure pain or difficulty with courage." There is an adjective form—fortitudinous—but it is rarely used.

- The point guard on the basketball team had the **fortitude** to play with an injured knee because he knew the team needed him to win the championship.
- Summoning up all of her **fortitude**, Joan of Arc refused to recant when she was burned at the stake.

7. **brazen** (BRAY zen) Coming from the Old English word meaning "made of brass," this adjective means able to undergo adversity with bold self-assurance. When people are brazen, however, they are insolent (rude), even shameless, in their audacity.

- The **brazen** woman, who was accused of murder, held her head high as she walked through the crowd, ignoring their insults and taunts.
- The ninth grader would have to be pretty **brazen** to plagiarize from the internet after several students had already been expelled for doing so.

8. **temerity** (tem ER it ee) From the Latin word meaning "rash," this noun is at one extreme of boldness. Someone with temerity exhibits a foolish disregard for danger. There is actually an adjective form of the word, "temerarious," but using this uncommon form would be a little bit audacious.

- Oliver Twist had the **temerity** to ask for some more porridge when he knew the directors of the orphanage were determined to feed the boys as little as possible.
- It took a lot of **temerity** for the soldier to cross No Man's Land in the middle of a skirmish.

9. **iconoclastic** (eye kon oh KLASS tik) This word describes a person (an icon-oclast) who seeks to overthrow popular ideas or institutions, which takes a certain amount of temerity. It comes from the Medieval Greek, which means "smasher of religious images." The noun form is "iconoclasm."

- Ever the **iconoclast**, Stephen was the only student in class who believed that cell phones were a foolish invention and a waste of money.

- Nietzsche revealed his **iconoclasm** when he announced to his nineteenth-century readers that God is dead.

10. **cheeky** (CHEEK ee) Like the synonymous adjective "saucy," this is a charming word for impudently bold. It's usually used to describe the flouting of social conventions and sometimes has a positive spin. Its roots are in the Old English, and the noun form is "cheek."

- Blanche had the **cheek** to call my mother a shrew right in front of my face.

- It was very **cheeky** of Hermione to wear a leopard-print jumpsuit to the ladies' luncheon; she made everyone else look dull by comparison.

Oddballs

15

Just as "enormity" doesn't mean huge (see section 11), many other words don't always mean what they sound like. Here are ten.

1. **jejune** (juh JOON) This adjective means dull, bland, or uninteresting and is usually used to describe speech or writing. It comes from the Latin word for "fasting," as in unsatisfying to the mind or soul. Another meaning of the word is "childish" or "immature." It is possible that this comes from the mistaken belief that the word comes from the French word *jeune*, which means young.

   • Professor Calabrini was known for giving lectures that were so **jejune** that most of his listeners were bored to sleep after ten minutes.

   • Alonso's bearing was so **jejune** that people thought he was a teenager when he was in fact in his twenties.

2. **niggardly** (NIG ard lee) This adjective is not a racial slur. Probably of Scandinavian origin, it means frugal (see the "Give and Take" section) or tightfisted in giving or spending. A stingy, miserly person is a niggard.

   • "You are so **niggardly**," remarked Marie Claire, upon hearing that her father had given her only a tiny sum with which to buy a prom dress.

   • The dieting supermodel's caloric intake was so **niggardly** that she began to lose weight at an alarming rate.

3. **forte** You may know the meaning of this noun—"something at which a person excels"—but do you know its proper pronunciation? It's FORT (rhymes with port). It comes from the Old French word for "strong." Only when it is used as a musical denotation to mean "loud and forceful," a meaning which derives from the Italian, is the "e" actually pronounced. Over time, more and more people have confused the two roots, however, with the result that the two-syllable pronunciation (FOR-tay) has become more acceptable.

   • Since words are her **forte**, I always defer to Jane when I want to know the correct use or pronunciation of a word.

- Gaston has finally decided to make a career move and open his own bakery; after all, butter creams, chocolate icings, flaky pastries, and fruit-fillings are his **forte**.

4. **hoary** (HOR ee) Someone who is hoary is not full of hair (hirsute)—unless it is gray hair. The adjective means gray- or white-haired and therefore quite old. The white-haired, white-bearded seaman in Samuel Taylor Coleridge's poem "The Rime of the Ancient Mariner" is described as "hoary." It can also simply mean ancient and worthy of respect as a consequence of age. It can only be used to describe people, not things.

- The chestnut-colored hair of Vladimir's youth had paled and turned **hoary** with age.

- Having lived more than a century, the **hoary** and withered man commanded respect wherever he walked.

5. **gadfly** (GAD fly) This noun is often confused with the word "gadabout," which is a person who roams about in search of amusement or social activity. A gadfly, on the other hand, is a person who acts as a provocative stimulus or catalyst to action, a goad (someone who prods or urges to action). A second meaning is an irritating critic.

- Though Mr. Skuggins was a good editor, his constant and irritating nitpicking often earned him the label of **gadfly**.

- Horace, the **gadfly** of the school, incited all of the faculty members to demand higher salaries and better benefits.

6. **piebald** (PYE bald) Here's an odd adjective that has nothing to do with either pastry or pates (from the Middle English word that means "top of the head"). Something that's piebald is spotted or patchy, especially in black and white.

- Smearing his ink-stained fingers across the fresh bedspread, Alfonso left behind a **piebald** pattern of black and white.

- The Dalmatian's **piebald** coat blended well with the spotted upholstery on the firehouse couch.

7. **toothsome** (TOOTH sum) Though something or someone that is toothsome might inspire a wide, toothy grin, the word has very little to do with teeth. This adjective actually means "delicious" or "luscious," as in a tasty meal, or "sexually attractive and exciting," as in a handsome woman or man.

- With her stunning good looks and impressive mind, Alexandra was certainly a **toothsome** girl.

- The **toothsome** lobster thermidor was cooked to a turn.

8. **caryatid** (CAH ree a tid) Although this noun sounds like the name of a grass-hopper or a more exotic insect, it's actually an architectural term. A caryatid is a structural column sculpted in the form of a draped female figure. The name comes from the priestesses of Artemis at Caryae in Greece, where there is a famous temple to Artemis.

- The statues of toga-draped maidens that support the lintel of one of the temples at the Acropolis are probably the most famous example of **caryatids** in Greek art.

- Dressed in flowing robes and carrying a fake slab of marble above her head, Hermione was sure she would be the only guest at the Halloween party who had come as a **caryatid**.

9. **adventitious** (ad ven TISH us) This adjective sounds as if it has to do with the arrival or "advent" of something, but it doesn't. The word means "not inherent, or coming from an external source." Another synonym is "accidental."

- A large, **adventitious** population of Ecuadorians has settled in central New York State, so the local school districts teach several courses in Spanish as well as in English.

- Truffles sometimes grow **adventitiously** in the woods beyond the Smiths' country house, enabling Hattie Smith to add a gourmet touch to her otherwise ordinary dishes.

10. **pulchritude** (PUL kri tood) Here's a noun that sounds ugly but means great beauty. The adjective form is "pulchritudinous."

- Helen of Troy's face was renowned for its **pulchritude**.

- Needing beauty in the midst of such horror, the soldiers in the trench were overwhelmed by the **pulchritude** of the sunset.

MAKE A MATCH #5

Sections 13–15

Match each word in the left-hand column with the phrase on the right that best suggests its meaning.

A. adventitious   1. _____ a proper code of behavior
B. boor   2. _____ embarrassing social error
C. caryatid   3. _____ unmannerly oaf
D. decorum   4. _____ subtle shade of meaning
E. fortitude   5. _____ always knowing what to do, socially
F. gadfly   6. _____ unchanging determination
G. gaffe   7. _____ courageous, daring
H. iconoclastic   8. _____ "stiff upper lip"
I. intrepid   9. _____ deliberately breaking taboos of society
J. jejune   10. _____ stingy, penny-pinching
K. niggardly   11. _____ dull, uninspired
L. nuance   12. _____ attractive, luscious
M. piebald   13. _____ weight-bearing statue of a woman
N. pulchritude   14. _____ beauty
O. resolute   15. _____ pattern of black and white splotches
P. savoir faire   16. _____ added on, accidental
Q. toothsome   17. _____ critical but provocative stimulus

Work Ethic

16

If you work hard, you deserve words describing your efforts. Happily, English supplies plenty of these.

1. sedulous (SED yuh lus) This adjective describes hard work, consistently applied to the task at hand. It originates in two Latin words meaning "without trickery," a fact that shows the sedulous person isn't trying to take any short cuts!

- Josh's high grades are due to a combination of natural intelligence and **sedulous** effort.
- The poet W. B. Yeats **sedulously** sought for beautiful images to use in his writing and was delighted when his new wife indicated help was available from the realm of the supernatural.

2. herculean (her kyoo LEE un) If you face a herculean task, you're going to need herculean strength. This adjective refers to something really difficult or really powerful, like the tasks confronted by the Greek hero Hercules or the physical power he used to complete them.

- We often say nothing good gets accomplished by a committee, but the seventeenth-century King James translation of the Bible is surely an exception: about forty-seven men worked together in the **herculean** task of translating both the Old and New Testaments of the Christian Bible.
- Around midnight, Phoebe completed the job of revising her part of the American history project, emailing the results to her partner, and writing a "procedural" page on how she and Lindsay had coordinated their **herculean** efforts.

3. stamina (STAM in ah) This noun refers to endurance, the strength—whether physical or mental—to keep going.

- The **stamina** to stay focused during a long college admissions test is an important skill.
- Lord Astor's racing horses possess speed but not **stamina**; they consistently lead at the start of a race and fall behind at the end.

4. **meticulous** (muh TICK yoo lus) This adjective emphasizes painstaking care with details. While it's always a compliment today, it has its roots in the Latin word for "fear."

- The fact that Lei has a wild artistic imagination does not conflict with the **meticulous** nature of his drawing techniques.
- Willingness to give **meticulous** attention to details and strong eyesight are the chief requirements of those attempting the ancient art of making lace.

5. **punctilious** (punk TIL ee us) Even a bit more than "meticulous," this adjective suggests attention to every minute detail or point. (And like the word "punctuation," punctilious is derived from the word "point," as in the dot at the end of this sentence.) It can be positive or negative, depending on the context.

- When George said "whatever" to his **punctilious** boss's outlining of the rules of the job, it was clear this was not a match made in heaven.
- If the recipe calls for an eighth of a teaspoon, only the more **punctilious** cooks will search for a measuring spoon.

6. **fastidious** (fast TID ee us) This adjective pushes meticulous (#4) and punctilious (#5) a little more toward the extreme. It can still be used in a positive context but often moves over into meaning "overly exacting" or "unnecessarily squeamish."

- Even as a small child, Fauntleroy was **fastidious**: his toys were arranged precisely on the shelf and the teddy bear was in the exact middle of the bed.
- Some consider **fastidious** people unfortunate, for they are so seldom pleased with anything.

7. **assiduous** (a SID yoo us) Like sedulous (#1), this adjective suggests diligence, persistence. Unsurprisingly, it comes from the Latin for "to sit," implying the ability to stay in your seat until the job is done.

- Yurah was so **assiduous** in her work on the Intel grant project that her parents had to remind her of the importance of food and sleep.
- "**Assiduous** I'm not," bragged Bo, whose work was frequently shown in Outsider Art Fairs. "But folks seem to like my stuff anyhow."

8. **tenacious** (ten AYSH yus) The tenacious person holds on, whether it be to an object, a goal, or a point of view. And, yes, the Latin root word means "to hold."

- Bud tried to loosen little sister Carole's hold on his precious iPod, but her grasp was surprisingly **tenacious**.

- **Tenacity** is usually a virtue, but not always: Howie, a major complaint collector, holds on to every slight and grievance he's ever suffered—to the benefit of no one.

9. **alacrity** (a LACK ri tee) This noun refers to speedy and cheerful willingness to do something. It's most often seen in the phrase "with alacrity." It comes from the Latin word for "lively."

- Slackers are not noted for performing with **alacrity** at school or at work.

- Mr. Dithers was delighted when Dagwood attacked the quarterly report with more than usual **alacrity**.

10. **frenetic** (fren ET ik) Even positive qualities can be taken too far. If your eager approach to work becomes too eager, you can describe yourself as being frenetic—in short, frenzied or wildly excited. The next time you're tempted to go overboard, remember that "frenetic" derives from the Greek word for "brain disease."

- Being a journalist on a weekly paper suits Dennie perfectly, except for the **frenetic** mood in the office as the deadline draws near.

- The longer the search for the missing child continued, the more **frenetic** grew the mood of the anxious parents.

Words for the Ages   17

Here's a list of words to describe the old and the young. Some describe age in terms of years, others in terms of spirit.

1. dotage (DOE tij) This noun means the deterioration of mental faculties that comes with aging. It can be used more or less interchangeably with "senility." A person who is in his dotage is called a "dotard."

- In his **dotage**, Seymour no longer had the attention span to read long novels and resorted instead to gossip magazines and television news programs.

- "Laura has married a **dotard**," her mother wailed. "He's not only fifty years older than she is, but he can barely remember her name. I hope she didn't marry him just because he is a billionaire."

2. venerable (VEN er uh bul) Unlike dotage, this adjective means "commanding respect because of old age or dignity." It also has a religious connotation. In the Roman Catholic Church, it is used as a form of address for a person who has reached the first stage of canonization. It comes from the Latin word for "worship."

- The mayor, a **venerable** man in his late seventies, was respected by the town for his dignified manner, his generous nature, and his years of experience as a legislator and a leader.

- Singing the praises of youthful innocence, the nineteenth-century writer Henry David Thoreau has described an infant as "more **venerable** than the oldest man."

3. puerile (PYOO ril) Though it comes from the Latin word for "boy," this adjective applies to males and females and means "childish" or "juvenile."

- Professor Larkin glared at his class of adult education students and shouted, "Don't be so **puerile**. This is no time for throwing spitballs!"

- The demure senator was ashamed of the **puerile** behavior of some of her campaign workers, who made prank phone calls to her opponent's headquarters.

4. **wizened** (WIZ end) This adjective means "dried up" or "withered." You can describe things, such as a piece of fruit that is no longer fresh, as "wizened," but it is most commonly used to describe a person who is wrinkled with age.

- In Coleridge's famous poem, an ancient mariner, stooped and **wizened** with age, returns from the sea to tell the story of his experiences.

- Whenever Marguerite purchased inexpensive tulips from the grocery store down the street, they **wizened** almost as soon as she put them in a vase. Now she buys them from the florist. They cost more, but they last longer.

5. **pubescent** (pyoo BESS ent) This adjective means "having reached puberty or the stage of adolescence in which an individual becomes capable of sexual reproduction." It also means "covered with short hairs or soft down"—perhaps a description of the cheek of a pubescent boy? The noun is "pubescence."

- "You're acting like a **pubescent** girl," Clothilde's fiancé insisted. "We're planning an engagement party, not a bat mitzvah."

- Sandy could tell by the braces, the pimples, and the budding mustache that Zachary had reached **pubescence**; she hoped he would now finally ask her to go on a date instead of playing "cowboys and indians" in his backyard.

6. **dowager** (DOW ah jer) From the Latin word for "dowry," this noun refers to "a widow who holds property or a title that comes from her deceased husband." It can also be used to describe any old woman of high social standing.

- Lady Entwhistle, a wealthy old **dowager** who grew up on the streets of London, moved to Knightsbridge when she married Lord Entwhistle and has lived there quite comfortably since his death several years ago.

- Miss Havisham, a character in Charles Dickens's novel *Great Expectations*, is a **dowager** who was left at the altar on her wedding day and waits for the rest of her life for a groom who never arrives.

7. **senescence** (sen ESS ense) This is a fancy noun that means "old age." It comes from the Latin word for "old man," but it applies to both genders. The adjective is "senescent."

- Having reached **senescence**, Laura felt it was time to think about whether she would spend the last years of her life sitting in a rocker and knitting or joining the Peace Corps and traveling through Africa.

- Dr. Hargrove is a geriatric doctor who specializes in health issues affecting **senescent** patients, such as high blood pressure, heart palpitations, and osteoporosis.

8. **callow** (CAL low) It's back to youth with this adjective. From the Middle English word for "bald," it means "immature" or "lacking adult experience." Perhaps it comes from acting like a bald baby or else from acting "baldly," that is, bluntly, without sophistication or sensitivity.

- "Ah, **callow** youth!" reflected the old man when he overheard a group of boys making fun of his long beard and bent walk. "They'll know better when they grow old."

- In a speech he made in 1933, Winston Churchill refers to the students of Oxford University as "**callow**, ill-tutored youths" and then goes on to blame the adults of England for setting a bad example.

9. **superannuated** (SOO per AN yoo ate ed) Although it comes from the Latin for "over one year old," this adjective means somewhat older than that. It connotes "ineffective or outmoded because of advanced age."

- "I'm tired of relying on **superannuated** forms of identifying plagiarism in our students' papers," announced the principal. "It's time we used the internet to help us locate the culprits and then punish them accordingly."

- George Bernard Shaw once defined a nap as "a brief period of sleep which overtakes **superannuated** persons when they endeavor to entertain unwelcome visitors or to listen to scientific lectures."

10. **ingénue** (ON jen oo) This noun comes to us from the French for "guileless" (see the "Oh, What a Tangled Web" section). It means "a naive or innocent young woman." It is also used to describe an actress who plays that role.

- Arriving in New York City for the first time, the **ingénue** from Alabama checked into a YWCA and asked at the front desk if there was someone available to be her chaperone as she took in the tourist sights.

- Marilyn Monroe's role in *The Seven-Year Itch* as a sexy **ingénue** who charms her married neighbor while his wife is away on vacation catapulted the beautiful young starlet to instant celebrity.

True Believers

18

I f you've ever felt intense devotion—for a person, an idea, or even a sports team—here's the real deal about real zeal.

1. **ardor** (ARE dur) The root of this noun is the Latin word *ardere*, which means "to burn," and it means burning passion or fiery devotion. The adjective form is ardent. You can feel ardent about a person or an idea as long as it is a very enthusiastic feeling.

- Romeo's **ardor** for Juliet was so overwhelming that he waited below her balcony in spite of her family's antipathy to him.

- An **ardent** admirer of Mozart, Fritz waited in line for two days to purchase tickets to the new production of *The Magic Flute*.

2. **zealot** (ZELL it) This is a noun for a person who feels extreme passion or devotion, sometimes to the exclusion of almost anything else. It is used almost exclusively to describe someone who is committed to an idea or series of ideas; it is not used to describe someone who is passionately in love with another person. The passion a zealot feels is "zeal." The adjective form is "zealous."

- The religious leader attracted a group of **zealots** whose devotion was so intense that they formed a commune in which they could live and work only with each other.

- An enthusiastic medical student, Praveen approached his residency at the hospital with **zeal**; he worked twenty-hour days and rarely took a day off.

3. **amorous** (AM or us) From the Old French word *amoureus*, which means "loving," this adjective describes a particular kind of passion—love or sexual attraction. It is used exclusively to describe feelings toward people. A similar word is "concupiscence" (con KYUP ih sens), which adds a bit more lust to the mix. The adjective form is "concupiscent."

- Popeye was so **amorous** about Olive Oyl that he saw hearts in the air around her whenever he looked in her direction.

- Jeffrey thought about Gladys's sweet soul and extraordinary beauty day and night; he was overwhelmed with feelings of **ardor** and concupiscence.

4. **fervent** (FER vent) We're back to hot passion for ideas as well as for people with this adjective. Like ardent, this adjective means burning with enthusiasm. In fact, it comes from the Latin word for "boil." The noun form is "fervor." A related word, which means the same thing, is "fervid."

- Luis's **fervent** desire to move to New York was fueled by his need to make enough money to support his large family.
- The audience applauded with **fervor** after hearing the candidate's galvanizing (see the "Eponyms" section) speech.

5. **fanatical** (fan AT ik al) This adjective comes from the Latin words that mean "temple" (*fanum*) and "being inspired by certain frenzied, devotional rites" *(fanaticus)*. It means to be possessed by enthusiasm to the point of being irrational. Another adjective form is "fanatic," which is also what you call someone who is possessed by these feelings. The word "fan" comes from "fanatic."

- Greg's **fanatical** (or **fanatic**) devotion to the Yankees ultimately cost him his job. He refused to remove his Yankees cap during executive meetings and called in sick several times a week to go to the ballpark.
- Carlos was **fanatic** about ballet. He attended several performances a week with Sidney, a fellow balletomane (see the "What's My Line" section).

6. **manic** (MAN ik) Like fanatical, this is an adjective that means "passion to the point of madness." The symptoms of "mania," as defined in the field of psychiatry, include excessive gaiety, loss of sleep, and wildly irrational behavior. These might also be the symptoms of someone whose passion is manic or maniacal. The noun form is "mania;" someone who feels manic feelings is, of course, a maniac.

- Elizabeth's passion for frogs bordered on **manic**. Hundreds of stuffed frogs lined her bookshelves; she wore T-shirts with pictures of frogs on them; and she nominated herself president of the Frogs' Rights Society.
- A **maniacal** coffee drinker, Lloyd drank ten cups a day, searching the city for the best cappuccinos, expressos, and lattes.

7. **evangelical** (ee van JEL ik al) Passion turns religious with this adjective. Although the word originally referred to anything relating to the Christian gospel and the zealous preaching of those beliefs, it has come to have a more generalized meaning than pure missionary work. Someone who is evangelical has an ardent or crusading enthusiasm for something.

- The congregation was mesmerized (see the "Eponyms" section) by the **evangelist** preacher's fiery sermon on sin and damnation.
- Their antiwar sentiments bordering on the **evangelical**, the student protesters marched through the streets of Washington with posters and leaflets, chanting "No more war!"

8. **vehement** (VEE heh ment) It is possible that this adjective comes from a Latin word for "to carry." It means characterized by (or carrying) an intense emotion or conviction. People are not vehement, but they do things *with* vehemence.

- At his trial, the accused man insisted on his innocence, **vehemently** denying he had ever seen the victim before.

- When Nikita Khrushchev felt strongly about something, he would take off his shoe and **vehemently** strike his podium to emphasize his words.

9. **effusive** (eff YOOSE iv) This adjective means "unrestrained in emotional expression" or "gushy." Anyone who is very passionate about something is likely to be effusive about it. It comes from the Latin verb for "to pour out." The noun form is "effusion;" the verb form is "to effuse."

- Whenever you mention Sarah's name to Josh, he blushes and becomes very **effusive**, extolling (which means "to highly praise") her beauty, wit, and intelligence.

- Thrilled with the cashmere sweater in her favorite color, Sandy wrote a very **effusive** note to Meg, thanking her for her generosity and thoughtfulness.

10. **hell-bent** This adjective, which can also be spelled without the hyphen, means recklessly determined to do or achieve something. Anyone who is truly ardent, zealous, or fervent is likely to be hell-bent about it.

- Teddy and Max, **hell-bent** on seeing the Nets win the basketball game, painted their faces and stood in the bleachers, screaming, "Go Nets!" until they were hoarse.

- **Hell-bent** on being the first to reach the North Pole, the explorers refused to turn back, even when the sea was clogged by glacial ice and the temperatures dropped to forty below.

MAKE A MATCH #6

Sections 16–18

Match each word in the left-hand column with the phrase on the right that best suggests its meaning.

A. alacrity   1. _____ hard-working for long periods
B. amorous   2. _____ characterized by romantic love
C. dotage   3. _____ loss of abilities because of age
D. effusive   4. _____ "gushy" in manner
E. frenetic   5. _____ attentive to small details of work

F. herculean	6. _____ forceful in manner
G. ingénue	7. _____ persistence, perseverance
H. pubescent	8. _____ overly devoted to a cause
I. puerile	9. _____ retired, outdated
J. punctilious	10. _____ frantic, harried
K. sedulous	11. _____ a young and innocent woman
L. stamina	12. _____ dried up, withered
M. superannuated	13. _____ childish, immature
N. tenacity	14. _____ ability to keep going
O. vehement	15. _____ quickness and eagerness
P. venerable	16. _____ respected because of age
Q. wizened	17. _____ adolescent
R. zealous	18. _____ requiring or possessing great strength

PRACTICE, PRACTICE, PRACTICE #2

Sections 10–18

For the blank in each of the sentences below, select the word that best fits meaning.

A. adventitious	K. herculean
B. adversary	L. piebald
C. callow	M. protocol
D. churl	N. recalcitrant
E. culinary	O. savory
F. detrimental	P. seemly
G. dogged	Q. superannuated
H. fastidious	R. temerity
I. fortitude	S. toothsome
J. frenetic	T. vehement

1. Talking a walk in the park, feeding the pigeons, talking to friends, shopping for the makings of a simple meal—these were all pleasant activities for the _____ man, freed from his work after forty-five years of dedication.

2. Her _____ search for just the perfect gift paid off: knowing that she had found just what her mother wanted made her effort worthwhile.

3. The ease with which he asked his classmate for a date was _____, for he was really very nervous about being rejected.

4. Those desserts in the bakery window all look very _____; I hardly know which one to select.

5. Being an ambassador means you must be very familiar with the _____ of other cultures because you don't want to commit a blunder.

6. Being asked by his parents to drop extracurricular activities in order to work harder on his grades made him feel _____, but he knew better than to argue back.

7. Getting the campaign materials organized requires a _____ coordination of efforts by all volunteers.

8. The _____ coat of the dog provided him with the rather unimaginative name of Spot.

9. Was his interrupting the author's meal in the restaurant to ask for an autograph _____ or just plain rudeness?

10. When he said, "No, in thunder!" to my request, I meekly said I hadn't known he felt so _____ in his opposition.

11. Only a real _____ could have refused the sweet little girl's request that we buy Girl Scout cookies from her.

12. Back in the 1960s, the surgeon general's report first offered scientific evidence that smoking is _____ to people's health.

13. Wayne is very _____, in that he keeps his office space very neat and doesn't like even his secretary to rearrange his desk.

14. On her birthday, Lauren wants every friend to be near her and every _____ to be far away.

15. The usually calm Ms. Howard grew quite _____ when the technician told her that her hard drive had crashed.

16. The chaplain of the church camp stressed to the campers the importance of _____ behavior in the weekly church service; he would speak privately to anyone behaving inappropriately.

17. Some people like to poke around hardware stores, but good cooks probably prefer to roam the aisles of stores with _____ equipment.

18. Alice made cookies for her son's friends, but she offered chips and salsa for those who preferred _____ snacks to sweet ones.

19. Ms. Blevins had thought that Simon was maturing, but his classroom prank yesterday was a regression to his earlier _____ manner.

20. Martina doesn't think of herself as particularly brave, but her friends have great admiration for the _____ she showed in working every day while undergoing painful medical treatments.

Enemies, Adversaries, and Antagonists

19

Whether you're only slightly angry or ready to declare war, there's vocabulary that offers you more than ample possibilities for ways to express your feelings.

1. **nemesis** (NEM ess iss) In Greek mythology, the goddess of vengeance and retribution was Nemesis. The noun means "an opponent that cannot be beaten or overcome" or "a source of harm or ruin."

- Throughout the comic book series, Superman was plagued by his **nemesis**, Lex Luthor.

- "Chocolate is my **nemesis**," declared Johanna. "Even when I am on a diet, I can't resist it so I never lose any weight."

2. **inimical** (in IM ih kal) From the Latin word meaning "enemy," this adjective means extremely hostile. There is no noun form.

- The **inimical** Genghis Khan was obsessed with war and conquest.

- Poised for a fight, the **inimical** gang waited on the street corner for the boys to pass them.

3. **enmity** (EN mitt ee) Here's a noun that means "deep-seated, often mutual hatred." When two people share enmity, peace is unlikely. The word shares a Latin root with "inimical."

- The **enmity** between North Vietnam and South Vietnam was so great that war was inevitable.

- Will and Jake felt a growing **enmity** as they drifted apart after college. One joined the Peace Corps; the other took a job on Wall Street.

4. **pugilistic** (pyoo jil ISS tik) This adjective refers to people who fight with their fists. It comes from the Latin word *pugil*, meaning "fighter." A related word, **pugnacious**, which means "combative in nature," comes from the Latin root *pugnus*, which means fist.

- Spear in hand, Achilles assumed a **pugilistic** stance before his foe.

- **Pugnacious** by nature, the young man refused to sit down on the bus, even when he was asked politely by the group leader.

5. belligerent (bell ij er ent) Here's a strong adjective that means aggressive or engaged in warfare. It comes from the Latin word that means "to wage war," the same root for "bellicose" (see #10). The noun form is "belligerence."

- By 1939, there could be no mistaking Germany's **belligerence** toward its neighbors.
- The boys in Mr. Sullivan's eighth grade class were so **belligerent** that he had to separate their desks in the classroom.

6. miffed (MIFT) This adjective describes someone who is annoyed or angry over a trivial issue. There is a noun form, "miff," which means a small spat (see the "Them Thar's Fightin' Words" section) but it is rarely used.

- Alexios was **miffed** when his sister Artemis ate the last of the chocolate chip cookies; she had already had two, and he had had none.
- "You were supposed to be here at noon," muttered a **miffed** James. "It's already one o'clock, and we have to be back at school in ten minutes."

7. animosity (ann ih MOS it ee) This noun comes from two Latin words that mean bold (*animosus*) and spirit or soul (*animus*). It means bitter hostility or active hatred. There is no adjective form.

- Sujata's **animosity** toward Rosie dates back to the time Rosie took the job that Sujata had applied for first.
- The **animosity** between the two brothers was so great that they didn't speak for almost twenty years.

8. antipathy (an TIH path ee) From the Greek word that means "of opposite feelings," this noun means a strong feeling of aversion or repugnance. It's a bit milder than belligerence or animosity. You might have an antipathy for skim milk, but you wouldn't want to wage war against it.

- The smoke-filled rooms and noisy music were **antipathetic** to Lynette. She asked her date if he could find a cleaner and quieter restaurant.
- Cats have a natural **antipathy** toward dogs, especially large, growling ones.

9. malice (MAL iss) This noun, coming from the Latin word that means "bad," connotes a desire to harm others or see them suffer. Someone who is malicious is deliberately harmful or spiteful.

- Stanley Kowalski had a **malicious** heart, and he detested the vulnerable Blanche DuBois.
- In the playground, the **malicious** child kicked the other children and bit the teacher when she tried to stop him.

10. **bellicose** (BELL ih kohs) From the Latin root that means "war," this adjective means about as hostile as you can get. Like belligerent, it means warlike.

- The **bellicose** Mohawk Indians were quick to use their hatchets on the white settlers.
- Eager to fight, the **bellicose** reporter documented all of the instances of discrimination in the corporation's hiring policies.

Comrades, Cohorts, and Companions

20

Here are some words to describe casual acquaintances, close pals, and intimate partners as well as some of the words we use for the feelings we have for them.

1. camaraderie (kahm RAD er ee) From the Old French word that means "roommate," this noun means a light-hearted rapport (another good word from the Old French that means "mutual trust") among friends.

- In the 1920s, there was widespread **camaraderie** among the American expatriates who congregated in the bars and cafes of Paris.
- The lonely graduate student drank her coffee alone, longing for even a moment of **camaraderie**.

2. gregarious (greg AIR ee us) This adjective, which means "sociable," comes from the Latin for "belonging to a flock." A gregarious person enjoys the company of others.

- Franz Kafka, who loved to live and work in solitude, was hardly what his acquaintances in Prague would call **gregarious**.
- The **gregarious** candidate greeted his constituency warmly from the podium.

3. affable (AF uh bul) From the Latin verb that means "to speak to," this adjective describes someone who is gracious and approachable, easy to speak to. The noun form is "affability."

- Always **affable**, Mr. Winterbottom said good morning to the doorman and shook his chauffeur's hand.
- Because of her **affability**, Sarah was elected president of the student council; she was good at improving communication between the students and the administration.

4. congenial (con JEEN ee al) Like "affable," this adjective means "agreeable and sympathetic, gracious." It can be used interchangeably with "genial"; they both come from the same Latin root, *genius*, which means "spirit of festivity." The noun for "congenial" is "congeniality." The noun for "genial," however, is either "geniality" or "genialness."

- With his bright smile and warm handshake, Smithers was known as the most **congenial** employee at Phonics R Us.

- Miss **Congeniality** was talented and beautiful but, most important, she was gracious and friendly.

5. **simpatico** (sim PA tee ko) This adjective comes from either the Italian or the Spanish word that means "sympathy," and it means "having like mind or temperament." People who are "simpatico" become friends because they have common interests. There is no noun for this word.

- Louise and Susan are very **simpatico**; they both love Italian cooking, going to the dog races, and playing jai alai.
- The two men are truly **simpatico**; they sit in Starbucks every day and discuss everything from politics and food to the state of their souls.

6. **veneration** (ven ur RAY shun) Suggesting a bit more feeling than friendship, this noun connotes "respect or reverence." It's usually used to describe feelings for someone older or more experienced. The verb form is "to venerate."

- The students at Pencey Prep **venerated** the headmaster not only for his intellect but for his warmth and generosity. They felt he created an inspiring atmosphere for learning.
- The patriarch basked in the **veneration** of his family and friends.

7. **adulation** (ad yoo LAY shun) Here's another noun that connotes a bit more feeling than friendship. From the Latin root which means "to flatter," this word means "excessive admiration or flattery." It's pretty close to adoration in meaning. There is a verb form, "to adulate," but it's never used.

- The fan's **adulation** for Derek Jeter was so great that he changed his own name to Derek.
- The students felt nothing but **adulation** for their history teacher until they found out that he belonged to an illegal extremist group.

8. **demonstrative** (dem ON strat iv) This adjective means "given to open expression of emotion." Someone who is "demonstrative" usually, but not always, demonstrates friendly or loving feelings. The noun form is "demonstrativeness," not "demonstration."

- The newlyweds were very **demonstrative** in public; they always held hands on the street and often kissed while seated in restaurants.
- The insurance salesman's **demonstrativeness** was apparent when he began to weep when his beloved Florida Marlins won the World Series.

9. **cohort** (KO hort) In Caesar's time, a "cohort" was a division of the Roman army made up of three to six hundred men. A legion consisted of ten cohorts, or three to six thousand men. The noun has now come to mean "any kind of group or band of people" and even to mean simply "a companion."

- "I expect you and your **cohorts** to appear in my office after school for detention," said the principal. "I know you all went out for sushi together instead of going to history class."

- The thief and his teenage **cohorts** broke into my apartment and stole all of my video games.

10. **kudos** (KOO doss *or* KOO doze) Here's a noun that means "the praise one might offer to a friend or to someone of exceptional achievement." It comes from the Greek word meaning "magical glory." Although it looks like a plural noun, it is not. There is no such thing as a single "kudo."

- The brave fireman sought no **kudos** for his heroic deeds.

- The teacher gave Belinda **kudos** for being the only student in the class to write the extra-credit essay. "Belinda is a thoughtful and hardworking student," she announced to the class. "She always goes the extra mile."

Sounds Like, Smells Like

21

W e think a lot about how to describe what things taste like. The words below should help with smells and sounds. (See also section 82, "The Body and Beyond.")

1. **resonant** (REZ uh nunt) Literally meaning "sounding again," this adjective can be used in a literal or figurative sense.

- Torrance's department store hired a Santa Claus with a reedy, piping voice, far from the ideal Santa who should have a deep, **resonant** tone when he asks children what they want for Christmas.

- The touching film showed the dying soldier clutching his buddy's hand while struggling to recite the **resonant** phrases of a Psalm he had learned as a boy.

2. **sonorous** (SON er us) This adjective has a meaning similar to that of #1— describing a full, rich sound—and may also describe spoken words that are impressive.

- Lying in the hammock, Iris relished the **sonorous** backdrop of humming bees and the drone of a lawn mower being pushed by someone other than herself.

- Washington's Farewell Address and Lincoln's Gettysburg Address are probably the most **sonorous** orations in the history of this country.

3. **reverberate** (re VER ber ate) This verb comes from vivid Latin roots meaning "to whip back." We must picture sound beating its way back through the air, whether we see the word used in its literal sense or its very common figurative sense where it becomes a synonym for "repercussion," literally, "striking back."

- As the nymph Echo shouted "Do you love me?" to the vain Narcissus, the air **reverberated** with the response, "Love me, Love me."

- Hiram felt the **reverberations** of his hasty decision to drop out of college for many years.

4. **acoustic** (uh KOOS tik) This adjective describes things which relate to sound, as suggested by the Greek root word. In the field of music, the word has the special sense of describing an instrument whose sound is free of electronic effect. Put an "s" on the adjective and you have the noun **acoustics**, referring either to the scientific study of sound or to the overall effect of sound in an enclosed space.

- Frank and Stanley and Allen all heard Bob Dylan in 1963 when he was still playing **acoustic** guitar; their younger friends who know only the later period are envious.

- The **acoustics** of newer, more architecturally impressive buildings often cannot match the quality of sound in older concern halls.

5. **timbre** (TAM ber *or* TIM ber) The word may be pronounced as its French origins suggest, or it may be "anglicized" (pronounced like an English word). Either way, the noun refers to the indefinable qualities of a sound that distinguish it from sounds identical in pitch and volume.

- The **timbre** of Placido Domingo's voice has deepened over the years of his long career, but he has sounded wonderful, young or old.

- Even the untrained ear can distinguish the **timbre** of a flute from that of a bassoon.

6. **tintinnabulation** (tin ti NAB yoo lay shun) You won't have many chances to use this noun meaning the sound of the ringing of bells, but when you see it in Edgar Allan Poe's poem "The Bells," you'll feel very learned. (If that doesn't impress your friends sufficiently, you can produce the fact that in earlier centuries Oxford University had on its staff a "tintinnabularius"—yes, a bell ringer.) A related additional bit of the lore of sound is the word **tinnitus** (tih NIGH tus) meaning a persistent ringing or buzzing sound in one or both ears.

- As Poe says, "...the **tintinnabulation** that so musically wells/From the jingling and the tinkling of the bells."

- While we generally think of the sound of bells as pleasant, anyone who has suffered even briefly from **tinnitus** can tell you the sound is maddening.

7. **noisome** (NOY sum) Sounds like a "sound" word, right? Surprise—it's generally used for smells, and unpleasant or dangerous ones at that. If it's a smell that an**noys** it's **nois**ome. (Not just a pun—"annoy" has the same root word.)

- Students sought out the source of the **noisome** odors in the second floor hallway and found it in the chemistry lab where experiments with sulfur were underway.

- Tenants complained about the **noisome** fumes coming from the basement of the Estcourt Building, fearing that an explosion might occur.

8. **redolent** (RED uh lunt) Another "smell" word and a more pleasant one. This adjective usually describes a good fragrance, an aromatic smell. It can also be used figuratively for an intangible quality, a memory, or an aura.

- A full day after Thanksgiving had passed, the kitchen remained **redolent** of the smell of roasted onions, sage, and spices used in pumpkin pie.

- Just opening his college yearbook transported Luke to memories **redolent** in equal measures of good times and anxiety about the future.

9. **pungent** (PUN junt) This adjective describes sharp smells that may be pleasant or otherwise, and the meaning may be extended to figurative uses. The Latin root word means "to sting."

- The **pungent** smell of burning leaves wafted through the lanes of the town, prompting many a resident to wonder what neighbor was violating City Code regulation #447.

- Enjoyment of the politically **pungent** satire of Garry Trudeau's *Doonesbury* may depend upon one's own political views.

10. **odoriferous** (oh der IF er us) If you want a five-syllable adjective meaning "having a smell," then this is the word for you.

- Walking hand in hand with the love of his life in the summer sunlight beneath the **odoriferous** trees of Charleston, Ben felt a heightened sense of the joy of being alive.

- A steady diet of goat curry followed by gorgonzola cheese could make someone a little too **odoriferous** for intimate companionship.

MAKE A MATCH #7

Sections 19–21

Match each word in the left-hand column with the phrase on the right that best suggests its meaning.

A.	acoustics	1. _____	ringing noise in the ears
B.	belligerent	2. _____	praise
C.	camaraderie	3. _____	enjoying being with a group
D.	cohort	4. _____	relating to the science of sound
E.	demonstrative	5. _____	suggesting through smell or memory
F.	gregarious	6. _____	prone to go to war
G.	kudos	7. _____	likely to fight
H.	nemesis	8. _____	close companionship
I.	noisome	9. _____	a perpetual opponent
J.	pugnacious	10. _____	pleasing in sound
K.	redolent	11. _____	a group
L.	resonant	12. _____	physically showing feelings
M.	sonorous	13. _____	uniqueness of a sound
N.	timbre	14. _____	almost reverent admiration
O.	tinnitus	15. _____	unpleasantly smelly
P.	veneration	16. _____	enduring through time

Them Thar's Fightin' Words

22

T here are lots of words for a good fight, from "tiff" (a kiss-and-make-up fight) to an epic war. Here is a group that will help describe all the types of battles in between.

1. spat (rhymes with mat) In this instance, it's a noun, not the past tense of spit. Quite simply, it means a brief quarrel, usually fought with a few mean words.

- After the two friends got into a **spat** over who would eat the last cookie, they resolved it by breaking it in half and sharing it.

- Though the couple was prone to **spats** over who would do the household chores, they always described themselves as "happily married."

2. bicker (BIK er) Here's a verb for what people who have spats do—they quarrel, usually over petty matters. Although people who bicker usually hurl words not spears, the word comes from the Middle English word that means "to attack."

- "Instead of **bickering** over who gets to sit in the front seat next to me," said the mother, "why don't you children walk to school this morning?"

- The couple's constant **bickering** drove their landlord crazy, and she finally asked them to move out of the building.

3. dispute (dis PYOOT) The Latin root of this word, *desputare*, means to examine. Therefore, when you dispute something, you engage in an argumentative discussion about its validity; you debate its truth. It can be used either as a verb or a noun.

- The student was certain that the word "tiff" meant quarrel so he **disputed** his grade on the vocabulary quiz when his teacher marked him wrong.

- A **dispute** over the existence of global warming was the focus of the environmentalists at the conference.

4. squabble (SKWAH bul) Also used either as a verb or a noun, a squabble is another way to say a verbal argument over something pretty trivial. Squabbles tend to be a bit more raucous (noisy) than disputes.

- On the day before Christmas, the two adults **squabbled** over who would get the last Scrabble set in the crowded toy store.

• A **squabble** between a police officer and a motorist illegally parked in the crosswalk tied up traffic for over an hour on the usually deserted street.

5. **tussle** (TUSS ul) A squabble takes on a physical aspect when you use this word, either as a noun or a verb. Derived from the Middle English word that means "to pull roughly," a tussle suggests a rough struggle.

• The police officers **tussled** with the bank robber, finally wrenching the gun from his hand.

• When the two football players fought for the ball on the forty-seventh-yard line, one of them lost his helmet in the **tussle**.

6. **wrangle** (RANG ul) Once again, the argument gets physical with this word. Whether it's used as a noun or a verb, it connotes a noisy quarrel. Even though a wrangler is a cowboy or a cowgirl who tends saddle horses, someone who wrangles is contending with words, not horses.

• The girls **wrangled** over their plans for the evening, unable to agree on whether to go to a movie or stay home and finish their homework so they would be free for the rest of the weekend.

• After spending an hour in a **wrangle** over what to do for the evening, they realized it was too late to go out at all.

7. **contention** (kon TEN shun) Deriving from the Latin verb *contendere* meaning "to strive," this noun means "the act of striving to win in a competition or debate." The word usually involves a verbal argument but not always. The verb form is "to contend."

• The soccer team played their hearts out in a fierce **contention** to win the cup.

• Most scholars **contend** that Shakespeare's *The Tempest* was the last play he completed.

8. **altercation** (all ter KAY shun) Here's another noun that means a vehement quarrel, usually verbal. Although there is a verb form—"to altercate"—which stems from the Latin word that means "to quarrel," it is rarely used.

• The judge ordered silence in the court after an **altercation** broke out between opposing counsel.

• The teacher stopped the **altercation** between the two students by showing them the correct answer in the textbook.

9. **dissent** (dis SENT) From the Latin *dissentire*, "to feel against," this verb means to disagree or differ in opinion. It can also be used as a noun, although the preferred form is dissension.

• The Protestants **dissented** from the church of Rome and established their own church.

- After the judge made his ruling, there was so much **dissension** in the courtroom that he was forced to call a recess.

10. **irreconcilable** (eer REK con SYLE uh bul) No self-respecting section about arguments would be complete without this adjective which means "impossible to bring into harmony or agreement." It's most frequently used in divorce court where couples insist that they should separate based on "irreconcilable differences." Consider the antonym: when people fight and make up, they "reconcile."

- Since one of the roommates was an inveterate slob and the other was a meticulous cleaner, their dispute was **irreconcilable**.
- The dispute between evolutionists and creationists is **irreconcilable**.

I'm Against That—
Or Am I Next to It?

23

W ords that deal with placement in space can be as simple as "by" or "in" or as complex as some of the words below.

1. **juxtapose** (JUX ta pose) This useful word describes placing items or abstractions next to each other for the sake of comparing or contrasting them. The noun form is "juxtaposition."

- The **juxtaposition** on the bulletin board of the pictures of the students as kindergarteners and as seniors intrigued many passersby, who attempted to match child with young adult.
- The old phrase "champagne taste on a beer budget" neatly **juxtaposes** the longing for expensive objects with a meager bank account.

2. **contiguous** (con TIG yoo us) This word refers to the condition of sharing an edge or of connecting without a break.

- As lab partners, Gillian and Chelsea had **contiguous** work areas.
- In British usage, **contiguous** houses are often referred to as "semidetached."

3. **proximity** (prox IM it ee) The condition of being physically close. (Memory trick: think "approximate"—an answer that would be "close.")

- Larissa was on the chaise longue and the bonbons were on the adjoining table; such **proximity** made her vow to eat healthfully all weekend almost impossible to keep.
- The real estate agent was quick to point out the **proximity** of the house to the best elementary school in the district in an attempt to offset the fact that the lawn was parched and ragged.

4. **athwart** (ah THWART) This is a very literary way of saying "across." You won't be hearing it on the street, but you will find it in older or poetic writing.

- A famous eighteenth-century poet refers to stars that shoot "**athwart** the sky."
- William Buckley says he founded the magazine *National Review* with the mission of "standing **athwart** history yelling STOP!"

5. **trajectory** (tra JEKT or ee) This word, meaning "a path through space," can refer to something as astronomical as a missile going through the skies or as figurative as an individual's career plan. (The word derives from the Latin for "throw" and is thus related to words such as "reject," "eject," and "projectile.")

- Conner found it difficult to fill out the college counselor's questionnaire about his hopes for the future, for he had never before contemplated the possible **trajectory** of his life.

- Air traffic controllers at any airport must be constantly aware of the **trajectories** of all planes scheduled to land.

6. **adjacent** (ah JAY sent) A fairly common word meaning "lying close to or next to."

- Since Alyssa's dorm room was **adjacent** to Pam's, the two girls were virtually roommates, constantly exchanging clothing and observations on life.

- What a bad idea—the rat poison and the aspirin were on **adjacent** shelves in the bathroom!

7. **periphery** (per IF er ee) This word denotes the outmost area—an area to the side—of something, either literal or figurative. The adjective form, "peripheral," may be even more common.

- Drivers need not only keen vision for seeing straight ahead but good **peripheral** vision that will detect traffic approaching from the side.

- Although Samantha was focusing on her academic responsibilities as the end of the semester drew near, her grandmother's illness was always in the **periphery** of her consciousness.

8. **perpendicular** (per pen DIK yoo ler) Possibly an old friend from math problems, this word describes either the formation of a right angle or a line that is vertical.

- Mr. McKean used a plumb line to make sure that the installation of the door frame was **perpendicular**.

- Churches in the English Gothic style have a sharp emphasis on the **perpendicular**; a viewer's eye is instinctively drawn from earth to the skies.

9. **oblique** (ob LEEK) Another word that frequently appears in math problems, this word has the literal sense of being neither vertical or horizontal but slanting. It is also frequently used to describe something that is indirect or downright misleading.

- Cynthia eyed the four unmarked streets entering the traffic circles at **oblique** angles and wondered which of these was Mt. Carmel Road.

- The politician's **oblique** reference to "mistakes that were made" is not what his frustrated constituents considered either an apology or an explanation.

10. **catercorner** (CAT er corn er) or **cattycorner** or **kittycorner**. In whatever form it appears, this word has nothing of the feline about it. Deriving from the Latin word for "four," it means simply "diagonal." The adjective form is catercornered.

- Nat, hungry because he had skipped breakfast, used his mid-morning break to run to the bagel shop **catercorner** to the school.
- Delighted to see her old friend Olivia at the banquet, Julia longed to speak to her immediately, but since they were at **kittycornered** tables in the ballroom, she settled for an enthusiastic wave.

24

We all need a touch of splendor—brilliance, grandeur, magnificence—in our lives. These words help us name or describe something dazzling.

1. **panoply** (PAN uh plee) This noun is used for a striking or splendid display, often used in association with events such as a coronation or a state funeral. It originally denoted a full suit of armor, which must, in its fully polished condition, have given off quite a sheen.

- When Doreen first visited the United Nations, she was delighted by the **panoply** of flags of all the countries represented there.
- The **panoply** of the funeral of Pope John Paul II fascinated even viewers who had no religious associations with the ceremony.

2. **coruscate** (KOR us kate) This verb comes from the Latin word meaning "to sparkle" and can be used either literally or figuratively.

- The film made sharp visual contrast between the life of poor Russian women in drab shawls and the luxury at the czar's ball where figures in shimmering taffeta wore **coruscating** diamonds, emeralds, and sapphires.
- Prof. McIntosh sets high standards for students in his classes, but they continue to sign up, for his **coruscating** wit makes his lectures a delight.

3. **éclat** (a KLA) This French noun has come straight into English to describe great brilliance of performance or the appreciation such a performance might receive.

- Dressed in a purple robe tipped with ermine, Prince Boyohboy entered the kingdom with great **éclat**.
- When the company gave the name "Éclat" to one model of their luxury cars, they probably hoped to evoke a sense of *both* sterling performance and admiration.

4. **flamboyant** (flam BOY ant) This adjective, which derives from the French word for "flame," can be used admiringly for something dashing and colorful in style or can shade over into criticism for that which is overly showy.

- About half of the faculty members defend Emily's **flamboyant** individuality as displayed through her spiky hair and equally spiky jewelry.

- The writer Truman Capote earned a lot of attention from the press for his **flamboyant** activities, such as his Black and White ball given for five hundred forty of his closest friends.

5. **sumptuous** (SUMP tyoo us) From the Latin word for "expense," this adjective describes things or situations that are lavish, marked by abundance, and, thus, are likely to have cost a lot.
- Fred's midday craving for a **sumptuous** meal is not likely to be fulfilled by the offerings of the salad bar and the sandwich stand.
- Marc Antony yielded quickly to the **sumptuous** effect of the regal Cleopatra in her golden boat with its perfumed-filled sails floating down the Nile.

6. **pyrotechnics** (PYE ro TEK niks) This noun, taken literally, is the technical term for fireworks ("pyre" equals "fire" in Greek). It can also be used for a display of wit or brilliance in the performing arts that might rival the sparkling effect of skyborne rockets and Catherine's wheels on the Fourth of July.
- The verbal **pyrotechnics** in Oscar Wilde's plays are a delight for a lover of language.
- Doc Watson's uniqueness as a performer of traditional American folk songs comes from the beauty and grace of his style rather than from technical **pyrotechnics**.

7. **burnish** (BURN ish) This verb means "to polish to a high sheen." You will often see "burnished," the adjectival form of the word, meaning "shining."
- The turkey served at the banquet, beautifully cooked, appeared **burnished** to a dull gold.
- The hair of Princess Myohmy was not so much brushed as **burnished**, for she had six handmaidens responsible for its gleaming appearance.

8. **sybarite** (SIB uh rite) This noun, which can be used admiringly or critically, fits an individual whose life is given over to pleasure and luxury. It has its origin in an ancient Greek city, Sybaris, notorious for its luxurious excess.
- "Those who criticize our **sybaritic** existence are merely envious," said Lady Gotalot, as she sent her footman out for caviar and peacocks' tongues.
- Being a counselor in many Girl Scout camps is great fun, but not for **sybarites**; you may be asked to shower in cold water and to sleep on an army cot.

9. **iridescent** (eer ih DESS unt) This adjective describes the appearance of a shining spectrum of colors. Its meaning and spelling (only one *r*) are easy to remember when you know the word comes from Iris, the classical goddess of the rainbow.

- Young John marveled at the **iridescent** display of colors in the feathers of so common a bird as the pigeon.

- Photographers may find beauty in unexpected places such as the **iridescence** of an oil slick.

10. **ostentatious** (os ten TAY shus) Anything, even splendor, can be carried too far. This adjective always conveys a negative tone in describing something that is perceived as overly showy, pretentious.

- Bernie likes cars as well as the next person, but he characterizes Brian, who possesses three luxury sedans, an SUV, and a convertible, as "completely **ostentatious**."

- Gore Vidal encourages writers to avoid verbal **ostentation** by "killing their darlings," i.e., getting rid of any overly cute or precious phrasing.

MAKE A MATCH #8

Sections 22–24

Match each word in the left-hand column with the phrase on the right that best suggests its meaning.

A.	altercation	1. _____	dramatic, showy
B.	athwart	2. _____	argument
C.	burnish	3. _____	fireworks
D.	dissent	4. _____	disagreement with a majority view
E.	éclat	5. _____	lavish, expensive
F.	flamboyant	6. _____	marked by a rainbow of colors
G.	iridescent	7. _____	slanting
H.	irreconcilable	8. _____	polish
I.	juxtapose	9. _____	course of movement
J.	oblique	10. _____	person devoted to luxury
K.	ostentatious	11. _____	physical closeness
L.	panoply	12. _____	to the side, not central
M.	peripheral	13. _____	brilliant performance
N.	proximity	14. _____	across
O.	pyrotechnics	15. _____	petty argument
P.	squabble	16. _____	not solvable
Q.	sumptuous	17. _____	impressive display
R.	sybarite	18. _____	place close together
S.	trajectory	19. _____	showing off

Farrago

25

This title word means "hodgepodge" or "mixture." The words below compose the second example of our "medley" theme.

1. miasma (mye AZ ma *or* mee AZ ma) From the Greek word for "pollution" or "stain," this noun means "a poisonous atmosphere or influence." It originally referred to the atmosphere thought to arise from swamps or putrid matter. The adjective form is "miasmic."

- The **miasma** of failure that hung in the locker room after the boys lost the football game was too much for the coach to bear without launching into a pep talk.
- In Henry James's *Daisy Miller*, Daisy catches malaria after walking through the **miasmic** atmosphere in the Roman Forum at night.

2. automaton (aw TOM at on) This noun means "a robot" or "a person who responds in a mechanical way." It comes from the Latin for "a self-operating machine."

- The requirements of basic training were so rigorous and so demanding that by the end of the first week, most of the men and women moved more like **automatons** than like human beings.
- Poet W. H. Auden has written: "One of the most horrible, yet most important, discoveries of our age has been that, if you really wish to destroy a person and turn him into an **automaton**, the surest method is not physical torture, in the strict sense, but simply to keep him awake, i.e., in an existential relation to life without intermission."

3. pomp (rhymes with romp) A noun that means "magnificent or dignified display," this word come from the Greek for "procession." It is often used to describe what occurs at wedding ceremonies, graduations, or royal events.

- "**Pomp** and Circumstance" is a fitting piece of music to be played at graduation ceremonies because it is both solemn and dignified.
- A symphony orchestra, a parade of soldiers in full-dress uniform, and a procession of flower girls bearing bouquets of orchids and roses were only part of the **pomp** at the retired general's wedding ceremony in Virginia.

4. **egregious** (e GREEJ us) Although this word comes from the Latin for "outstanding," it means only "outstandingly bad or offensive."

- Looking quite doleful, Marjorie handed in her essay exam and said to her teacher, "Please forgive my **egregious** grammar and punctuation, but I had a lot to say and not enough time to proofread what I wrote."
- Robertson Roofers did such an **egregious** job of repairing the slate roof on the Kandinskys' house that they had leaks in their kitchen all winter long.

5. **ululation** (ull yoo LAY shun) This noun comes to us from the Latin and means a "howl" or "wail of lamentation." If you say it fast and loud, it sounds like what it means.

- When Marlowe arrived at the edge of the village, he could hear the **ululations** of the natives emerging from deep in the jungle and wondered if there had been a death among the tribesmen.
- As Tulik made her way through the smoke of the funeral pyre, she heard the **ululations** of the women who had gathered in mourning around the coffin of the village elder.

6. **minuscule** (MIN us kyool) From the French, this adjective originally meant "small, as opposed to capital, letter," but it is generally used now to mean "very small, tiny."

- The doctors discovered **minuscule** traces of mercury in the preservative used for the vaccinations but determined that they were not harmful.
- While she was in Venice, Laura purchased a collection of **minuscule** glass animals which she now displays on a mirrored shelf on her bedroom wall.

7. **attenuate** (ah TEN yoo ate) This verb means "to reduce in force, value, size, or degree." It comes from the Latin for "to make thin." A verb with a similar meaning is "to truncate," but it is used only to mean "to shorten." The adjective form is "truncated."

- Niko's robust health was **attenuated** by poor eating habits, a lack of exercise, and his high-stress job as an emergency medical technician.
- Ms. Nichols took her class to see a modern and **truncated** version of *Hamlet*. The play was set in a computer software company in Palo Alto, and the entire performance lasted only an hour and a half.

8. **nugatory** (NOO gat or ee) This adjective originally comes from the Latin word for "jokes" or "trifles," but it has come to mean "of little or no importance" or "trifling." When you make something "nugatory," you render it "futile" or "invalid." It has nothing to do with the word "nugget."

- "Now that you're in tennis camp, you will spend all of your time strengthening your serve and improving your speed," said Lars, the tennis pro. "All other activities—including eating, drinking and sleeping—are **nugatory**."

- The new administration's lax environmental policies will render **nugatory** all of the previous laws regarding carbon dioxide emissions.

9. **recrudescent** (ree kru DESS ent) This adjective means "to revivify" or "to come back to life after a period of quiet inactivity." The verb form is "to recrudesce."

- After a long summer of lazy beach days and afternoon naps, Walter Jimcrack is **recrudescent** and ready to reassume his position as the vigilant security guard at P.S. 117 in the South Bronx.

- Like a phoenix emerging from the ashes, Arnold **recrudesced**, returning to his job as a construction worker after suffering what his doctors thought might be a fatal brain tumor.

10. **sallow** (SAL oh) Here's an adjective that means "of a sickly, yellowish color or complexion." No one who is healthy is ever described as "sallow."

- After spending weeks in the hospital in Singapore fighting a rare blood disease, Hortense was **sallow**, weak, and rail thin.

- At Yasger's ranch, the men who herded the cows and rode the horses were ruddy and strong, but the women who worked inside the dairy all day looked **sallow**, exhausted, and depressed.

Persuading or duping may help you get your way, but sometimes plain old begging does the trick.

1. **importune** (im por TOON) This verb refers to the making of insistent requests, pleading so often that the person on the receiving end may become irked. The word origin—Latin for "not a refuge" seems to foresee the likeliness of an unhappy outcome.

  • His teacher's repeated assertions that his midterm grade was accurate did nothing to stop Vance from continuing to **importune** her to change it.

  • Shakespeare's Desdemona repeatedly **importuned** her husband Othello to forgive Cassio's drunken behavior, thus unknowingly playing into the hands of the plotting of evil Iago.

2. **supplicate** (SUP lih kate) To supplicate is to ask in a very humble manner. If you think of the related word "supple" (limber, bendable), you'll get an image of someone begging on bended knee—that's supplication.

  • In the opening of Sophocles's play *Oedipus Rex*, the inhabitants of Thebes appear before King Oedipus as **supplicants**, begging him to save them from the plague that is destroying the city.

  • All of Marcy's **supplication** was in vain: her parents steadfastly refused to allow her to have her own car.

3. **cajole** (ka JOLE) Sometimes teasing and flattery work where begging fails. Cajolery attempts to nudge someone jokingly into doing what you ask. Its possible Old French origin combines the ideas of chattering like a jay and of luring someone into a cage.

  • "Oh come on, Dad, let me have $20 more," said Scott **cajolingly**. "You know you feel good about yourself when you're a really generous guy."

  • In eras when married women had almost no legal rights, many became expert **cajolers**: they knew how to sweet-talk their husbands into giving them their own way in various matters.

4. **beseech** (be SEECH) Related to the word "seek," this verb emphasizes the earnest and humble nature of a request.

- When Oliver Cromwell wrote on theological matters to the Synod of Scotland in 1650, "I **beseech** you in the bowels of Christ to think it possible you may be mistaken," he probably didn't foresee the day his words would be available on a T-shirt.
- After the McCorkle family lost Beau, their older son, in the war, they **beseeched** Jeb, the younger boy, not to follow in his brother's military footsteps.

5. adjure (a JOOR) This "begging" verb has the formal and solemn connotation of swearing, the taking of an oath, as implied in the "jure" root word. (Think of a jury member taking an oath.)
- "I **adjure** you by all you hold holy not to believe Mr. Badguy's allegations," said Bartholomew Upright.
- The speaker in Poe's "The Raven" dares "to **adjure** Hope" but is answered by the equally allegorical Despair.

6. implore (im PLORE) This verb of earnest entreaty has at its Latin root the idea of weeping: the person making the request cares so much that he or she is, at least figuratively, near tears.
- The Lims **implored** their teenaged daughter to leave off the excessive partying and aim for a more balanced life—some hard work, some fun, some time for family.
- "See yourselves as serious students, writers, even poets," said Mr. McCarron **imploringly** to his young students, "and you're more likely to become what you have envisioned."

7. woo (rhymes with boo) This wonderfully short word carries the olden-times sense of a man seeking a woman's affections, but it is still used in a larger sense of begging, entreating, seeking an end.
- Nancy and Virginia are doing a project on Longfellow's poem, "The Courtship of Miles Standish," in which John Alden attempts to **woo** a woman for the bashful Miles Standish but ends up winning her heart himself.
- The St. Louis Chamber of Commerce is attempting to **woo** business back into the downtown area where many attractive buildings are available for low rent.

8. entreat (en TREET) "Earnestness" is the keynote here. If you make an entreaty, you ask in a very sincere manner.
- The coaches **entreated** the administration to allow student athletes to leave classes early for Friday afternoon games.
- A line that has been used in many a marriage ceremony— "**Entreat** me not to leave thee, nor to return from following after thee"—has its biblical origin not between a wife and her husband but in the widowed Ruth's plea to her mother-in-law Naomi.

9. **mendicant** (MEND ih kant) This noun moves us from begging as general pleading into begging for money, for help. A mendicant is a formal term for a beggar. It derives from the Latin word for "needy" and an associated root for "physical defect."

- Jon has been reading about **mendicant** friars, those who took an oath of poverty and depended on their belief in the providence of God and the kindness of others for their very survival.

- Laurie and Lily had seen beggars in large cities in the United States, but they were unprepared for the number of **mendicant** children coming up to them on their foreign travels last summer.

10. **cadge** (rhymes with badge) This verb associated with begging for money may derive from an old word for "peddler." The slang term "sponge" is a rough synonym.

- It is sad to see a man who once had such dignity **cadging** change from passersby.

- Although Mark has officially quit smoking, he can be caught **cadging** the occasional cigarette from a colleague.

A re you an egotist or a rebel? All these words give us a focus on the individual instead of the group.

1. **narcissist** (NAR sis ist) A negative word for those people (not you!) who go too far in "being into themselves." Narcissists, being in love with themselves, lack empathy with others. The word comes from Greek mythology where Narcissus fell in love with his reflection in a pool. His punishment was to be turned into a flower, a very pretty flower.

- Some sociologists believe we are becoming a culture of **narcissism**, what with the rise of the "self-esteem" movement and the growing popularity of blogs that chronicle the lives of average individuals.

- "If you feel you're falling in love with a **narcissist**," counseled Dr. Dougherty, "run the other way, head for the hills. It's a prescription for disaster."

2. **solipsist** (SOL ip sist) The philosophical idea behind solipsism is that only the self has reality or the possibility of being verified. Popularly, "solipsist" is used as a rough synonym for "narcissist," an individual who is completely focused on him or her self. Even the root words reflect that: Latin for "alone" (*solus*) plus Latin for "self" (*ipse*).

- Did you read the jazz critic who referred to John Coltrane's playing as "**solipsistic** caterwauling (screeching)"? Many would disagree!

- "You only exist because I believe you do," said Ricky to Avery, before adding, "Just kidding! I'm not really that much of a **solipsist**."

3. **autocrat** (AW toe krat) An autocracy is government by one individual, so an autocrat is either a ruler of that sort or, more generally, a person whose power and authority have no limit.

- In 1858 Oliver Wendell Holmes published his *Autocrat of the Breakfast Table*. These essays pretend to record accounts of the morning meal in a boarding house by the presumed "ruler" of the group.

- Was Craig bragging or complaining when he stated that his household became an **autocracy** when his son was born? "Nancy and I do whatever little Ryland wants or needs," he said.

4. **autonomous** (aw TAHN uh mus) This adjective describes something or someone who acts independently.

- "Everyone has the right to be free / May we all live **autonomously**!" said Mike, making up an impromptu rhyme to help him remember the word.
- The Trans' oldest child is out of college and is fully **autonomous**; when the younger two complete their education, Nam and Julie plan to travel extensively.

5. **autodidact** (AW toe DIE dakt) This noun refers to someone who is literally self-taught, has not had formal education in a certain field.

- When the character Ishmael in Herman Melville's great novel *Moby-Dick* says, "A whale ship was my Yale College and Harvard," he could be speaking for the author as well. As a writer Melville was a complete **autodidact**.
- The most organized of **autodidacts** might work his way alphabetically through a library; a minor version of this scheme is A. J. Jacobs, who recently wrote a book about his experience of reading his way straight through the *Encyclopædia Britannica*.

6. **soliloquy** (so LIL uh kwee) If you talk to yourself, you're soliloquizing. More literarily, a soliloquy is a speech given by a character alone on the stage. "Monologue" would be a rough synonym.

- The most famous Shakespearean **soliloquy** is probably Hamlet's speech beginning with the words, "To be or not to be, that is the question."
- "Don is a pretty good storyteller, but how can I tell him that some of his **monologues** just go on too long?" asked his friend in a query to Miss Manners.

7. **idiosyncrasy** (id ee oh SIN kra see) This noun refers to some characteristic of behavior that is limited to one person or group. It may be lovable or annoying. The various Greek roots of the word reinforce the meaning: an individual mixture of personal characteristics.

- "Lee has to look at the sports page before he'll sit down to breakfast," said his wife. "It's just his little **idiosyncrasy**."
- Charles Dickens often makes his minor characters memorable by giving them an **idiosyncrasy** that marks their appearances; for example, Mr. Pecksniff always puts himself down as a way of making himself important.

8. **recluse** (REK loos *or* rek LOOS) Recluses are people who choose to live in solitude as much as possible. The root word in Latin means "closed in." "Hermit" would be a good synonym whereas its root "eremite" is a fancy word used mostly for one who withdraws from the world for religious reasons.

- Probably the best-known **recluse** in twentieth-century literature is Arthur "Boo" Radley of *To Kill a Mockingbird*. He emerges from his house only in an unusual situation such as saving a child from the murderous attack of the evil Bob Ewell.

- Milton's poem *Paradise Regained* refers to the biblical John the Baptist as a "glorious **eremite**."

9. **renegade** (REN uh gade) The original meaning of this noun was "a deserter." Now, it's used mostly with the more flattering meaning of "a rebel or outlaw." You can find, among others, a car model and a hiking boot named "Renegade," and you can be sure the marketing folk probably aren't thinking much about the appeal of traitors!

- Secrets'R'Us screens its employees for loyalty carefully before they are hired, but there's no way to be sure someone won't later turn **renegade** later.
- Adrian likes to think of himself as a **renegade**, but his rebelliousness is mostly limited to boasting and to slogans on T-shirts.

10. **heterodox** (HET er oh dox) This adjective describes statements, behavior, or opinions that vary from accepted or popular belief. A renegade would have heterodox opinions. "Orthodox" would be an opposite.

- With the developments in the Middle East in the past few years, most Americans have had to do some fast learning about Islam, the mainstream beliefs as well as some of the more **heterodox** variations.
- The poetry critic gave the phrase "a morning stippled with birdsong" as a charming example of "**heterodox** word use," since "stipple" is a word most often employed for short strokes or dots in painting.

11. **cynosure** (SY no shoor) A cynosure is something or someone that everyone looks at, so narcissists or solipsists (see #1 and #2) would doubtless like to have it applied to them. An earlier use was limited to the idea of something, such as the North Star, that people use to guide and direct them (so, obviously, they have to look at it). (All you lovers of word history, get yourself to a dictionary to understand why "cynosure" literally means "dog's tail"!)

- Even students who considered themselves "celebrity-proof" felt the **cynosural** power of the star of *Saturday Night Live* as he made his way through the lobby and hallways of the school, heading for the auditorium where he would speak on techniques of satire.
- When Thomas Carlyle writes of the French Revolution, he refers to Marie Antoinette as "the fair young queen, the **cynosure** of all eyes."

MAKE A MATCH #9

Sections 25–27

Match each word in the left-hand column with the phrase on the right that best suggests its meaning.

A.	autocrat	1. _____	a beggar
B.	automaton	2. _____	an outlaw or rebel
C.	cajole	3. _____	a hermit
D.	cynosure	4. _____	magnificent display
E.	egregious	5. _____	flattering and teasing way of asking
F.	idiosyncrasy	6. _____	humble way of requesting
G.	mendicant	7. _____	a robot
H.	miasma	8. _____	worthless, of no value
I.	narcissist	9. _____	cut off sharply
J.	nugatory	10. _____	outstandingly bad
K.	pomp	11. _____	center of attention
L.	recluse	12. _____	one who rules alone
M.	recrudescent	13. _____	egotistical person
N.	renegade	14. _____	small, personal way of doing something
O.	supplicate	15. _____	poisonous atmosphere
P.	truncate	16. _____	bouncing back after inactivity

PRACTICE, PRACTICE, PRACTICE #3

Sections 19–27

Place the letter of the appropriate word in the blank for the sentence that it best suits.

A.	adulation	K.	minuscule
B.	antipathy	L.	narcissist
C.	autonomous	M.	nemesis
D.	burnish	N.	periphery
E.	cadge	O.	pomp
F.	camaraderie	P.	recluse
G.	contiguous	Q.	reverberate
H.	importune	R.	sumptuous
I.	irreconcilable	S.	sybarite
J.	miffed	T.	wrangle

1. Pam felt like a _____ when she used her gift certificate at the spa to have a massage, a facial, and a swim in the indoor pool.

2. The robot was completely _____, needing nothing but batteries to keep him fully functioning.

3. Ms. Hauk learned a lot at the conference but mostly she enjoyed the _____ of workers in the same field who always understood what she was talking about.

4. The amount of zinc needed by your body is _____ but nonetheless very important.

5. After the upsetting breakup with his girlfriend, Jed was something of a _____ for a couple of weeks, refusing to leave his bedroom except for an occasional meal.

6. Lance Armstrong had won the _____ of people in many countries for both his athletic prowess and for his fight against illness.

7. All efforts to _____ his boss for a raise ended with her snapping, "I said no. Don't keep asking."

8. Although she spends a lot of time looking at the mirror, she's no _____, for she's very aware of the concerns of other people.

9. Eric and Phil held amazingly similar records of victories in wrestling each other; each regards the other as his _____.

10. The recently discovered manuscript of the writer will further _____ her already high reputation.

11. Adepeju is not one of the central figures on this project, but she does much unrewarded work on the _____.

12. The reenactment of the Renaissance banquet featured a table loaded with wonderful food and many guests dressed in _____ costumes.

13. The two brothers tended to _____ every night over who would do what kitchen clean-up chore; finally, their mother posted a schedule.

14. The Thompsons felt _____ that they were not invited to the neighbors barbecue, since they had invited them over to their cookout the previous month.

15. Beverly had such a feeling of _____ about her former employer that she eagerly accepted the new offer that came her way.

16. George can easily pass on the message to Ned because their workspaces are _____.

17. The television coverage of the royal wedding, which was celebrated with much _____, drew millions of viewers.

18. The negative effects of the unfair dismissal of Ms. Lyons still _____ through her institution, although over five years have now passed.

19. Although the couple hoped that counseling would help their marriage, their _____ differences eventually caused them to divorce.

20. James had several dollars in his wallet but had to _____ spare change in order to use the vending machine.

I Just Don't Understand You

Reasons for misunderstanding are many and go beyond the verbal, but each of the following words offers a possibility for having a negative effect on communication or comprehension.

1. abstruse (ab STROOS) This adjective describes something that is hard to understand because of its intellectual difficulty or its obscurity. The root word is the Latin meaning "to push away, to hide."

- The fact that Greek uses a different alphabet gives it an **abstruse** appearance lacking to, say, German.
- A bright young man, Jeremy breezed through the beginning weeks of advanced physics, but as the degree of **abstruseness** increased, he intensified his study regime.

2. byzantine (BIZ uhn teen) (sometimes capitalized) This adjective is in increasingly common use to describe something excessively complicated, especially when the complexities come about through intrigue or scheming. The origin, of course, lies in the word Byzantine as referring to the eastern part of the later Roman Empire. Was the Byzantine Empire byzantine?

- Although the company has very few written rules, the informal structure is **byzantine**, leaving new employees bewildered until they figure out whom to see about what.
- Sociologists are increasingly interested in the rather **byzantine** social codes of preadolescent girls: if Millie insults Mollie, will Maggie snub Millie?

3. inscrutable (in SCROOT uh bul) If a person or thing is inscrutable, it's mysterious, hard to fathom or penetrate. Good synonyms would be "puzzling," or "enigmatic." In Latin, the root word means something like "not searching through the rags or the trash." (Would a dumpster diver be able to figure things out?)

- Characters in many Joseph Conrad novels know there is nothing more **inscrutable** than the sea.
- Victoria prides herself on amateur psychoanalysis of her teachers, but Prof. Holmes remained **enigmatic**, even to her.

4. mendacity (men DASS ih tee) Mendacity is dishonesty, plain and simple.

- Is the character of Dill in *To Kill a Mockingbird* **mendacious** because he is just basically dishonest or because he wants to use his fabulous imagination?
- In Tennessee Williams's play *Cat on a Hot Tin Roof*, the characters Brick and Big Daddy have a memorable exchange about **mendacity**, each having good reason to be well acquainted with the quality.

5. apocryphal (a POK ruh ful) This adjective describes things of questionable truth or authenticity. (The root word, from the Greek "hidden," refers to scriptural texts accepted by some Christians but not all.)

- The story of George Washington and the cherry tree is **apocryphal**; he may never have come near a hatchet, but the tale illustrates a larger truth about Washington's honesty.
- "If it isn't true it ought to be" is another way of describing **apocryphal** tales: either they are in the spirit of truth or they are irresistibly good stories.

6. elliptical (e LIP tik ul) This adjective, usually used for written or oral expression, describes a verbal structure where some element is left out, either intentionally or by error. The context determines whether the word expresses praise or blame. The origin is from the Greek for "falls short of"—just as the mathematical "ellipse" falls short of being a circle.

- If you shout, "Help!" you have uttered an **elliptical** sentence; you did not need to say, "I need help!"
- A major difference between poetry of the late nineteenth century and the late twentieth century is that the latter is much more **elliptical**. The reader must often supply the implied connection between two lines or passages.

7. esoteric (ess oh TER ik) Something esoteric is known only to a small group, to a few.

- The word "esoteric" is not a common word, but it is far less **esoteric** than the word "omphaloskeptic"—"meditating while staring at your navel." Now *that's* **esoteric**.
- Joelle, not being a sports fan, is intrigued by real sports enthusiasts who exchange **esoteric** bits of lore such as "most home runs hit by a left-handed batter being pitched to by a left-handed pitcher."

8. arcane (ar KAIN) Similar to "esoteric," this adjective implies a sense of exclusivity, something not known by people in general. It carries an even further sense of being something at least mildly mysterious, appropriate for a word whose roots mean "secret chest."

- Since Mr. Douglas has taught at his school for over thirty years, he knows many **arcane** facts such as what boy in the 1970s wore a short wig to hide his long hair and what physics teacher was fired after only a few weeks on the job.

- The spelling of "rhythm" may be difficult but it's hardly **arcane**; look it up in any dictionary.

9. **disingenuous** (diss in JEN yoo us) Don't play dumb with me! That's what someone who is disingenuous does. An ingénue (see section #17, "Words for the Ages") is an innocent young woman, and a male or female *pretending* innocence is being disingenuous.

- "I had no idea I would hurt your feelings when I called you a 'total dunderhead,'" she said, smiling **disingenuously.**

- When former President Clinton defended himself from attack by saying much depended "on what the meaning of 'is' is," was he being a clever legal strategist or just being **disingenuous**?

10. **factitious** (fak TISH us) This adjective describes something *lacking* in authenticity, so don't be fooled by the fact that the first syllable is "fact."

- Jim Dixon moved from his seat on the stage to the podium with **factitious** ease; in reality, he was terrified about giving this speech on Merrye Olde England, a subject dear to his boss's heart but a concept he himself found **factitious**.

This group of words is all about comfort and solace.

1. **palliative** (PAL ee ah tiv) This word can be used as a noun or an adjective and comes from the Latin word for "cloak." It means "soothing the symptoms of a disorder without effecting a cure." The verb form is "to palliate."

- Chicken soup is just a **palliative** for the flu. The hot liquid temporarily clears the sinuses, but the virus doesn't really go away.
- "I don't like to take cold medicines," Charlene said. "They **palliate** my symptoms so I go to work because I think I am feeling fine, but they don't cure my cold and I end up getting sicker."

2. **assuage** (ass WAGE) This verb means "to soothe" or "to make less painful or burdensome," and it comes from the Latin for "to sweeten." The adjective form is "assuasive," but it is rarely used.

- Marla tried to **assuage** her daughter's fears about getting her wisdom tooth pulled by telling her it wouldn't hurt a bit.
- The principal **assuaged** Alex's parents' concerns over their son's failing grades in geometry by offering to give him help in the school's learning center during his free periods.

3. **emollient** (ee MOLL yent) Here's another noun that means "soothing," but it is used mostly to describe something that softens or soothes the skin.

- After a day of gardening without gloves, Emilia rubbed a special **emollient** she purchased online over her hands to ease the blisters and chafes on her fingers.
- Many people say that a popular **emollient** used for moisturizing the hands works quite well as an insect repellant.

4. **ameliorate** (ah MEEL ee or ate) Here's a more general verb that simply means "to improve." The noun form is "amelioration."

- "We have had many complaints about delays in our arrival and departure times," said the public relations spokesperson for Cross Country Buslines.

"We hope to **ameliorate** the situation shortly by adding more buses to the fleet and hiring more experienced drivers."

- Surveying the devastation that resulted from the recent hurricane in the area around Palm Beach, Florida, Red Cross workers were doubtful that there would be any **amelioration** of the wreckage in the immediate future.

5. **alleviate** (al LEEV ee ate) This verb is pretty much a synonym for "palliate" or "alleviate." It means "to ease symptoms" without providing a cure and comes from the Latin for "to lighten."

- Dr. Harvey suggested that Allegra take a strong pain medication to **alleviate** the back pain caused by her fall during last week's horse show, but she refused, insisting the medicine made her too dizzy to ride.

- "I know you are upset that you can't go to the ballet because of our board meeting," said Jorge's boss. "I hope these two tickets to next week's performance will **alleviate** some of your disappointment."

6. **conciliate** (con SILL ee ate) This verb means "to overcome distrust or hostility" or "to try to gain or regain someone's friendship." It comes from the same Latin root as the word "reconciliation," which has a similar meaning—"to reestablish a close relationship between two parties." The adjective form is "conciliating." The noun form is "conciliation."

- After telling Kate that her remarks in class were superficial and dull, Michael thought it best to **conciliate** her by bringing her an ice cream soda and a doughnut during lunch.

- Not only did the subcommittee on environmental impact brutally denounce the president's policies on emissions control, they refused to make any **conciliating** remarks in the subsequent hearings.

7. **foster** (FAWS ter) This verb means "to nurture" or "to promote the growth and development of." "Foster parents" are called that because they nurture children who are not related to them by blood. The word comes to us from the Old English word for food or nourishment.

- Headmaster Owens insists on a stringent dress code because he believes that a tidy appearance in school **fosters** a student's respect for his teachers, for his peers, and for his academic work.

- Carmine brushed his teeth three times a day, remembering the words of his dentist, Dr. Payne: "Proper dental hygiene **fosters** healthy gums and teeth."

8. **mollify** (MOLL ih fye) From the Latin word for "soften" this verb, like "conciliate," means "to calm in temper" or "to soothe hostile feelings." The noun "mollification" is too much of a mouthful; nobody uses it.

- When Daisy dropped her ice cream cone, she began to wail. Nothing would **mollify** the four-year-old, not even a new scoop of double chocolate chip.

- When Rover ate Ian's new loafer, Ian became enraged and could not be **mollified**; we had to take the dog to a neighbor's house to keep him safe from Ian's fury.

9. **placate** (PLAY kate) There seem to be plenty of verbs that mean "to lessen someone's anger or hard feelings," and here's another one. One "placates" under the same conditions that one "mollifies."

- A man of integrity, William made a point of never **placating** his enemies with lies or empty promises.

- Almost any political office involves a fair amount of groveling and manipulating in order to **placate** a constituency with a broad range of demands and needs.

10. **succor** (SUK or) This noun comes from the Latin for "to run to the aid of," and it means just that—"relief" or "comfort in a time of distress." One can "offer" succor, "receive" succor, or, in the verb form, "succor" someone else. Don't confuse it with "sucker."

- Madeline took some **succor** in knowing that although she didn't win the spelling bee, she was elected "Best Speller Under the Age of Twelve" in a nationwide vote.

- After the dashingly handsome Juan was proven innocent and released from the dungeon, most of the women in the village rushed to **succor** him, bringing food and drink and the offer of a warm bed.

Bad Guys

30

Bad guys come in both genders and in many different forms. Here's a sampling of types.

1. curmudgeon (ker MUJ un) This bad guy is a grouch, a grump. He (or she) is in a perpetually bad mood. Weirdly enough, no one seems to know the origin of this noun that suggests a growling cur.

- If Bobbie Sue doesn't lose some of her **curmudgeonly** ways, she will find herself without any friends or professional allies.
- Before his conversion to kindness, Dickens's Ebenezer Scrooge was the embodiment of a **curmudgeon**—and stingy, to boot.

2. booby (BOO bee) This noun serves as an all-purpose term for a person who is perceived as being foolish or stupid. Modern slang often shortens it to **boob,** making it a short trip to "boob tube" as a slang term for a television set.

- Catherine wondered what **booby** at her school had arranged her schedule in a way that gave her no period for lunch.
- The women in James Thurber's short stories all tend to regard their husbands as **boobies**, men who deserve a good lecture in order to set them straight.

3. ninny (NINN ee) Roughly synonymous with the word above, this noun has perhaps an even stronger sense of lack of intelligence or of overall silliness. Dictionary makers think it may be a shortened form of the dark side of innocence.

- Why, Brad wondered, should he be required to attend a session on career counseling and have some **ninny** who didn't even know him tell him what he should do to earn a living?
- The title of John Ashbery and James Schuyler's novel *A Nest of **Ninnies*** is self-explanatory: it concerns the doings of some very silly people.

4. nincompoop (NINN com poop) This noun, whose origin is also unknown, sounds much like ninny but seems to be a completely different word for a silly or stupid person. Some find that just saying the word gives a sense of satisfaction.

- Only a **nincompoop** would leave his expensive new jacket in the lounge while he went to class and expect to find it when he returned.

- What **nincompoop** stapled a confidential internal memo to Senator Quillen's press release?

5. **martinet** (mar tin ET) This noun refers to a person who demands strict adherence to all regulations, however small. Its use was originally limited to the field of military endeavor, but today martinets can be found almost anywhere.

- In the film *Dead Poets' Society*, the teacher, played by Robin Williams, encourages his young charges to rebel against **martinets** they encounter in their classrooms.

- As an office supervisor, Ms. Jennings prides herself on what she calls "running a tight ship"; those unfortunate enough to work for her see her as a cruel **martinet**.

6. **roué** (roo A) The history of this single-sex noun suggests it is a man evil enough to be cruelly tortured by being broken on a wheel. Today a roué is merely lecherous, perhaps more pitiable or self-deceiving than evil.

- Christopher Walken comically portrays a would-be **roué** who vainly attempts to win women with an accent and champagne that are both French.

- A young **roué** might be mildly amusing, but an aging **roué** is merely pathetic.

7. **miscreant** (MISS kree ent) In times and places where religious toleration was lacking, this noun could describe those who were considered infidels or heretics. Now it is more generally understood as a more equal-opportunity wrongdoer.

- On any given afternoon the waiting area of Principal Shattuck's office is filled with young **miscreants** sent there by their frustrated teachers.

- In Leonard Bernstein's musical *Candide*, set in the time of the Spanish Inquisition, the cruel Spanish priests round up the **miscreants** while the chorus sings "It's a Glorious Day for an Auto-da-fe."

8. **poltroon** (pol TROON) Simply put, a coward.

- Jordana was tired of dealing with **poltroons** who offered elaborate false rationales for their failure to confront their oppressors.

- Those serving in the British Army in the eighteenth century may have been ardent patriots or arrant **poltroons**.

9. **buffoon** (buff OON) A person who enjoys clowning, joking around, or one whose normal behavior is perceived as ridiculous. This noun comes from the Italian word "buffa" meaning "jest." (A comic opera is, even in English, referred to as an "opera buffa.")

- J. D. enjoyed playing the **buffoon** in study hall, mimicking Ms. Springer's facial expressions behind her back, then feigning total innocence as she turned to glare at him.

- Tony thinks his antics are original and witty, but most people regard him as a complete **buffoon**.

10. **scapegrace** (SKAPE grace) The English origin of this noun is self-evident; it describes a person who has "escaped" a condition of "grace." It's used for a scoundrel, a rascal, but often with the sense of describing mischief, not evil.

- MJ and McKenzie were the leading **scapegraces** of the playground in the park; their mothers often had to extricate them from tussles over whose turn it was at the swings or who had the right to the last cookie.

- Were women attracted to Don Juan in spite of his being a **scapegrace** or because he was such a rascal?

MAKE A MATCH #10

Sections 28–30

Match each word in the left-hand column with the phrase on the right that best suggests its meaning.

A.	abstruse	1. _____	very strict disciplinarian
B.	apocryphal	2. _____	to give help or comfort
C.	assuage	3. _____	known only to a select group
D.	buffoon	4. _____	of dubious origin
E.	byzantine	5. _____	lecherous man
F.	conciliate	6. _____	a coward
G.	curmudgeon	7. _____	calm or soothe a worry
H.	disingenuous	8. _____	excessively complex
I.	esoteric	9. _____	phenomenon of lying
J.	inscrutable	10. _____	intellectually obscure or difficult
K.	martinet	11. _____	someone you might laugh at
L.	mendacity	12. _____	to help make peace
M.	poltroon	13. _____	a grumpy person
N.	roué	14. _____	a lovable rascal
O.	scapegrace	15. _____	falsely playing innocent
P.	succor	16. _____	hard or impossible to figure out

Not-Quite-Naughty Words

31

A lthough they nudge up to a naughty wink, these words for mild sexual references can be found in scholarly literature as well as the daily paper.

1. ribald (RIB uhld *or* RYE buhld) This adjective describes something or someone that is characterized by witty hints at sexual content.

- The puppet show is suitable for families, but adults may get a sly laugh or two from some mildly **ribald** jokes.
- The **ribaldry** in the ancient Greek comedy *Lysistrata* doesn't come through in older English translations.

2. bawdy (BAWD ee) This word can be an adjective or noun and derives from the word "bold." Like "ribald," it refers to humorously coarse language or allusions. "Risqué" is a near synonym.

- Julia was startled to learn that the original words to "Yankee Doodle Dandy" were rather **bawdy**.
- Shakespeare has so many **bawdy** lines that scholar Eric Partridge wrote an entire book about them.

3. prurient (PRUR ee unt) This adjective may describe an inappropriate variety of interest in sexual matters, such as overt curiosity about other people's private lives. Appropriately, it derives from the Latin word meaning "to itch."

- In an earlier era some communities forbade the circulation of literature that caused "**prurient** interest," but lawyers had difficulty finding common ground on the exact definition of "prurient."
- In Shakespeare's *Hamlet*, the character Polonius has a **prurient** interest in what his son Laertes is up to in Paris, even hiring a spy to check things out.

4. profligate (PROF li gut) Adjective or noun, this word refers to "wild" behavior that may be in the monetary or the sexual realm—or both.

- Her **profligate** spending habits had to cease after she lost her high-paying job as flower-arranger to the stars.

- The Thompsons brought up their son, George, to observe a very strict code of morality, so it has been hard for them to witness his adult transformation into a **profligate**, specializing in wine, women, and song.

5. **tryst** (TRIST) A secret meeting planned by lovers, often a couple whose love is not approved by society. If you know the operatic lovers Tristan and Isolde, you have an instant memory device for yourself.

- After Romeo and Juliet secretly marry, they make an elaborate plan for a **tryst** in the vault where members of her family, the Capulets, are buried.

- The storyline of the sitcom focused on Desiree's fear that her husband was plotting a **tryst** with an old girlfriend, when in reality his secretive actions were part of arranging a surprise party for her, Desiree!

6. **dissolute** (DISS uh lute) A person whose sense of moral restraint has *dissolved* may be called "dissolute." You have a root word and memory device all in one here.

- The **dissolute** friends of the prince of Wales helped to cause a negative transformation of English court life in the late eighteenth century.

- While some popular novels about college life in the early twenty-first century suggest that all students are living a completely **dissolute** life, the reality is quite different.

7. **racy** (RAY see) This adjective describes neither speeding competitions nor matters of skin pigmentation; instead, it describes something bordering on the improper and serves as a rough synonym for ribald (#1) or risqué. Does R rated stand for "racy"?

- Lucille's first encounter with the beautiful images of love in the Song of Solomon made her feel this book was rather too **racy** to be part of a Bible study class.

- Chris's posters advertising his race for class president relied on **racy** words in big print followed by a coy, "Now that I've got your attention…"

8. **dalliance** (DAL ee unce) This noun suggest a sense of playful flirtation. It comes from the verb "to dally," which can have a general sense of "wasting time" or the more specific spending of time in an amorous mode.

- Marc Antony's attraction to the Egyptian Cleopatra may have begun as a **dalliance** but ended up changing Roman history.

- Karen had a period of treating men like charms for her charm bracelet; she would **dally** with one guy's affection and then move on to the next.

9. **carnal** (KAR nul) This adjective describes matters relating to the physical, particularly to the sexual. It often has a legal tang to it. It comes from the Latin word for "flesh": think "chili con carne."

- The judge kept sealed all testimony about **carnal** matters.
- The phrase "**carnal** knowledge" as a formal way of referring to sexual union has been in the English language since 1450.

10. **smut** (rhymes with gut) This noun can refer to something as simple as a bit of soot, but these days it is more often associated with figurative dirt—obscenity, pornography.

- One problem with a campaign to ban or label CDs with "**smutty** lyrics" is that few can agree on how to define "**smut**."
- Humorous poet Ogden Nash had a field day when a senator whose last name was "Smoot" began an anti-obscenity drive: "Smoot Smites **Smut**," he wrote.

That's how nineteenth-century writer Henry David Thoreau described "time." These words describe its passage in less poetic fashion.

1. evanescent (ev an ESS sent) From the Latin for "vanishing," this adjective means "disappearing like vapor." It can be used to describe something literal, like a fragrance, or something more figurative, such as love. The verb form is "to evanesce."

- "If I had known your feelings for me would be so **evanescent**, I should not have allowed myself to fall in love with you," Darcy murmured. "I am a man who remains true to his feelings and foolishly expected the same of you."

- As the fog gradually **evanesced**, the Golden Gate Bridge shimmered in the morning light, awing Jack and Neil with its beauty.

2. ephemeral (ee FEM er al) This adjective comes from the Greek word that means "day" and, though it originally meant "lasting only a day," it now describes anything short-lived or fleeting. The noun form "ephemera" refers to printed matter—such as newspapers, greeting cards, or calling cards—that have relevance or hold interest for only a passing amount of time.

- The Peruvian novelist Mario Vargas Llosa once said, "No matter how **ephemeral** it is, a novel is something, while despair is nothing."

- At the antiques fair on the pier, we visited the stall of a dealer who specializes in **ephemera**, including old maps, nineteenth-century women's magazines, Victorian postcards, and daguerreotypes.

3. chronic (KRON ik) From the Greek kronos (see #2), this adjective is the opposite of ephemeral. It means "of long duration" or "frequently recurring."

- Because of **chronic** financial problems, the Penniworths were finally forced to sell their spacious brownstone overlooking the park and move into a small apartment on the outskirts of the city.

- Phoebe suffers from **chronic** and painful migraines from which she can find no relief. As a result, she rarely travels far from home and limits her social life to occasional lunches or dinners out.

4. **dilatory** (DILL ah tore ee) This adjective means tending toward postponing or delaying. The noun form is "lateness."

- Katy spends most of her afternoons in detention because her **dilatory** habits make her constantly late for school.

- "You're fired!" Mr. Hardy shouted at Nathan, citing his careless filing methods, his unkempt appearance, and his **dilatory** attendance record as the reasons.

5. **diurnal** (dye UR nal) This adjective means "occurring in a twenty-four-hour period" or "daily" or "occurring or active in the daytime, rather than at night" (see "nocturnal" in the "Darkness, My Old Friend" section). It comes from the Latin word for "day."

- Norman's **diurnal** routine included a two-hour weight-lifting session at the gym, a five-mile run, and one hundred sit-ups and still he was overweight. "It must be all those cream puffs I eat," he sighed, looking down at the scale.

- Many poets, such as William Wordsworth, have written about earth's "**diurnal** course" to describe the passage of a day.

6. **antiquated** (AN ti kwayt ed) This adjective means "very old" or simply "too old to be fashionable, obsolete." It comes, of course, from the same Latin root as "antique."

- The headmistress held such **antiquated** views of teenage social behavior that she had never even heard the expression "hooking up" and thought it simply meant "to meet up with."

- Men who hold **antiquated** views of women's role in society expect that it is their job to bring home the bacon and women's place to clean the house and cook the meals.

7. **archaic** (ar KAY ik) From the Greek word meaning "ancient," this adjective describes something that belongs to a much earlier period of time, often a classical period of civilization. It is similar to "antiquated" in that it usually describes something that is no longer in use, but it suggests something even older. Something antiquated is "old-fashioned"; something that is archaic is "out of use altogether." It is commonly used to describe language that is no longer used.

- The belief that all human disease can be explained by the four humors—blood, phlegm, yellow bile, and black bile—and that most illness can be cured by bloodletting is **archaic**; we have since discovered more sophisticated methods for diagnosis and healing.

- The psychologist Carl Jung believed in a "collective unconscious," that the human mind contains **archaic** images that are part of the most ancient, universal thoughts of all mankind.

8. **passé** (pass AY) This adjective comes to us from the style-conscious French and means "no longer current" or "out of fashion." When something is passé, its time has come and gone.

- "Little white gloves are so **passé**," declared Jeanne, observing her sister's party clothes. "Take them off immediately. You'll look like a dork!"

- "Cocktail parties are **passé**," wrote Hal Hampden in his gossip column for the *Evening Star Tribune*. "The latest craze is the breakfast get-together. It's a far more stylish way to meet the great and the near-great."

9. **gloaming** (GLOW ming) This noun is a lovely literary term for "dusk" or "twilight." You won't hear it much in conversation, but it comes up quite often in novels, even contemporary ones.

- The narrator of Joseph Conrad's novel *Heart of Darkness* tells his story on board a ship in the **gloaming**; the setting of the sun foreshadows the impending darkness of the tale.

- I watched Jeremy, his shoulders hunched in despair, walk the desolate beach at sunset and disappear into the **gloaming**.

10. **anachronism** (an AK kron is im) This is a noun for the fairly common literary technique of representing someone or something as existing in other than chronological or historical order. So, for instance, a play that includes a scene in which Sigmund Freud has a dinner conversation with William Shakespeare relies on anachronism to make a point. The adjective form is "anachronistic."

- Iago's horn-rimmed eyeglasses were an **anachronism** that marred the student production of *Othello* currently being performed at P.S. 119.

- The audience is so familiar with the idea of personal computers that they didn't realize how **anachronistic** it was to have a clue sent by email in the detective film set in the 1950s.

C onfusion can be mild puzzlement or absolute mayhem. (That latter word comes from the Old French to "maim" and expresses riotous disorder.)

1. **obfuscate** (OB fuss kate) This verb comes from the Latin for "to darken over" and means to make confusing or difficult to understand. One often obfuscates intentionally in order to hide the truth. The noun form is obfuscation.

- "Do not **obfuscate** the truth," Mr. Gekko's lawyer advised him. "The jury will know when you are trying to cover up your intentions to embezzle money from the company."

- When Sam's mother asked him where he was going so late at night, his answer was so full of **obfuscation** that she was sure he was up to some trouble.

2. **melee** (MAY lay *or* meh LAY) From the Old French word for "to mix," this noun means a brawl, a confused and violent battle. There is no verb or adjective form.

- When the referee called a foul in the second quarter, a **melee** broke out on the court; both teams rushed onto the floor and began throwing punches at each other.

- "We'll never be able to find each other in the rush hour **melee** at Grand Central Station," said Tom. "Let's meet at a nearby coffee shop instead."

3. **anarchy** (AN ark ee) Confusion takes a political turn with this word. From the Greek for "without a ruler," anarchy is a noun which means "the absence of any form of political authority" or a more general "absence of order or control." The noun "anarchism" means something slightly different; it is a theory that all forms of government are oppressive and should be abolished. Someone who believes in anarchism is an "anarchist."

- When the principal called the teacher into the hallway, **anarchy** broke out in the classroom. The students began throwing spitballs and tossing papers out of the window.

- An avowed **anarchist**, Rachel was opposed to creating a student council in the middle school.

4. **bedlam** (BED lem) Though we now use this noun to mean "any place or situation of utter confusion or noisy uproar," it once referred to only one such place. Bedlam is a contraction of Hospital of Saint Mary of Bethlehem, a former institution for the mentally ill in London.

- There was **bedlam** on the senate floor when Senator Whistlebottom declared his resignation; his was the deciding vote on the new transportation bill.

- When the prison guards went on strike, there was **bedlam** in the cellblocks; the prisoners began shouting for food and banging their cups on the bars of their cells.

5. **confounded** (con FOUND ed) This adjective is a synonym for "confused" or, another nice word, "befuddled." It comes from the Latin for "to mix together" or "confuse." People are generally confounded, not situations. It may also be used as a verb to mean "to confuse or cause to be mixed up" or "to damn someone or something." When someone is angry or frustrated, a polite way of expressing that feeling is to cry, "Confound it!"

- The seventeenth-century English poet Sir Henry Wotton once said, "Tell the truth so as to puzzle and **confound** your adversaries."

- Although she had studied hard, Julianne was utterly **confounded** by the math problems on her final exam.

6. **convoluted** (con vol OOT ed) This adjective doesn't mean confused; it means "confusing." Something that is convoluted is intricate or complicated. It actually means "coiled in overlapping folds," like the inside of a seashell or the petals of a flower or the folds in the brain. When we come across something that is convoluted, we feel confused.

- Marina's directions to her house were so **convoluted** that Roger was certain he would get lost.

- Jean-Paul used such **convoluted** logic to explain existentialism that Babette had no idea what he was talking about.

7. **perturbed** (per TURBD) From the Latin for "to throw into disorder," this adjective means both "to throw into confusion" or "to be anxious, agitated, or confused." Something can be a force of perturbation (the noun form) or someone might be perturbed by coming across something that is convoluted.

- The researchers were **perturbed** by the results of the experiments. They could not explain why rats found their way through the maze more easily than humans.

- The heat outside in the park **perturbed** Mr. Olmstead. It was January in New York, and he expected it to be another cold and wintry day.

8. **labyrinthine** (lab er IN thin *or* lab er IN theen) If you remember the maze that confined the minotaur in Greek mythology, then you'll understand this adjective. It describes something that has the qualities of a labyrinth or maze—an intricate structure of interconnected passages. Like something that is convoluted, something that is labyrinthine can be very confusing. It describes situations or places, not people.

- The inside of the school was so **labyrinthine** that Megan could not find her way to her history class and wandered the halls for hours.

- Christos's excuse was so **labyrinthine** that no one was convinced that he was innocent.

9. **awry** (ah RYE) This adjective doesn't quite mean confusing but it belongs here because it means "away from the correct course" or amiss—and that can be confusing. A synonym is "askew," which means "twisted to one side." People are not awry; things are.

- The wind blew in through the door, leaving the papers on the desk **awry**.

- Caitlin's plans went **awry** when she decided to drive across country in her mother's old Chevy; she spent more time in the repair shop than on the road.

10. **quagmire** (KWAG myre) Though this noun literally means "a swampy, muddy piece of land" (from the Middle English word for "bog"), its figural meaning is "a difficult predicament." When things go awry, you often find yourself in a quagmire.

- Jake found himself in a **quagmire** when he purchased the last three tickets to the ballgame but had already invited three of his best friends.

- America's involvement in the Vietnam War was an infamous **quagmire** that inspired protests and debates across the country.

Sections 31–33

Match each word in the left-hand column with the phrase on the right that best suggests its meaning.

A.	anarchy	1. _____	lasting a very brief time
B.	archaic	2. _____	twilight
C.	awry	3. _____	pertaining to physical aspects
D.	bedlam	4. _____	secret meeting
E.	carnal	5. _____	attempt to obscure, confuse
F.	convoluted	6. _____	inappropriate interest in others
G.	dilatory	7. _____	complete confusion
H.	ephemeral	8. _____	subtly witty about sex
I.	gloaming	9. _____	absence of government
J.	melee	10. _____	delaying in action
K.	obfuscate	11. _____	gone off-track
L.	profligate	12. _____	belonging to distant past
M.	prurient	13. _____	dirt, literal or figurative
N.	ribald	14. _____	confused fighting
O.	smut	15. _____	unrestrained behavior
P.	tryst	16. _____	confusingly complicated

Earth, Air, Fire, Water 34

L acking the periodic table of elements available to students today, the ancient Greeks concerned themselves with only the four named above.

1. **terrestrial** (tuhr ES tree uhl) This is the Latin-derived adjective for referring to the planet Earth or to land. Think "terra firma"—solid land—or "extra-terrestrial," a being from another planet.

- While Caroline enjoys an occasional bit of bird-watching, most of her scientific research is focused on **terrestrial** creatures.
- Everyone living in 1969 marveled at the first photographs of this **terrestrial** blue ball floating in space.

2. **firmament** (FER ma ment) This noun might sound as if it referred to terra firma, the earth, but instead it refers to the sky, the heavens. It's usually used in a religious, historical, or poetic context.

- The boys' school retained its traditional ways, starting chapel every day with the eighteenth-century hymn "The Spacious **Firmament** on High."
- Herman Melville, in his powerful novel *Moby-Dick*, describes the sperm whale as having "one broad **firmament** of a forehead."

3. **ethereal** (eh THEER ee al) This adjective describes things that are heav-enly, delicate, insubstantial, as if they were "of the air."

- Although Arthur Rackham, a nineteenth-century English artist, excelled in drawing countless varieties of **ethereal** beings, I have looked only at his *Blue Fairy Book*.
- Angela dwelt on this earth with the rest of us mortals, but she had a sort of **ethereal** aspect to her, perhaps suggested by her name.

4. **celestial** (suh LES tee uhl) Deriving from the Latin word for "sky," this adjective can describe things literally relating to the concept of the sky or the heavens, or it can take the meaning of extremely good, figura-tively "heavenly."

- The young astronomy buffs enjoyed their campout, forsaking sleep for attempts to identify the **celestial** formations over their heads.

- The **celestial** aroma of frangipani delighted the aristocratic nostrils of Count Almaviva.

5. **conflagration** (con fla GRAY shun) This noun refers to a really big fire. It derives from the Latin for "to burn" that also gives us the adjective "flagrant." In English, the adjective form refers not to a literal burning but to something conspicuously offensive, perhaps *as if* it were on fire.

- As Dennis slid down the fire pole, he heard the special ringing of the alarm in the firehouse that signaled a huge **conflagration**.
- Her mother would have forgiven lateness of ten or fifteen minutes, but when Hepsie strolled in over an hour late, she was grounded for this **flagrant** violation of their curfew agreement.

6. **incendiary** (in SEND ee air ee) In its literal sense this adjective describes substances that can cause a fire. It can also describe anything that figuratively inflames.

- Don't leave those oily rags in the garage! They are highly **incendiary**.
- Peter tried hard to keep his temper, but when Ralph used the **incendiary** words, "You're not man enough to fight with me," he instinctively came out swinging.

7. **torrid** (TORR id) If it's torrid, it's intensely hot, burning. The adjective may also be used figuratively.

- The **torrid** midday sun blazed down unmercifully on the commandos doing training exercises in the desert.
- Cinematic love scenes formerly allowed audience members to use their imagination, but now the most **torrid** duo may enact their passion for the audience.

8. **febrile** (FEE brul) From the Latin word for "fever," this adjective describes just that—something related to or characterized by fever, whether literal or figurative.

- Parents are understandably frightened if their child has a **febrile** seizure, but this natural response to a high fever does not cause brain damage.
- The "Letters" page of the newspaper has published a number of **febrile** responses to the controversial article supporting human cloning.

9. **deluge** (del OOZH *or* DEL yoozh) This word refers to a flood or a heavy rain, either literal or figurative. History buffs may know Louis XIV's self-centered, "Apres moi, le deluge" (After me, the flood—in short, I don't care what happens later). A pleasantly quirky related word is "antediluvian," "before the (biblical) flood" or "a really long time ago."

- The television station has been **deluged** with calls protesting the news report graphically showing cruelty to animals.

- Mira's English teacher frequently digressed into accounts of her **antediluvian** childhood, a time before color television.

10. **sodden** (SODD en) This adjective describes something literally soaked through or something so dull and unimaginative that one might imagine a flood had carried away anything potentially good.

- The messenger rode horseback for two hours in the driving rain, proudly handing over the **sodden** envelope to the general.

- Why are you reading the **sodden** prose of that textbook when you have access here to some of the best novels ever written?

T hese words help us describe actions such as lightening up, seeing the light, or doing something with a light touch.

1. **banter** (BANT er) This word, which can be noun or verb, deals with the light touch in conversation. "Banter" refers to good-humored, playful conversation.

- Cindy and Phil talked about their hometowns, their academic majors, their astrological signs—the usual first-date **banter**.

- Fans of Monty Python laugh at this group's satirical routine on **bantering**; somehow the comedians make this exchange of playful remarks into a difficult skill.

2. **badinage** (bad in AZH) More lightweight conversation...this import into English serves as a synonym—with a French twist—for banter.

- Late nineteenth-century wits Oscar Wilde and James McNeill Whistler were famous for their elegant **badinage**, each topping the other with an inconsequential witty remark.

- The awkwardness of two strangers in an elevator is sometimes lessened by **badinage** about the weather or the equally fascinating topic of the slowness of the elevator.

3. **repartee** (rep ar TAY) Yet another French word for a light exchange of conversation, this one emphasizing the retort or reply of the person addressed, which may, in turn, inspire yet another clever remark.

- Most people can eventually think of a clever retort, but those skilled at **repartee** possess the essential skill of responding immediately.

- Shakespeare matches his witty male character Benedick with a female, Beatrice, equally talented at **repartee**.

4. **gingerly** (JIN jer lee) Here we move from lightness of conversation to lightness of touch. This adverb describes a cautious, delicate approach to something, either literally or figuratively.

- When Dr. Pruitt encouraged Thomas to pick up the centuries-old Chinese vase that was the center of his collection and examine it, Thomas did so very **gingerly**.
- Brian, who longed to marry Felicia, knew he must approach the topic of matrimony **gingerly**, for she had often expressed her delight in her independence.

5. **lambent** (LAM bent) This adjective describes the lightness of...well, light. It might tell of something flickering or something glowing, a literal "lick" of light. It can also be used figuratively.

- By the **lambent** glow of the lantern, Randy was thrilled at last to see the cave paintings he had been reading about ever since he was a teenager.
- Ian prefers comedians with a **lambent** wit that makes him smile over the cruder sort that send their audiences into instant guffawing.

6. **leaven** (LEV en) To leaven is to lighten, either in a literal sense of causing bread dough to rise or the metaphorical sense of lightening up a figuratively heavy topic. (The same root word leads to "alleviate," meaning to lighten the pain or burden of something.)

- **Unleavened** bread such as matzos has had no yeast or baking powder used in its preparation.
- Dr. Lester's imparting of ethical instruction was always **leavened** by his sense of humor, which thus **alleviated** any potential sense of "ho-hum" on the part of his students.

7. **elucidate** (eh LOOS ih dayt) This verb means to make clear ("lucid") through explanation, to shed light on the subject. The root word "lucid" is itself an adjective coming from the Latin word for "bright" or "shining."

- The scholarly edition of Virgil's *Aeneid* had only a few lines of Latin per page; many annotations to **elucidate** the text followed.
- Paula carried her letter of apology personally to Mrs. Coleman, hoping to get a chance to **elucidate** any parts that were unclear in what she had written.

8. **epiphany** (eh PIF uh nee) This noun refers to any instant perception, sudden comprehension, spontaneous revelation. A cartoonist might indicate the epiphany of a character by drawing a light bulb over his head. The root word in Greek means "to show." When capitalized, the word has the specific meaning of a Christian holiday observed on January 6, when, as tradition expresses it, the Magi or Three Kings arrived in Bethlehem to see the newborn Jesus.

- Tiffany asked me if her realization that Chip just wasn't that into her could count as an **epiphany** like those in the stories of James Joyce.

- The secular concept of the Twelve Days of Christmas has its origins in the religious holiday of **Epiphany**.

9. **diaphanous** (die AF uh nus) Literally applied, this adjective usually describes cloth that is so fine in texture as to allow one to see through it. The root, "phan"—to show—is the same as in "epiphany" (#8). It can also have the figurative sense of "easily seen through."

- The chorus girls in *Ziegfeld's Folies* wore **diaphanous** garments in varying pastel shades.
- The invention of the cell phone has allowed liars to get away with tales such as, "I'm working late tonight, honey," that would formerly have been less **diaphanous**.

10. **benighted** (be NITE ed) Today this adjective is always used figuratively to describe a person or an argument in moral or intellectual darkness; the "night" of ignorance has descended. (Would an epiphany change things?)

- Prejudices that today seem utterly **benighted** may once have been considered merely opinions.
- "Latin is not a dead language," said the esteemed Miss Elmore, "and those who call it such are themselves **benighted**."

H ow do you express your displeasure or anger?

1. **diatribe** (DYE ah tribe) The root of the Greek word "diatribe" or "learned discourse" is *diatribein*, which means "to consume or wear away." In English, the noun means "a bitter, abusive lecture."

- Stalin's speech was a furious **diatribe**, harshly critical of his political opponents.
- Xiao Xiao's cutting humor and brutal sarcasm made each of her movie reviews a hilarious **diatribe** against contemporary culture.

2. **harangue** (ha RANG) Although the Old French, Old Italian, and Middle English roots of this noun simply mean "a speech to an assembly," the word now means a long, pompous, public speech with a particular point of view. It can also be used as a verb.

- Though Willis intended to deliver a calm and focused speech, he quickly lost control of his emotions and **harangued** his colleagues about the dangers of grade inflation.
- Ralph has always longed to be a dictator, but his awkward mannerisms caused assemblies to laugh at his brutal, fascist **harangues** rather than be frightened by them.

3. **tirade** (TYE raid) Like "diatribe," this noun means an "angry or violent speech, denouncing someone or something." It comes from the French word for "torture," the same root as for the word "martyr."

- Cicero, the Roman orator famous for his public speaking skills, delivered many brilliant **tirades** in front of the Roman senate.
- When Ed was late for dinner for the third night in a row, his wife launched into a furious **tirade** about the importance of punctuality and respect for family routines.

4. **rant** (rhymes with can't) Unlike tirade or harangue, a rant is not only an angry or violent speech, but it can also be used to describe a piece of writing that is angry or that inspires anger or violence. It can also be used as a verb.

- The editorial in the school paper was an impassioned **rant** about the lack of school spirit during the homecoming game.

- As the ball sailed through the pane of glass and Melvin broke his fourth window of the summer, he could already hear his mother **ranting** at him about keeping his games confined to the schoolyard.

5. **vituperation** (vye TOOP er ay shun) This noun also means "a sustained speech of harshly abusive language." The emphasis here is more on abusing rather than on arguing or correcting. The adjective form is "vituperative."

- After years of being called "a cow" and other nasty names, Muffy grew tired of her husband's **vituperation** and decided to leave him.

- Judge Wilkinson grew tired of the prosecutor's abusive style of cross-examination and warned, "If you continue with this **vituperative** behavior with the witnesses, I shall have you removed from the courtroom."

6. **castigate** (CAST ih gate) From the Latin word for "pure," this verb means "to harshly scold," "criticize severely," or "punish." Other words from the same root include "chastise," which means "to punish by beating" or "harshly criticize," and "chasten," which means to "correct by punishment" or "verbally subdue."

- In her letter to the urban planning department, Katya used all of the harsh language she had learned in law school to **castigate** city officials for failing to supervise the proper installation of wheelchair ramps in most of the apartment buildings on her block.

- With her voice raised in anger and her finger wagging with fierce disapproval, Martha **chastised** her boyfriend for having yet again forgotten their anniversary.

7. **fulminate** (FULL min ate) This verb, from the Latin for "to strike with lightning," means to issue an explosive verbal attack, either in speech or writing. A good way to remember it is to think of a "fulminate of mercury," which is a chemical powder that explodes under heat and is commonly used in detonators. The noun form is "fulmination."

- The group of first graders **fulminated** against the teacher who was responsible for the lengthening of nap time, the shortening of recess, and the decrease in the frequency with which ice cream was served in the cafeteria.

- Having heard his local newspaper's **fulmination** against the president after he increased the number of troops being sent overseas, the congressman decided to articulate more extreme opposition to the war.

8. **excoriate** (ex CORE ee ate) From the Latin word that means "to take off the skin," this verb means not only literally "to remove the skin" but to censure strongly, as if flaying with words.

- Simon's brutality as a talent show judge was so severe that contestants would often burst into tears as he **excoriated** them for the mistakes they had made during their performances.

- When Mara fell from her bike, her ankle was cut and her knee was **excoriated**.

9. **admonish** (add MON ish) This verb expresses a milder form of anger than most of the other words on this list. When you admonish someone, you "gently caution" them or "warn" them against something. There is a noun form—"admonishment"—but it is a bit formal.

- Because his mother never paid attention to him when he was well-behaved, Joshua became a chronic mischief-maker, savoring his mother's **admonishments** each time she caught him misbehaving.

- Mr. Talleyboggin, Stephanie's mentor, **admonished** his protégée to apply herself to her thesis work and push the university for more research funding.

10. **invective** (in VEK tive) This noun is not so much an angry speech as it is a description of harsh and abusive language. The verb form "to inveigh" (in VAY) is used with "against." When one inveighs against something, one vehemently protests against it or attacks it.

- In a speech full of **invective**, Mr. Watson criticized his employees for their lack of creativity and their unwillingness to work overtime under deadline pressure.

- **Inveighing** against the long hours, minimum wages, and poor benefits, Mr. Watson's employees went on strike, refusing to manufacture any more widgets until conditions improved at the plant.

MAKE A MATCH #12

Sections 34–36

Match each word in the left-hand column with the phrase on the right that best suggests its meaning.

A.	banter	1.	_____ feverish
B.	castigate	2.	_____ violent speech
C.	conflagration	3.	_____ glowing
D.	deluge	4.	_____ of the earth
E.	diaphanous	5.	_____ a large fire
F.	diatribe	6.	_____ light conversation
G.	elucidate	7.	_____ delicately handled
H.	epiphany	8.	_____ to make clear
I.	ethereal	9.	_____ a spontaneous revelation
J.	febrile	10.	_____ to attack verbally
K.	fulminate	11.	_____ bitter lecture
L.	gingerly	12.	_____ to scold harshly
M.	lambent	13.	_____ heavenly
N.	rant	14.	_____ easily seen through
O.	sodden	15.	_____ intensely hot
P.	terrestrial	16.	_____ a flood
Q.	torrid	17.	_____ soaked through

PRACTICE, PRACTICE, PRACTICE #4

Sections 28–36

Directions: Select a word from the list below that best fits the blank in one of the sentences and place the letter in the blank.

A.	antiquated	K.	martinet
B.	assuage	L.	melee
C.	banter	M.	mendacity
D.	byzantine	N.	obfuscate
E.	castigate	O.	perturbed
F.	celestial	P.	placate
G.	dalliance	Q.	ribald
H.	diaphanous	R.	tirade
I.	evanescent	S.	torrid
J.	inscrutable	T.	tryst

1. The instructions for setting up her new answering machine were so _____ that Mildred asked her daughter to do it for her.

2. Caroline's expression was so _____ that Sam didn't know if she liked his gift or thought it was ridiculous.

3. Prone to _____, Hal lied about his previous experience during his job interview.

4. Susan decided to _____ her disappointment over the canceled picnic by taking herself out to dinner.

5. Not even a double scoop of chocolate chip ice cream would _____ Madeline after she fell and scraped her knee.

6. Mr. Caine was such a _____ that he gave his students detention if they were one minute late for class.

7. A passionate advocate for protecting the environment, Richard launched into a _____ against gas-guzzling SUVs.

8. The mildly _____ one-act play included a romantic scene between a seductive student and her naive tutor.

9. Forbidden to see his girlfriend on school nights, Dan arranged a _____ with her at the public library.

10. Cara's and Tom's relationship began as a _____ over coffee but developed into a passionate romance.

11. The beauty of fresh-cut flowers is _____; enjoy them while you can.

12. "Don't _____ me for being late," Justine cried. "There was a lot of traffic on the thruway."

13. That map is so _____ that it still refers to Sri Lanka as Ceylon.

14. David thought his son's explanation for the broken window was so confusing that he was deliberately trying to _____.

15. On the first day of the sale, Sheets & Towels R Us hired extra security guards to control the _____ of customers.

16. When she returned home, Fran was _____ when she saw several police cruisers with flashing lights parked in her driveway.

17. We hired an artist to paint a _____ scene, including all of the major constellations, on the ceiling of our attic.

18. The _____ temperatures drove most of the families to the beach or to air-conditioned movie theaters.

19. The English teachers engaged in a few minutes of clever _____ before settling down to discuss the curriculum for the coming year.

20. The _____ curtains in the boardroom enabled the junior partners in the firm to partially view the president's meeting with the firm's biggest client.

Speech Therapy

37

D oes your manner of speech need help or does it already possess the virtues and avoid the pitfalls of the words described below?

1. **bombast** (BOM bast) This noun refers to padded, pretentious speech (and now extended to use in writing). It's no coincidence that the word is related to an old French word meaning "cotton padding."

- Jeremy would make a good president of the student council, but the **bombast** in his recent speech really turned me off.

- Shakespeare's character Pistol is given to **bombastic** utterances such as, "Let not hemp his windpipe suffocate." Why doesn't he just say, "Don't hang him"?

2. **pontificate** (pon TIFF i kate) This verb, meaning to speak in an over-authoritative manner, might suit many who are bombastic (#1). Only a pontiff (a pope) deserves to talk in such a manner without giving offense.

- Hilary enjoys having a drink with her coworkers except when Jay comes along, for he always grabs the center of attention and **pontificates** on politics.

- Mr. Calabro is the best-informed man I know, and I admire not only his knowledge but the fact that he never **pontificates** on any of his many fields of expertise.

3. **stentorian** (sten TOR ee un) This is a fancy adjective meaning "extremely loud speech." It is an eponym (see section 75), deriving from Stentor, a Greek herald in Homer's *Iliad* whose voice was said to be as loud as the voices of fifty men combined.

- Why do those who use their cell phones in public places tend to be so **stentorian**?

- In earlier eras the ability to be **stentorian** was prized, but in this day of microphones and public address systems it is not required.

4. **panegyric** (pan e JYRE ik) Originally a speech of praise, this noun now extends to the written form as well. Its Greek root words, *pan* (all) and *agora* (gathering place, marketplace), allow us to see the origin—a man addressing an assembled crowd, perhaps at a funeral, where praise comes most easily—and help us remember the meaning.

- In 431 BC, Pericles delivered a now famous **panegyric** for those soldiers fallen after the first battles of the Peloponnesian War.
- "Should college recommendations for my students be pure **panegyric**?" mused Mr. Isaacson as he began the daunting task of helping his students complete their college application requirements.

5. **eulogy** (YOO luh jee) This noun can be seen as a rough synonym for panegyric (#4), except that modern usage of eulogy is generally restricted to a speech made at a funeral. Perhaps this fact is true because "eulogy"—which literally means "good words"—sounds so much like "elegy," a poem lamenting a death.

- When circumstances allowed Huckleberry Finn to attend his own funeral, did he get to hear a **eulogy** for himself?
- At the service for Ms. Dougherty, she will be **eulogized** by one family member and one coworker.

6. **histrionic** (his tree AHN ik) This adjective literally means "relating to actors or acting," but is coming more to mean "overly dramatic or emotional," an ineffective mode of speaking of writing.

- Mr. Ryshke had an excellent point to make at the meeting, but his **histrionic** manner of presentation undercut its effectiveness.
- Indulging in **histrionics** in the workplace is never a good idea; tears or yelling isn't likely to win the respect of a boss or coworkers.

7. **grandiloquence** (grand IL uh kwenss) This noun, literally meaning "grand speaking," could in theory be positive, but in fact it is always negative, denoting pompous speech.

- Anyone who wants to be more familiar with examples of **grandiloquence** might look at Independence Day speeches from the nineteenth century—a heavy use of long sentences and flowery abstractions.
- Erica longs to be an eloquent speaker but her over-reliance on artificial phrasing makes her merely **grandiloquent**.

8. **embellish** (em BELL ish) The verb "embellish" means "to decorate," presumably with the end of making something beautiful. A speech that is appropriately embellished is effective, but if the number of embellishments is too great, bombast (#1) may be the result. The use of "embellish" is not limited to language.

- Job-seekers may be tempted to **embellish** their résumés, but they should attempt to resist that temptation.

- The Veneerings don't merely hang curtains. No, the drapery at their windows is **embellished** with cornices, valances, tiebacks, and more.

9. **testimonial** (test ih MOAN ee uhl) You can give a testimonial for a person, a faith, or a product. In short, it is a spoken or written statement of tribute. (Like all words in the "testify, testament, testimonial" category, it has a male-centered origin in the word "testes" or "testicles"; presumably, a man holding a hand on that portion of his anatomy was speaking even more frankly than if placing a hand on his heart.)

- I like Mr. Powell, but I don't want to give a **testimonial** for him at the rally, for I also like his opponent.

- Joella spoke so enthusiastically about her Hairsheen, her new shampoo, that I fleetingly wondered if she had been paid by the company to give her dorm-mates a **testimonial**.

10. **sermonize** (SER muh nize) While this verb could mean simply "to give a sermon," it's more frequently used, with a negative sense, for a speech or bit of writing that is inappropriately like a sermon. In short, it assumes an air of moral superiority over the person listening or reading.

- Happily, the film doesn't **sermonize** about the importance of the arts in a school curriculum. It makes the point in a more subtle and effective way.

- All of Aunt Sally's **sermonizing** made Huck Finn want to light out for the territory, and many adolescents identify with that feeling when well-meaning adults talk *at* them.

How Deep Is the Ocean, How High Is the Sky?

38

T his section deals with heights, depths, and in-betweens.

1. **apogee** (AP uh jee) This noun has complex scientific aspects but is also used by the common person to mean, simply, "highest point." (The "gee" at the end of the word comes from "Gaia," a term for the earth.)

- Costas's camera caught the ballerina at the **apogee** of her leap—what a beautiful image by a talented photographer!

- Those at the **apogee** of their careers may have to wonder if descent is inevitable.

2. **acme, apex** (AK mee, AY pex) Here are two more nouns starting with "a" that are synonyms for apogee, highest point.

- **Acme** Hardware, **Acme** Office Products, **Acme** Pesticides—do these names in the telephone book try to persuade the consumer that they represent the highest point of their respective trades, or did the owners just hope the company would get the first listing alphabetically?

- The hikers climbed steadily in near darkness for over an hour, reaching the **apex** of the hill just in time to be rewarded by the beautiful sunrise.

3. **zenith** (ZEE nith) From the three "A" words meaning "highest point" to a "Z" word of the same meaning. This noun originally had an astronomical sense of the highest point of a celestial body and comes from Arabic, the language of many great early astronomers.

- Many scholars consider the thirteenth century to have marked the **zenith** of Islamic literature.

- When Giuseppe Verdi wrote music for the operas *Otello* and *Falstaff*, he was chronologically elderly but was at the **zenith** of his powers.

4. **pinnacle** (PIN a kul) Yet another word for "highest point" as well as a common term for a mountain peak.

- When Cliff finished the difficult climb to the **pinnacle** of Mt. Katahdin, he proudly recorded in his journal, "Today I completed my hike of the entire Appalachian Trail."

- "If I may speak frankly, my dear Miss Ashley," said the impoverished nobleman courting the American heiress, "I think you have reached the **pinnacle** of perfection."

5. **nadir** (NAY deer) This noun, meaning "lowest point" stands alone against the quartet of words for its opposite. Like "zenith" (#3), it comes into English from the Arabic word for "opposite"; it originally had an exclusively astronomical meaning.

- Robby felt he had reached the **nadir** of his high school years when his girlfriend broke up with him on the same day he received his disappointing test scores.
- Hannah's unbounded optimism allowed her to view the **nadir** of her fortunes as a challenge to find a new direction for her life.

6. **bathos** (BAY thoss) This singular noun, coming from the Greek word for "deep," refers to a literary effect that is overly commonplace or grossly sentimental. Less talented authors unintentionally fall into it, but parodists or satirists may seek it out for effect. (It neatly rhymes with "pathos," the Greek word for "feeling.")

- The poet Edgar Allan Poe wielded a mean hatchet when he turned critic, not hesitating to condemn bad verse as "barbaric," or "full of **bathos**."
- Erica's spoofing version of an episode in Homer's *Iliad* featured a successful moment of **bathos**: Achilles almost lost the battle with Hector when he had to excuse himself to go to the bathroom.

7. **abject** (AB jekt *or* ab JEKT) This adjective describes either a low condition or status or describes something most contemptible or most wretched. Appropriately, it comes from the Latin meaning "thrown aside."

- The writer Richard Savage lived many years in the most **abject** circumstances, often walking all night for want of a place to lay his head.
- To run away from a friend in need is one example of the most **abject** varieties of selfishness.

8. **liminal** (LIM in ul) Neither high nor low, neither in nor out—liminal describes something in between, on the edge. It comes from the Latin word meaning "threshold."

- When the lovers in *A Midsummer Night's Dream* leave the city of Athens, they find themselves in the uncharted forest, a **liminal** area not bound by values established by the laws of the city.
- Many ethical questions related to new developments in science are in a **liminal** state: many sincere people do not know what position to take.

9. **consummate** (kun SUM it *or* KAHN sum it) Note the pronunciation; we're talking about the adjective form, not the verb (KAHN sum ate). The adjective describes the highest, most complete or perfect form of some quality, whether positive or negative.

- The Roman poet Horace wrote a satire about the **consummate** bore, a person many readers have met in a twenty-first-century embodiment.

- Writers of a **consummate** artistic temperament must be admired, but family and friends may find them hard to deal with, for they leave practical matters to others.

10. **quintessence** (kwen TESS enss) This noun refers to something that is not at any extreme except the extreme of being purely or perfectly itself. The origin of the word had the literal meaning of having been purified five ("quint-") times.

- In his melancholy, Hamlet described mankind as being the "**quintessence** of dust."

- Andrea and Catherine are good examples of the **quintessential** student— one who is always curious, always looking to add knowledge onto what he or she already knows.

Sycophants Galore

39

Sycophants are people who hope to gain advantages for themselves for flattering people with power or influence. Formal English offers a rich array of language to supplement the slang terms for this type of person.

1. **smarmy** (SMARM ee) This adjective describes a person who smears phony charm all over the person he or she hopes to flatter.

- Dr. Idzal, faculty advisor for the yearbook, sees right through **smarmy** students who think insincere compliments are the road to the position of editor-in-chief.

- The musical *My Fair Lady* describes a character this way: "oozing charm from every pore, he oiled his way across the floor"—it doesn't get any **smarmier** than that.

2. **servile** (SER vile) This adjective describes the behavior of someone willing to act like someone's slave in hopes of getting a payoff later.

- As Alphonse works his way up the corporate ladder, he tries to keep his dignity intact, but even he has **servile** moments of getting coffee or running small errands for his supervisor.

- Whenever the director of his lab starts to tell a joke, Nat **servilely** laughs long before the punch line.

3. **obsequious** (ob SEE qwee us) Among the many words to describe falsely humble behavior, this adjective offers the most syllables. Its root word is the Latin verb "to follow," and the obsequious follow with a vengeance.

- **Obsequious** people get the reward they aim for only if their acting is superb or if the object of their attention is imperceptive or vain enough to believe them.

- For lovers of the novels of Charles Dickens, the character Uriah Heep, who talks nonstop about how "'umble he is," has become almost synonymous with **obsequiousness**.

4. **blandishment** (BLAND ish ment) This noun is used for flattering language subtly designed to coax the hearer into complying with the hopes of the speaker. Not surprisingly, it comes from the Latin word meaning "to flatter."

- Peter told his boss that her introduction to the annual report reminded him of the style of the Gettysburg Address; will Ms. White fall for **blandishments** like this?

- Prof. Ray enjoys students' notes of a complimentary nature when they arrive after grades have been given; otherwise, he fears they may be mere **blandishments**.

5. **minion** (MIN yun) This noun is always used contemptuously to describe a "yes-man," a person who unquestioningly serves another. (The cut of meat, filet mignon, preserves the original French spelling and the more positive meaning of "dainty" or "darling.")

- Mr. Blunderbuss never personally fires anyone; one of his **minions** always does it for him.

- The head of the division never sat at a meeting without his **minions** flanking him as courtiers of a Renaissance king might do.

6. **henchman** (HENCH man) Originally bearing a neutral sense of a trusted follower, this noun has increasingly come to have a negative sense like that of minion (#5), suggesting sycophancy.

- The king and his **henchmen** traveled by horseback through the north of Scotland, looking to shore up support among the nobility there against a threatened invasion.

- While no proof is yet available, the press strongly suspects that the leader of the oil lobby is a **henchman** of Sen. Phogbound, who receives enormous support from owners of oil wells.

7. **fulsome** (FULL sum) This adjective, meaning "offensively insincere," had a happier past of meaning simply "abundant." If you use it in that latter way today, you'll be seriously misunderstood and seen as absolutely oleaginous (slimily flattering).

- After Mr. Brown made a false step with his boss, he wrote an apology that was so **fulsome** that it offended more than the original error.

- Ms. Milnor's **fulsome** request that we give a standing ovation to the speaker wiped out any possibility of a spontaneous show of appreciation.

8. **wheedle** (WEE dul) This verb describes a process of flattery or guile to achieve a desired end. Sycophants are good at wheedling.

- With minimal skills and a genius at **wheedling**, Nanette turned a temporary part-time job into a permanent high-paying position.

- His big smile and his double-talk rhetoric allowed the unscrupulous salesman to **wheedle** the couple out of their savings.

9. fawn (rhymes with dawn) This innocent word for a baby deer has an accidental double in a verb referring to the display of affection designed as a trade-off for favor.

- Abigail **fawns** shamelessly on her dissertation advisor, hoping for extra-special letters of recommendation from her.

- What a **fawner** Jed is! He practically slavers when his boss joins him at the cafeteria table.

10. toady (TOW dee) This noun is no accidental twin of the amphibian creature the toad. A toady is an obvious flatterer, the term for which comes from the graphic noun "toadeater," occasionally heard today.

- The original **toadeaters** literally ate or seemed to eat poisonous toads in sideshows, a move designed to allow the audience to see that their partner could expel the creature from their system.

- Tim was initially disappointed when his company transferred him to a small town, but he solaced himself with the thought of no longer working with a bunch of **toadies**.

MAKE A MATCH #13

Sections 37–39

Match each word in the left-hand column with the phrase on the right that best suggests its meaning.

A.	abject	1. _____	slavish
B.	apogee	2. _____	to flatter
C.	bathos	3. _____	in between
D.	bombast	4. _____	wretched
E.	embellish	5. _____	highest point
F.	eulogy	6. _____	loud speech
G.	fulsome	7. _____	overly dramatic
H.	grandiloquence	8. _____	offensively insincere
I.	henchman	9. _____	sycophant
J.	histrionic	10. _____	lowest point
K.	liminal	11. _____	to decorate
L.	nadir	12. _____	funeral speech
M.	servile	13. _____	gross sentimentality
N.	stentorian	14. _____	pompous speech
O.	wheedle	15. _____	pretentious speech

Today, most people try to avoid gender-specific name-calling, but you'll come across some of these words in your reading.

1. **hag** (rhymes with bag) This word is actually an abbreviation of *haegtesse*, an Old English word that means "witch" or "hag." The noun is reserved solely for women and, although it once meant "soothsayer" or "oracle," it has since retained only the negative meaning of "witch" or "frightful, ugly old woman."

- In many fairy tales, a nobleman's reward for helping an old **hag** is to see her transformed into a beautiful, young maiden, ready to offer her hand in marriage.
- With a cackle, the **hag** mounted her broomstick, donned her pointed, black hat, scratched her wart-covered nose, and flew off into the night sky.

2. **misogynist** (miss OJ in ist) Dating back to the early seventeenth century, this noun means "woman-hater."

- People always suspected that Otto would inherit his father's hatred of women and, by the time the boy turned twenty, there was no question that he was a full-blown **misogynist**.
- It did seem ironic that Gabriel, who had chosen to work at a women's rights center, should be such an incorrigible **misogynist**.

3. **shrew** (rhymes with screw) Although this noun applied to both men and women as far back as the thirteenth century and meant "spiteful person," it has since come to mean "a peevish, spiteful, nagging woman." The word comes from the Old English for a "shrew mouse," which was once believed to have a venomous bite.

- Before her marriage to the gallant prince made her an altogether happier woman, Gwendolyn had been a mean-spirited, pestering **shrew**.
- In Shakespeare's *Taming of the Shrew*, the character of Katherina, dubbed a "**shrew**" for her stubborn and critical nature, is eventually tamed by the suitor Petruchio, who transforms her into a tender wife.

4. **chauvinist** (SHOW vin ist) This noun has two meanings. First, it describes anyone who is fanatically patriotic. It also means someone with a prejudiced belief in the superiority of his or her own gender or group, and it is most commonly applied to males.

- Because Arthur was wary of being labeled a **chauvinist** and ruining his political career, he tried to hide his belief that men were more intelligent and more competent than women.
- The fact that Aidan continued to sing the praises of his country even after it became apparent that its government was committing terrible atrocities abroad made people realize that he was not only a patriot but a **chauvinist**.

5. **misanthrope** (MISS an throwp) Here's one of the few nouns on the list that's not gender-specific. Anyone can be a misanthrope since it means "one who hates or mistrusts humankind."

- Julian had turned into such a **misanthrope** that he could not stand to speak to people, let alone see them, and so he spent most of his days locked up in his room.
- Only a **misanthrope** would believe that no one would be willing to donate money to the tsunami relief fund.

6. **crone** (rhymes with moan) We're back to misogyny (#2) with this noun. It means a "cantankerous, old, withered woman" and comes from the Old French word for "carrion," or dead and decaying flesh.

- Years of hard labor and misery had transformed Roberta from a buxom, sprightly lass to a wretched, hunchbacked **crone**.
- In the myth of the golden fleece, Jason helps a **crone** to cross a flooded river, only to discover that the withered old woman is none other than the Greek goddess Hera in disguise.

7. **misandrist** (miss AND rist) Here's the other side of the coin from misogynist—in short, a man-hater.

- When Lisa and Margot started the **misandrists'** club at college, they chose as the club's symbol a picture of a man's face with a red "X" superimposed over it.
- Patty had been abandoned by three husbands and was cruelly treated by her father; it was no surprise that she was such a **misandrist**.

8. **harridan** (HARR ih den) Here's another antiwoman noun that dates back at least as far as 1700. It means a "vicious, scolding old woman" and may come from the Old French word for "old horse" or "nag."

- After years of being hounded, scolded, and maligned by his **harridan** of a wife, Mr. Snogworth snapped and had to be committed to the local psychiatric institution.

- As Malcolm lay in his bed, he could hear the landlady trudging up the steps, ready to reveal her true **harridan** nature by demanding the rent, complaining about his playing loud music, and chastising him (see the "Don't Yell at Me" section) for smoking cigarettes in the apartment.

9. **fishwife** (FISH wife) This noun can mean literally "a woman who sells fish," but it more generally means "a course, abusive, nagging woman."

- "Go tell that **fishwife** of a mother to stop hounding us about how we raise our children," exclaimed Howard, tired of listening to his mother-in-law's unsolicited advice.
- George heard Martha's gruff voice calling for him through the open window and wondered why he ever married such a **fishwife**; she was always nagging him to do chores when he was trying to relax.

10. **philanderer** (fil AND der er) This noun describes a male flirt, that is, a man who carries on many love affairs with women that he does not take seriously. Most philanderers engage in extramarital affairs with women they have no intention of marrying. The word actually comes from the Greek for "lover of men." The adjective form is "philandering."

- All of Hortense's friends knew that her husband was a **philanderer** but no one could talk her into divorcing him; she loved him, no matter how many times he was unfaithful to her.
- When Nancy threatened to leave him, Marco promised to stop his **philandering** ways and remain faithful to her; he was ashamed of his uncontrollable habit of flirting.

Oh, What a Tangled Web

Sir Walter Scott, writing two hundred years ago, noted: "Oh, what a tangled web we weave, when once we practice to deceive!" These words help describe means to those tangles.

1. ruse (ROOSE *or* ROOZE) From the Middle English word for "detour," this noun means "a crafty scheme," "a sneaky plan."

- Unable to pay his rent, Herman came up with several **ruses** to avoid bumping into his landlord, including climbing out of the window and using a ladder to leave his apartment building every morning.

- So that her husband wouldn't know she was planning a surprise party for him that evening, Jessica came up with a clever **ruse** to get him to the restaurant. She told him they were going to a party for his best friend.

2. guile (rhymes with style) This noun means "skillful cunning" or "deceit" and comes from the Old English word for "sorcery." "To beguile," a related verb, comes a bit closer to the word's original roots; though it also means "to deceive," it often suggests a kind of cunning that is more charming than treacherous.

- The German philosopher Friedrich Nietzsche once said, "The most dangerous physicians are those born actors who imitate born physicians with a perfectly deceptive **guile**."

- Caught taking an extra cupcake off the food line in the cafeteria, Rasheen **beguiled** the server with a bright smile and a shrug and said, "It's for my friend who forgot to take one when she picked up her lunch."

3. clandestine (clan DES tin) Probably formed from the Latin for "internal secret," this adjective is used to describe something done secretly in order to conceal a private plan or an improper purpose. People aren't clandestine; actions are.

- In a **clandestine** meeting that took place in his London war rooms, Winston Churchill met with his cabinet to discuss the impending deployment of British troops.

- Knowing their parents would forbid their union, Romeo and Juliet arranged a **clandestine** marriage by Friar Lawrence, who saw in their love the possibility of ending the age-old feud between the Capulets and the Montagues.

4. **surreptitious** (SUR rep TISH us) This adjective means clandestine or stealthy, in short—sneaky. Just like "clandestine," it is more often used to describe the actions people do, not the character of the people who do them. The noun form is "surreptitiousness," but it's never used.

- The pickpocket sidled up to the commuter on the packed subway car and **surreptitiously** removed the wallet from the man's back pocket.
- Sylvester the Cat, known for his **surreptitious** gait, tiptoed up to Tweety Bird's cage, carefully opened the gate, and swiped the little yellow bird into his paw. "I tought I saw a puddy cat," Tweety Bird cried, as he slipped free of Sylvester's claws.

5. **innuendo** (in yoo END oh) This noun may or may not qualify as "deception." From the Latin for "hint" or "give a nod to," it means "a subtle or indirect expression" or "an insinuation." If it's true, of course, it doesn't qualify as deception, but all too often it suggests the kind of half-truth that leads to rumor or gossip. In fact, in a legal sense, it means "allegedly libelous or slanderous material."

- "This article is full of rumor and **innuendo**," shouted Brad Pitt. "I was not married in a secret ceremony in Las Vegas; nor am I the playboy it makes me out to be."
- The defense attorney in the murder trial attacked the prosecution's case as relying on **innuendo** as opposed to fact.

6. **subterfuge** (SUB ter fyooj) The Latin root of this noun means "to escape secretly," but the word, like ruse, has come to mean "any secret plan or strategy."

- "Telling me you had to work late last night was pure **subterfuge**," Alyssa shouted at her husband. "I know you were out playing cards with the boys instead of having dinner with my mother."
- Through careful **subterfuge**, including dipping his thermometer into a cup of hot tea when his mother wasn't looking, Harvey managed to convince his parents that he was far too sick to go to school.

7. **finagle** (fin AY gul) This verb isn't quite slang, but it's a more informal way of saying "to take by dishonest means" or "to swindle." It's sometimes used to suggest actions that are a bit more manipulative and a bit less deceitful than out-and-out cheating.

- Babs managed to **finagle** a day off from work by saying that she had to visit a sick relative in the hospital.
- In a crooked real estate scheme claiming to offer cheap condominiums in South Florida, the two crooks managed to **finagle** millions out of their clients.

8. **furtive** (FUR tiv) This adjective means "sneaky" or "shifty" and comes from the Latin word for "thief." It can describe a person or, more often, the way a person acts.

- In a **furtive** effort to get closer to Cindy, Max shifted in his seat and casually threw his arm around the back of her chair.

- Afraid that she would fail the history test, Olivia glanced **furtively** at her neighbor's paper and was immediately caught by the teacher and accused of cheating.

9. **bamboozle** (bam BOOZ ul) The origins of this odd-sounding verb are unknown. Like "finagle," it is an informal way of saying "to swindle" or "to deceive." It has the same almost playful feeling as "to hoodwink."

- In *Adventures of Huckleberry Finn*, the King and the Duke attempt to **bamboozle** some townspeople by pretending to be great Shakespearean actors and charging money for their performance.

- Luke **bamboozled** Chip out of his vintage Mickey Mantle baseball card by trading him a reproduction of a Babe Ruth card and telling him it was an original.

10. **temporize** (TEMP er ize) From the Latin for "to pass one's time," this verb has a slightly more sinister quality. It means "to act evasively in order to gain time or to avoid an argument."

- The congressman **temporized** during a discussion of stem cell research at a White House conference in order to delay the vote and create more time for his committee members to lobby opponents of the upcoming bill.

- In an effort to help their accomplice steal some chips from the corner deli, the two hoodlums **temporized** with the man at the cash register, distracting him with stories about the old neighborhood.

I magine a world where all these words could be used only as metaphors or in reference to history.

1. martial (MAR shul) Mars, the Roman god of war, left his mark on this adjective. Unsurprisingly, it means "related to or characteristic of war or warriors."

- **Martial** arts are not part of war, but they do infuse a warrior-like state of discipline on those who practice them.
- The **martial** blare of trumpets led off the triumphal procession that featured exotic animals from the conquered land and chariots full of the golden spoils of war.

2. carnage (KAR nej) This noun refers to the slaughter inevitable in any war. The root word is the Latin for "flesh."

- Although Homer's *Iliad* glorifies the victorious warrior, it does not spare the reader the sense of the terrible **carnage** of the Trojan War.
- After the birthday party for ten four-year-olds, the family room looked more like a scene of **carnage** than one of celebration.

3. subjugate (SUB ju gate) This verb expresses the action of conquering, enslaving. The Latin root word comes from the yoke that subdues animals.

- Although the French **subjugated** the inhabitants of England in the eleventh century, the French language melded with the English language rather than replacing it.
- Toni looked longingly at the German chocolate cupcakes in the bakery but **subjugated** her hunger by thinking of the form-fitting prom dress she had just purchased.

4. internecine (inter NES en *or* inter NEES en) This adjective has come to mean intra-group struggle or destruction. (Should you see it in literature earlier than the late eighteenth century, it will lack that "internal" sense. A famous seventeenth-century poem uses "intestinal" to describe civil war.)

- The War between the States is one of the bloodiest examples of **internecine** conflict in military records.

- My very literate mother yelled down to my brother and me that we should stop our **internecine** squabbling.

5. **besiege** (be SEEJ) An army besieging a town surrounds it with armed force and waits. The verb can also be used figuratively for any mental or emotional pressure.

- When Ms. O'Brien announced that she could assist students in finding high-paying summer jobs, she was **besieged** with requests for help.
- When the Turks **besieged** the city of Vienna in 1683, the results went beyond the military: this was the occasion for the introduction of coffee to the European world, or so some experts believe.

6. **mercenary** (MER sin err ee) As a noun, this word refers to a professional soldier, one who fights for pay for any country. As an adjective, it describes any "just for money" motive.

- Thousands of Hessian soldiers from north Germany were sold to England to fight as **mercenaries** against the rebellious colonists in America.
- When Rosa asked Raoul how much his summer internship paid, he snapped, "Don't be so **mercenary**. I'm doing it for the experience."

7. **plunder** (PLUN der) This verb refers to the seizing of property during war or some similar act of force. It comes from the German word meaning "household goods." The word is often associated with the words "pillage" and "sack," both of which describe the forceful taking of property.

- Many towns and villages were **plundered** during the Thirty Years War when soldiers could be seen carrying out everything from knickknacks to bed linen while distraught owners wailed.
- The evangelist encouraged his followers to "**plunder** hell" by depriving Satan of possible inhabitants.

8. **ballistic** (buh LIST ik) This word's formal meaning refers to the dynamics of projectiles; the ancestry goes back to the Greek word "to throw"—think "throw a *ball*." This word is best known today in its slang meaning of really really angry—angry enough to *throw* something.

- The ancient Romans had a machine of war called a *ballista*; its job was to hurl heavy projectiles, just as modern **ballistic** weapons do.
- My physics teacher nearly went **ballistic** when I told him I didn't have my project done on time.

9. **hegemony** (huh JEM uh nee) Many wars are fought over power, what state will have hegemony over another. This noun, which became very trendy in the late twentieth century, means just that: predominant influence of one nation over another. The origin is the Greek word for "leader."

- The movie *Dr. Strangelove* satirically displays the leaders of the United States and Russia having to choose between **hegemony** and survival.

- Athenian **hegemony** first emerged in the aftermath of the wars with Persia.

10. **ordnance** (ORD nuns) This noun refers to items as dissimilar as weapons, ammunition, vehicles—whatever is needed to keep the military going. Do not confuse it with **ordinance**; this word sounds similar but has the entirely different meaning of a city regulation.

- During World War II, Dennis, whose health barred him from serving in the military, left his sales position for a job at the **ordnance** factory; he wanted to feel part of the war effort.

- City **ordinance** #1415, forbidding the possession of "exotic animals," required that Sebastian divest himself of his cheetah if he wished to continue living in Pleasantville.

MAKE A MATCH #14

Sections 40–42

Match each word in the left-hand column with the phrase on the right that best suggests its meaning.

A.	carnage	1. _____	dominant influence
B.	chauvinist	2. _____	to forcefully seize
C.	clandestine	3. _____	woman-hater
D.	finagle	4. _____	frightful woman
E.	hag	5. _____	fanatically patriotic
F.	hegemony	6. _____	man-hater
G.	innuendo	7. _____	crafty scheme
H.	martial	8. _____	secretive
I.	mercenary	9. _____	indirect expression
J.	misandrist	10. _____	to swindle
K.	misogynist	11. _____	to act evasively
L.	ordnance	12. _____	related to war
M.	plunder	13. _____	slaughter
N.	ruse	14. _____	to enslave
O.	subjugate	15. _____	professional soldier
P.	temporize	16. _____	ammunition

Bored and Lazy

re you bored or are you lazy? These low energy words help pinpoint your exact status.

1. **ennui** (ahn WEE) This noun is the French import for referring to boredom, listlessness. If you're bored, you can at least give a Gallic shrug to express your state.

- Jean Paul had planned to drop by Les Deux Magots in the afternoon for an apertif, but once **ennui** set in, he merely sat quietly in his room listening to Edith Piaf songs.

- The gray sky and cold wind fed into Annette's sense of **ennui**, and the warm gloves and umbrella she had planned to purchase that afternoon remained on the shelves of the store.

2. **enervated** (EN er vayt ed) This adjective (from the verb "enervate") describes a sense of weakened vitality, a loss of energy, letting you feel as if some vital nerve had been removed.

- After the soccer team lost to their archrival, Jason, the team captain, felt **enervated**, not so much from physical exhaustion as from emotional depletion.

- Many Roman leaders believed that an excess of luxury had **enervated** civilizations such as Egypt and that too much contact with these nations could **enervate** Rome itself.

3. **jaded** (JAY ded) This condition of world-weariness may come from over-familiarity or overindulgence in something originally pleasant. The word has nothing to do with the gemstone "jade" but derives from an old word for a broken-down or useless horse.

- Having a world-famous chef for a grandfather had given little Morgan a prematurely **jaded** attitude toward food. At ten he was heard to utter, "Fish quenelles? Again?"

- Those who are overly self-indulgent pay the price of becoming **jaded**, unable to enjoy exotic travel or fancy clothing, pleasures that would delight most people.

4. **lassitude** (LASS ih tood) Another noun for emotional fatigue or a dreamy, lazy mood, "lassitude" comes from the Latin word for "weary."

- As the whispered phrase "Nichols is coming" went from cubicle to cubicle, workers interrupted their state of **lassitude** to assume the time-honored posture of looking busy when the boss approached.
- Jess had studied so hard for her exams that the end of exam week found her in a state of complete **lassitude**, barely able to do more than reach toward her bedside table for her mug of cocoa.

5. **otiose** (OH tee ose) This adjective may describe a condition of idleness or laziness or a person or thing that is ineffective. The word derives from the Latin word for "leisure."

- Linda has no religious motivation for observing a day of rest, but she feels a spate of being **otiose** benefits both body and soul.
- Do those marks over the letters of that brand of ice cream mean anything, or are they merely **otiose** eye-catchers?

6. **pall** (rhymes with wall) This verb describes the fact of a phenomenon's becoming boring or wearying. (It is a verbal cousin to appall, to be filled with shock or dismay.)

- Simon liked the first act of the new play, but as the villain grew more and more wicked, it began to **pall** on him.
- There is a satisfaction in making your living environment neater, but those who are not true neatniks find the pleasure of organizing the closet **palls** after half an hour.

7. **banal** (buh NAL or buh NAHL or even BAY nul) This adjective describes the predictably trite, the ordinary.

- E. B. White could take the most **banal** of thoughts (such as "big cities can be lonely") and turn them into fascinating essays.
- Hannah Arendt's concept of the "**banality** of evil" has received a lot of attention in the last half century.

8. **somnolent** (SOM no lent) This adjective is a fancy way of saying "sleepy." (Memory trick: think of "insomnia," not getting any sleep.)

- Patrick wanted nothing more than to spend a **somnolent** afternoon in the hammock, possibly working up to reading a newspaper headline or two.
- Although Rita likes the idea of books on tape, the narrator's voice often has a **somnolent** effect on her, possibly a holdover from years of bedtime stories.

9. **phlegmatic** (fleg MAT ik) Here is an adjective describing a person who is slow to act, slow to get angry—more or less the far extreme from temperamental. While it can have the positive sense of "calm," today it more often has a negative feel, possibly as suggested by the feel of a throat full of phlegm. (Word historians may enjoy knowing the long pedigree of this concept: as early as 400 BC it was regarded as one of four basic "humors" or temperaments.)

- Sarah likes to stir up an occasional feeling of jealousy in her boyfriends, but Ned's **phlegmatic** nature has conferred immunity on him thus far.
- The stereotype of a certified public accountant as somewhat **phlegmatic** certainly does not apply to Mel: he may crunch numbers all day but on the weekend he skydives and bungee jumps.

10. **torpid** (TOR pid) If you're torpid, you have no energy. If you're a certain kind of animal, you might be hibernating, but if you're a plain old human being, you've let yourself get bored stiff. And that's what the Latin root means.

- "So far as I know," said Jack, school expert on music of the last twenty-five years, "the only song with '**torpor**' in the lyrics is 'Like the Weather' by 10,000 Maniacs."
- Sean had promised his parents he'd clean out the garage on Saturday afternoon, but the sight of piled up, rusting yard equipment and stacks of old *Saturday Evening Posts* put him into a **torpid** frame of mind, and he took a nap instead.

See What I Mean?

44

I f you're looking for the right word to describe how you perceive things, peruse (a verb that means "to examine with great care") or at least have a glance at the list here and see what you think.

1. **scrutiny** (SCROO tin ee) From the Middle English for "to take a formal vote," this noun means "careful examination or study" or "close observation." On the other hand, something that is "inscrutable," is "difficult to understand" or "impenetrable." The verb form is "to scrutinize."

- The orthopedist **scrutinized** Carol's X-rays in search of a cause for her excruciating shoulder pain, but she could find nothing out of the ordinary in the images.

- After careful **scrutiny** of the crime scene, the detective determined that the burglar must have entered through the kitchen door with a key since there were no signs of forced entry.

2. **scan** (rhymes with pan) Oddly enough, this verb has two opposing meanings. After much debate by word scholars, it was decided that it is acceptable to use it to mean "to examine closely" or "to look over or leaf through hastily." It is also used by English and Classics students to mean "to analyze verse into metrical patterns." It comes from the Latin word for "to climb," because one could beat the rhythm of a poem by tapping one's foot.

- Max **scanned** the school newspaper to see if there was an article on last week's soccer game since he scored the winning goal; sadly the sports section covered only the girls' swim team and the recent junior varsity lacrosse games.

- **Scanning** the first book of *The Aeneid* takes up the first month of Mr. Tobin's AP Latin class because the students have difficulty determining the poem's meter after a summer without practicing Latin.

3. **discern** (DIS sern) From the Latin word for "to separate," this verb connotes a particular kind of seeing. When you "discern" something, you distinguish it from something else. You perceive it to be different or distinct. The noun, "discernment," means "having good judgment or keen insight."

- "Your new toupee looks terrific," Alice told her husband Morris. "I can't **discern** any difference between the hairpiece and the fringe of natural red hair around your ears."

- Known for her **discerning** taste in *haute couture*, Coco was hired as a consultant for the photo shoot for the May issue of *Vogue* magazine.

4. **monitor** (MON it or) This word has many meanings as a noun, including the screen on which you watch television or view the contents of your computer. In this context, however, it's a verb which means "to supervise" or "keep a close watch over." It comes from the Latin for "to warn."

- After his heart attack, the doctor told Paul to carefully **monitor** his diet, avoiding all foods that are high in sodium or cholesterol.
- As the new security guard for 124 Park Avenue, John has the job of **monitoring** whoever comes into the building and stop any strangers from entering the elevator without a guest pass.

5. **descry** (dih SCRY) This verb comes to us from the French word for "to call out." It means "to catch sight of something that is difficult to see" or "to discover something by very careful scrutiny" (see #1). It should not be confused with "decry," which comes from the same French root but means "to openly condemn."

- In the dusky distance, Marlowe **descried** a ship heading out toward the horizon, its sails golden in the sunset.
- After carefully examining the hieroglyphics in the cave, Indiana Jones **descried** directions that would lead directly to the secret vault containing the treasures of the lost ark.

6. **gander** (GAN der) Aside from being "a male goose," this noun is an informal way of saying "a look or glance."

- On the first day of school, Hal nudged the boy sitting next to him in homeroom and said, "Get a **gander** at the new girl in the front row. She's hot."
- All of the telephone operators at the telemarketing company were required to eat lunch under the **gander** of the supervisor so as to guarantee they would not take more than the allotted thirty-minute break.

7. **askance** (ah SKANS) The origin of this adverb is unknown, but it describes the way a person looks at something. It means "with disapproval or suspicion" or "sideways" (which suggests that it might come from the Italian for "slantingly" or "obliquely").

- There is a fairly well-known, ribald (see the "Not-Quite-Naughty Words" section) limerick that begins: "There was a young fellow called Lancelot, Whom his neighbors all looked on **askance** a lot."
- Stephanie's elite summer camp was so snobby that the girls looked **askance** at anyone who was not wearing the right designer jeans or the latest style in sneakers.

8. **ogle** (OH gul) This verb comes to us from the German word for "eye." It means "to stare at," usually in a rude or flirtatious way.

- In a famous photograph by Ruth Orkin, a beautiful Italian woman walks down a narrow city street while men **ogle** her from the sidewalk, from a parked motorbike, and from a neighboring café.
- When Chet is the lifeguard on duty at the town pool, all of the girls sit on their beach towels and **ogle** his perfect tan and huge arm muscles.

9. **espy** (es SPY) Like descry, this verb that means "to glimpse something partially hidden." It comes to us from the French, using the same root as the word "espionage," which means "spying in order to obtain secret information."

- In the gloaming (see "The Stream I Go A-Fishing In." section), Captain Ahab **espied** the tail of a white whale breaking the water in the distance and headed further out to sea.
- The game of hide-and-seek was over when Julie **espied** the purple sleeve of Penny's party dress peeking out from behind the pale yellow curtains in the living room.

10. **myopic** (my OPP ik) From the Greek word for "nearsighted," this adjective can be used both literally and figuratively. Someone who needs glasses because they cannot see clearly at a distance is "myopic," but so is someone who is "short-sighted" and "lacks long-range perspective."

- Because she was so **myopic**, Ramona couldn't see more than two feet in front of her nose and had to wear thick lenses to correct her vision.
- "Don't be so **myopic**," advised the Millers' stockbroker. "It's foolish to put all of your money in high-tech stocks because they are popular right now. You've got to think about which industries will be successful in the years to come."

I n addition to technical terms for diseases or medicines and states of health, the language has useful non-technical words.

1. **placebo** (pla SEE bo) A substance that contains no medicinal value but one which the patient believes has such value. (In English it is a noun but comes directly from the Latin verb form meaning "I shall please.")

- The pharmaceutical company tested the new drug in a trial where half the subjects received the medication and half received a look-alike **placebo**.
- Psychologists are interested in the so-called **placebo** effect wherein some patients who falsely believe they are receiving a useful medication demonstrate relief from their symptoms.

2. **elixir** (ee LIX er) A liquid potion or medicine falsely believed to cure any ailment.

- In earlier centuries, dishonest traveling salesmen peddled **elixirs** that would cure all ills—or so they promised before they quickly left town.
- Could love be the true **elixir**? The composer Donizetti wrote an opera based on just such a premise.

3. **panacea** (pan ah SEE ah) Literally, a "cure-all," a substance believed to be a remedy for any disease or difficulty.

- How wonderful it would be if doctors could prescribe a **panacea**, regardless of the patient's symptoms.
- Worrying about an exam the night before it is, unfortunately, not a **panacea** for neglecting to study throughout during the semester.

4. **nostrum** (NOS trum) In past eras, an ineffective potion or pill sold by a dishonest person; now, any possible remedy, not scientifically proven, for a minor ailment or bodily condition.

- The old-timey "medicine man," who often traveled with a carnival-like show, offered glowing promises and an array of **nostrums** to an uneducated audience.

- The shelves of today's drugstores allow today's overweight consumers to select their favorite **nostrum** for possible help with losing weight.

5. **salubrious** (sal OO bree us) Describing circumstances or conditions favorable to good health.

- Devon found that listening in class and taking notes had a **salubrious** effect on his grade.
- The poet John Keats, ill with tuberculosis, left the foggy weather of London for the more **salubrious** climate of Rome.

6. **prognosis** (prog NO sis) A prediction concerning the course of a disease, particularly of the possibilities for recovery. (Compare with "diagnosis"; both contain the root of the Greek word for "knowing.")

- Although Jeremy continued to have symptoms of his illness, he took comfort in the fact that the **prognosis** for his recovery was excellent.
- The second "talking head" on the Sunday morning television shows disagreed sharply with the speaker before him concerning a **prognosis** for society's ills.

7. **malinger** (ma LING ger) To pretend to be ill in order to get out of unpleasant work.

- Students who habitually **malinger** do not win the sympathy of harder-working classmates.
- Some films about World War II depict sergeants in the U.S. army as being particularly skillful in distinguishing the truly ill from those who were **malingering**.

8. **benign** (be NINE) Used in a general sense to mean kind or friendly, this word has the specific medical sense of meaning not dangerous to health.

- Mr. Reynolds was understandably relieved when his doctor told him the tumor on his lungs was **benign**.
- The **benign** face and helpful words of her counselor raised Gina's spirits on an unhappy day in her life.

9. **noxious** (NOK shus) and **innocuous** (in NOK yoo us) Describing, respectively, that which does harm and that which does no harm.

- Federal inspections work to keep **noxious** chemicals out of our food supply.
- Physicians must adhere to the first principle of the ancient Hippocratic oath, "First, do no harm." Their treatment, ideally, will be helpful, but it must be **innocuous**.

10. **dyspeptic** (dis PEP tik) Literally, descriptive of a person suffering from indigestion but often used more generally for a person who is grouchy or ill-tempered.

- Selina's doctor recommended that she see a specialist for her recurring bouts of **dyspeptic** distress.

- Sharing a workspace with the perpetually **dyspeptic** Oscar did not increase Elmo's pleasure in his summer job.

MAKE A MATCH #15

Sections 43–45

Match each word in the left-hand column with the phrase on the right that best suggests its meaning.

A. banal	1. _____ boredom		
B. benign	2. _____ weak		
C. descry	3. _____ world-weary		
D. dyspeptic	4. _____ trite		
E. enervated	5. _____ sleepy		
F. ennui	6. _____ to stare at		
G. jaded	7. _____ careful examination		
H. malinger	8. _____ short-sighted		
I. myopic	9. _____ to feign illness		
J. nostrum	10. _____ cure-all		
K. noxious	11. _____ harmless		
L. ogle	12. _____ poisonous		
M. panacea	13. _____ healthful		
N. salubrious	14. _____ suffering indigestion		
O. scrutiny	15. _____ quack remedy		
P. somnolent	16. _____ to catch sight of		

PRACTICE, PRACTICE, PRACTICE #5

Sections 37–45

Directions: Se ect a word from the list below that best fits the blank in one of the sentences and place the letter in the blank.

A.	abject	K.	histrionic
B.	banal	L.	lassitude
C.	carnage	M.	misogynist
D.	clandestine	N.	obsequious
E.	crone	O.	ogle
F.	descry	P.	philanderer
G.	embellish	Q.	pinnacle
H.	ennui	R.	pontificate
I.	eulogy	S.	ruse
J.	guile	T.	scrutiny

1. Obsessed with baseball, Josh like to _____ about the strengths and weaknesses of the various players.

2. At the funeral, Mark delivered a moving _____ about his mother's generosity and compassion.

3. Penny stamped her feet and pounded her fists in a _____ display of disappointment at not winning the science award.

4. Marlowe did not _____ his story with unnecessary details or exaggerations.

5. Many think the Nobel Prize for Literature signifies the _____ of an author's career.

6. Thousands live in _____ poverty in the crowded slums of Rio de Janeiro.

7. The _____ servant bowed deeply before the king each time he entered or left the room.

8. James was such a _____ that he wanted to ban women from his eating club.

9. Dressed in rags, the _____ pointed a bony finger at the children and demanded that they help her across the street.

10. Everyone knew that Esther's husband was a _____ who was never faithful to her.

11. Using all the _____ she could summon, Phoebe convinced her principal that she hadn't plagiarized her essay even though she had copied portions from the encyclopedia.

12. In a _____ meeting on the outskirts of town, the two men made plans for their impending bank robbery.

13. Although her son Billy hated baths, Margaret devised a clever _____ that lured him into the tub.

14. The photographer's images of the _____ on the battlefield were a powerful antiwar statement.

15. The construction workers like to take their lunch hour right on the street so they can _____ the women who pass by.

16. It was almost impossible to _____ the lights of the village in the thick fog.

17. Since all of her friends were away for the summer, Allison spent her nights at home suffering loneliness and _____.

18. The chaplain's talk was so _____ that most of the students fell asleep during the morning assembly.

19. Overcome by _____, Steve spent most of his winter vacation at home watching DVDs.

20. Topher's careful _____ of the morning newspaper revealed no mention of his team's victory on the soccer field.

Mad as a Hatter

46

The term "mad as a hatter" was in the English language almost thirty years before the Mad Hatter appeared in *Alice's Adventures in Wonderland*. Real mental trouble is no laughing matter and deserves serious expression.

1. lunatic (LOON ah tik) This adjective comes from the Latin word for moon. Because it was originally believed that the cycles of the moon could trigger periods of intermittent insanity, the word means insane or wildly foolish. The noun is "lunacy." Oddly enough, the related word "loony," which also means crazy, may have a different root, coming from "loon," a diving bird noted for its wild cry.

- "Staying up all night to study right before an exam is sheer **lunacy**," cried Peter's mother. "You'll be too tired to think straight and you'll surely fail the test."

- The naive critic said that Jackson Pollock must have been a **lunatic** to think that dripping paint on a canvas was a form of serious art.

2. irrational (ir RASH on al) This adjective means "not rational or reasonable." It may describe a person who is guided by other forces, such as instinct or feeling, but it more often suggests an absence of mental clarity or madness.

- Afraid of commitment and nervous about her impending marriage to Melvin, Carla had an **irrational** desire to flee the country and join the Peace Corps.

- "Fearing that everyone wants to harm you is **irrational**," said the psychiatrist. "You have done nothing to inspire such negative feelings in others."

3. incoherent (in ko HEER ent) This adjective describes someone who is unable to think or express his or her thoughts in a clear or orderly manner. It comes from the Latin for "unable to stick together." Someone who is drunk or sleepy or confused may be incoherent but not insane, but the word is often used to describe a symptom of madness.

- The homeless man walked down the street, gesticulating wildly and mumbling to himself **incoherently**; the pedestrians avoided him, thinking he was insane.

- The label on the pain medication warns users not to operate heavy machinery as it may cause drowsiness or **incoherence**.

4. **deranged** (dur RAYNJD) As a verb, this word means "to disturb the order of" something or "to upset the normal condition" of it. Most often, however, it is used as an adjective to mean "insane," as in having one's mental order upset or disturbed.

- The **deranged** man ran through the streets of the city, crying for his mother and threatening to harm anyone else who came near him.

- "Clarissa became quite **deranged** after her husband died," explained the doctor. "Her grief was so extreme that she could no longer take care of her basic needs and had to be hospitalized."

5. **demented** (duh MEN ted) Here's an adjective that means "loss of intellectual faculties such as memory, concentration, or judgment." People suffering from dementia (the noun form) have a kind of illness that comes from an organic disease of the brain.

- Mrs. Wilson's **dementia** had progressed to the point where she needed a full-time companion who would make sure she didn't wander out of the house in her pajamas.

- In his **demented** state, Harry Lyme could not remember the name of his wife or the address of their home.

6. **neurotic** (nur OT ik *or* nyoor OT ik) Although a century ago, this adjective was considered a scientific term for various emotional or mental disorders, such as hypochondria, it is now only used informally to mean excessively anxious or upset. A related word, which you might run across in a nineteenth-century novel, is "neurasthenic," which referred to nervous exhaustion and breakdown. Both words share the prefix which means "having to do with the nervous system."

- Meg's dog Georgia was a bit **neurotic**; every time Meg left the house, Georgia would begin to howl and paw frantically at the door.

- Joel's friends called him **neurotic** because he was always so anxious before taking an exam, but Joel believed his anxiety helped him to study hard and do well.

7. **psychotic** (sy KOT ik) This adjective suggests a much more severe madness than neurotic. Someone who is psychotic has a severe mental disorder characterized by a loss of contact with reality and consequent inability to function in social situations. The noun form is "psychosis."

- The **psychotic** serial killer was captured by the police and found guilty of murdering twelve women.

- *I Never Promised You a Rose Garden* tells the true story of a **psychotic** young woman who suffered from multiple personality disorder.

8. **berserk** (ber SURK *or* ber ZURK) This adjective, which means destructively deranged or wildly unrestrained, comes from the Old Norse word *beserkr*, "a wild warrior or champion." These Norse warriors wore hides or shirts (*serkr*) of bears (*bera*) and became frenzied in battle, howling like animals and foaming at the mouth. Ironically this word only appeared in English in the nineteenth century, long after these warriors were said to live. It is often used to describe wild animals as well as mad people.

- When Suzanne discovered that her brother Ben had borrowed her iPod and broken it, she went **berserk**, screaming loudly and threatening to break one of his favorite toys.

- One of the elephants at the zoo went **berserk**; he broke out of his cage and rampaged through the cafeteria, knocking over tables and chairs and frightening the visitors.

9. **delusional** (deh LOOZH en al) Originally, a psychiatric term, this adjective means having a false belief in something despite strong evidence to the contrary. Like the psychotic, the delusional person has lost touch with reality.

- The **delusional** Adolf Hitler believed he could successfully invade Russia; ultimately he was forced to abandon his plan.

- The **delusional** drug addict donned a cape and insisted that he was Count Dracula.

10. **amuck** (a MUK) Also spelled amok, this adverb comes from the Malay and means "doing something in a frenzied or uncontrolled state."

- During the blackout, rioters ran **amuck** in the streets, looting shops, breaking windows, and burning trash.

- The soldiers ran **amuck** in the village, killing women and children and destroying civilian property.

ll these words deal with repetition. We hope you don't find this list redundant (a nice word for "repetitive").

1. rehash (REE hash) This verb means "to do something over again, often with minor alterations." It is usually used to describe the retelling of a story or something that involves language.

- Despite rave reviews from the critics, Scott was very disappointed in the film, calling it "a **rehash** of the novel without any of the sexy parts."

- Karla couldn't believe how badly her date with Jamal went; she **rehashed** the evening with each of her friends, detailing Jamal's flat tire, her lost wallet, and their dreadful goodnight kiss.

2. alliteration (al LIT er AY shun) This noun is a literary term that refers to "the repetition of the same sound, usually a consonant, at the beginning of words in a phrase or sentence or in stressed syllables in a phrase."

- A poem entitled *Alliteration, or the Siege of Belgrade: A Rondeau* is written entirely in **alliteration**. The first three lines are: "An Austrian army, awfully array'd,/Boldly by battery besiege Belgrade;/Cossack commanders cannonading come," and each successive line uses the next letter in the alphabet alliteratively.

- Using **alliteration** in his poem "Exposure," the World War I poet Wilfred Owen writes: "Worried by silence, sentries whisper, curious, nervous."

3. recurrent (ree CUR ent) This adjective means "to occur repeatedly." The verb form is "to recur," not "to reoccur."

- Timothy had **recurrent** nightmares about his chemistry teacher; each night he dreamed that Ms. Crossbones told him he failed his final exam and would have to take chemistry again next year.

- The individual's struggle for identity within the confines of old-fashioned and often oppressive social conventions is a **recurrent** theme in the American novel.

4. **doppelgänger** (DOP el GANG er) From the German for "double-goer," this noun means "a ghostly double of a living person," usually one that stalks or haunts its real-life counterpart.

- Joseph Conrad's novella *The Secret Sharer* is about a sea captain who is haunted by a **doppelgänger,** a naked swimmer named Leggatt, who mysteriously comes aboard his ship and shares all of the intimate details of his life.
- Clothilde was increasingly bothered by Holly, who became her **doppelgänger,** dressing like her, wearing her hair in the same style, and even taking a job in the same advertising agency.

5. **reprise** (rih PREEZE) From the Old French for "to take back," this noun means a "a return to an original theme." It is used predominantly in music to describe a repetition of a phrase but it can mean the repetition of any action. It is also used as a verb.

- The thrilled audience gave a standing ovation to the orchestra of *Kiss Me, Kate* and shouted for a **reprise** of "It's Too Darn Hot" and "Wunderbar."
- Mr. Kachtick's Middle English recitation of the "Prologue" to *The Canterbury Tales* was so popular that he **reprised** it each year for his Medieval Literature elective.

6. **recapitulate** (ree cah PICH yoo late) This verb means "to repeat in concise form." It's slightly different from "rehash," which can be an exact or even longer recounting of the same event. The noun form is "recapitulation."

- "Can you please **recapitulate** how you discovered that your house was burglarized?" Detective Olsen said to Mrs. Butterworth. "Stick to the facts, Ma'am, just the facts."
- After a brief **recapitulation** of the novel's plot, the women in the book club began a serious discussion of its central themes and its relevance to contemporary life.

7. **tautology** (taw TOL oh jee) Like "redundancy," this noun means "a needless repetition of the same words or phrases." It can also be used to describe an empty statement composed of simple statements that make it *logically* true, whether the simple statements are *factually* true or not.

- "The general consensus of opinion" and "7 a.m. in the morning" are both **tautologies**; one only needs to say "the consensus" and "7 a.m."
- "I am either in love with you or I'm crazy about you," Harry said, offering a meaningless **tautology** rather than an expression of his deepest feelings.

8. **reprobate** (REP row bate) This noun is included here because it means "a hardened criminal" or, in the terms of this section, "a repeat offender." A reprobate has no hope of salvation.

- An incorrigible **reprobate**, Lefty McGee was arrested for robbery only weeks after he was released from prison.

- The prison on the hill had a minimum security block for juvenile offenders and a maximum security cell block for the more serious **reprobates**.

9. **perennial** (per EN ee al) From the Latin for "throughout the year," this adjective means "lasting an indefinitely long time" or "appearing again and again." "Perennial" plants come back and flower each year, while "annual" plants have one season only.

- "Finding good teachers is a **perennial** problem at Highgate Academy," said Headmaster Wiggins. "Our best teachers tend to move on to university-level jobs after a year or two and we've got to replace some of them every September."

- Dahlia has planted a lovely **perennial** garden of roses, irises, and azalea bushes. The flowers bloom every season and all Dahlia has to do is weed the garden and keep it well-watered.

10. **replicate** (REP lih kate) This verb meaning "duplicate" or "reproduce" comes from the Latin for "to fold back." The noun form, "replication," also means "echo" or "a reply to an answer," but it is rarely used this way now.

- The research biologists at the Immunology Center all agreed that they should repeat their experiments several times to see if they could **replicate** the results of their first experiment.

- Worthington carefully considered his colleague's decision to duel and offered only a silent nod of agreement in **replication**.

Thehe words listed here add a little refinement to the ways in which you can call something "soiled." Consider these possibilities:

1. **besmirched** (buh SMERCHD) Here's a verb that means "to make dirty" or "stain." You can physically besmirch something as when you spill gravy on a tablecloth or make something more figuratively dirty such as when you besmirch a reputation through gossip.

- "Put your drink down on a coaster," cried Helena, "before you **besmirch** my mother's antique mahogany end table."

- After he was caught cheating at poker, Arnold's reputation was **besmirched**; nobody wanted to play with him anymore.

2. **sully** (SUL lee) From the Old French word *souiller*, which means "to soil," this verb also can be used to describe both physical dirtying or more figurative tainting or corrupting. The adjective form is "sullied."

- Thanksgiving dinner was delicious, but the turkey was **sullied** by gravy that was way too salty.

- We spilled so much gravy and coffee on the tablecloth that Bill had to wash all of the **sullied** linens immediately before the stains set in.

3. **defiled** (duh FILED) This verb comes from the Middle English for "to trample on, abuse, or pollute." It means to corrupt or take away the purity of something. It is often used specifically to describe the polluting of a consecrated area.

- "One of our employees spilled soda on the assembly line and **defiled** a whole batch of cookies," explained the company spokesman, "so we will have to recall all oatmeal cookies manufactured on that date."

- The hooligans **defiled** the church by spray-painting graffiti on the statues on the altar.

4. **squalid** (SKWAH lid) This adjective means "dirty or wretched" caused by poverty or negligence. It can also mean dirty in the sense of being morally repulsive. The noun form is "squalor."

- When he first joined the Peace Corps, Paul was horrified by the **squalor** in which the natives lived. Many of them slept on the floor in mud huts and had no electricity or flush toilets.

- The principal decided to ban several of the books on the reading list because he considered the material too **squalid** for high school freshmen.

5. **slovenly** (SLOV en lee) Here is a milder form of dirty, an adjective that means sloppy. Someone who is not neatly dressed is slovenly. It can also be used to describe something done in a "slipshod" (or careless) manner.

- Trip's mother refused to allow him to join the family at the restaurant because he was dressed in such a **slovenly** manner. She sent him home to put on a clean shirt and pressed pants.

- Rachel's boss fired her for doing such a **slovenly** job. None of her files were in alphabetical order and her desk was covered with unopened mail and old food wrappers.

6. **unkempt** (un KEMPT) From the Middle English word that means "uncombed," this adjective, like slovenly, means disorderly or untidy. It can be used to describe people or things.

- The English garden surrounding the cottage in Martha's Vineyard was carefully cultivated to look wild and **unkempt**, as if it naturally grew that way.

- Although Liz paid a fortune to be styled at a chic salon, her hair always looked dirty and **unkempt**.

7. **disheveled** (dih SHEV eld) This adjective comes from the Old French for "disarranged hair." Like unkempt, which literally means "uncombed," it can mean more than disorderly or untidy hair. People who are sloppily dressed are disheveled, as are things that are not neatly arranged. It can also be used as a verb.

- Professor Krupiak was as **disheveled** as his office. His clothes were rumpled and his hair was uncombed, and his books and papers were scattered all over the desk and floor.

- Carla carefully **disheveled** her hair to give it a windswept look because she didn't want to appear too prim when she went backstage to meet the rock band.

8. **slatternly** (SLAT urn lee) A slattern is a dirty, untidy woman, and the adjective is slatternly. Oddly, the word is used only to describe females. It comes from "to slatter," a word used in an English dialect to mean "to spill or splash wastefully," but it may also have its roots in the Swedish word *slata* or "slut," which did not originally have a sexual connotation.

- As the couple was leaving the opera, a **slatternly** woman dressed in rags approached them, murmuring, "Alms for the poor?"

- Having fallen on hard times, Gwendolyn Greystone looked more like a **slattern** than a society hostess. Her hair was unkempt, her clothes were dirty and wrinkled, and she looked as if she needed a bath.

9. **mire** (rhymes with tire) Both a noun and a verb, this word comes from the Old Norse word for "bog." It means both "a wet, soggy, muddy place" (a bog) and "to soil with mud or filth." It also means to get stuck or entangled in something as in "mired in hours of math homework."

- The fisherman waded through the **mire** to find the river stocked with trout.
- **Mired** in poverty, the natives were unable to afford medicine or proper health care for their children.

10. **bedraggled** (beh DRAG gld) This adjective is a fitting follow-up to the word "mire," because it means "wet" or "limp" or "soiled as if having been dragged through mud."

- Our puppy Lucy looked so **bedraggled** after she was caught in a rainstorm out in the woods. Her shiny coat was covered in mud and leaves.
- After camping in the Okeefenokee for a week, Alexa and Danielle returned home tired, hungry, and **bedraggled.**

MAKE A MATCH #16

Sections 46–48

Match each word in the left-hand column with the phrase on the right that best suggests its meaning.

A.	alliteration	1. _____ insane
B.	amok	2. _____ not reasonable
C.	doppelgänger	3. _____ disorderly
D.	incoherent	4. _____ in a frenzy
E.	irrational	5. _____ do over again
F.	lunatic	6. _____ repetition of sound
G.	mire	7. _____ ghostly double
H.	perennial	8. _____ needless repetition
I.	rehash	9. _____ hardened criminal
J.	reprobate	10. _____ lasting a long time
K.	slattern	11. _____ to soil
L.	slovenly	12. _____ wretched
M.	squalid	13. _____ sloppy
N.	sully	14. _____ untidy woman
O.	tautology	15. _____ bog

Keep It Clean

49

Below is a neat and tidy list of words about keeping clean. Some involve literal filth while others deal with editing language.

1. **ablution** (ab LOO shun) This noun means "a washing or cleansing of the body" and is most often used to describe a religious rite. It can also be used to describe any washing that is done in a ritualized way.

   • Before entering the temple, the women were required to remove their street clothes and engage in a series of **ablutions** in a special bathing room in order to be clean for prayer.

   • Before going to work each morning, Lola performed her **ablutions**—brushing her teeth, showering with scented bath gel, applying foaming cleanser and toner to her face—with consummate care in order to showcase her legendary beauty.

2. **immaculate** (im MAK yoo let) This adjective comes from the Latin word for "not blemished" and means "impeccably clean" or "flawless." Although the word is best known from the idea of "Immaculate Conception," the doctrine in the Roman Catholic Church that dictates that the Virgin Mary was conceived free from all stain of original sin, it is perfectly all right to use it to describe a more secular purity.

   • "I want this room to be **immaculate** before you leave," Mildred announced to her daughter Alex. "Pick up all the dirty laundry and put it in the hamper, make your bed, and vacuum the cookie crumbs off the carpet or you're not going anywhere!"

   • Carrie's school record was **immaculate**. Her test scores were perfect; her grades were excellent; and she was involved in numerous extracurricular activities, including sports and community service work.

3. **purge** (PERJ) The verb, which comes from the Latin word for "pure," means "to cleanse or purify." It can be used in many different contexts. One can be purged of sin (the word "purgatory," for instance, is a place of remorse or purging). It can be used in the law to mean "cleared of charges." It can mean "to get rid of impurities" in a more general way.

- The vegetables at the health food store are carefully washed and **purged** of all of their impurities before being pressed into fresh juice at the juice bar.

- Orthodox Judaism requires that women be **purged** in a *mikvah*, a ritual purification bath, before the Sabbath prayers.

4. **expurgate** (EX purr gate) Purging turns literary with this verb. It means to "remove erroneous, obscene, or otherwise objectionable material from a book or other piece of writing before publication." More often than not, we hear the word "unexpurgated" to describe works that have not been tampered with by overzealous editors.

- In the early twentieth century, one had to go to Paris to obtain **unexpurgated** copies of James Joyce's novel *Ulysses*.

- As late as the 1970s, many American schools only taught **expurgated** copies of *The Catcher in the Rye* because parents and school administrators objected to J. D. Salinger's use of foul language.

5. **bowdlerize** (BODE ler ize) Like expurgate, this verb has to do with literary cleansing. It comes from Thomas Bowdler (1754–1825), who published an expurgated version of Shakespeare "in which those words or expressions are omitted which cannot with propriety be read aloud in a family." It means to "cleanse a manuscript of what is deemed 'offensive' material" or to "shorten it so as to skew the content in a certain way." The noun form is "bowdlerization."

- The novels of Henry Miller are too explicit to **bowdlerize**; by the time a conservative editor finished removing offensive material there would be little left to read.

- Horrified by the **bowdlerization** of the Shakespeare editions at her school, the English teacher collected them all and burned them.

6. **unadulterated** (UN ad DULL ter ate ed) The best synonym for this adjective is "pure," but unlike immaculate, which means "spotless," "unadulterated" means "not diluted with irrelevant or unnecessary material."

- "Just tell us the **unadulterated** truth," said Jamie's father. "We want to know what happened at the party and why the neighbors called the police."

- The fresh cranberry juice, **unadulterated** by sugar or other fruit juices or flavorings, was almost too tart to drink.

7. **fumigate** (FYU mih gate) From the Latin word that means "to make smoke," this verb means a particular kind of cleaning—"to employ smoke in order to disinfect or exterminate."

- There were so many spider nests in our basement that we had to call Bugaway Pest Exterminators to **fumigate** the house.

- After the students in Mr. Peppiat's chemistry class performed their sulfur experiments, he had to have the lab room **fumigated** to eliminate the horrible smell of rotten eggs.

8. **hygienic** (hi JEN ik) This adjective means "sanitary" or "sufficiently clean so as to promote or preserve health." The noun form is "hygiene."

- Meticulous about oral **hygiene**, Barnaby brushed his teeth twice a day, flossed after every meal, and rinsed his mouth with plaque remover before bed every night.
- The chef at *Le Café Sal* set a high standard of personal **hygiene** for his staff.

9. **pristine** (priss TEEN) This is another good adjective that means "clean and pure, free from dirt or decay." It also means "original or uncorrupted."

- "This copy of Dante's *Inferno* is in **pristine** condition," said the rare book dealer. "The binding is perfect and the pages are clean. It looks as if it has never been opened."
- After the masterful restoration work, the Renaissance frescoes seemed to return to their **pristine** condition.

10. **winnow** (WIN oh) From the Old English word for "wind," this verb once meant literally "to separate the grain from the chaff" by means of a current of air. It has since come to have a more figurative meaning—"to rid of undesirable parts" or "to separate the good from the bad."

- After weeks of rigorous interviews, the list was **winnowed** down to the three most experienced job candidates.
- "I have finally **winnowed** my book down from three thousand pages to one thousand pages," said Fabienne. "Maybe now I can get a publisher to read it before rejecting it."

I n this book, "cleanliness" is literally next to "godliness." We hope you find the list inspirational.

1. **apotheosis** (ah POTH ee OH sis) This noun comes to us from the Greek and means "glorification" or "giving God-like stature to." A good synonym is "deification." The verb form is "apotheosize."

- Many people believe that Michelangelo's towering sculpture *David* **apotheosized** manly perfection.
- In his essay "Uses of Great Men," the nineteenth-century writer Ralph Waldo Emerson has written: "There are no common men. All men are at last of a size; and true art is only possible, on the conviction that every talent has its **apotheosis** somewhere."

2. **apostate** (ah POSS tayt) From the Greek word for "to revolt," this noun is used to describe someone who has abandoned either his or her religious faith or political party or cause, in other words, "a turncoat."

- After they closed down the factory, the strikers divided into two groups: those who still believed in unionizing the workplace and the **apostates**, who chose to go back to work the next day because they desperately needed the income.
- When Carl finally decided to abandon the beliefs of his local church and find a minister who would marry him and Robert, he was despised as an **apostate** by the people he thought were his friends.

3. **heretic** (HEH ret ik) This is another noun with a Greek root. It comes from the word for "to choose," and it means "a person who holds controversial opinions." It was originally used to describe anyone who dissented from the official dogma of the Roman Catholic Church, but it has come to have a broader use. The adjective form is "heretical."

- The other teachers at the Hewlett Academy, a conservative prep school in Massachusetts, called Mr. McPhee a **heretic** when he stopped giving weekly exams and abandoned traditional grades in favor of pass/fail evaluations with written comments.

- The headmaster, who supported Mr. McPhee's decisions, was later fired for being a **heretical** thinker who was unable to control his faculty and preserve the academy's rigorous academic policies.

4. theocracy (thee OK rass ee) This noun means "a government ruled by religious authority."

- "Allowing religious issues to determine our legislative policy is tantamount to a **theocracy**," shouted the senator, determined to fight the president's policy on stem cell research.
- Before the election of Saul as king, Moses essentially ruled Israel as a **theocracy**, claiming all law was determined by God.

5. numinous (NOO min us) This adjective means "having a supernatural presence" or "spiritually elevated." It may come from the Greek word for "to nod," as in expressing divine approval by nodding the head.

- Dressed in a diaphanous (meaning "translucent" or "delicate") white gown and appearing suddenly at the top of the stairs, Belle's figure took on a **numinous** appearance in the candlelight.
- Nature was **numinous** for the transcendental philosophers of the nineteenth century who believed that it was only through nature that individuals could know their own souls.

6. ecumenical (EK yoo MEN ik al) This adjective means "universal" or "of worldwide scope." It is very similar to the word "catholic" (see the "Together/Apart" section). Its more specific religious meaning is "promoting unity among churches or religions."

- The community in northwestern Alaska was so small that the only church in town was truly **ecumenical**, offering services for Catholics, Jews, Protestants, and Unitarians.
- The Saturday religious services at Janice's summer camp were always about **ecumenical** topics that would appeal to the diverse group of campers.

7. redemption (ree DEMP shun) This noun's specific religious meaning is "salvation from sin through the sacrifice of Jesus," but it also can be used more broadly to mean "to rescue or save" or "deliverance upon payment of a ransom." In its most secular usage, it can mean "recovery of something that has been pawned or mortgaged." The verb form is "to redeem."

- After ruining his father's tennis racquet by using it as a fly swatter, Josh **redeemed** himself by getting a job as a golf caddy and earning enough money to buy his father a new and better racquet.
- In the movie *Rocky*, the protagonist seeks his **redemption** and self-respect by "going the distance" with the heavyweight champion Apollo Creed.

8. **sanctimonious** (SANK tih MOAN ee us) Although this adjective comes from the Latin for "sacred," it means "pretending to be sacred" or "excessively righteous." It connotes a kind of hypocritical piety. The noun form is "sanctimony."

- The **sanctimonious** businessman maintained his veneer of innocence, but the judge knew he was lying all along.

- The politician's smarmy **sanctimony** about the importance of family values in determining political policy earned him the mistrust of his more liberal constituents.

9. **transcendent** (tran SEND ant) This adjective is most often used to mean "lying beyond the ordinary range of perception" or "not part of the material universe." In his theory of knowledge, the philosopher Immanuel Kant uses the word to mean "beyond the limits of experience and therefore unknowable." The word should not be confused with "transcendental," which means "concerned with the intuitive basis of knowledge," a term which forms the basis of a nineteenth-century literary and philosophical movement associated with Ralph Waldo Emerson, among others.

- According to most religions, God is a being of **transcendent** power who is ultimately unknowable to human beings.

- Because of the unbroken horizon line and the excessive moisture in the air, the sunsets along the beach in Key West have a **transcendent** glory that renders them as spectacular as any sunsets in the world.

10. **ecclesiastical** (ek LEEZ ee ASS stik al) This adjective means "of or relating to a church" or "appropriate for use in a church." The noun form, "ecclesiastic," means "a minister" or "priest."

- Dressed in **ecclesiastical** robes and carrying a book of hymns, the bishop stood out in the crowd of children and parents at the school's December Christmas party.

- Because **ecclesiastics** from all over the world were in Rome to attend a special mass at the Vatican, it was impossible to obtain a hotel room at a reasonable price anywhere in the city.

Godliness Redux

R edux" means "led back" or simply "again." Readers may know it from novelist John Updike: he gave the name *Rabbit Redux* to his sequel to *Rabbit, Run*. Our language has so many terms from religion that it warrants two sections.

1. **pantheon** (PAN thee ahn) Literally, "all gods." Today you'll see it used in two ways: (a) spelled with a capital, it names an ancient and beautiful circular building, once a temple, later a church, in Rome or (b) a general term for a group of people regarded as most important (figuratively, "gods") in a certain field or era.

- Although not originally buried there, the artist Raphael now has his tomb in the **Pantheon**, as readers of Dan Brown's *Angels and Demons* know.

- Alvin told me that his personal **pantheon** of twentieth-century figures includes Martin Luther King Jr., Mother Teresa, Winston Churchill, and Joe DiMaggio.

2. **sacrilegious** (sac ri LEEJ us *or* sac ri LIJ us) This adjective describes behavior that is disrespectful toward things many consider sacred, either literally or figuratively. The surprise word history is that it is *not* related to the word "religious" (note carefully the slightly different spelling!).

- "I know you're not religious," said Brenda to her husband Woody, "but please try not to use religious oaths while my sister is visiting. She'd regard it as not only **sacrilegious** but disrespectful to her personally."

- "For a painting so tied in with the history of New York to be sold and sent out of state is a **sacrilege**," said Prof. Silver, distraught at the auction of the Asher B. Durand painting *Kindred Spirits*.

3. **canon** (KAN un) Originally, this word referred to church law or codes as established by a church council. It is now frequently used metaphorically.

- Hamlet, suggesting that only his religious beliefs restrain him from suicide, laments that God has "fixed his **canon** 'gainst self slaughter.'"

- For years schools taught only the best-known of literary works, highly praised for decades, but now many allow teachers to choose non-**canonical** texts, including some recent and controversial titles.

4. **laity** (LAY uh tee) Sometimes you'll hear "layman" or "layperson." All these words refer to people who are not members of the clergy or, by extension, those who are not part of some specialized group. A modern synonym would be close to "the man in the street."

- "'Twere profanation of our vows / To tell the **laity** our love," writes the poet John Donne, who at one period of his life saw erotic love as a kind of religion.
- "When professional dance critics use phrases like 'the nodes of intensity ambush the formality' or write of 'structuralizing spatial velocities,'" said Casey, "I'm happy to be a **layman** who just really enjoys ballet and modern dance."

5. **credo** (KREE doe) The Latin for "I believe," this verb has become a noun that serves as an elegant synonym for the simpler "creed," a formal statement of beliefs.

- "If you obey the **credo** that form follows function," said the ceramics instructor, Ms. Rush, "then you won't make the handle of that mug a thorny vine."
- The Iago in Shakespeare's play never overtly states a philosophy of evil, but his counterpart in Verdi's opera sings a powerful **credo** about his belief in a cruel god.

6. **messianic** (MES ee AN ik) Literally, this adjective refers to a Messiah, a figure in the Judeo-Christian tradition that is or will be a savior of the world. By extension it's often used to refer to zealous or overzealous belief in a cause or a leader. The word comes from the Hebrew for "anointed."

- "There's nothing wrong with green algae," noted Don, "but when Doug starts talking about it he gets that **messianic** gleam in his eye as if taking algae could cure all the ills of the world."
- Some earlier interpreters of Virgil saw a **messianic** theme in one of his early poems, but skeptics argue he was merely flattering a Roman leader, suggesting that his child would be remarkable.

7. **incarnation** (in car NAY shun) Religiously speaking, this noun means "a fleshly version of the divine." Thus, in Christianity, it refers to Mary's conception of Jesus—and the initial letter is capitalized. More generally, it's used for the giving of bodily form to something abstract.

- F. Scott Fitzgerald intensifies the religious feel of Gatsby's near-worship of Daisy when he writes, "He kissed her and the **incarnation** was complete."
- "You don't have to look at me as if I were the devil **incarnate** when I suggest going off your diet long enough to have a bite of my birthday cake," said Angela huffily to her friend Adele.

8. **venial** (VEEN ee uhl) Deriving from the Latin word for "forgiveness," this adjective is used within the Roman Catholic church to describe a sin that is, roughly speaking, "minor," "easily forgivable." Like all the other words in this list, it's also used figuratively, here to mean "unfortunate but not terribly offensive."

- "Okay, Tonya, I'll admit I was twenty minutes late for our date," said Huey, moving from defense to offense, "but don't you think that's rather **venial** compared to your calling up your old boyfriend the minute I went out of town?"

- When his supporters forgave or overlooked many of his **venial** transgressions, Senator Goofball moved slowly but more inevitably to greater breaches of the trust they had placed in him.

9. **conclave** (KON klave) In Roman Catholic use, this is a meeting of the cardinals of the church to select a new pope. By extension, it refers to any highly secret meeting. The origin is interesting: the key word is "key"— Latin, "clavis." (Think of keys on the musical instrument "the clavier" or the key-shaped "clavicle/collarbone.") The original conclaves had to be held in a locked room.

- Is it true that the Sistine Chapel was the setting for the **conclave** that chose Pope Benedict?

- "This is a good afternoon to work on the senior prank," said Hal impishly to Mort. "All of the faculty members and administrators are in a big **conclave** to choose the senior prize winners."

10. **hagiography** (HAG ee OG ruh fee) This interesting noun has nothing to do with "hags." Literally, it's the life of a saint and more generally it refers to a biographical account so uncritical as to make the subject sound too good to be human.

- James Boswell's eighteenth-century life of Samuel Johnson was far from a **hagiography**: although Boswell held Johnson in the highest esteem, he did not hesitate to show him gobbling down his food or "tossing and goring" those in a conversation with him.

- Campaign lives are often in the **hagiographical** tradition: any less than wonderful acts of the presidential candidates may be omitted or fancifully reinterpreted.

Sections 49–51

Match each word in the left-hand column with the phrase on the right that best suggests its meaning.

A.	apotheosis	1. _____	not a member of the clergy
B.	canon	2. _____	rule by a religious body
C.	ecclesiastical	3. _____	without any flaws
D.	ecumenical	4. _____	life of a saint
E.	expurgate	5. _____	becoming a god or godlike
F.	fumigate	6. _____	to cleanse, remove the offensive
G.	hagiography	7. _____	smugly holy
H.	heresy	8. _____	separate good from bad
I.	immaculate	9. _____	violation of the sacred
J.	laity	10. _____	promoting unity in religion
K.	messianic	11. _____	relating to church matters
L.	pantheon	12. _____	violation of church belief
M.	sacrilege	13. _____	to use smoke for cleansing
N.	sanctimonious	14. _____	overzealous belief in a cause
O.	theocracy	15. _____	official church rules
P.	winnow	16. _____	a group of revered figures

L ike section 25, this is a grab-bag section, one that offers ten fine
words that are NOT thematically related. Here goes:

1. **susurrus** (soo SUR us) An unusual word, and an interesting one, whose
sound hints at its meaning. It refers to a soft rustling noise, a whisper, a
murmur. It comes into English directly from the Latin, but a more anglicized form is **susurration**.

  • Just as Geordie, lolling in the hammock, was almost nodding off from the
    soft moaning of the breeze and the gentle **susurrus** of the insects, a mosquito
    bit him on the neck, sharply ending his sense of harmony with nature.

  • The newspaper described the opposition to the prime minister's speech as
    being "a **susurration** of protest, not a gust of anger."

2. **epitome** (e PIT uh mee) This noun refers to a typical representative or
example of some category. Dictionaries are just beginning to recognize it
as a synonym for "embodiment," a use long frowned on by purists. (See
second sentence below.) And in older literature you may see it used in its
literal sense as an abridgment or summary.

  • This particular church was identified by art historian John Ruskin as an
    epitome of the changes that occurred in Venetian architecture after the
    thirteenth century.

  • "Tad thinks he's the **epitome** of 'cool,' but I've got news for him—he's not,"
    said Scarlett scornfully.

3. **striation** (stry A shun) Some call this a fancy word for a "stripe," and
that may serve as a memory device. But it might also refer to a ridge, a
groove, or a furrow. Usually you'll see it in the plural, referring to parallel
groupings of the thing.

  • McDermott's plastered-down hair still bore the marks of the **striations** made
    by his comb.

  • The **striated** pattern on the rock was "beautiful" to Lars, the artist, and
    "interesting" to Lara, the geologist.

4. **holistic** (hole IST ik) There's no "w" at the start of the word, but the meaning has to do with "wholes" not "holes." A holistic approach emphasizes the overall quality of something, the interdependence of its parts.

- When Toby asked his new English teacher if she "took off for spelling," she answered, "No, I grade **holistically**; I look at the overall quality of your writing rather than tallying up errors."

- Dr. Ning's lecture on **holistic** medicine clarified for the audience this alternative approach to medical treatment: a doctor using the holistic approach would not merely look at the nose and throat of, say, patients with a bad cold but would ask them about their eating, sleeping, and exercising.

5. **stipulate** (STIP yoo late) If you stipulate, you make an express demand as part of an agreement; you specify exactly what's required.

- When Harriet agreed to marry Peter, she made the specific **stipulation** that he would never kid her (or, worse, criticize her) about her love of shoes and her possession of many, many pairs.

- Rules for the operation of the Godivan Embassy **stipulate** that all meals served there must end in the presentation of a dessert made of chocolate, whether milk or bittersweet.

6. **extant** (EK stant *or* ek STANT) This word offers a one-word way to say "still in existence."

- Fossil records show us that many ancient forms of life were quite different from **extant** life.

- The fact that there are eighty **extant** manuscripts of Chaucer's poetry from the early fifteenth century testifies to his popularity.

7. **tribulation** (trib yoo LAY shun) This noun refers to a hardship, an affliction, a form of suffering. It's not related to "tribes" or "tribunes" or "tributes." Its surprising (to most of us, at least) origin is the Latin word for "threshing sledge"—a device that pressed on the wheat just as an affliction might press or oppress your spirit. It's sometimes used in a specialized sense within the Christian religion as a period of great suffering for believers.

- Those working for a greater degree of racial equality in the 1960s were sustained in their **tribulations** by their belief that this important change *would* come.

- When Martin went to the administration of his school to protest the absence of a soft drinks machine, the principal said gently, "Martin, I don't think that going without a cola for six hours ranks as one of the great **tribulations** of all time."

8. **recrimination** (re crim in AY shun) This noun refers to the fact of countering one accusation with another.

- Ernest Hemingway made unpleasant and unfair statements about F. Scott Fitzgerald in his book *A Moveable Feast*. Since Fitzgerald was already dead at that time, I don't feel that Hemingway's own death should protect him against a reader's **recrimination**.

- Amy thought she would feel better after she lashed out at Jessica, but instead her ugly statement has sent her into a fit of self-**recrimination**.

9. **conundrum** (cuh NUN drum) A conundrum is a challenging puzzle, a dilemma, a riddle. Even the origin of the word is unknown.

- Bert accidentally goofed up his electronic calendar and now realizes he has two social engagements at the same hour on Friday night; he's now dealing with the **conundrum** of which to cancel.

- "I'll never understand Al," sighed Jan. "He'll always be a complete **conundrum** to me."

10. **belie** (be LIE) This verb refers to misrepresentation, to self-contradiction. Although it's based on the word "lie," it isn't used to convey a sense of deliberate deception.

- Although Carrie was falsely accused of cheating on the French exam, the tears welling in her eyes **belied** the calm of her denial.

- **Belying** Dick's statement that he "always traveled light" were the big suitcase and the overstuffed duffel bag that he was cramming into the trunk of the car.

M ae West though too much of a good thing was wonderful. She'd probably agree that the wealth of words to express an abundance or a superabundance is a very pleasant phenomenon.

1. surfeit (SUR fit) As a verb or as a noun, this word expresses the idea of "over-muchness."

- The hosts meant well with their repeated offers of food, comforts, or entertainment, but their constant attention to his welfare **surfeited** the guest, who longed for a little benign neglect.

- The grandparents, remembering their own cherishing of one or two toys in their Depression-era childhood, saw the many stuffed animals, games, and electronic gear in Miranda's room as a **surfeit** that might be unappreciated or meaningless to the child.

2. superfluous (soo PERF loo us) Literally "overflowing," this adjective can describe either literal objects or more abstract qualities. Shakespearean English allowed for the noun "superflux," but we've lost that pleasing word.

- "Yes, you'll need a hat to protect you from the sun," said the tour organizer, "but taking a straw hat, a cotton hat, a plastic hat, and a baseball cap is just downright **superfluous**."

- A **superfluity** of fragrance to a hypersensitive nose might make one "die of a rose in aromatic pain," or at least poet Alexander Pope thought so.

3. plethora (PLETH uh ruh) From the Greek for "to be full," this noun is a good synonym for "excess." Creeping into the language is a tendency to use the word simply to mean "a lot," but you'll do well to keep it in the category of superabundance.

- "It's feast or famine," sighed Mrs. Treadwell. "First I didn't have enough stationery so I told everyone I wanted it for my birthday. And now I have a **plethora**! Where will I put all these boxes?"

- The **plethora** of choices in the six-page menu at the diner made things difficult for the indecisive Earnestine, who kept changing her mind between "farm-raised pork loin with cream-filled potatoes" and "dieter's special Jell-o with cottage cheese."

4. **myriad** (MEER ee ud) Perhaps not *too* much, this noun expresses the concept of an indefinite but huge quantity. It comes from the Greek for "ten thousand," but is never used in that literal way in English.

- Nothing can make an individual feel so small as to contemplate the **myriad** stars in the sky and to reflect on the distance the light has traveled to reach us.

- Even people unfamiliar with much poetry may know William Wordsworth's poem about his delight, after he "wandered lonely as a cloud," in coming upon a **myriad** of daffodils dancing in the breeze.

5. **sate** (rhymes with ate) and **satiate** (SAY she ate) How appropriate to have not one but two verbs to express the idea of being fully or excessively satisfied!

- Leroy was looking forward to the "all-you-can-eat" buffet and felt disappointed that he was completely **sated** after just one refilling of his plate.

- Belinda, an ardent devotee of the Ramones, had thought she could never learn enough about them, but midway through the five-day conference, she was startled to realize she was on the verge of being **satiated**.

6. **exorbitant** (ex ORB ih tant) From the Latin for "out of orbit," this adjective expresses the concept of something that exceeds all fair bounds. It's most commonly used to describe prices or numerical quantities.

- "That new specialty food store has good things," noted Nelson, "but the prices are truly **exorbitant**. I mean, how special can cole slaw *be*?"

- The **exorbitant** number of demands his boss made of him lessened Selwyn's pleasure in the new job.

7. **gratuitous** (gra TOO ih tus) It can mean "free," "given without obligation," (as in "There's no such thing as a gratuitous mid-day meal," but it's chiefly used today to mean "unwanted" or "unjustified." The fancy word for a "tip"—gratuity—is related, at least ideally, to the older meaning.

- "If I need his help, I'm glad to know he's there to answer my questions," said Vivian. "But his hanging around my cubicle, offering **gratuitous** advice about how to get ahead in the company is just plain annoying."

- Nickleby's **gratuitous** criticism of Selby's work was beginning, subtly, to undermine his confidence. Was that the effect Nickleby had hoped for?

8. **supernumerary** (SOO per NOO mer air ee) Literally, this noun refers to a person who is in excess of a required number, but it is most often used as an elegant word for an "extra" in a movie or dramatic work. Opera slang sometimes calls such a person a "spear-carrier."

- Sam, sensing his lovebird friends wanted to be alone, avoided the cliché of "Three's a crowd," by saying dryly, "I'm something of a **supernumerary** here so I'll see you later."

- Glynis hoped someday to become an actress herself, so she was delighted to get a job as "townsperson" in the regional summer production of *Horn the West*. "So, I'm a **supernumerary**," she says. "I still get to hang around actors and, don't forget, I do say 'Look, is that Daniel Boone?' on stage!"

9. **aggrandize** (uh GRAND ize) This verb can mean "to make greater," but today it's almost always used to refer to someone's making himself seem greater by exaggerating or by belittling others.

- Renee wondered if Jason believed his own self-**aggrandizing** statements or if he just hoped to fool others.

- When Shirley, a so-so singer, told me she had "performed at Carnegie Hall," I was impressed. I later learned this was a bit of **aggrandizement**: her chorus had rented out the hall for one night, as any group with enough money can do.

10. **lagniappe** (LAN yop) This noun first referred to a small gift a storeowner might give a customer but is coming increasingly to be used as "an unexpected extra gift or benefit." With roots in New World Spanish and Quechua, it was originally used in the Creole dialect of Louisiana.

- Customers gave Bolling's Department Store a lot of repeat business because their children enjoyed the lollipops Mr. Bolling gave them as a **lagniappe**.

- To be true to the spirit of a **lagniappe**, this item in the vocabulary book should have been an eleventh entry in the section, an extra, above and beyond what's expected.

T he complement to excess is dearth (see #1). All these words suggest a quality of absence or deficiency.

1. dearth (rhymes with earth) The meaning of this noun is simple. There's not enough of something or maybe there's simply none of it. The origin is in the Middle English word for "costly," kept also in the British use of "dear"—"I'd like to buy mince pies, but they're so dear lately."

- The committee was surprised by the **dearth** of applicants for the Bedriomo Travel Grant: Isn't any student traveling this summer? Couldn't some student use a little financial help?

- The **dearth** of food in the Netherlands during World War II caused residents to use the term "Hunger Winter" when they recalled the worst of that era.

2. paucity (PAW suh tee) From the Latin word for "few," this noun expresses just that in English.

- The **paucity** of supplies available for classrooms meant that dedicated teachers often paid for crayons and rolls of paper for class projects out of their own pockets.

- Since he had anticipated an abundance of curiosity about his new invention, the **paucity** of responses was not only disappointing but startling.

3. exiguous (ex IG yoo us) This adjective describes something that is just barely enough for the purpose. It comes from the Latin for "measured out," suggesting a measuring cup that was never overflowing.

- When the young boy became aware of his family's **exiguous** economic circumstances, he insisted on getting after-school jobs to help as much as he could.

- There was an **exiguous** outcropping of grass among the rocks; otherwise, the terrain was bleak.

4. eke (EEK) As a verb, "eke" carries two senses: the older one expresses the idea of "adding to" or "increasing" while the one more in use today carries the sense of "managing but with difficulty." (Extra trivia for word-lovers:

our word "nickname" was originally "an eke-name," an "additional" name. The "n" of "an" moved over and became part of the next word. "Umpire" went the other way: it was originally "a numpere.")

- Mr. Compton **eked** out a living as a teacher by continuing to work on the family farm in the summers.

- Although Lynette had never studied Italian, she could **eke** out the meaning of a newspaper article in a Roman newspaper through her knowledge of Latin and French.

5. **stint** (rhymes with hint) The verb "stint" expresses the concept of "restricting" or "limiting." (The stingy measuring cup of #3 is at work here as well.) The noun describes a length of time spent on a particular task, presumably with the sense of "not considering lengthening the appointed time." The word originates in older English meaning "to blunt" or "to stop."

- "When you make Scottie's birthday cake," said Mrs. Meyers to her cook, "don't **stint** on the cream. Scottie loves cream."

- Ms. Amendola did a two-year **stint** in the military before returning to the pursuit of her original career goal, becoming a dancer.

6. **scant** (rhymes with pant) Whether used as an adjective or as a verb, the word carries the idea of "barely sufficient" or "in short supply." The related adjective form, "scanty" echoes that sense.

- Porter received **scant** attention from his father when he was growing up and is determined not to repeat that pattern: he lavishes love on his own children now.

- Alison was always trying to balance her work as wife and mother and her work as wage-earner; she felt she was always **scanting** one at the expense of the other.

7. **nominal** (NOM in uhl) From the Latin word for "name," this adjective suggests something exists in name only; in other words, it's minimal, token.

- While Lord Redlinghuys is the **nominal** chair of the fund-raising committee, a professional staff does all the hard work of contacting possible donors, publicizing the benefits, and the like.

- "I receive a **nominal** salary as a spokesperson for bass fishing," said Rick. "But I earn my real living by writing articles for men's magazines."

8. **meager** (MEE ger) This adjective can refer to something that is scanty (#6) in either quantity or quality. The word derives from the Latin for "thin."

- Some would have described Henry Darger as living a **meager** existence, for he lived in one room and worked as a cleaning person at a hospital. But the richness of his inner life is revealed in his paintings, now being collected by folk art museums.

- "Callie, I'm disappointed in the **meager** amount of reading you did this summer. Should you really be taking on an Advanced Placement English class?" said Ms. Zak, the concerned teacher.

9. **pittance** (PIT unss) This noun refers to a tiny amount, whether, as frequently, of money or of some more abstract entity. Tellingly, the origin of the word is in the Latin *pietas* (think "piety"), suggesting that amounts people give to charity may be minimal.

- "I was insulted that I was offered so little money, a mere **pittance**, to do the research for the television show about the opening of the West," said Walt. "You know they must have some 'deep pockets' sponsoring it."

- The song "I Felt Nothing" from the Broadway hit *A Chorus Line* describes the satisfaction of feeling not a **pittance** of concern for the difficulties of someone who earlier denied you a needed helping hand.

10. **titular** (TICH yoo lar) Like #7, this adjective carries the sense of "in name or title only," not possessing any real substance. It can also be used in the simpler sense of "referring to the title."

- The phrase "head of the family" that once had such powerful meaning has now become merely **titular** and is probably on its way to nonexistence.

- Ivan, one of the **titular** brothers in Dostoevsky's great novel *The Brothers Karamazov*, has a frightening encounter with a figure called The Grand Inquisitor.

MAKE A MATCH #18

Sections 52–54

Match each word in the left-hand column with the phrase on the right that best suggests its meaning.

A.	aggrandize	1. _____	to be fully satisfied
B.	belie	2. _____	a puzzle
C.	conundrum	3. _____	not looking at separate parts
D.	epitome	4. _____	hardship, trial
E.	exiguous	5. _____	in name only
F.	gratuitous	6. _____	a return accusation
G.	holistic	7. _____	hatred of foreigners
H.	lagniappe	8. _____	tiny little bit
I.	nominal	9. _____	to exaggerate
J.	pittance	10. _____	more than necessary
K.	recrimination	11. _____	unexpected benefit
L.	sated	12. _____	unwanted
M.	stint	13. _____	to misrepresent
N.	superfluous	14. _____	just barely enough
O.	tribulation	15. _____	a defined period of time
P.	xenophobia	16. _____	a typical representative

PRACTICE, PRACTICE, PRACTICE #6

Sections 46–54

Directions: Select a word from the list below that best fits the blank in one of the sentences and place the letter in the blank.

A.	belie	K.	paucity
B.	conundrum	L.	rehash
C.	defile	M.	reprobate
D.	ecclesiastical	N.	sanctimonious
E.	eke	O.	squalid
F.	hagiography	P.	striation
G.	heretic	Q.	susurrus
H.	immaculate	R.	titular
I.	incoherent	S.	unkempt
J.	nominal	T.	winnow

1. Because her study partner's explanation of the math sections was _____, Barb failed the review test.

2. After telling his mother about how he got a black eye in the playground, Ivan had to _____ the story when his father came home.

3. The juvenile detention center on Route 54 is currently being used as a halfway house for _____ and serious offenders.

4. Melinda did not want to _____ her collection of Hummel figurines with cheap imitations.

5. The _____ apartment was furnished with a worn sofa, a threadbare carpet, and dingy curtains.

6. After Nick wrestled with his brother on the lawn, his hair was _____ and his clothes were covered in grass stains.

7. Mrs. Bisby kept her kitchen as _____ as a hospital room; everything was swept, polished, and put in its place.

8. "Perhaps you can _____ the weak sections out of the manuscript and rewrite the introduction," advised Sara's editor.

9. Considered a _____ for her views on abortion, Cynthia was ostracized by her classmates at her parochial school.

10. Tired of cleaning up after her roommate, Cecilia delivered a _____ speech on the virtues of cleanliness.

11. The store specialized in _____ products such as chalice cups, hymnals, and votive candles.

12. James searched for a book on _____ to learn about the life of St. Jude.

13. You can see the level of the sea at high tide by studying the _____ on the rocks along the shore.

14. Flossie's enthusiastic efforts preparing food would _____ her feigned indifference to the upcoming picnic.

15. "There is a _____ of educational programming for children on the television networks," complained a spokesperson for the Children's Learning Center.

16. After years of trying to _____ out a living as a poet, Florence decided to go to medical school.

17. Janice was vexed about how to solve the _____ of why she was always on a diet but never lost any weight.

18. Karla was paid a _____ salary for her internship at the magazine, but the experience made it worthwhile.

19. Mrs. Peabody's job as principal was merely _____ since she had very little say in the day-to-day running of the upper school.

20. Rose enjoyed feeling the breeze on her neck and listening to the _____ of the tall grass underfoot as she wandered across the meadow.

Send in the Clowns

55

W e all know what a clown is, but did you know that there is actually a variety of interesting words for those who make us laugh?

1. raconteur (ra kon TER) This noun describes a person who inspires laughter through his or her verbal talents. The word comes directly from the French and means "a storyteller of skillful wit." (Memory trick: a raconteur *recounts* things well.)

- Osborne is such a **raconteur** that he had everyone at the dinner table guffawing at his tales.

- When Jay Leno told the anecdote about the chicken, everyone laughed, but when I tried to repeat it to my buddies, there was an awkward silence. I'm just not the **raconteur** Leno is, in case you hadn't noticed.

2. harlequin (HAR le quin) This fellow is recognizable by his clothing of brightly colored diamond shapes and his mask. His outfit goes back to the clown figure in Italian acting troupes several centuries ago. (Romance novels now sometimes associated with the word have no direct connection.)

- The bright costume of the **harlequin** figure in the ballet contrasted dramatically with the all-white outfit of Pierrot.

- In Karl's extensive teddy bear collection is an automated **harlequin** bear; if he's a bit chubby in his traditional outfit, he deftly juggles three wooden balls—so long as his battery is working.

3. stooge (STOOJ) Our immediate association may be to the trio of Larry, Moe, and Curly, but a literal stooge is one who helps a comedian to be funny by feeding "straight" lines to him. An audience may or may not be aware that the stooge is part of the act. By extension, the word may leave the world of clowns entirely and come to mean those who allow themselves to be used by others, presumably in exchange for some kind of gain.

- While the skill of Cox, the **stooge**, was the secret to the success of the comedy duo, it was Box, his partner, who received most of the applause.

- Rafferty's press secretary was a complete **stooge**: he habitually took the blame for his boss's bad decisions, always willing to say, "I misunderstood Mr. Rafferty's instructions."

4. **card** (rhymes with lard) This noun, mostly used in informal contexts, describes a person who is not a professional clown but who is eccentrically amusing in his or her behavior.

- Carol Ann is such a **card** that everyone in our grade enjoys hanging out with her. She's the one who tricked Mr. Hipkens into taking a big bite of a dog biscuit.

5. **wag** (rhymes with tag) Another amateur clown, a wag is similar to card (#4) in being a habitual joker, a bit silly in his or her mischief. The word has a longer history and higher verbal status than the more recent arrival card.

- A Shakespeare character punningly suggests that a certain young **wag** will one day "wag" from a noose because of his mischievous ways.

6. **wit** (rhymes with bit) This short noun not only denotes the quality of being verbally clever but can also denote the person who is intelligently and subtly amusing. Wits can easily trade quips, witty remarks made on the spur of the moment.

- O for a time machine that would allow us to sit in the same room with such eighteenth-century English **wits** as Alexander Pope and Jonathan Swift.
- While Georgie secretly longs to be perceived as a **wit**, the low-level caliber of her humor qualifies her only as a class clown.

7. **mountebank** (MOUNT uh bank) Examples of this particular type of clown are largely found in accounts of earlier eras: they told stories and jokes, even did some magic tricks in order to attract a crowd of folk to whom they could attempt to sell ineffective medicines. The history of the word—Italian for "jump up on the bench"—allows us to visualize the start of their crowd-gathering tactics. Today the word might be used for any unscrupulous salesperson, whether joke-telling or not.

- Perhaps Michiko is romanticizing the past when she says she finds the nerve and skill of marketplace **mountebanks** somewhat appealing.
- That used car salesman turned out to be a bit of a **mountebank**; his dashing flattery faded when I realized the car I bought was a lemon.

8. **droll** (rhymes with roll) This adjective describes words, facial expressions, or acts that are amusing in an odd way, perhaps somewhat whimsical. The fact that it comes from a medieval English word for *goblin* may help us sense its flavor.

- The audience responded very favorably to Louis's **droll** presentation of Puck; at first they weren't sure whether to laugh or not.
- The **droll** look on Jeff Foxworthy's face made his supporters laugh even before he began his comic routine.

9. **antics** (AN tiks) This noun describes acts that are perceived as either amusing or not, depending on the context or on the personality of the beholder. Strangely enough, it derives from the same root word as *antique*, although modern uses have no hint of age about them.

- The **antics** of the trained dog wearing a tutu had even the most sophisticated audience member hee-hawing.

- Ms. Ford has just about had it with the **antics** of her last period class: is secretly signing a classmate's yearbook really more important than passing the algebra exam?

10. **prankster** A prankster plays pranks, that is, mischievous tricks, practical jokes. As with antics (#9), these pranks may or may not be perceived as humorous.

- Writer Tom Wolfe captured in his book *The Electric Kool-Aid Acid Test* the antics of Ken Kesey, well-known author of the 1960s, who traveled cross-country with friends who called themselves the Merry **Pranksters**.

- What group of **pranksters** filled the principal's office to the ceiling with bright-colored balloons? Will she be amused?

Dionysian or Apollonian?

This mouthful of a title alludes to a split between the intuitive (embodied in the Greek god Dionysus) and the rational (embodied in the Greek god Apollo) as described by nineteenth-century philosopher Friedrich Nietzsche.

1. **bacchanal** (back uh NAL) This noun refers to any drunken or riotous celebration. It derives from a Roman celebration in honor of Bacchus, another name for the god Dionysus, particularly in his role of god of wine.

   - "Mom," said Ian, impatiently, "it's just a bunch of us from the calculus class getting together over at Cameron's house to study for the test. You're talking like I'm asking to go to some kind of **bacchanal**."

   - The literate detective surveyed the crime scene—empty bottles of wine and champagne, scattered items of clothing, and a trampled party hat or two— and deduced that a **bacchanalian** evening had moved from joy into violence.

2. **hedonist** (HEE dun ist) Derived from the Greek word for "pleasure," this noun denotes a person devoted to having a good time.

   - Eddie was something of a **hedonist**, living it up to all hours, until he surprised his friends by being accepted into a pre-med program and hitting the books with equal fervor.

   - For Joe and Deedee, devout lovers of the printed word, a **hedonistic** day in London consists of visiting as many used bookstores as possible.

3. **carouse** (kuh ROWZE) This verb refers to taking part in noisy partying. The noun form, "carousal" (kuh ROWZ uhl) refers to merrymaking but should not be confused with "carousel" (KARE oh sel), the merry-go-round. "Carouse" derives from a German expression for the last glass a drinker could order before the bar closed down.

   - Paula's parents, themselves quiet and hard-working, are distressed by the fact that Paula, now supporting herself, chooses to spend her free time **carousing** with like-minded cronies.

   - The weekend **carousals** of the tenants in the neighboring apartment continue, despite Kenny's irate calls, first, to them and, then, to the landlord.

4. **revelry** (REV uhl ree) Another term for a loud "good time," in the Dionysian sense. The verb, "revel" (REV el), has a milder sense of the enjoying or relishing of anything, even a thought.

- College officials are less than thrilled with the sounds of **revelry** streaming forth from on-campus residences every Saturday night
- Liam **reveled** in the announcement that he had won the Lucio Piccolo poetry award.

5. **libertine** (LIB e⁻ teen) This noun refers to a person who acts without moral restraint, a debauchee (DEB oh SHAY)—is Deb O'Shea a debauchee?

- According to the musical *The King and I*, the English governess to his son and heir does not like "polygamy or even moderate bigamy" and thus considers the many-wived King of Siam to be a **libertine**.
- One of the most famous compulsive seducers is the Spanish Don Juan, whose very name has become a synonym for a male **libertine**.

6. **chaste** (rhymes with based) From the Latin word for "pure," this adjective describes a person who is morally pure in thought and conduct. The meaning is often simplified to mean simply "not sexually active." It can also be used figuratively for a pure and simple design in art of architecture. The noun form is "chastity."

- "Some students can never remember," said Prof. Strauss punningly, "that the Fielding hero Tom Jones was chased, but not **chaste**."
- After viewing so many pictures of heavily ornamented cathedrals for her presentation on Gothic art, Maggie relished all the more the **chaste** design of the Greek temple whose photograph hung on her office wall.

7. **celibate** (SEL ih but) Now used as a synonym for "chaste" in the sense of "not sexually active," this adjective, from the Latin word for "bachelor," formerly denoted only the legal fact of being unmarried. You'd probably be misunderstood if you used it that way today.

- The deeply loving husband and wife voluntarily agreed to occasional periods of **celibacy** to help them focus on the spiritual aspect of their union.
- Shakespeare's heroine Hermia, who refuses to marry the man her father has selected for her, is given the choice between death and lifelong **celibacy** in the service of the unmarried goddess Diana.

8. **ratiocination** (RASH ee os in A shun) This noun refers to a methodical and logical process of thinking. And, yes, it derives from the same Latin word as the mathematical term "ratio."

- Edgar Allan Poe's detective M. Dupin solves the crime of the murders in the rue Morgue through his talent at **ratiocination**.

- "**Ratiocination** is not my thing," said Billy Ed. "I do okay by going with my gut feeling."

9. **staid** (rhymes with layed) This adjective is most often used as a compliment to mean "dignified" or, more frequently in a negative sense, "overly prim and proper."

- Mr. Alford encouraged his eighth graders to reread Atticus Finch's **staid** but passionate defense of the judicial system in the novel *To Kill a Mockingbird*. "It's all the more tragic," said Mr. Alford, "that his faith is unjustified."

- The **staid** appearance of Abby and Martha, the elderly aunts in the comedy *Arsenic and Old Lace* is indeed mere appearance, for they delight in poisoning visitors with their homemade wine.

10. **spartan** (SPAR tun) If you're spartan in your way of life, you're far from hedonistic (#2). You're self-disciplined, self-restrained, content with a simple, spare way of life. The adjective also may suggest "stoicism" (STO ih siz um), the ability to bear difficult physical or emotional circumstances without showing distress. The word derives from the ancient Greek city of Sparta, whose inhabitants supposedly possessed such traits.

- In early twentieth-century England, wealthy families often sent their sons to somewhat **spartan** boarding schools featuring hard mattresses, cold showers, and corporal punishment for offenses.

- "Matt has been positively **spartan** in his response to disappointments in the college admissions process," said Ms. Pleshette, his counselor. "No whining or moaning—I wish more were like him."

L ove, trouble, support, grief—what don't we get from our families? It's no surprise that many words exist to express types of family connections.

1. **scion** (SIGH un) This noun is a fancy way of referring to a descendant or heir, most often to a male of a wealthy family.

- "Being a **scion** of the McBucks family is enviable in many ways but not without its own set of problems," sighed Bucky McBucks on a tough day.

- A **scion** of a family known for a successful investment business, James Merrill made his own reputation as a distinguished poet.

2. **epigone** (EP in gon) If being a scion is tough, being an epigone is tougher, for "epigone" always has a negative connotation of "second-rate follower." From the Greek word for "child," this noun is now used for a figurative "second-generation," an imitator, a copier of an earlier pathbreaker. A modern slang equivalent might be "wannabe."

- No one disputes Mick Jagger's originality, and no one can count the number of **epigones** following palely in his glow.

- Plato was an ardent disciple of Socrates, but he transcended the undesirable possibility of being a mere **epigone**.

3. **filial** (FIL ee uhl) This adjective describes the relationship of a son or daughter to the mother or father. (And think of a related word such as "affiliated.")

- Although Martina does not have warm feelings for the father who was absent for much of her childhood, she does her **filial** duty, checking to make sure he's in good health and seeing him on family holidays.

- LuAnne's **filial** bond with her mother is more than hereditary or legal: LuAnne really enjoys her company.

4. **avuncular** (uh VUNK yoo ler) As the second and third syllables suggest, this word describes a relationship with an uncle. By extension, it's used even more often to describe the kind, friendly manner of an unrelated man, a manner like the kind uncle you remember or wish you had had. (Aunts—time for a protest. There's no equivalent word for you. Take solace in the fact that in Latin even some uncles were left out, for the word referred only to an uncle on the mother's side!)

- "I can't wait to see my brother and his son at the family barbecue," said Horace. "Nothing like renewing those fraternal and **avuncular** ties!"

- "McFadden's **avuncular** manner doesn't fool me," confided Sandra. "Underneath those corny jokes is a man conspiring to keep me from my next promotion."

5. **nepotism** (NEP oh tiz im) This noun refers to favoritism shown to relatives in practices such as business matters. While it comes from the Latin word for "nephew," it now refers to any family member.

- "My sister is better qualified for this job than anyone I know," lamented Edwina. "Too bad the company has a strict policy against **nepotism**."

- Colleges that give preference in admissions to children of alumni practice an open form of **nepotism**, a practice outlawed in some companies.

6. **posterity** (pos TER uh tee) In a limited sense, this noun refers to a person's descendants (children, grandchildren, etc.). In a larger sense it is used for a general sense of "future generations." (It derives from the Latin word for "coming after," the same root that makes "posterior" an elegant way to refer to a person's rear end.)

- The Smith family, immensely wealthy, has set up a trust to guarantee comfortable living for their **posterity**.

- The Nobel Prize for Literature was not bestowed on James Joyce or Marcel Proust. **Posterity** has had the last laugh, for those writers draw higher esteem than most of the winners.

7. **lineage** (LIN ee ij or LIN ij) Generally speaking, this noun means "ancestry," the "line" going back to your forebears on the family tree. A chart of the family tree is a called a "pedigree," from the foot-of-a-crane appearance of such a chart. "Pedigree" is sometimes used informally to refer to an individual's education or training or to a "purebred" animal's background.

- Petra brags of tracing her **lineage** back to Charlemagne, ignoring hundreds of other ancestors who didn't make the history books.

- "I don't care about his **pedigree**," huffed Mr. Stormer when his daughter began detailing her fiance's educational background. "Is he a man who'll treat you right?"

8. **progenitor** (pro JEN ih ter) A progenitor is a direct ancestor, or by extension an originator. The other end of the spectrum gives us "progeny," a Latinate word for offspring, literal or figurative.

- Historians of classical music regard Arnold Schoenberg as the **progenitor** of modern music.

- Nell sat back in her easy chair, happy to look again at her holiday cards from Calvin, Russell, and Lila, each surrounded by their bright-faced **progeny**.

9. **prolific** (pro LIFF ik) This adjective describes someone with many offspring, either literal children or figurative children such as books.

- Farm families of the previous century were often **prolific**, with each of the many children assigned farm chores as soon as they were old enough.
- Joyce Carol Oates is an amazingly **prolific** writer, her fans can barely keep up with her output.

10. **posthumous** (POS tyoo mus) Literally meaning "after death," this adjective has a special "family sense" in referring to a baby born after the death of his or her father. It can also be used in nonfamily contexts.

- Modern-day psychologists have written about the childhood of eighteenth-century writer Jonathan Swift: not only was he a **posthumous** child, but his mother was geographically distant from him in his early years.
- Sicilian writer Giuseppe Lampedusa's only novel, *The Leopard*, was published **posthumously** to great acclaim; the writer knew only the sadness of having his manuscript rejected twice.

MAKE A MATCH #19

Sections 55–57

Match each word in the left-hand column with the phrase on the right that best suggests its meaning.

A.	antics	1. _____	skillful storyteller
B.	bacchanal	2. _____	Italian clown figure
C.	carouse	3. _____	whimsically amusing
D.	chaste	4. _____	practical joker
E.	droll	5. _____	drunken celebration
F.	epicene	6. _____	person devoted to pleasure
G.	harlequin	7. _____	to party
H.	hedonist	8. _____	morally pure
I.	lineage	9. _____	methodical thinking
J.	nepotism	10. _____	after death
K.	posthumous	11. _____	having many offspring
L.	prankster	12. _____	ancestry
M.	prolific	13. _____	overly prim and proper
N.	raconteur	14. _____	self-disciplined
O.	ratiocination	15. _____	heir
P.	scion	16. _____	imitator
Q.	spartan	17. _____	favoritism shown to relatives
R.	staid	18. _____	amusing or outrageous behavior

Yield...Or Don't Yield

 All these words are adjectives describing elasticity or its absence. Whether you're describing someone supple enough to do the most difficult yoga exercises or someone flexibly open-minded—or their opposites—there's a word for it.

1. resilient (rez ILL ee ent) From the Latin for "to leap back," this word describes the ability "to recover readily from illness or misfortune" or to "get back into shape." The noun form is "resiliency."

- "Children are quite **resilient**," Joey's pediatrician told his mother. "Though he's got quite a bad case of the flu, he should be back on the soccer field in no time."

- Although Gloria told Herb he was "dull" and "unattractive" after one date, Herb's **resiliency** enabled him to go back to Meet Your Mate Online and try another date the following weekend.

2. adamant (AD ah ment) Since this word comes to us from the Greek for "unconquerable" and "diamond," it's no wonder it means "impervious to reason" or "stubbornly unyielding." There's even a stone named "adamantine," that was thought to be impenetrable.

- After hearing reports of terrorist threats at the airport, Belle's parents remained **adamant** about her not attending the spring break party in Cancun.

- Although Rajneesh thought his history grade was unfair and complained to Mr. Lombardy, his teacher, Mr. Lombardy remained **adamant**, insisting that his class participation was poor and his final paper was inadequately researched.

3. lithe (rhymes with writhe) A good word for "limber" or "flexible," this word can be used to describe people or things. Another form of the adjective is "lithesome" or "lissome (LISS um)."

- Carmella's long, **lithe** body and natural grace made her a skillful ballet dancer.

- The **lissome** elephant grass, bent double in the tropical breeze, formed pale green loops that waved gently in the morning sun.

4. **implacable** (im PLAK ah bul) We're back to unyielding with this adjective. It means "unable to be appeased or mollified" (see the "What a Relief" section). The noun form is "implacability" or "implacableness."

- Even though Greg brought her a bouquet of roses and apologized profusely for missing her piano recital, Jessica remained **implacable**; she just couldn't forgive him for missing her big night.
- Fully aware of Lotta's **implacability** when she was upset or frustrated and fearful of her having another tantrum, her mother made sure to take an extra cupcake in case Lotta dropped hers.

5. **stringent** (STRIN jent) From the Latin word for "to draw tight," this word means "strict or severe" or "constricted." It is used to describe actions rather than people.

- The school imposed **stringent** rules regarding dress code. Absolutely no shorts or tank tops were allowed, even on the hottest days of the year.
- Samuel Smiles, the nineteenth-century Scottish political reformer, once said: "No laws, however **stringent**, can make the idle industrious, the thriftless provident, or the drunken sober."

6. **stalwart** (stal WART) This word, from the Old English word for "steadfast," means "firm" and "resolute" and can be used to describe people or actions. It can also be used as a noun to mean "one who loyally supports a party or a cause."

- The band of striking workers remained **stalwart**, marching in front of the factory and refusing to enter until they were given higher wages and better benefits.
- The antiwar rally was attended by students, conscientious objectors, and a large group of liberal **stalwarts**.

7. **compliant** (com PLY ant) Someone who is compliant is "flexible," "adaptable," or "willing to agree to the demands of others." It is generally used to describe someone who is "submissive." A good synonym, which comes from the same Latin root for "to fold" or "to bend" is "pliant." "Pliant" is often used to describe flexible things rather than flexible people. The noun form is "compliance."

- When Henrietta insisted that her husband come with her to see a doctor, he came along like a **compliant** child; he must have been feeling very ill since he generally distrusts the medical profession.
- "We expect full **compliance** with the rules and regulations of the country club," explained the club president. "That means no bare feet in the lobby or sitting rooms."

8. **obeisance** (oh BAY sense) This is not the noun form of "obey." That's "obedience." "Obeisance" is what you do to express your obedience or respect. Like a bow or a curtsy, obeisance is "a gesture that expresses homage or a willingness to serve."

- Embarrassed by their **obeisance** and never remembering when it was appropriate to return their small bows with bows of his own, Walter had a difficult time doing business with his colleagues in Asian countries.

- Jeeves bowed every time he entered Mr. Carnegie's study, certain that his employer would be pleased by his **obeisance**.

9. **malleable** (MAL ee ah bul) From the Latin word for "hammer," this adjective means "capable of being shaped or formed (as if by hammering, either literally or figuratively)." It can be used to describe things or people who easily adjust to differing circumstances.

- Bernard was an extremely **malleable** child, which made him easily liked by the other children, particularly the bullies who always wanted to have their way.

- The jewelry designer preferred working with silver because it is an extremely **malleable** metal, making it ideal for creating unique and intricate settings.

10. **inexorable** (in EX or ah bul) This adjective means "relentless" or "not capable of being stopped or changed."

- Acutely aware of the **inexorable** passage of time, Ronak shouted "*Carpe diem!* Live for today!"

- "In the end, nature is **inexorable**," said the nineteenth-century Russian novelist Ivan Turgenev. "It has no reason to hurry and, sooner or later, it takes what belongs to it."

59

In a previous chapter, you'll find many words that suggest an abstract sense of lightness, as opposed to something heavy (or "ponderous"). Think, for example, light conversation ("banter" or "repartee") or a light touch ("gingerly"). The examples in this section offer words that focus on the "not dark" meaning of light.

1. translucent (tranz LOO sent) This adjective comes from the Latin word meaning "to shine through." People often confuse it with "transparent," which means "perfectly clear." Translucent things, such as the glass often used for shower doors or bathroom windows, diffuse light in a way that prevents seeing something perfectly clearly.

- Phineas peered through the window of the art room to see what the class was doing, but the **translucent** glass prevented him from seeing the nude model.

- The *Daily Record* reporter could not get permission to photograph everyone at the rally so he used a **translucent** filter on his camera to blur the images of the faces in the crowd.

2. pellucid (peh LOO sid) Here's an adjective that, like transparent, means "perfectly clear." It can describe something literal, like a windowpane, but it is often used more figuratively to describe a writing style or an explanation.

- The **pellucid** prose style of Ernest Hemingway, much of it drawn from his experience as a journalist, makes him a favored author in high school and college English classes.

- Dr. Garfield's **pellucid** explanation of the patient's symptoms enabled the medical students at the teaching hospital to gain a fuller understanding of the diagnosis.

3. luminous (LOO min us) Like "pellucid," this adjective can also be used to describe a clear verbal style; perhaps more often it is used to describe something full of light—or illuminated—from within.

- On Halloween, the **luminous** windows of the houses along the dark street helped the children to trace their way home.

- The critics praised the poet for her **luminous** style that captured the essence of the human condition without excess words.

4. **incandescent** (in kan DES sent) This word means "shining brilliantly." Sometimes it means "bright or glowing as a result of being heated" (like a light bulb which shines when the filament inside heats up), but it can also be used figuratively to mean "lit from within by strong emotion or intensity."

- The bride's face was **incandescent** with joy and excitement at the prospect of their honeymoon in Thailand and their future life together in Brooklyn.
- When the coals turned an **incandescent** orange, Mark knew it was time to put his chicken on the grill and cook up his famous "chicken noir."

5. **effulgence** (ee FULL jens) This noun comes from the Latin "to shine out" and means just that—"a glow or radiance." It can be used literally or figuratively.

- In the first half of its visible course, the comet emitted a high degree of **effulgence**.
- The candidate, whose good looks and commanding manner contributed to his **effulgent** presence, dominated his dull rival throughout the debate.

6. **limpid** (LIMP id) This adjective has two slightly different meanings. Like many of the words in this section, it means "perfectly clear or easily understood." It can also be used to describe an untroubled, serene state.

- The house was situated on the banks of Lake Winnepesaukee, whose **limpid** waters were rarely troubled by wind or currents.
- Professor Milstein's **limpid** explanation of string theory enabled the first-year physics students to apply very complex formulas to everyday processes.

7. **luminary** (LOO min air ee) This noun comes from the same Latin root as "illuminate" and "luminous" and means "an object that produces light." Perhaps more commonly, however, it refers to people—experts in their field—who serve as an inspiration to others.

- The panel on the meanings and uses of slang was hosted by Noam Chomsky and various other **luminaries** who specialize in linguistics.
- Candles, lanterns, sconces, and other **luminary** devices are sold online at discount prices at a website called "Lights R Us."

8. **resplendent** (reh SPLEN dent) This adjective is best used to describe someone or something that is brilliant or dazzling in appearance.

- The paparazzi's cameras flashed as the movie star emerged from her limo, **resplendent** in a sequined gown and a diamond choker and clutching a pink poodle wearing a tiara.
- Wordsworth was awestruck by his view of the Alps, **resplendent** in the glitter of the rising sun.

9. radiant (RAY dee ent) This adjective means "emitting heat or light from within." It is frequently used to describe stars or planets, which outshine other astral forms.

- According to the New Testament, a **radiant** star guided the wise men to a manger in the little town of Bethlehem where Jesus was born.
- The child's delight in wearing her new sweatshirt embossed with the face of Peppa Pig was evident in her **radiant** smile.

10. chiaroscuro (kee ar ah SKOOR oh) This noun is used to describe the contrast of light and shade in certain works of art. Although it was originally a Renaissance technique made famous by artists such as Rembrandt, Caravaggio, and Leonardo da Vinci, it now also describes high contrast in many visual forms, especially in modern photography.

- The twentieth-century photographer Robert Mapplethorpe used **chiaroscuro** in his photographs of the human form to create stunning, high-contrast images that have earned him much critical acclaim.
- The sun filtered through the parted curtains, creating a **chiaroscuro** of deep shadow and bright light that highlighted the vase of chrysanthemums against the dark mahogany of the table.

Darkness, My Old Friend

60

H ere's a list of dark words to brighten a dim vocabulary. The offerings here will help you to describe everything from a poorly lit room to a dark mood to a hard-to-see solution to a difficult problem.

1. **obscure** (ob SKYUR) This adjective means "so dark as to be barely visible" or "indistinct." It can also mean "hidden" or "not well-known," "not easily understood," or "inconspicuous." You can use the word to describe a little-known town or author or even a dense piece of writing that's hard to comprehend. When it's used as a verb, it means "to make indistinct or dark." The noun form is "obscurity."

- Albert thought the reading assignments in his philosophy class were so **obscure** that he started a weekly study group so that he could go over the material with his classmates.

- A solar eclipse occurs when the moon comes into alignment with the sun and **obscures** it, preventing it from being seen from the earth.

2. **crepuscular** (crep US kyoo lar) This adjective means "dim" or "like twilight." Unlike "obscure," it is used solely to describe the quality of physical light.

- Having only one small window, the basement was damp and **crepuscular**, even on a bright summer morning.

- More car accidents occur at dusk than at any other time of day because it is more difficult to judge distances or see other drivers in **crepuscular** light.

3. **nocturnal** (NOK turn al) From the Latin word for "night," this adjective means "occurring at night" or "most active at night." A related word is "nocturne," which is a painting of a night scene or "a piece of piano music with a pensive, dreamy mood."

- A **nocturnal** creature, my cat Bruiser wanders around the neighborhood at night, searching through trash cans for food and getting into fights with the neighbors' pets.

- Most pianists aspire to play Chopin's pensive but difficult piano **nocturnes.**

4. **tenebrous** (TEN ah brus) This adjective means "dark and gloomy" and is used exclusively to describe literal darkness. There is a noun— "tenebrosity"—but it is rarely used.

- The children looked out of the nursery window at the **tenebrous** woods behind the house and, imagining ghosts in the trees, called for their nanny.
- The mansion, shrouded in a **tenebrous** fog, most definitely looked like the setting for a gothic novel.

5. **swarthy** (SWAR thee) Here's an adjective reserved for describing dark complexions. The noun form is "swarthiness."

- The poet Walt Whitman described himself as "**swarthy**" from so many days spent outdoors under a hot sun.
- When scholars write about Shakespeare's *Othello*, they often refer to him as "the **swarthy** moor."

6. **shrouded** (SHROWD ed) A shroud is something that conceals, protects, or screens, whether it's a cloth used to wrap a body for burial or a natural screen such as a "shroud of fog." This adjective, therefore, means "wrapped in darkness." The word comes from the Middle English word for "garment."

- **Shrouded** in the shade of the weeping willow tree, the lovers had a picnic in the grass and read poetry to each other.
- We were late to the party because we couldn't find the house; **shrouded** in the crepuscular evening light, it was barely visible from the road.

7. **dusky** (DUSK ee) Since "dusk" is the darkest hour of twilight, "dusky" means "dark" or "shadowy." Like swarthy, this adjective is also used to describe a dark complexion.

- The Ethiopian's **dusky** skin and strong features stood out in the crowd of Irish boys seated behind the goal line at the soccer match.
- Tess made her way home in the **dusky** light, fearful that her fragile figure and innocent expression made her an obvious target for muggers.

8. **opaque** (oh PAYK) From the Middle English word that means "shady," this adjective means several different kinds of dark. First, it means "impenetrable by light." It also means "so obscure (see #1) as to be unintelligible." Finally, it means "dense," as in mentally unintelligible. The noun form is "opacity."

- The drawing room was so bright that Leslie hung **opaque** drapes on the windows so that the sun would not shine through and fade the upholstery on the couch and chairs.
- No longer in love with Chloe but afraid to tell her so, Will responded to her invitation to her parents' house for dinner with an **opaque** "We'll see."

9. **lowering** (rhymes with flowering) Don't confuse this word with the "lowering" (first syllable rhymes with "go") that means "lessening" or "moving downward." This verb means "to appear dark or threatening." It can be used to describe a stormy sky or an angry, sullen look. The noun form is "lower."

- Inspecting the **lowering** sky and feeling the sudden gusts of wind against his face, Heathcliff spurred his horse to move faster through the heath.
- After the teacher chastised Philippe for talking in class, he gave her a **lowering** look but stopped chattering with Kevin.

10. **penumbra** (pen UM bruh) A word often used in astronomy, this noun means "partial shadow," the area between complete illumination and total eclipse. It can also be used figuratively to mean "an area in which something exists to an uncertain degree."

- "Although our dress code is very strict," said the headmaster, "wearing certain items of clothing, such as shorts, on warm-weather days falls under the **penumbra** of 'exceptions due to climate.'"
- Anxious to avoid the summer heat but wanting to tan herself, Danielle sat down in the **penumbra** under a leafy tree.

MAKE A MATCH #20

Sections 58–60

Match each word in the left-hand column with the phrase on the right that best suggests its meaning.

A.	adamant	1. _____	easily able to recover
B.	crepuscular	2. _____	stubbornly unyielding
C.	inexorable	3. _____	limber
D.	lithe	4. _____	strict
E.	lower	5. _____	relentless
F.	luminary	6. _____	allow light to pass diffusely
G.	nocturnal	7. _____	dazzling
H.	obscure	8. _____	not easily understood
I.	opaque	9. _____	an object that produces light
J.	penumbra	10. _____	like twilight
K.	resilient	11. _____	active at night
L.	resplendent	12. _____	of dark complexion
M.	stringent	13. _____	impenetrable by light
N.	swarthy	14. _____	to appear threatening
O.	translucent	15. _____	partial shadow

hough not everyone knows how to spell it, most of us know the word "chic" (SHEEK) comes from the French and means "stylish" or "fashionable." Below is a list of other words that convey elegance and sophistication and just might add style to the way you say "style."

1. **panache** (pan OSH) From the Latin word that means "plume," this noun means a touch of added style or dash. Just picture a brilliantly colored feather emerging from a Roman helmet, and you'll get the idea.

- Jeanette decided to tie a crimson (see the "Over the Rainbow" section) scarf around her neck to add **panache** to her otherwise dull gray business suit.
- "The rhinestone buttons add **panache** to this wool coat," said the salesgirl at the Chic Boutique. "You'll wow them on opening night."

2. **charisma** (kar IZ ma) This noun, which comes from the Greek word for "divine favor," means "personal magnetism" or "charm." It's used to describe someone's personality rather than their fashion sense. The adjective form is "charismatic."

- The president's **charisma** made him a powerful public speaker and garnered him many admirers, despite his scandalous romantic affairs.
- The pop singer's **charismatic** stage presence led to her becoming a spokeswoman for a number of national charities and an outspoken political activist.

3. **brio** (BREE oh) From the Italian word for "fire" or "life," this noun means "vivacity" or "spirit." It is generally used to describe a way of doing something. It may have entered the English language from the musical instruction "con brio," which means "with energy."

- "Let's go, everybody!" Dan shouted with **brio** as he led the tired scouts up the mountain. "We can make it!"
- The performer recited Homer's *Odyssey* with **brio**, galvanizing (see the "Eponyms" section) the students with his engaging recounting of Odysseus's struggle with the Sirens.

4. **élan** (ay LAN) This noun comes from the Old French word for "rush," originally from the Latin for "to throw a lance." Like brio, it means "enthusiastic liveliness," but it can also be used, like panache, to mean "a dash of style."

- With his bright yellow scarf and beret, Pierre's **élan** was obvious to everyone at the biology fair; it was clear he was no ordinary scientist.
- Although she was the only woman to wear her Easter bonnet to the post-parade luncheon, Gladys dressed with so much **élan** that the hat seemed perfectly appropriate.

5. **esprit** (ess PREE) From the French word for "spirit," this noun means "liveliness of spirit" or "sprightliness." You may have heard it used in the expression "esprit de corps," which means "a common spirit of enthusiasm or devotion to a cause among the members of a group."

- Professor Steinbach's **esprit** so charmed her students that they managed to be passionate about all aspects of chemistry, even the densely written lab analyses.
- The *esprit de corps* was so high in the avant-garde dance troupe that they didn't seem to mind that no one showed up for their performances.

6. **cachet** (cash AY) This noun originally meant "a seal affixed to a letter or document to mark its authenticity" but it has since come to mean "a mark of quality or a distinguishing feature." It comes from the Old French word for "to press."

- The nosegay he wore in his buttonhole gave **cachet** to Mr. Giovanelli's otherwise indistinguishable blue suit.
- Lots of teenagers like to buy clothing with a designer label prominently displayed because they think it gives **cachet** to their outfits.

7. **flair** (rhymes with care) This noun means "a distinctive elegance or style" and comes from the Middle English word for "fragrance." It can also mean "a particular aptitude or talent."

- Blair has a **flair** for the dramatic; when she waltzes into a room, dressed to perfection, everyone takes notice.
- "Catherine will be our new It Girl," exclaimed the cosmetics company executive. "Her fresh face and natural **flair** will convince all women to buy our new Luscious Lips lipstick."

8. **raffish** (RAFF ish) Coming from the Swedish word for "rubbish," this adjective can mean "cheaply or showily vulgar in appearance" or "tawdry" (see the "Eponyms" section). It is often used today, however, to mean "characterized by a carefree or fun-loving unconventionality."

- When Jack walked into the classroom wearing a fedora at a **raffish** angle, his classmates were amused and his teacher made him remove it immediately.
- Chet's **raffish** behavior at parties and other social gatherings earned him the admiration of Claire, the beat poet, and Stanley, the existentialist philosopher.

9. **rakish** (RAKE ish) This adjective means "self-confidently stylish" or "jaunty" and probably derives from the word "rake," one of whose meanings is "an angle of incline from the perpendicular" and is a term used to describe the tilted masts of pirate ships. It is probably not related to another meaning of the word "rake," which is "an immoral or dissolute person."

- Charlie Chaplin was famous for his duck-footed walk, his bowler hat, and the **rakish** way he swung his cane.
- **Rakishly** dressed for a day of sailing, Alex wore white sneakers and slacks, a striped sailor's shirt, and a admiral's hat tilted at a raffish angle.

10. **verve** (VERV) From the Old French word for "fanciful expression," this noun means "energy and enthusiasm in the expression of ideas, especially in an artistic performance." One uses this word to describe how a person does something, not to describe the person.

- Roberta's zither performance lacked the **verve** she brings to her piano playing; the audience found the concert completely lackluster (a good word for "dull").
- "There's no **verve** in your step," shouted the dance instructor as she watched the budding ballerinas trip haltingly across the dance floor. "Your audience will expect a little enthusiasm, girls!"

Scary Things

Y ou're scared of spiders, he's scared of public speaking, they're scared of noises in the night. Fear is subjective, but the following ten words conjure up concepts that might win a wide following of fear.

1. **jeremiad** (jer uh MY ad) This noun refers to a speech or written work that mournfully laments the wrongdoings of mankind and predicts a kind of wholesale doom to descend on mankind. The bitter tone is associated with the writings of the Hebrew prophet Jeremiah (seventh and sixth centuries BC), who lamented man's evil ways. Today it may be transferred to a lighter variety of doleful complaints.

- The sociology class seemed to be going pretty well until the last week of the term when Prof. Ausmus broke into a kind of **jeremiad** about "your generation," calling us self-centered and self-serving—ouch.

- Some African American writers in the 1960s thought James Baldwin's **jeremiad** of despair left little room for the possibilities of hope and change in racial relations.

2. **Armageddon** (arm a GED un) This noun, also of biblical original (here, the Christian New Testament), refers to a projected final battle between the forces of good and evil to occur at the end of time. Like #1, the word is also used today in reference to more secular concepts. The word itself comes from a variation of the name of a Palestinian mountain range.

- Michael is such a passionate follower of political matters that he views every presidential election as an **Armageddon.**

- Many disagreed with the speaker from the large investment firm who predicted a kind of economic **Armageddon** in the near future if current trends persisted.

3. **apocalypse** (a POK a lips) From the Greek word for "revelation," this noun is also of biblical origin. It refers to a vision of the total destruction of the world, cosmic devastation. (#2 would be one of various possibilities). The adjective form is "apocalyptic."

- "The choice of your prom dress is important," said my mom, "but not one of **apocalyptic** importance, not the end of the world."

- Ancient Persians, who were not part of the Judeo-Christian tradition, also had visions of an **apocalypse**, some that frightened and some that comforted with their prediction of the destruction of enemies of the Persians.

4. **Gorgon** or **gorgon** (GOR gun) This noun, which now can refer to a woman who is regarded as terrifying, has its origin in the Greek myth of three sisters, each with a head full of serpents and the ability to turn beholders into stone.

- Depressed by her low grade on her Spanish project, Helena privately lashed out at her teacher: "Señora Ehrhardt is a **gorgon**, a monster without being a myth!"

- Visual artists enjoy the challenge of depicting the snaky-haired Medusa, the most famous of the **Gorgons.**

5. **chimera** (kai MEER ah *or* kai MAIR ah) and **chimerical** The noun form denotes another scary female from Greek mythology. The mythological chimera was a fire-breathing monster; part lion, part goat, and part snake. A chimera became the more generalized word for any creature of the imagination, any unfounded concept. The adjective form may be seen more often today.

- Sometime in the eighteenth century the concept of a giant sea snake ceased to be a **chimera** and became a zoological fact.

- Andrea traded in her **chimerical** hopes of becoming a second Madonna for work on an MBA degree.

6. **incubus** (IN kyoo bus) In medieval folklore, this malevolent demon could sexually attack women in their sleep. Now time has transformed that frightening image into any oppressive burden that torments an individual as a nightmare might. And indeed the word derives from the Latin word for "nightmare."

- After the Civil War there was much rejoicing that America had at last freed itself from the **incubus** of slavery.

- My twenty-page term paper on endangered species oppressed me all semester. I'm glad to be free of that **incubus.**

7. **juggernaut** (JUG er not) This noun refers to any overwhelmingly powerful, unstoppable force, usually destructive. Most people today don't know that it was originally a title for a Hindu god.

- Has the **juggernaut** of desire for instant gratification overcome the time-honored principle of working for a long-range goal?

- The Dyersburg Trojans had hoped to win the regional football championship this year, but the **juggernaut** force of the Union City Golden Tornadoes has prevailed.

8. **specter** (SPEK ter) Literally, a ghost (or wraith or apparition), this noun is now often used for any "disturbing" image of a future problem.

- On the night before the battle in which he was killed, Richard III was visited by **specters** of all those whom he had murdered, at least in Shakespeare's version of his life.

- The **specter** of a lifetime of minimum wage jobs kept Lenore motivated to continue prepping to pass the bar exam.

9. **feral** (FAIR ul) This adjective can describe either an animal in the wild or one returned to living in such a state. It can also describe human behavior that is more like the savagery of an animal.

- Brad and Susanna, ardent cat lovers, wanted to adopt one of the **feral** cats prowling the garbage dump, but they worried about the response of Moggy and Lily, their pampered Persians.

- The **feral** smile of the salesperson was almost more disturbing than a leer, thought Candace.

10. **anathema** (ah NATH eh ma) This noun comes to us from the Greek word that came to mean "doomed offering" or "accursed thing." Today the meaning is roughly synonymous with a strong curse, a near wish for damnation. (Oddly, its original meaning was positive—a thing set apart as an offering to the gods—but the purely negative sense is all that's left now.) The word can refer to either the curse itself or the person or thing that is cursed. In the latter case, it is not necessary to include an article when using it in a sentence.

- To Dorothy, a confirmed luddite, the idea of spending hundreds of dollars on a laptop computer is **anathema**; she would rather use the money for a fountain pen, some fine stationery, and an antique writing desk.

- In the opening act of *Macbeth*, the three witches gather on the heath and revel in the **anathemas** they have placed upon a sailor and his wife.

S ometimes the end is desired, sometimes not. The words below offer terms for either situation.

1. **interminable** (in TERM in uh bul) Literally meaning "not able to end," this adjective is chiefly used to describe something tedious, a situation you wish *would* end.

- During the seemingly **interminable** lecture on Habits of Twelfth-Century Monks, Dustin contemplated the state of his fingernails and mentally made a list of girls he'd had a crush on.
- Rosetta endured her mother's **interminable** questions about her whereabouts and her companions only by thinking of how soon college life would prevent these inquisitions.

2. **indefatigable** (in de FAT ig uh bul) If you're indefatigable, your energy never ends; you're incapable of becoming fatigued. Lucky you!

- Is it true that Julius Caesar was virtually **indefatigable**, dictating his observations on the Gallic Wars while riding on horseback?
- "Even if I were **indefatigable**, I don't want to work a sixteen-hour day," mused Frederick as he once again contemplated a career change from corporate lawyer to deep sea diver.

3. **abiding** (uh BIDE ing) If it abides with you, it lives with you, and thus it doesn't end.

- Stephanie has an **abiding** love of board games: as a child she played Candyland and Sorry for hours, and now she's a chess fanatic.
- His **abiding** distrust of strangers has caused Leon difficulties in casual social encounters.

4. **limbo** (LIM bo) Modern use of this noun refers to a state that *feels* as though it will never end because you're getting no attention or information that might enable you to move on. The word originated in Roman Catholic theology as an afterlife space of neither punishment nor reward (usually capitalized when used in this sense). Souls placed there remained for eternity. (No relation to the West Indian dance of the same name!)

- "Yes, I'm staying on the waiting list for Exley, my first choice college," said Alf. "But I hate being in **limbo**, not knowing whether I'll be there or at Wiley, my second choice school."

- In Dante's poem *The Divine Comedy*, written from a Christian perspective, the pilgrim's tour of the afterlife reveals the Roman poet Virgil in **Limbo**; he suffers only by knowing that others have a chance at greater happiness.

5. **incessant** (in SES unt) This adjective is a variant form of "unceasing."

- The **incessant** banal cell phone conversations by fellow passengers made Juan's train trip less of a pleasure than it had been in less advanced technological times.

- Prof. Roskelly worked **incessantly** on her new book on rhetoric, determined to meet the publisher's new deadline.

6. **ineluctable** (in e LUCT uh bul) This adjective is a formal word for "inevitable," "inescapable." In that sense, the end *is* in sight.

- The Fall of Troy was foredoomed by Fate, but each generation of inhabitants sought to postpone the **ineluctable** event.

- The seductive Lola in the musical *Damn Yankees* seeks to persuade her chosen victim that struggle is meaningless, for his surrender to her is **ineluctable**.

7. **unremitting** (un re MIT ing) This is another adjective for something that never stops, never slackens. Memory tip: it's not "in remission."

- The **unremitting** pain of Tim's fractured wrist dented his pleasure in the ice fishing expedition with his buddy Geoff.

- Darby's **unremitting** pleasure in Joan's company made him quote Antony's lines on Cleopatra, "Age cannot wither nor custom stale her infinite variety."

8. **pertinacious** (per tin AY shuss) This adjective means "holding on to a belief or a plan," "persistent." It's a near-twin of **tenacious**. (That there should be two such similar adjectives—and with varying spelling—is one of the mysterious delights of the English language.)

- No one is so **pertinacious** as a four-year-old who wants his parent to purchase the Whameroo, a toy advertised every three minutes on television.

- Edison's **tenacious** belief that he could invent a light bulb sustained him through several false attempts.

9. **unflagging** (un FLAG ing) When something flags, it tires, possibly stops. So the adjective describes something that does not tire, does not stop. The root word is Scandinavian.

- Dinner party conversation began to **flag** with dessert; everyone had already said whatever they had to say, which was, in the case of several guests, not much.

- Sisyphus's efforts to push the huge boulder up the hill left him with a rolling stone but with **unflagging** spirits, if we believe philosopher Albert Camus.

10. **relentless** (re LENT less) There's no stopping the adjectives for "unstopping" (#4 is the exception). The root word derives from a word meaning "to melt," but the "relentless" never melts, never slows. You can also say "unrelenting."

- The **relentless** pressure on Margaret to succeed had begun when she was three months old: her parents played the music of Mozart in the nursery because they had read that it aided development of an infant's brain.

- The **unrelenting** beat of the drum resounded through the tropical night, delighting the dancers (Were they doing the limbo?) and frustrating the would-be sleepers.

MAKE A MATCH #21

Sections 61–63

Match each word in the left-hand column with the phrase on the right that best suggests its meaning.

A.	anathema	1. _____	inescapable
B.	apocalypse	2. _____	endless
C.	Armageddon	3. _____	tireless
D.	brio	4. _____	personal magnetism
E.	cachet	5. _____	vivacity
F.	charisma	6. _____	distinguishing feature
G.	chimera	7. _____	stylishly unconventional
H.	feral	8. _____	jaunty
I.	incubus	9. _____	battle between good and evil
J.	indefatigable	10. _____	vision of cosmic devastation
K.	ineluctable	11. _____	creature of the imagination
L.	interminable	12. _____	malevolent demon
M.	juggernaut	13. _____	unstoppable force
N.	pertinacious	14. _____	ghost
O.	raffish	15. _____	savage
P.	rakish	16. _____	a curse
Q.	specter	17. _____	persistent

PRACTICE, PRACTICE, PRACTICE #7

Sections 55–63

A.	adamant	K.	lithe
B.	carouse	L.	lowering
C.	chaste	M.	nepotism
D.	crepuscular	N.	panache
E.	effulgence	O.	pertinacious
F.	hedonist	P.	posthumous
G.	inexorable	Q.	raconteur
H.	jeremiad	R.	ratiocination
I.	juggernaut	S.	spartan
J.	limpid	T.	stringent

1. On a windless day, Huck and Jim traveled up the _____ waters of the Mississippi, quickly making up for lost time.

2. Jeremy could feel the arrival of final exams pressing on him like some kind of _____.

3. During the eclipse, the _____ of the afternoon sun gradually dimmed.

4. Mr. Skirball was _____ about the fact that the document had to be ready by 5:00 p.m.

5. In the _____ light one could just make out the fact that three men were walking along the road.

6. I have never seen anyone as _____ as Maude; once she gets an idea for a project, she just doesn't let go.

7. The monkey's _____ body was draped around Al's head and shoulders.

8. How did your irresponsible friends get you to _____ until 3:00 a.m. on the night before your big test?

9. The clouds _____ on the horizon made us feel that we should not set out for a long hike.

10. Although the living conditions were _____, there was a compensating air of good fellowship at the camp.

11. The social critic came close to delivering a _____ about the future of the country; he's really very gloomy about things.

12. Those with a strong sense of _____ will be able to use their deductive abilities and solve this case quickly.

13. I love Ethan's stories; he's a great _____.

14. The poet Robert Southey talked about writers' need to earn a living, saying they could not exist on "_____ bread and cheese."

15. The society kept the women closely chaperoned to ensure they would remain _____ until they married.

16. He seems to be living entirely for pleasure these days—what a _____.

17. There are very _____ penalties for anyone who violates the honor code because we take cheating very seriously.

18. The _____ with which Alison performs has made her much in demand, for everyone enjoys a confident sense of style.

19. The _____ passing of time makes most people aware of the importance of treasuring every day.

20. Ruth had hoped her husband could work for her company some day, but then she learned there was a policy against _____.

T his list makes a good preparation for the "Oy" section, which comes next. These words offer ways to express more pacific (or "peaceful") feelings.

1. halcyon (HAL see yon) The "halcyon" was a Greek mythological bird, a type of kingfisher that was supposed to have the power to calm the wind and the waves. It's no wonder, then, that the adjective has come to mean "calm" and "peaceful." It is also used to refer to the "golden days," the peaceful and happier days of the past. In fact, the adjective is generally not used to describe people at all but rather to describe places or periods of time.

- The nineteenth-century British poet Christina Rossetti has written: "My heart is like a rainbow shell / That paddles in a **halcyon** sea."
- "I remember the **halcyon** days," Ruby's grandfather reflected, "when it was possible to find an affordable apartment in this city and walk the streets without fear of being mugged."

2. somnolent (SOM no lent) From the Latin word for "sleep," this adjective means "sleepy" or "sleep-inducing." A good synonym is "soporific."

- Their faces pale and **somnolent** in the moonlight that shone in through the nursery window, the children waited for their mother to come in and kiss them each goodnight.
- During the lecture series on the subject of finding happiness, the microbiologist gave a speech so **soporific** that half the audience was out like a light after the first half hour.

3. ruminate (ROO min ate) This verb means "to chew cud," as cows do, and comes from the Latin word for "throat." It belongs in this section because it also means "to reflect on carefully" or "to chew over" in the mind, "to meditate upon."

- "You look like Rodin's *Thinker*," Juliet said as she watched her father **ruminate** about the recent events in the Middle East.
- Albert Camus, the French philosopher, **ruminates** about the absurdity of the human condition in his famous essay, "The Myth of Sisyphus."

4. **repose** (ree POHZ) This noun means "the state of being at rest." It can also be used to suggest extreme rest, that is, "death," as when a body is "in repose." The adjective form is "reposeful."

- Lying in **repose** on the divan in her sitting room, Charlotte looked as if she were posing for Manet.
- "The body is in **repose** at the Happy Rest funeral parlor," read the obituary in the local newspaper.

5. **equilibrium** (EE kwil IB ree um) In physics, this noun means "the state of a physical system at rest"; in chemistry, it means "a chemical reaction in which its forward and reverse reactions occur at equal rates." The word is here, however, because we also use it to describe a state of mental balance. Someone with equilibrium is stable and calm; he or she has "equipoise" (a good synonym).

- Tom took one look at the maple tree that had fallen on his roof in the storm and lost his **equilibrium.** "It's going to cost me a fortune to repair that slate roof," he wailed in despair.
- After falling clumsily on stage in the first act of *Swan Lake*, the girl picked herself up with perfect **equipoise** and got back in line with the rest of the swans.

6. **equanimity** (eek wan IM it ee) This is another good noun for "equipoise" or "equilibrium," but it is used only to describe a state of mind. It means "the quality of being calm and even-tempered, of having composure."

- With a look of perfect **equanimity** on his face, the yogi sat on the floor, closed his eyes, crossed his legs, and began to meditate.
- Batman met the Joker's hostile glare with a look of perfect **equanimity** before taking off in his Batmobile with a screech of rubber.

7. **concord** (KON kord) Part of the root of this noun is the Latin *"cord"* or "heart." It's no surprise that it means "harmony" or "total agreement." A related noun is "accord," which means the same thing.

- It's not true that cats and dogs are natural enemies. My dog Daisy and my cat Henrietta live together in perfect **concord**.
- After hours of debate, the two senators finally reached an **accord** about revamping the Social Security system.

8. **sedate** (seh DATE) As an adjective, this word means "calm, composed, or dignified in manner." It can also be used as a verb to mean "to calm by means of a drug that has a tranquillizing effect."

- Lawrence was a **sedate** young man in his mid-twenties who dressed quite soberly and never acted rudely or aggressively in the company of others.

- When the emergency medical team discovered that Stella was in shock after the car accident, they thought it best to **sedate** her and bring her to the emergency room.

9. **quiescent** (kwee ESS ent) A good synonym for this word is "quiet," not in the sense of "not noisy" but in the sense of "peaceful" or "at rest." The noun form is "quiescence."

- Many of the shops in the mall have big sales in February to drum up business in the **quiescent** period after the Christmas rush.

- Samuel Johnson, the eighteenth-century writer and lexicographer, said: "Great abilities are not requisite for an historian; for in historical composition, all the greatest powers of the human mind are **quiescent**. He has facts ready to his hand; so there is no exercise of invention."

10. **sinecure** (SYNE ek your *or* SIN ek your) This noun means "a job or similar position that provides a salary but little work"—a great deal if you can get it.

- Kareem's position as the ambassador of good will was little more than a **sinecure**; he was paid well and given a beautiful apartment in town, but he rarely had to offer his good will to either visitors or natives.

- Damian was officially hired to be a landscape gardener at Shea Stadium, but the position turned out to be a **sinecure** as he was able to watch all of the Met games for free but did very little actual gardening.

Oy

65

T he Yiddish expression "Oy vey" literally translates as "Oh woe," as in: "Oh, woe is me!" and is often shortened to a simple "Oy!" The words on this list are all about being agitated, annoyed, or aggravated, about the feeling that inspires a yelp of "Oy!"

1. exacerbate (ex ASS er bate) When you "exacerbate" something, you "aggravate" it or "increase its severity." Its Latin root means "to make harsh." The noun form is "exacerbation."

- The swelling in Mrs. Cunningham's knee was **exacerbated** by the fact that she had to keep bending down to pick up the toys left on the floor by her twin sons, Aiden and Frank.

- The antics of disc jockeys like DJ Hamentashen **exacerbate** the pop music industry's image as contrived, superficial, and manic.

2. exasperate (ex ASS per ate) Though it sounds like "exacerbate," this verb's meaning is slightly different—"to irritate" or "annoy" or to *feel* "irritated" or "annoyed." Think of it this way: a situation is "exacerbated" (or "exasperated") and then a person feels "exasperated."

- Celia was **exasperated** after hours of conversation with a support technician from her online service provider; no matter what he told her, she still couldn't sign on to the internet.

- Disneyland **exasperated** Charles. The lines were long, the weather was brutally hot, and he was tired of being waved at by Mickey Mouse.

3. harass (har ASS *or* HAR ass) This verb means "to persistently torment or irritate" or "to wear out with repeated attacks." There are lots of almost synonyms, including "pester," "badger," and "hound," but none quite evoke the intensity and persistence of "harass." The word comes from the Old French *harer*, which means "to set a dog on."

- Desperate for some fresh photos for the next issue of *Celebrity Face* magazine, the paparazzi **harassed** the film star by following her all over town; he even collided into her Mercedes with his truck in order to photograph her irritation when she saw the damage.

- The landlord was always **harassing** his tenants for the rent, convinced that they wouldn't pay on time if he didn't keep reminding them.

4. **provoke** (pruh VOKE) This verb means "to incite to action or feeling," more specifically to feelings of anger or frustration. It comes from the Latin for "to challenge." The adjective form, "provocative," means "stimulating," sometimes in a specifically sexual way. The noun form is "provocation."

- "Merwin Williams's **provocative** new book about global warming will make you seriously reconsider before buying a car that isn't fuel-efficient," said one reviewer.

- "You are dressed too **provocatively**," Melissa's father insisted. "Go back upstairs and put on a blouse that covers your bellybutton and a skirt that's at least knee-length."

5. **goad** (rhymes with road) In Old English, a "gad" was "a long stick with a pointed end, used for prodding animals." The word "goad" which comes from this root has a more general meaning—"to urge" or "to prod," but it retains some of its negative connotation. It can be used as a noun or a verb.

- The anticipation of summer vacation is a good **goad** for making students study for their final exams.

- **Goading** their team to victory, the crowd in the front row at the basketball game shouted words of encouragement and waved banners proclaiming: "Go Tigers!"

6. **prickly** (PRIK lee) One definition of this adjective is "marked by jabs or pricks," and this suggests its more figurative meaning, which is "irritable" or "grouchy."

- Knowing her husband could be **prickly** in a traffic jam, Mrs. Simpson suggested a back route that avoided highway congestion.

- The **prickly** owner of the local soup shop shouted "No soup for you!" when his customers made too much noise while waiting on line.

7. **cantankerous** (can TANK er ous) This adjective may come from the Latin word *contingere* for "to touch." It means "very touchy" or "ill-tempered" and "disagreeable."

- Though he is often **cantankerous** to the residents of Sesame Street, Oscar the Grouch has a secret heart of gold.

- The **cantankerous** Mrs. Noodlesburg frequently reprimanded the Miller boys for playing softball on the street in front of her house.

8. **testy** (TEST ee) Another adjective that means "irritable," this word comes from the French word *tête*, meaning "head." Someone who is "testy" is "impatient" or "exasperated" or, considering the root, "headstrong."

- "Don't get **testy** with me!" shouted Grandmother Vargas when her grandson Victor rolled his eyes and refused to stay home for the evening to watch his little brother.

- **Testy** after a long day at work and a suffocating subway ride in the heat, Mr. Sugarman was in no mood to hear about his daughter's request for a new car.

9. **beleaguer** (be LEEG er) This verb comes from the Dutch for "around the camp." Like "harass," it means, "to persistently torment" or, given the root, figuratively "surround with troops." One can beleaguer or pester someone or be beleaguered by them.

- The **beleaguered** mother made herself a cup of coffee after her colicky infant again woke her in the middle of the night.

- The **beleaguered** Confederate troops were forced to retreat after their crushing defeat at the Battle of Little Roundtop.

10. **irascible** (ear ASS uh bul) This adjective means "ill-tempered" or being *near* but not quite *in* a state of anger (think "irate"). It's a stronger feeling than "prickly," more along the lines of "cantankerous." The irascible person conveys a sense of "I might get angry if you push me any further."

- I like Ginger, but her **irascible** nature makes me a little frightened of her, for I don't like to be yelled at.

- Konrad may indeed have an artistic temperament; does that give him the right to be **irascible** much of the time?

The words on this list all have to do with learning or teaching. They should be instructional to both the novice ("a person who is new to a field or activity") and to the veteran ("a person who is well-experienced or practiced in an activity").

1. **erudite** (ERR yeh dite) This adjective has an interesting history. It comes from the Latin roots for "untaught" or "rude." In English, however, it was used to mean "learned" as early as the fifteenth century and, though it was used only sarcastically for periods of time, it was ultimately used only to mean "learned" or "scholarly." The noun form is "erudition."

- The students at State College love Professor Krupotkin because he is generous with his time, creative in his teaching methods, and so **erudite** in the field of Russian history.
- Isabella's **erudition** became quite obvious during her lecture at the Archaeological Institute; she has translated more than twenty-five languages, including Sanskrit, Mandarin, and ancient Greek.

2. **recondite** (REK on dite *or* rek ON dite) Here's an adjective that describes something that is not easily understood or very "obscure" (see the "Darkness, My Old Friend" section). The noun form is "reconditeness." "Recondition," on the other hand, means "to restore" something or put it back into good condition.

- The writings of Danish philosopher Søren Kierkegaard are **recondite** not only because of the complexity of his ideas but because of his dense writing style and its awkward translation into English.
- "The operating manual to my new DVD player is as **recondite** as a page out of a medieval history text," wailed Ben. "I can't figure out how to play anything, let alone set the timer."

3. **pedagogue** (PED ah gog) From the Latin word for "a slave who supervised children and took them to and from school," this noun has come to mean "schoolteacher" or "educator." Although the adjective "pedagogical" means "having to do with educational matters," the noun form often has a slightly negative connotation. A "pedagogue" often instructs in a "pedantic" (see #4) or "dogmatic" (see the "Stubborn as a Mule" section) manner.

- Always the **pedagogue,** my father turned breakfast into an excuse for teaching. Every morning, my sisters and I had to listen to a lecture on the nutritional value of corn flakes or the relative merits of raising chickens organically.

- The teachers' conference being held in Phoenix next June will deal with various **pedagogical** matters, ranging from the use of PowerPoint in the teaching of poetry to ways to make the curriculum more multiculturally diverse.

4. pedant (PED ant) This is a not very complimentary noun for a person who pays too much attention to book learning and formal rules. A pedant is ostentatiously learned and narrow minded. The adjective form is "pedantic."

- Gregory was such a **pedant** that when Sarina sent him a love letter, declaring her passion for him, he corrected the spelling and sent it back to her.

- Professor Carismundi's teaching methods were so **pedantic** that few students signed up for his classes. He taught the history of philosophy but never discussed the ways in which the various philosophers' ideas were relevant to human experience.

5. didactic (dye DAK tik) From the Greek word for "taught," this adjective means "intended to instruct." It, too, is sometimes used negatively to describe someone who teaches or moralizes excessively. The noun form is "didact."

- Though the minister often gave interesting sermons during weekly chapel, he had a tendency to be too **didactic,** forcing the students to focus on facts and academic issues rather than to reflect on their spiritual lives.

- Maggie's mother was **didactic** about everything; even preparing dinner could turn into a lecture about nutrition and healthful eating habits.

6. docent (DOE sent) This noun represents a specific kind of teacher. It is someone who lectures at a university without being a regular faculty member or a tour guide who lectures at a museum or cathedral.

- Although Karen was hoping to get a full-time job as an English professor at the university, there were so few positions available that she finally took a job as a **docent** in the humanities department for one year and waited on tables in her spare time to increase her income.

- After four years as an art history major in college, Julie got a job as a **docent** at the Dia Arts Center in upstate New York, leading tours of new exhibitions by contemporary artists.

7. tyro (TY ro) From the Latin word meaning "squire" or "recruit," this noun means "a beginner in learning something." It's a good synonym for "novice."

- "There are three levels of hills at this resort," explained Sven, the ski instructor. "There's the Bunny Run for the **tyros,** Pleasure Hill for the moderately experienced skiers, and Break-A-Leg Mountain for the experts."

- Since he was just a **tyro** at the guitar, Devon wasn't yet able to play the more complicated Beatles songs. His teacher told him he would need a couple of months of lessons before he could take on "Norwegian Wood."

8. **savvy** (SAV ee) This adjective may well be the only word in the English language with a double "v." It comes from the Old Spanish for "to know" and from the Latin for "to be wise," but it means more than "smart." Someone who is "savvy," is "well-informed and perceptive." There is even a touch of shrewdness in the word's connotation.

- A **savvy** investor, Herb made a fortune in the corn futures market by studying weather conditions in the Midwest and reading *The Farmer's Almanac*.

- Having worked as a buyer for several clothing boutiques and department stores, Anne was a **savvy** shopper; she knew where to shop for the newest fashions at the lowest prices.

9. **edify** (ED if fye) This verb means more than just "teach"; it means "to instruct morally, intellectually, or spiritually." It comes from the Latin word for "to build" and suggests the building of character.

- The rabbi's lecture to the group of Hebrew school students was **edifying** as he attempted to teach them what it means to be devout in a world that is increasingly secular.

- "You might not think playing video games is an **edifying** experience, but I do," Ralph said to his father. "Super Mario has taught me not to give up in the face of adversity. I think that's a pretty morally uplifting message."

10. **empirical** (em PEER ik al) This is an adjective about learning, not teaching. A student who learns empirically is "guided by practical experience or observation rather than by precepts or theory." It comes from the Greek word for "experienced." The noun form is "empiric."

- Andrew's psychology professor taught him the textbook definitions of psychotic behavior, but **empirical** evidence suggested that his anxiety was perfectly normal.

- The university president was shunned by the public for insisting that women are weaker in math and science than men without any real academic basis or **empirical** proof for his assumptions.

MAKE A MATCH #22

Sections 64–66

Match each word in the left-hand column with the phrase on the right that best suggests its meaning.

A.	cantankerous	1. _____	intended to instruct
B.	concord	2. _____	peaceful
C.	didactic	3. _____	sleepy
D.	equilibrium	4. _____	to reflect on
E.	erudite	5. _____	mental balance
F.	exacerbate	6. _____	total agreement
G.	goad	7. _____	composed
H.	halcyon	8. _____	a job with a salary but little work
I.	harass	9. _____	to aggravate
J.	pedagogue	10. _____	to torment
K.	recondite	11. _____	to urge
L.	ruminate	12. _____	ill-tempered
M.	savvy	13. _____	scholarly
N.	sedate	14. _____	obscure
O.	sinecure	15. _____	educator
P.	somnolent	16. _____	beginner
Q.	tyro	17. _____	shrewdly perceptive

Y ou don't have to be an artist, a fashion designer, or an interior decorator to know the right word to describe a particular shade or hue. Here is a list of adjectives for a spectrum of colors that will give you a much broader palette to choose from.

1. azure (AH zhur) This word comes from the Persian word for "lapis lazuli," a brilliant blue stone first mined in Turkistan. It is a light, purplish blue, the color most often used to describe the sky on a sunny day.

- Dorothy and the Tin Man romped through the field of poppies under an **azure** sky.

2. vermilion (ver MILL yen) From the Latin word for the "larvae of a worm" from which the dye was first obtained, this is a vivid red. This word is often used when you want to say something more interesting than "fire-engine red."

- Many visitors to Key West stroll to the boardwalk at sunset to watch the sky turn a brilliant **vermilion** and see the sun drop below the horizon.

3. teal (TEEL) This is actually the name for a small, short-necked, freshwater duck with bright plumage. As a color, it is a dark bluish-green, the color of the feathers usually found on the head and wings of these ducks.

- The window dresser had difficulty with the display of the new **teal** fashions; the clothes were too blue to blend with the green backdrop but clashed with the light turquoise floor.

4. crimson (KRIM zun) This color ranges from a bright red, like vermilion, to a vivid, purplish red. It comes from the Old Spanish word for "a shield-louse insect," from which the dye was first obtained. You often find crimson used to describe the color of blood.

- Daisy's cheeks flushed a bright **crimson** at the mention of Giovanelli's name.

5. cobalt (KOH balt) This is a deep, vivid blue, which sometimes ranges to a greenish-blue. The metallic element cobalt is often used to create the blue glass used for bottles of imported designer water.

- Rebecca held the **cobalt** bottle up to the light, but it was such a deep blue that it was difficult to determine how much perfume was still left inside.

6. **puce** (PYOOS) This word comes from the French word for "flea," and is said to be the same color as the wings of a flea—a deep red to dark, grayish purple.

- The **puce**-colored walls of the apartment were meant to be subtle and elegant but appeared instead to be a dreary gray.

7. **sepia** (SEE pee ah) This is a dark brown ink or pigment that was originally prepared from the secretion of the cuttlefish. In fact the word comes from the Latin for "cuttlefish." It is most often seen in old documents or manuscripts, which were written in sepia-colored ink, or in old photographs.

- Andreas perused his parents' old photo albums, studying the **sepia** images for nineteenth-century costume designs.

8. **heliotrope** (HEEL ee oh trope) Ranging from a brilliant violet to a deep, reddish purple, this color takes its name from the Latin word for a Peruvian plant with small, fragrant, bright purple flowers that turn toward the sun.

- Emma wore a **heliotrope** silk gown to the ball which brought out the violet in her eyes.

9. **cerulean** (sir ROO lee an) This color ranges anywhere from a brilliant sky blue to a deep blue to a bluish green. It was often used by classical writers to describe the sky, the Mediterranean Sea, and, occasionally, leaves or fields.

- At twilight, the aqua-colored sea turned **cerulean**, contrasting sharply with the white sails of the passing ships.

10. **chartreuse** (SHAR troose) This color comes from the name of a brilliant yellow or green liqueur from the monastery of the Carthusian order and is an apple-greenish yellow color, popularly used in DayGlo-colored paint.

- Emile used differently colored highlighting pens for each of his textbooks: hot pink for math, **chartreuse** for history, and blue for English.

How Sweet It Is

68

J ust as there are different kinds of sweetness, there are many ways to express the variations. Below you'll find a range of words for sweet tastes, sounds, or acts.

1. confection (con FEK shun) Not only does this noun mean "a sweet concoction like a piece of candy or a cupcake," but it also means "any kind of object that displays a splendid craft or skill." The adjective form is "confectionary."

- The bakery's shelves were stocked with delectable (see #8) **confections** such as raspberry tarts, pecan rolls, and seven-layer cakes.
- Sandra's frilly ballgown was a delightful **confection** of organza, silk, and lace.

2. treacly (TREE klee) From the Middle English word that means "antidote for poison," this adjective means "cloyingly (see #3) sweet or overly sentimental." It can be used literally or figuratively. Treacle is literally a sweet syrup.

- The **treacle** was particularly tasty on the salty biscuits.
- "You are the kindest police officer I have ever met," Simone said in a **treacly** voice. "Are you sure you want to give me a speeding ticket?"

3. cloying (KLOY ing) This adjective originally comes from the Latin meaning "to drive a nail into." It's no wonder it means something that is so overly sweet and rich that it tastes bad. It can be used literally or figuratively.

- Allison loves her boyfriend, but she is overwhelmed by his **cloying** expressions of fidelity.
- I only put lemon in my tea because I find the taste of honey too **cloying**.

4. maudlin (MAWD lin) This adjective is a contraction of the second name of the biblical figure Mary Magdalene, who was frequently depicted as a weeping penitent. It means "effusively (or gushily) and tearfully sentimental."

- I knew that Margaret was capable of somewhat **maudlin** behavior, but I was stunned when I saw that telephone commercials made her cry.

- Henry found the production of the Yiddish play **maudlin** and melodramatic and gave it a bad review.

5. **unctuous** (UNK chew us) This adjective comes from the Latin word for "ointment" and actually means "oily or slippery." It's in this section because it also means affected or insincere earnestness. Someone who is unctuous often acts too sweet.

- The **unctuous** politician not only kept the graft money; he was actually reelected.

- "I'll be your best friend if you help me," Mary Ann said **unctuously**. "Please, please, please!"

6. **dulcet** (DULL set) From the Old French word for "sweet," this adjective means "sweet or pleasing to the ear, melodious." It can describe a voice or a musical sound. Though there is a verb form—"dulcify"—which means "to sweeten," no one ever uses it.

- Phoebe played **dulcet** tones on her harp, but her husband kept right on reading the newspaper.

- "I love your azure eyes, your delicate earlobes, the **dulcet** tones of your voice," Tristan crooned, hoping to win his lady's affections.

7. **euphonious** (yoo FONE ee us) Like dulcet, this adjective means "sweet or pleasing to the ear." It comes from the Greek meaning "sweet-voiced." The noun form is euphony.

- Irving Bodolowsky changed his name to Johnny Rocket because he thought it sounded more **euphonious**.

- Because of the **euphony** of the soprano section, the choir leader placed the altos and the tenors in the back rows.

8. **delectable** (de LEKT uh bul) This adjective doesn't necessarily mean sweet, but it does mean "pleasing to the taste buds." It can be used as a noun as well as an adjective.

- The juicy mango slices were **delectable** on the scorching hot July afternoon.

- The hostess of the mah-jongg game brought in a platter of **delectables**; they weren't all sweet, but there was a generous assortment of candied ginger, caramel toffees, and chocolate-filled cream puffs.

9. **winsome** (WIN sum) Not to be followed by "lose some," this adjective means "charming in a sweet or child-like way." Only people are winsome, not things. The word comes from an Indo-European root which means "to desire or strive for."

- The **winsome** child looked so longingly at the pony that the ranch hand took her for a ride.
- "How do I look?" Blanche asked with a **winsome** expression on her face. "I haven't worn this dress since I left Belle Reve."

10. **saccharine** (SAK a rin) A cross between cloying and maudlin, this adjective means "excessively sweet and overly sentimental." People who are saccharine are probably not being genuine. Like the artificial sweetener, it's a contrived replacement for the real thing.

- "She's so sweet, butter wouldn't melt in her mouth," hissed Leonore, referring to Phyliss's **saccharine** words about her new haircut.
- With a **saccharine** smile, Harvey told his new boss that her criticism was extremely helpful.

For every word that evokes sugar, there may well be a matching one that connotes vinegar. Here's a group of words you can use to describe the bitterest sourpuss you know.

1. **acerbic** (ah SERB ik) This adjective can be used to describe something that literally tastes sour, or it can used more figuratively to describe a bitter character or cutting expression. "Acerbity" is the noun, but it is rarely used.

   • H. L. Mencken's **acerbic** wit was beloved by intellectuals and social critics.

   • The **acerbic** tarragon vinegar prevented the cole slaw from tasting too sweet.

2. **acrimonious** (ak ri MO nee us) If you want to describe bitterness in someone's language, tone, or even behavior, use this adjective. It comes from the Latin word for "sharp." The noun form is "acrimony."

   • The couple broke into an **acrimonious** battle in divorce court, forcing the judge to shout, "Order in the court!"

   • The **acrimony** between the competing players on the court forced the referee to threaten to pull them out of the game.

3. **astringent** (ah STRIN jent) Based on its medicinal use, which means "to draw together or constrict tissues," this adjective means "sharp" or "penetrating, severe." The noun form is "astringency."

   • The teacher's **astringent** comments on Angus's history essay convinced him to rethink his thesis and write a new analysis.

   • The **astringency** of Orwell's commentary on life as a policeman in Burma earned him praise from the lower classes.

4. **embittered** (em BIT erd) Like it sounds, this adjective means "having bitter or negative feelings aroused by something." The noun form is not "bitterness" but "embitterment."

   • **Embittered** by defeat, the Italian army had no kind words for the German officers.

   • Crushed by **embitterment**, Alexis vowed never to marry.

5. **acidic** (ah SID ik) This adjective can also be used literally or figuratively. Something that is acidic can have a high chemical acid content, but it can also be used to describe a sour personality or a sharp humor. The simple adjective "acid" is also acceptable.

- The Chateau Margaux tasted so **acidic** that James was forced to call over the sommelier to help him choose a new bottle.
- The Speaker of the House's **acid** remarks forced the Republican senator to retract his argument.

6. **captious** (CAP shus) Based on the Latin word for "seizure," this adjective means "marked by a tendency to find and point out (catch) trivial faults."

- The **captious** English teacher corrected his student for saying, "It is me" instead of "It is I."
- "It is impossible to work for such a **captious** man," wailed Mary Ann. "He makes me type everything over twice before he is satisfied."

7. **vitriolic** (vit ri OL ik) Here's a particularly strong adjective that means "scathing" or "bitterly cruel." It's reserved for the most acidic humor or criticism. The noun form is "vitriol."

- The humor of comedian Lenny Bruce could be particularly **vitriolic** when he was mocking conventional mores and ideas.
- Put off by his **vitriol**, Angela decided not to see Charles anymore and began dating a very gentle pharmacist.

8. **caustic** (CAW stik) From the Greek word meaning "to burn," this adjective means "biting or cuttingly sarcastic." Caustic comments really sting on an emotional level. The noun "causticity" is pretty much only used in scientific writing.

- "If I were you, I'd put a paper bag over my head before going out with that haircut," said Richard **caustically**. "But don't worry; it will grow."
- Many students appreciate the **caustic** humor of *The Daily Show*; they get a kick out of Trevor Noah's criticism of our administration.

9. **rancor** (RANK or) This noun means "bitter, long-lasting anger or resentment" and comes from the Latin word meaning "to stink" or "be rotten" (see #10). The adjective form is "rancorous."

- Gwendolyn's **rancor** at her sister was so intense that she agreed to go to her party but refused to wish her a happy birthday.
- Ben's **rancorous** remarks drove his wife to seek a marriage counsellor who could help him learn the art of gentle criticism.

10. **rancid** (RAN sid) Rancid comes from the same Latin root as rancor but is used slightly differently. It means "repugnant" or "nasty," but it doesn't describe people, only their remarks or behavior. It can also be used to describe food that has gone bad.

• After two weeks in a warm refrigerator, the milk was **rancid**.

• The valedictorian's **rancid** remarks about the school's curriculum embarrassed the principal at the graduation ceremony.

MAKE A MATCH #23

Sections 67–69

Match each word in the left-hand column with the phrase on the right that best suggests its meaning.

A.	acerbic	1. _____	pleasing to the ear
B.	azure	2 _____	describing food "gone bad"
C.	captious	3. _____	artificially sweet
D.	cerulean	4. _____	dark brown in color
E.	cloying	5. _____	bitter in tone
F.	dulcet	6. _____	fault-finding
G.	euphonious	7. _____	long-standing bitterness
H.	maudlin	8. _____	deep blue in color
I.	puce	9. _____	overly sweet in taste or manner
J.	rancid	10. _____	very angry
K.	rancor	11. _____	weepily sentimental
L.	saccharine	12. _____	flatteringly hypocritical
M.	sepia	13. _____	the color of a flea
N.	unctuous	14. _____	sky blue in color
O.	vitriolic	15. _____	sweet in tone

O ligarchy, oenology, opaque—many words start with "O" but a select few end in "O." You may have limited use for the dingo (wild dog of Australia) and the fandango (Spanish American dance), but the ten listed here should be in your hoard of words.

1. bravado (bra VAD oh) This noun refers to a swaggering variety of pretended courage. If you're faking bravery, you're displaying bravado.

- Kyle wanted to back down from the taunt he had thrown at the stranger, but the code of **bravado** known to many teenagers prevented his doing so.
- When Samuel Johnson said, "He who would be a hero must drink brandy," was he implying that alcohol reinforces **bravado**?

2. braggadocio (brag a DOE see oh *or* she oh *or* sho) A step above bravado in swaggering, this noun implies a cocky kind of bragging. It sounds Italian, but it comes into English from the sixteenth-century poem "The Faerie Queene," where it is the name of a boastful character.

- When Mel told Merry, "You've never known anyone like me before," she quickly responded, "I've never known anyone with your sense of **braggadocio**, you mean."
- Although Mr. Fite's words were unassuming, the audience sensed an underlying **braggadocio** in his manner.

3. virago (veer AH go) This noun refers to a woman seen as (a) bossy and domineering or (b) strong and courageous. Context (or viewpoint) is all. It derives from the Latin word for "man."

- Casper Milquetoast scribbled in his diary, "I am surrounded by vicious **viragos**. If only I had the courage to stand up to them!"
- The **Virago** Press specializes in the printing of literature by women.

4. crescendo (creh SHEN doe) Think "increase," for this noun comes from the Italian word of that meaning. Its original use is to describe a steadily growing loudness of sound, but it is now also used for any increase in intensity or force. (Purists still frown on the growing use of "crescendo" as a synonym for "peak" or "climax.")

- As Tchaikovsky's music began its **crescendo** and the fireworks simultaneously rose in the sky, the crowd in the park set off a spontaneous cheer.
- Caroline Gordon taught her students of writing to build a **crescendo** in their sentences, holding for last the word most deserving emphasis.

5. **libretto** (lib RET oh) As suggested by the suffix, a libretto is literally a little book. Its use is reserved to name the text of an opera or similar work.

- When Mrs. Stoopy termed "pretentious" the fact that Mr. Stoopy had brought the **libretto** of *Aida* with him to the performance, he snapped, "You're lucky I didn't bring the score."
- Is it fair that Giuseppe Verdi gets all the praise for the opera *Otello* while his **librettist** Arrigo Boito goes almost unmentioned?

6. **farrago** (fah RAHG oh) This is one of many nouns to mean "a mixture, a hodgepodge, an olio, a potpourri, an olla podrida, a gallimaufry."

- The sentence above contains a **farrago** of synonyms for "farrago."
- Jackie went to Dr. Smollett with a **farrago** of complaints: his leg hurt, he sometimes couldn't move his elbow, his eyelid tickled, and the like.

7. **peccadillo** (pek a DIL oh) A little sin, a small fault, this word comes into English from the Spanish.

- Ms. Armstrong never dreamed she could be fired for a **peccadillo** such as playing one game of solitaire on her office computer, especially a game she had lost!
- Fans of W. C. Fields relish his famous line, "None of your **peccadilloes**, my little chickadee."

8. **folio** (FOAL ee oh) A folio is a large book. You'll probably most often hear it in the phrase "The First Folio," which refers to the first printing of all of Shakespeare's works. It's a large book because the leaf (think foliage) is folded only once to produce the two folio pages. (Extra knowledge: if the leaf is folded again, you get a quarto, four pages, a smaller book. Folding it yet another time produces an even smaller book, an octavo.)

- His grateful students presented Mr. Bruner-Smith with a facsimile of Shakespeare's First **Folio** as a retirement gift.
- While she admired the hard-backed **quarto** version of her favorite novel, the **octavo** paperback was both less expensive and more portable.

9. **rococo** (ro KO ko *or* ro ko KO) Formally, this adjective describes styles of art and music (originating in the eighteenth century) characterized by ornamentation. By extension, it can describe anything, ornate, elaborate, or complicated.

- "Maybe something a little less **rococo**?" suggested Elaine, when her room-mate asked for her opinion on the dress with the flounced ruffles and lacy bodice with a contrasting furbelow.
- The music of Couperin and Rameau will be featured at the "**Rococo** Rocks" concert this weekend.

10. **bibelot** (bee buh LO) (The sound of the word ends in "o," if the written word does not!) The word names a decorative little object, a tchotchke.

- Mimi was disappointed when the beautifully wrapped box Rodolpho gave her contained not a diamond ring but only a tasteful **bibelot**.
- Mrs. Stuk-Upp was annoyed when the domestic staff referred to her expensive **bibelot** vitrine as a "whatnot shelf."

S hakespeare's Hamlet uses a play to reveal the guilty conscience of his murderous uncle, but our task is simpler: we'll use the theatrical realm to give us ten useful, interesting words.

1. repertory (REP er tor ee) *or* **repertoire** (REP er TWAR) Whether you choose the English or the French version of this noun, you are referring to a collection of plays (or poems or songs) that an acting company or a performer is prepared to enact. Figuratively, the word can refer to any skills or aptitudes of a person or a group.

- The Whitworth Acting Company not only has all of Shakespeare's English history plays in its **repertory**, but during intermissions two of the actors display their fencing skills.

- When they asked the short order cook at P. D.'s Grill if he could make a special order of lobster thermidor, he smoothly replied, "Sorry, guys, that's just not in my **repertoire**."

2. denouement (day noo MON *or* day NOO mon) This French import refers to a working out of all the factors that made the plot thicken. It can be used for a play, a novel, or real life. Literally, it means "un-knotting," getting the kinks out of the thread of the plot following the climax. Sometimes it's used more loosely to mean "the final result."

- The playwright had so many different plots going in the first half of the play—pirates, vampires, and spacemen—that the audience was not surprised that the **denouement** was unbelievable.

- Xenia's first three years at Hedgepeth University were marked by a trip abroad, a broken leg, and a major love affair; can the **denouement** of her college years be any more dramatic?

3. thespian (THESP ee un) This noun is a fancy term for, simply, an actor. It derives from the poet Thespis, who supposedly originated Greek tragedy. It can be used as an adjective meaning "related to plays."

- "All you **thespians** out there, listen up," blared the public address system. "There will be tryouts Friday afternoon for the Springfield High School version of *Spam-a-lot*."

- Jo is equally interested in acting and singing; so far no critic has encouraged her as a vocalist, but her **thespian** aspirations have met with some success.

4. **proscenium** (pro SEEN ee um) Literally, the area in a theater between the curtain and the audience or the orchestra pit. This noun is sometimes used as a word of contrast with more innovative "theater in the round," which lacks any such space.

- "I'm tired of Shakespeare productions on the **proscenium** stage," said Mr. Williams. "Let's eliminate that fourth wall and get right next to the audience in our beatnik version of *Romeo and Juliet*."
- The **proscenium** was jammed during the final curtain call, as actors, stagehands, and technicians clustered together in a democratic "all-together" bow.

5. **tableau** (tab LOW) Originally, this noun referred to actors "freezing" in position as if forming a painting for the audience. More often these days you'll see it used for a striking scene or even a vivid description.

- The photograph of the smiling baby in front of his father, his grandfather, and his great-grandfather presented a kind of **tableau** of the last ninety years.
- The early parts of the novel *Jane Eyre* gives readers a **tableau** of the life of a nineteenth-century English governess.

6. **protagonist** (pro TAG un ist) A protagonist is the most important character in a play. The character in conflict (the Greek word "agon") with the protagonist is called an "antagonist." In extended usage each word can be used, respectively, for a leader of a cause and his or her opponent.

- In Shakespeare's tragedies the **protagonist** is dead by the end of the play.
- Abraham Lincoln's **antagonist** in his race for a seat in the Senate, Stephen Douglas, is little remembered today.

7. **catharsis** (ka THAR sis) Greek tragedies, said the philosopher Aristotle, cause viewers to undergo a figurative cleansing—a catharsis—of emotions such as pity and fear. We still use the word to talk about Greek tragedy, and we also use it for any experience that leaves an individual with a feeling of release from emotional tension.

- The innovative musical *The Gospel at Colonus* uses a gospel choir to express the viewers' sense of **catharsis** after the death of the protagonist, Oedipus.
- Stephen's argument with his dad at the Thanksgiving dinner table was embarrassing to the guests, but both father and son found it **cathartic**; by the pumpkin pie they were cracking jokes together.

8. **hubris** (HYOO bris) This classical Greek word for "an excess of pride that may lead to a downfall" is used both for what happens within Greek tragedy and for what happens in modern day life.

- Whenever a protagonist declares himself as equal to the gods, the audience may expect that such **hubris** will be punished.

- Mona's claim that she'll be CEO of General Motors someday seems **hubristic**, for she has only been out of business school for three years.

9. **pathos** (PAY thoss *or* PAY-thohs) Another word straight from classical Greek, pathos is the Greek word for "suffering" (think "sym**pathy**" or "em**pathy**"). A play or other work of art that arouses feelings of pity, concern, or tenderness in the viewer or reader may be said to possess pathos.

- A sense of **pathos** welled up in the hearts of the usually tough members of the team when they saw the photographs of famine victims, and they vowed to raise money for the relief effort.

- Dostoevsky has scenes of great **pathos** in his novels: who can read, without pity, of a poverty-stricken widow, herself ill, forcing her little children to dance and sing for money in the streets?

10. **farce** (FARSE) A farce is a comic play characterized by improbable but humorous elements. By extension, the word can describe anything so absurd as to be laughable, whether by its humor or the fact that it makes a mockery, a joke, of an undertaking. (And isn't it a little bit funny that the origin of this word means "seasoned stuffing"?)

- The French **farce** featured three swinging doors, a trapdoor, and four windows: characters repeatedly missed each other by seconds, causing the audience to roar harder each time.

- "Student government at Montrose High is **farcical**," complained Annemarie. "Kids just run for office so they can list it on their college applications."

D on't misunderstand. The words are fully defined, but each of them expresses a concept that, for varying reasons, is not immediately seen as fully shaped or precisely expressed. Is it chaotic or merely inchoate (see #1)?

1. **inchoate** (in KO it) This adjective describes anything that is in a very early state of development. An early stage could be chaotic, but it's more likely to be simply vague or unformed. In short, you're just "hitching up," as the history of the word confirms: it comes from the technical term for a strap that's hitched to a harness.

- Polly asked the student senate to give her plans for the homecoming celebration a vote of confidence even though they were too **inchoate** at the time of the meeting to permit her to give the specifics.

- Judith and Glenn, engaged for three weeks, know they're going to have a big wedding in some exotic spot, but plans are **inchoate**, so don't press them for details.

2. **amorphous** (ay MORF us) To describe something that lacks a defined shape or organization, this is the right word. It comes from the Greek prefix "a," meaning "absence of" and the word "morph" for "shape."

- In the new film production of *Hamlet*, the ghost is not an actor in armor but an **amorphous** area of lightness with a commanding voice.

- Anais has some **amorphous** ideas for the required intellectual autobiography for her graduate school application, but hasn't yet developed an organizing concept.

3. **nebulous** (NEB yoo lus) Cloudy. That's both the definition and the word history of this adjective.

- Aaron wants to take a "gap year" between high school and college, but he has only the most **nebulous** of concepts of how he wants to spend the time.

- "What do you want to buy with your $200 reward money?" queried the officer. "Oh, stuff," said Megan, **nebulously**.

4. **intangible** (in TAN ji bul) If it lacks material shape or form, it's intangible. You can't touch it. In short, you can't tango with the intangible.

- Good will is certainly **intangible**, but savvy business owners know it is important to the success of their operation.

- Maria looks at the next ten years of her life and knows she wants a career, a home of her own, children, and a reasonable chance at **intangibles** such as health and happiness.

5. **allusive** (al LOOS ive) Something allusive is characterized by an indirect reference. The speaker or writer assumes the hearer or reader will understand a statement that is not fully spelled out. (Don't confuse this word with the similar word "elusive," meaning "tending to escape one's grasp.") "Allusive" comes from the Latin word meaning "to play," and indeed allusions are playfully enjoyable—as long as you understand them.

- As we drove across the Delaware River, Alice's dad, ever the amateur historian, said **allusively**, "I hope you're all feeling like George Washington."

- When Ms. Witherspoon added a tray of diet soft drinks to the buffet table, she said, "Let there be lite." When everybody but me laughed, I knew that once again I had failed to comprehend an **allusive** reference.

6. **ambivalent** (am BIV a lent) If you're feeling ambivalent, you can see equal merit in more than two opposing courses of action. The root words are the Latin words for "both" and for "weigh."

- The Roman poet Catullus's **ambivalent** phrase "I hate and I love" (*Odi et amo*) has been a solace to generations of **ambivalent** lovers since.

- Lara says she feels **ambivalent** about her preference for a presidential candidate the next time around, but Tristan is already quietly campaigning for his choice.

7. **cryptic** (KRIP tik) A crypt is a place where bodies or treasure may be hidden away. As an adjective, "cryptic" describes that which has a hidden or a puzzling meaning.

- The pirates puzzled over the **cryptic** markings on the map, longing to believe a store of gold doubloons was waiting for them on the island.

- Rory's airs of superiority and **cryptic** utterances such as "Some day you'll understand" do little to win friends.

8. **sophistry** (SOF iss tree) If you engage in sophistry, you seem good at arguing your case with superficially good reasoning that turns out to be full of holes. The sophist is out to display his or her cleverness and enjoys fooling others. The root word is the Greek word for "wisdom," but sophistry is a poor substitute for the real thing.

- If Mr. Claxon wants to play the **sophist** with his friends, fine, but he has no business coming into a junior high classroom and misleading students not yet able to rebut his superficially clever logic.

- One may fool others with **sophistical** thinking, but one must be very clever not to indulge in self-deception.

9. **ineffable** (in EF uh bul) Something ineffable cannot be expressed in words. While it may occasionally have the sense of the taboo, something forbidden, it's most often used to describe thinking about the abstract, the transcendental.

- Poets and mystics may try to get at the **ineffable** through allusion, hint, or image.

- Claire's grandfather died shortly after she turned thirteen, and she found herself puzzling over **ineffable** matters such as life, death, and a possible hereafter.

10. **spurious** (SPYUR ee us) From the Latin word describing an illegitimate child, this adjective now describes anything "of dubious origin."

- Ian kept trying to impress Guy with his vocabulary by telling him how "cromulent" everything was with him. Finally, he confessed that "cromulent" was a **spurious** word made up by a character on *The Simpsons*.

- While Ye Olde Antique Shoppe was well-stocked, Aunt Augusta felt sure that many of their items were **spurious** and that the buyer should beware.

MAKE A MATCH #24

Sections 70–72

Match each word in the left-hand column with the phrase on the right that best suggests its meaning.

A.	ambivalent	1. _____ a small misdeed	
B.	amorphous	2. _____ the working out of a plot	
C.	bibelot	3. _____ a mixture, an assortment	
D.	bravado	4. _____ abstract	
E.	catharsis	5. _____ seeming wisdom	
F.	cryptic	6. _____ having mixed feelings	
G.	denouement	7. _____ lacking a defined shape	
H.	farrago	8. _____ evoking feeling	
I.	hubris	9. _____ puzzling, mysterious	
J.	ineffable	10. _____ relating to acting	
K.	intangible	11. _____ a fierce woman	
L.	pathos	12. _____ excess of pride	
M.	peccadillo	13. _____ a cleansing or purging	
N.	repertoire	14. _____ ornate, elaborate style	
O.	rococo	15. _____ small decorative object	
P.	sophistry	16. _____ pretended air of courage	
Q.	thespian	17. _____ unable to be put in words	
R.	virago	18. _____ collection of material	

PRACTICE, PRACTICE, PRACTICE #8

Sections 64–72

Put the letter of the most appropriate word in the blank space of each sentence.

A.	amorphous	K.	goad
B.	astringent	L.	hubris
C.	beleaguered	M.	recondite
D.	catharsis	N.	sinecure
E.	crescendo	O.	spurious
F.	cryptic	P.	teal
G.	equanimity	Q.	thespian
H.	erudite	R.	tyro
I.	euphonious	S.	unctuous
J.	farrago	T.	vitriolic

1. It's fine to have a healthy sense of pride, but when it comes to border on _____, then it's excessive.

2. Prof. Maxwell is an excellent teacher and can make even the most _____ historical events come to life.

3. I know Mickey didn't mean the things he said, but I'm having a hard time forgetting those cutting and _____ comments he made.

4. Most people recognize and dislike flattery, but for some people no behavior is too _____ to be seen as insincere.

5. When you're a _____ in a certain field, you need to try hard to learn from the more experienced people.

6. Slowly the _____ blobs took on a more defined shape and became coordinated into a clear picture.

7. She's not aiming at being deeply _____ about the presidency, but she does want to understand the most common references.

8. People who can regard all of life's hardships with a sense of _____ are to be admired.

9. The bluish-green neck of the duck has supplied it with its name; it's referred to simply as a _____.

10. The poet had selected words for the opening line of the poem that were particularly _____; many people memorized it to have the pleasing sounds in their head.

11. Her desk contained examples of the many types of books she like to read. Quite a _____.

12. You must be feeling particularly _____ with so much work to do and so little time to do it.

13. He's the leading _____ of the school and is certain to win the drama award.

14. The fact he doesn't get paid until he finishes the work serves as a _____ for the completion of the project.

15. The alarm clock began its _____ of noise, getting louder and louder as the sleeper failed to rouse herself to turn it off.

16. Janine enjoys tricky word puzzles—the more _____ it is, the better she likes it.

17. The document is undergoing tests to determine whether it is genuine or _____.

18. His _____ anger has a particularly wounding quality to it.

19. Evelyn is willing to work hard on a summer job; she's not looking for some kind of _____.

20. Although Clay found it difficult at first to talk about his overpowering father, getting his feelings out may have served as a kind of _____.

The English language has many words for states of happiness—
and perhaps even more for various types of unhappiness. Let's
look at some.

1. lachrymose (LAK rih mose) This adjective can mean either "weeping,
inclined to weep" or "tending to cause weeping." It comes into English
directly from the Latin word for "tears."

• Certain types of novels feature **lachrymose** heroines; these frail creatures are
equally likely to pull out their lace handkerchiefs at news of the death of a
distant relative or the sight of frolicking puppies.

• Logan could not abide such **lachrymose** literature. Give him a robust novel
about battle at sea!

2. morose (more OSE) This adjective describes someone who is melancholy,
gloomy, generally down in the dumps.

• While there is little pleasure in the company of those who are **morose**, those
who are unflaggingly cheery can also be tiring.

• Shakespeare's play *The Merchant of Venice* opens with a line by Antonio, a
morose character, who is bewildered by his mood: "In sooth, I know not
why I am so sad."

3. apathetic (ap uh THET ik) This adjective describes someone who lacks feeling, lacks interest, has a bad case of "the blahs." It comes into English from
the Greek root word "path" (feeling) and the prefix "a" (absence of). The
noun form is apathy.

• Although Mattie claimed to be **apathetic** about political disputes, she cared
very much when the issue touched her life directly.

• The humor of the old joke line "I'm not **apathetic**; I just don't care."
requires that the hearer know the meaning of the key word.

4. listless (LIST less) This adjective, which comes from Middle English where
"list" could refer to interest or desire, works as pretty much as a synonym
for apathetic. Unlike that word, however, listless can refer to a physical as
well as an emotional state.

- After her best friend Sheila moved hundreds of miles away, Lola felt lonely and **listless** for a time without the daily pleasure of her company.

- A bad case of flu left Allan both looking and feeling **listless** even after the doctor allowed him to return to school.

5. **despondent** (de SPON dent) This adjective meaning "discouraged," "dejected" comes into English from a Latin verb meaning "to give up, to despair." The noun form is "despondency."

- The ancient philosophy of stoicism urged against **despondency**. Its followers sought to remain calm, whatever circumstances life might bring.

- After a few days of feeling **despondent** that he had not gotten the job he had sought, Mr. Van Zandt rallied his spirits and began a new series of interviews.

6. **lugubrious** (lug OO bree us) This adjective means "gloomy," often to an exaggerated degree, and comes from the Latin word meaning "mournful."

- Just because you had to miss the track meet is no reason to drag your **lugubrious** attitude around the hallways, making no attempt to pull yourself out of a bad mood.

- The **lugubrious** tone of the card Lauren sent to Dan was more worthy of a sympathy note than a thirtieth-birthday card.

7. **morbid** (MOR bid) This adjective comes from the Latin word for "disease" but in English refers more often to a disturbed state of mind, an emphasis on or preoccupation with unwholesome thoughts.

- Rory listened patiently while, at the breakfast table, his sister read him bits of newspaper articles about the recall of contaminated food and on the spread of child abuse; when she started in on the dangers of avian flu, he cried out, "Please, sis, something less **morbid**!"

- Edgar Allan Poe's story "The Fall of the House of Usher" features a character with a **morbid** acuteness of his senses: this fellow would have a tough time at a club with strobe lights and a disco ball.

8. **querulous** (KWER uh lus *or* KWER yoo lus) This adjective comes from the same Latin root as "quarrel," but rather than seeking the possible release of an argument, the querulous person whines, complains, grumbles.

- Until you've spent your birthday taking care of a pair of **querulous** toddlers, you don't know the full beauty of a few moments of solitude.

- Some see the character of Hamlet as **querulous**, but most Shakespeare lovers would claim the beauty of his language and his wit redeem him.

9. **petulant** (PET yoo lunt) This adjective describes one who is generally irritable, bad-tempered. If you're reading older literature, you may come across it as meaning "contemptuous or childishly rude," and it may contain a shade of that feeling today.

- Mr. and Mrs. Oldham privately lamented the spoiled nature of their neighbors' young child: "Nothing makes little Reynard happy. He remains **petulant** even when given chocolate ice cream and a red balloon."

- All of us crave attention from our friends and our family, but an air of **petulance** is likely to be counterproductive.

10. **peevish** (PEEV ish) Most people have a pet peeve, something that frequently annoys us, but we should try not to act peevish in response. This adjective describes the mood of one who is unpleasant to be around. It's roughly synonymous with "petulant" (#9), but if that word retains some sense of sending a bad mood outward onto others, a "peevish" mood may go more inward into a crabbed, grumpy state of mind.

- When Dana was in a **peevish** mood, all efforts to draw him out only made him retreat further into his mental cave.

- Although Clarice turned down Randy's request that she accompany him on his trip, she did offer to drive him to the airport. He **peevishly** replied, "It's the least you can do."

11. **dolorous** or **doleful** (DOLE ur us *or* DOLE ful) If you are feeling dolorous or doleful, you're grieving or feeling sad or sorrowful. The words can also be used for situations that cause the sadness. Both words come from the Latin word for pain.

- The **dolorous** expression on young Buddy's face displayed the sadness he was feeling at the death of his beloved dog.

- What a **doleful** situation—Ann's sister had to have emergency surgery on the day of the planned family reunion.

H appiness is just a thing called X and Y and Z. There are many ways you can experience your sense of well-being and many words you can use to describe it. Let's look at some of these.

1. **euphoric** (yoo FOR ik) This word generally suggests an extreme of happiness, a "wow" feeling. (Its origins in Greek are more modest; it literally means having good health, and indeed that should be a cause of great happiness.) The noun form is "euphoria."

- Mary Lou was understandably **euphoric** when she learned that she had just won the state lottery.

- Ms. Bosco claims that her cat feels **euphoric** when he gets a fair ration of catnip; while it's hard to know about an animal's feelings, jumping up and down and tossing the shreds of catnip in the air does indeed suggest intense happiness.

2. **ebullient** (e BULL yent) This word describes an outward manner of high enthusiasm that would presumably come from a feeling of joy and high spirits. Its Latin root word is a verb meaning "to bubble up," so we might say you're figuratively "boiling over" with happiness when you're ebullient. The noun form is "ebullience."

- Lucretia's good mood was evident to us all from her **ebullient** greeting of each of us with a newly coined, affectionate nickname.

- When his accountant told him about the large tax refund he would receive this year, Mr. Gadda's resulting **ebullience** prompted him to make an immediate booking of a trip to Patagonia.

3. **buoyant** (BOY unt) If you're buoyant, you're feeling lighthearted, uplifted. Figuratively, we might say you're floating on air, but the word derives not from air, but from water: think "lifebuoy," a device that enables one to float in water. In short, whatever floats your boat could make you buoyant. The noun form is "buoyancy."

- When Romeo learned that Juliet returned his feelings of love, he felt positively **buoyant**.

- Sanjay's **buoyancy** when he received a contract for his novel came partly from the money he received but mainly from his pride at being a published author.

4. **ecstatic** (ek STAT ik) This word implies an extreme of happiness. While today it can be used as a synonym of euphoric, its early history often finds it used negatively, almost a synonym for being mad, deranged. (Indeed its Greek roots suggest more the idea of "being beside yourself.") But this word has left all that negativity behind, and pure joy is what remains. Noun form: ecstasy.

- Ingrid was **ecstatic** when she learned that her science project had been awarded a top prize in the Intel competition.
- The prospect of floating along the canals of Venice in a gondola was for Lila a great pleasure; when she learned the usual high fee would be canceled, her feelings moved closer to **ecstasy**.

5. **jubilant** (JOOB ill unt) The modern meaning of this word is, like the words before it, the simple idea of being very happy. The history of this word has religious overtones within both Christianity and Judaism (it's ultimately from the Hebrew word for "a ram's horn") and you may encounter older uses with this shade of meaning. The noun form, "jubilee," is equally complex. In addition to its more common meaning of a celebration, it can have a formal meaning of a celebration of a fiftieth anniversary.

- Ms. Zak was **jubilant** when she learned that her son, her daughter, and all three grandchildren would be able to spend the holiday weekend with her.
- Didn't Queen Elizabeth II of England celebrate a **jubilee** fairly recently?

6. **exultant** (ex ULT unt) Here is yet another word meaning "extremely happy." It has not very common noun forms (exultance and exultancy) and, unlike the five adjectives before it, there is a common verb form, exult, meaning, "to be very happy." (Its Latin root—"a leaping dance step"—suggests its meaning.)

- An **exultant** look came onto Ben Hur's face as he realized that victory in the chariot race was certain.
- One of W. B. Yeats's poems paradoxically challenges a friend whose work has come to nothing to **exult**; we more ordinary folk are more likely to **exult** when our hard work pays off.

7. **jocular** (JOK yoo lar) A different variety of "smiley face" is represented by this word. "Jocular" has nothing to do with "jocks"; rather, it means "tending to make jokes." There are two close verbal cousins: "jocose," which can be synonymous or can carry a more generalized meaning of "merry" and "jocund" is a somewhat more literary word meaning "lighthearted." All three have their roots in the Latin word for "joke."

- Bartholomew was normally a serious fellow, but April Fool's Day brought out his **jocular** side.

- Lana's mood is somewhat more **jocose** than it was during exam week.

- If months had personalities, the month of May might be called **jocund**.

8. **risible** (RIZ uh bull) This word meaning "relating to laughter" can describe a person who is feeling inclined to laugh, but it is more frequently used to describe remarks or situations that are likely to provoke laughter. (Coming from the Latin for "laugh," this word is the cheery relative of a negative word, "derisive," which means laughing at in the sense of "mocking" or "jeering.") The not very common noun form is "risibility."

- On another night Niko would probably have laughed at the stand-up comedian's jokes, but he was not in a very **risible** mood the day he learned about his low grade in physics.

- The cartoonish stereotype of a **risible** situation is that of a man in a top hat slipping on a banana.

9. **complacent** (com PLACE unt) While the literal meaning of this word derived from Latin is "pleased with," today it always carries the negative sense of being unpleasantly self-satisfied, smug. The noun form is "complacency."

- When Roger was hungry for success as an artist, he was a stimulating person; now that he has won blue ribbons in a number of art competitions he has grown **complacent** and dull.

- The married couple's sense of **complacency** about having a life partner was sometimes irritating to their singleton friends.

10. **complaisant** (com PLAZE unt) This near-twin of the word above has taken on an equally negative meaning of its own: it describes a person who is overly eager to please or who calmly accepts mistreatment. The noun form is "complaisance."

- Patricia's well-meaning **complaisance** was annoying to her hosts: instead of expressing some preference when asked how she would like to spend the day, she routinely said, "Whatever you want to do."

- The subplot of the French play focused on the **complaisant** husband; why didn't he care that his wife was consistently unfaithful?

Eponyms

T he first word to learn here is the name of this section. An eponym is a word that was originally a person's name. When policemen ask if a suspect has been "mirandized," they want to know if the suspect has been made aware of his rights, as established in the court case of *Miranda v. the State of Arizona*.

1. **dunce** (rhymes with once) This noun is a good name for a stupid person, a dolt. It derives from Duns Scotus, a thirteenth-century Scottish monk, whose writings became the subject of ridicule long after his death. The eponym extends to the "dunce cap," which you may have seen in cartoons, a cone-shaped piece of paper placed, in crueler schooldays, on the head of an unprepared student.

- What a **dunce** I am! I left the tickets for the senior play at home on the mantel, and now we'll all be late for the opening.
- The twentieth-century novel *A Confederacy of Dunces* drew its name from Jonathan Swift's assertion that we can recognize a true genius from the fact that **dunces** will form a confederacy against him.

2. **luddite** (LUD ite) (sometimes **Luddite**) A person who opposes technology has come to be called by this interesting noun. It derives from one Ned Ludd, an English workman who, around 1779, destroyed machinery for weaving when it threatened his livelihood.

- If this book were being written with a quill pen, its authors could be called modern-day **luddites**.
- Some consider *Frankenstein* the ultimate **luddite** novel, for it shows the ghastly results of technology gone wrong.

3. **pyrrhic** (PEER ik) This adjective is most often used in the phrase "a pyr-rhic victory," meaning a technical win achieved at a high cost. The word derives from an ancient Greek named Pyrrhus who defeated the Romans in 280 BC but lost nearly all his own troops in the process.

- Daniel, in a rather rude manner, pointed out his teacher's mispronunciation of "tyranny" in front of the class; he was correct about her error, but I'd call it a **pyrrhic** victory since he needs her good will in writing his college recommendation.

- Some historians point out that most slave societies were able to abolish slavery without violence and that the Union triumph in the American Civil War was **pyrrhic**.

4. **spoonerism** (SPOON er is im) This unusual-sounding noun refers to humorous transpositions of sounds such as saying "blushing crows" when you meant to say "crushing blows" or "queer dean" when you meant "dear queen." We owe the term "spoonerism" to the Rev. William Spooner, an English clergyman who, supposedly, frequently committed such blunders.

- Lucy delights in all forms of word play, especially puns and **spoonerisms**.
- Laughter at **spoonerisms** is seldom long-lived, but the mayor is still being kidded for saying he knows "every crook and nanny in this town."

5. **draconian** (dra CONE ee un) This adjective describes treatment that is seen as exceedingly harsh or severe. The severe legal code of Draco, a seventh-century BC Athenian politician, is here memorialized; no dragons are involved.

- Georgia knew she had violated the curfew her parents had set for her, but she still felt that grounding her for a month was a **draconian** punishment.
- Those who believe strongly in the right to bear arms will probably judge gun laws in the United Kingdom to be **draconian**.

6. **maverick** (MAV rik *or* MAV er ik) This noun fits a person who dissents from group opinion and goes his or her own way. It derives from one Samuel Maverick (1803–1870), an American cattleman who chose not to brand his cattle.

- We could detect a streak of the **maverick** in Ian when he attended his classes on the day the other seniors had agreed to cut.
- When we asked Ms. Fanslow if she was a Republican or a Democrat, she said, "You'd have to call me a **maverick**. I decide how to vote on the merit of the candidate, not his or her label."

7. **quixotic** (quik ZOT ik) This adjective, meaning overly idealistic, derives directly from the fictional Spanish hero Don Quixote, who displays that trait. (The adjective takes on English pronunciation while the Don retains the "kee HOTE ay" pronunciation befitting the Man of La Mancha.)

- Mr. Hanly admired his **quixotic** young student, so he spoke very gently in saying it might be difficult to win the Nobel Peace Prize as well as write a great novel before he was thirty-five.
- One side of Caitlin's personality is **quixotic**, but she tempers that with a highly practical streak.

8. **mesmerize** (MEZ mer ize) This verb, now meaning "to enthrall, to capture fully someone's attention," originated in a literal form of hypnotism. Franz Mesmer (1743–1815), an Austrian doctor who believed he possessed magnetic curative powers, won many followers who became literally hypnotized while attending his sessions.

- Mr. Lipscomb **mesmerized** his students with accounts of personal meetings with Salman Rushdie and J. D. Salinger; he later scolded them for not asking for more proof about these untrue tales.

- Although Abraham Lincoln could never completely shake his skepticism about religion, he remained **mesmerized** by the idea.

9. **galvanize** (GAL va nize) This verb originally had the literal meaning of "shocking someone with an electric current." Today, it carries only the figurative meaning of "spurring someone into thought or action." The existence of the word bears permanent tribute to Luigi Galvani, an eighteenth-century doctor whose early research stimulated further experiments with electricity.

- The school principal used her assembly talk about poverty in this country to **galvanize** her students into an understanding of the importance of compassion.

- Some groups that once gloried in gaining the right to vote are no longer **galvanized** by the importance of using that privilege.

10. **tawdry** (TAW dree) This adjective describes something literally cheap or gaudy in appearance of something more figuratively shameful. It enshrines St. Audrey (think sain-TAW dree), a seventh-century English saint whose name was given to a fair that sold decorative items such as lace. Alas for St. Audrey, the word degenerated into a completely negative meaning.

- At twelve, Jenny attempted to acquire glamour by using all her mother's cosmetics but achieved only an unappealing, **tawdry** look.

- Why is it that some people enjoy revealing their **tawdry** secrets to a nationwide television audience?

MAKE A MATCH #25

Sections 73–75

Match each word in the left-hand column with the phrase on the right that best suggests its meaning.

A.	apathetic	1. _____	feeling like weeping
B.	complacent	2. _____	disapproving of technology
C.	complaisant	3. _____	independently minded
D.	draconian	4. _____	having no opinion
E.	euphoric	5. _____	being overly idealistic
F.	galvanize	6. _____	cheaply gaudy
G.	jocular	7. _____	deeply fascinated
H.	lachrymose	8. _____	extremely harsh
I.	luddite	9. _____	whiny, complaining
J.	lugubrious	10. _____	smugly content
K.	maverick	11. _____	very, very happy
L.	mesmerized	12. _____	relating to laughter
M.	pyrrhic	13. _____	gloomy, mournful
N.	querulous	14. _____	a win that's really a loss
O.	quixotic	15. _____	content with bad treatment
P.	risible	16. _____	in a kidding, joking mood
Q.	tawdry	17. _____	move someone to action

T his word (pronounced GAL ee MO free) comes from the Old French word for "sauce" or "stew." It names the third of our mixed word sections not related by theme.

1. fallow (FAL oh) The source of this adjective is agricultural as it comes from the Old English word for "fallow land." It refers to a piece of land that is plowed but left unseeded during a growing season. It can be used in a more figurative sense, however, to refer to any situation that remains uncultivated.

- Farmer MacDonald decided to build a new barn and a horse corral on the back five acres since that land has lain **fallow** for the past five years and he is no longer thinking of cultivating it.

- The American writer Henry Miller has written: "There is a time for play and a time for work, a time for creation and a time for lying **fallow**."

2. pallid (PAL id) This adjective means "abnormally pale" or "lacking vitality and dull." It can be used literally to describe a pale person's complexion or figuratively to describe something bland and dull, such as a pallid-tasting slice of beef.

- After catching sight of a caped figure grimacing at her in the window, Lorraine returned to the dinner table with trembling hands and a **pallid** face.

- The editors of the school paper decided not to run Mr. Bleg's editorial about grade inflation because the prose was **pallid**, the ideas were inane, and the argument was politically incorrect.

3. supine (soo PINE) From the Latin, this adjective means "lying on the back with the face upward." It is sometimes used to mean "showing lethargy or indifference." In any case, it should not be confused with "prone," which means "lying on the stomach with the face downward" or "having a tendency toward something," as in a child's "being prone to" tantrums.

- Lying **supine** on the couch with one arm draped dramatically over her forehead and one hand resting on her stomach, Victoria was the picture of exhaustion, which is exactly how she felt after a day of babysitting the triplets.

- The guard asked the prisoners to lie **prone** on the ground, their faces pushed into the mud, and threatened to shoot anyone who moved a muscle.

4. **atavism** (AT ah viz im) The best synonym for this noun is "throwback." It means "the reappearance of a trait or a form of behavior in an organism after several generations of absence." The adjective form is "atavistic." It comes from the Latin word for "ancestor."

- Social Darwinists, who claimed that there were inferior races which displayed more primitive traits than other human beings, often relied on the concept of **atavism** to explain their theories.

- "Those boys are so **atavistic**!" Julienne whispered to Maggie. "All they do is sit around, scratching their bellies and eating peanuts with their fingers. They're like a bunch of apes."

5. **imbroglio** (im BROL yo) This noun comes to us straight from the Italian word for "tangle." It means "a confused or complicated disagreement" or, quite simply, "an entanglement." You might use it to describe a small battle such as a fare dispute with a taxi driver or a larger argument with complicated international implications.

- What an evening! Hernando accidentally left his wallet in the taxi; we arrived late at the theater; and we got into quite an **imbroglio** with the box office manager over his letting us in without our tickets.

- The political **imbroglio** surrounding the controversy over same-sex marriage will most likely remain a strong issue in future presidential races.

6. **enigma** (en IG ma) "A puzzling, inexplicable, or ambiguous situation" is the meaning of this noun. You can use it to describe a person or a thing. The adjective form is "enigmatic."

- In a 1939 radio broadcast, British statesman Winston Churchill said: "I cannot forecast to you the action of Russia. It is a riddle wrapped in a mystery inside an **enigma**."

- Professor Arfer's grading policies were a complete **enigma** to his students; he seemed to weigh class participation, attendance, and exam grades in different combinations each semester.

7. **bumptious** (BUMP shuss) This adjective means "pushy" or "rudely assertive." Think of it as a cross between "presumptuous" and "bump," which may well be where the word comes from.

- "I really hate to shop at Toy World during the holidays," Amy remarked with a sigh. "It always involves dealing with nasty salespeople, long lines at the cash register, and **bumptious** customers who try to get ahead of you in line."

- It's hard to believe that Lee and Dorothy are sisters. Dorothy is shy, cautious, soothing, and calm whereas Lee is loud, annoying, **bumptious**, and aggressive.

8. **cicerone** (SIS eh RONE ee *or* CHI che RONE eh) We've borrowed this word that means "guide for sightseers" straight from the Italian. It originally refers to Marcus Tullius Cicero (106–43 BC), the famous Roman orator, statesman, and philosopher. You're more likely to see it in literature than hear it commonly used today.

- It will be terrific to have Julie as our **cicerone** when David and I visit Florence in April since she's lived there for two years and really knows her way around the city.

- It is impossible to visit the famous temples of Ankgor Wat in Cambodia without a **cicerone** as the ruins need to be protected from plundering by thieves and vandals.

9. **perambulate** (per AM byoo late) Here's a fancy verb for "to walk" or "to stroll." It can also mean "to walk through" as in "to inspect on foot." It comes from the Latin for "walk" and "through." The British have found another use for it. They call a baby carriage "a perambulator."

- After the company picnic, the park service staff **perambulated** the grounds, making sure there were no lost or left items and no damage done to park property.

- Every evening after a light supper, Mr. Bartleby takes a constitutional, during which he **perambulates** the streets along the waterfront and watches the ships unload their cargo.

10. **ancillary** (AN sill air ee) From the Latin for "maidservant," this word was once used as a noun to mean "servant." It is now used as an adjective to mean "of secondary importance" or, alternatively, "something that is auxiliary or helpful to something else," such as a workbook is to a textbook.

- "While you are in Paris," said Catherine's mother, "I'd like you to learn something about French art and architecture. Whether you actually learn to speak French is **ancillary**."

- On the first day of class, the teacher gave Catherine her art history textbook and several **ancillary** materials, including a collection of slides from the Louvre and a book about the French Impressionist painters.

Bright Lights!
Loud Music!

Yes, there must be moods where you want your nerves to be jangled, but the words in this list are negative, all describing a feeling of "too-muchness" about sight or sound or overall atmosphere.

1. **garish** (rhymes with parish) An adjective that describes something loud (in color or design), flashy, or glaring.

- The shocking pink shirt worn with the chartreuse pants certainly caught the eye; only the addition of an orange belt could have made Mason's outfit more **garish**.

- The community of Oldest Oaks was horrified when the new residents painted their picket fence fire-engine red. The Neighborhood Association is sending Mrs. Oldschool around to discuss with them their **garish** taste.

2. **gaudy** (GAW dee) This adjective means tastelessly showy, suggesting overly bright colors, overly flashy design. Coming from the Latin word for "enjoyment," "merry-making," it illustrates the linguistic phenomenon of *pejoration* (PEJ or A shun), whereby a positive word becomes a negative.

- **Gaudiness** is in the eye of the beholder: large quantities of bright primary colors please some, while to those who prefer grays and tans they are unbearable.

- "Do you find the work of Spanish architect Antonio Gaudi (GOW dee) **gaudy**?" asked Mr. Zavatsky, determined to get as close to a pun as possible.

3. **lurid** (LOOR id) This adjective meaning "causing shock or horror, grue-some" gains its overkill effect through a glaring, unsavory sensationalism. Perhaps anticipating the potential effect of something lurid, its origin is a Latin word for "pale."

- "Please, spare me the **lurid** details of the horrible things Rosemary said to you. They're just too painful to hear," Luke said sympathetically to Nora.

- The **lurid** headlines of the tabloid papers blazoned forth phrases like "body parts" and "sex fiend."

4. **cacophony** (ka KOF uh nee) Literally "bad sound," this noun refers to harsh, displeasing noises.

- "One man's music is another man's **cacophony**," said Bryan's father, clomping off to the refuge of his study to escape the sounds of heavy metal that his son relished.

- The school dining room, with the **cacophonous** buzz of the voices of hundreds of fifth and sixth graders, was not the place for a leisurely repast.

5. **raucous** (RAW kus) This adjective refers to harsh sounds or any atmosphere of rough boisterousness.

- The street was filled with a **raucous** mixture of the cries of street vendors clashing with car horns and the motors of Vespas.

- The principal cautioned the children to maintain a respectful silence when they entered the historic building: "Our usual **raucous** playground atmosphere is *not* appropriate in the Robert E. Lee Chapel."

6. **strident** (STRY dent) If it's harsh and grating in its sound, it's strident.

- When King Lear refers to a voice that is "soft, gentle, and low" as being "an excellent thing in woman," we wonder if he found a **strident** voice objectionable in everyone or only in women.

- "You'll clean up this pigpen and you'll clean it up now," Sergeant Maldonado said **stridently**, horrified that the new recruits had not learned that a barracks must be kept neat at all times.

7. **dissonant** (DIS on ant) Sounds that are unharmonious are called dissonant; in a more generalized sense varying opinions may also be so described.

- Twenty-first-century listeners find it strange that the **dissonance** in Stravinsky's *The Rite of Spring* caused a riot among those attending the Paris premiere in 1913.

- One of the factors that made Mr. Robinette such an effective leader was that he welcomed **dissonant** voices into a discussion; he did not regard differences of opinion as a threat to his ego.

8. **meretricious** (mer uh TRISH us) The meretricious item attracts the viewer's attention but in a showy, vulgar manner. Appropriately enough, the adjective derives from the Latin word for "prostitute."

- Fitzgerald's Jay Gatsby, who is described as being in the service of "a vast, vulgar, and **meretricious** beauty," is prone to excess—too much alcohol served at too many parties, too many unread books, even—some would say—too many shirts.

- "A little more restraint," said Kelly, "makes you more appealing. Any more sequins on that outfit and the effect will be positively **meretricious**."

9. **barrage** (buh RAZH) Literally referring to a heavy burst of gunfire or artillery, the noun can be used for any kind of overwhelming outpouring.

- The publishers knew the book would be controversial because of its support of the testing of drugs on animals, but they were unprepared for the **barrage** of angry criticism that demanded it be removed from bookstore shelves.

- Blanche shuddered as she entered the nightclub: a **barrage** of strobe light effects assaulted her eyes as completely as the thumping bass attacked her ear.

10. **pandemonium** (pan de MOAN ee um) This noun names an atmosphere of uproar, wild noises, confusion. Having nothing to do with "pandas" or "Pandora," it literally means "(place of) all the demons." It was coined in 1667 by the great epic poet John Milton as the name for the newly built city in Hell in his poem *Paradise Lost*. It quickly became a part of secular language, a five-syllable word that is widely known.

- **Pandemonium** broke out when the promoter announced at the assembly that free tickets to the David Bowie concert would be available to the first ten people to show up in the lobby.

- When the traffic lights at the busy intersection failed, there was a period of **pandemonium** as cars hesitated, roared forward, hesitated again, and drivers honked and cursed.

Crime and Punishment 78

Y ou don't have to be a lawyer to use the words in this list, but you might use them in any given conversation about law and order. To not include them in this book would be criminal.

1. jurisdiction (joor iss DIK shun) Here's a noun that means "the right and power to apply the law." In other words, when you have "jurisdiction" over something, you have "authority" over it.

- "The casinos are located in the suburbs, beyond the **jurisdiction** of the city," explained the judge, dismissing the case.

- In his essay "On Vanity," the French essayist Michel de Montaigne describes "the human creature" as "a magistrate without **jurisdiction**" to emphasize his idea of the individual's impotence in the great scheme of Nature.

2. recidivist (ree SID iv ist) From the Latin word for "to fall back," this noun means "someone who returns to a previous pattern of behavior, especially criminal behavior." The adjective form is "recidivistic."

- The Department of Motor Vehicles punishes **recidivists** more severely than first-time offenders. Drivers who are caught for moving violations must pay more for each succeeding ticket.

- The American Cancer Society suggests different measures for **recidivistic** smokers, ranging from hypnosis to nicotine patches.

3. exculpate (EX kul pate) This verb means "to clear from guilt or blame." The adjective form is "exculpable." "Culpable," on the other hand, means "guilty."

- The accused man was **exculpated** of the murder when he provided the perfect alibi; he was in the hospital having an appendectomy at the exact time of the shooting.

- Whistling cheerfully with an innocent expression on his face, Max came downstairs with chocolate all over his lips; I knew he was **culpable** for the missing brownies.

4. vindicate (VIN dih kate) Pretty much a synonym for "exculpate," this verb means "to clear of accusation or blame with supporting arguments or proof." It can also mean "to avenge," which is the meaning of its Latin root. The noun form is "vindication."

- Ben was **vindicated** for missing his varsity basketball game when he produced a note from his dentist, detailing his emergency root canal.
- In her work *Vindication of the Rights of Woman*, the eighteenth-century British feminist Mary Wollstonecraft said, "I do earnestly wish to see the distinction of sex confounded in society, unless where love animates the behaviour."

5. **impunity** (im PYOO ni tee) This noun means "exemption from punishment or harm." There is no such word as "punity"; we use "punishment."

- In his ill-received poem "Sordello," the nineteenth-century British poet Robert Browning wrote, "Any nose may ravage with **impunity** a rose."
- "In celebration of our last day of school, you may eat cupcakes and doughnuts in the classroom with **impunity**," announced Mrs. Marm. "Just make sure you clean up after yourselves or you'll get in trouble with the principal for making a mess."

6. **indict** (in DITE) This verb means "to accuse of wrongdoing" or "charge." The noun "indictment" is used in the legal profession to mean "a formal charge of wrongdoing by the findings of a jury."

- In *Adventures of Huckleberry Finn*, Mark Twain **indicts** the so-called civilized behavior of pre-Civil War society in the American South, pointing out its racism and hypocrisy.
- After her **indictment** on charges of embezzling thousands of dollars from The Wilson Widget Company, Agnes Smith, the company's bookkeeper, was sentenced to ten years in prison.

7. **contumely** (KON toom lee) Though it looks like an adverb, this word is a noun that means "rudeness" or "arrogance." You don't hear it much today, except if you're reading a nineteenth-century novel or if you're in a courtroom, where it is used to describe behavior that constitutes being in contempt of court. The adjective form is "contumacious."

- "If you continue with this **contumely**," Woolsey asserted, "I shall not have to take you home from the ball. Such discourteous remarks are inappropriate, especially from a respectable girl."
- The defendant's outburst of hostility toward the judge was considered **contumacious** behavior, and he was severely punished for it.

8. **litigate** (LIT ih gate) This verb means "to engage in legal proceedings" or "to bring a lawsuit." The noun form is "litigation," and the adjective form is "litigious."

- After he accidentally backed his car into his neighbors' picket fence and ran over their rare Japanese maple tree, Dr. Peron was engaged in **litigation** with them for months.
- "I don't see why they have to get so **litigious** about a little tree," Dr. Peron's wife said, "just because it was planted over one hundred years ago."

9. **pilfer** (PIL fur) From the French word for "spoils," this verb means "to steal a small amount or item." Stealthily taking a wallet filled with $100 is "stealing"; sneaking a couple of cookies off a platter which your mother was saving for guests is "pilfering." A good synonym is "filching."

- Although she wasn't caught by the police, Alice was punished when her mother found out she **pilfered** a glittery ornament off the Christmas tree in the lobby of the public library.

- Because he was such a sloppy eater, Jack **pilfered** a few extra napkins from the pizzeria when he ordered a chicken parmesan sandwich to go.

10. **injunction** (in JUNK shun) The general meaning of this noun is "a command" or "order." In law, it specifically means "a court order prohibiting a party from a specific course of action." The verb form is "to enjoin."

- After her husband's repeated threats of violence, the court issued an **injunction** preventing him from coming within a mile of the house.

- Because of its potential effect on the Hudson River striped bass, the proposed construction of a sewage treatment plant was **enjoined**.

MAKE A MATCH #26

Sections 76–78

Match each word in the left-hand column with the phrase on the right that best suggests its meaning.

A.	ancillary	1. _____	gruesome, shocking
B.	atavistic	2. _____	a mystery, a puzzle
C.	barrage	3. _____	falling back into an old pattern
D.	bumptious	4. _____	lying flat on your back
E.	cacophony	5. _____	complicated entanglement
F.	contumely	6. _____	helpful in a secondary way
G.	enigma	7. _____	showy, vulgar attractiveness
H.	garish	8. _____	a throwback
I.	imbroglio	9. _____	wildly chaotic situation
J.	injunction	10. _____	arrogant rudeness
K.	litigation	11. _____	brightly colored, flashy
L.	lurid	12. _____	lightweight theft
M.	meretricious	13. _____	clear of accusation
N.	pandemonium	14. _____	legal proceedings
O.	pilfer	15. _____	harsh, discordant sounds
P.	recidivist	16. _____	"pushy," demanding
Q.	supine	17. _____	overwhelming repetition
R.	vindicate	18. _____	legal order forbidding

H umanity's capricious nature is reflected in the number of words that suggest types and degrees of changeability.

1. **metamorphosis** (met a MORF oh sis) This noun means "a complete transformation in appearance, character, or function." The plural is metamorphoses. It often suggests a change that occurs by magic or sorcery, as in the mythological stories recounted in Ovid's *Metamorphoses*.

- According to Ovid, the gods **metamorphosed** the handsome Narcissus into a flower after he faded away, admiring his reflection in a pool.

- Dina's **metamorphosis** into a beautiful young woman occurred after a particularly awkward and painful adolescence.

2. **capricious** (cah PRISH us) This adjective comes from the Italian for "fright" or "sudden start" and means "unpredictable," "impulsive," or "subject to whim." The noun form is "caprice."

- **Capricious** by nature, Samantha was warm to her friends on Monday morning but quite aloof in the afternoon.

- Ruled by **caprice**, Professor Mason was sometimes an easy grader and other times quite strict, frustrating his ambitious students and amusing the indolent ones.

3. **volatile** (VOL a til) Another word that derives from chemistry (volatile chemicals evaporate readily at normal temperatures), this adjective also means "fickle" or "inconstant." Since it comes from the Old French word for "flying," it also suggests a person who is flighty or an emotion that is fleeting. More often than not, that fleeting emotion is violent or explosive, either literally or figuratively. Volcanoes are volatile; so are political situations.

- Stephen's **volatile** nature led him to break up with Dierdre after proclaiming his love to her the day before.

- Market **volatility** made it possible to make a fortune quickly or lose one.

4. **mutable** (MYOOT uh bul) Another adjective that means "prone to frequent change," this word can be used to describe people as well as things. The verb form is "mutate."

- The weather was so **mutable** that Daisy left the house with sunglasses and an umbrella.

- If the pollution in the river continues to increase, the fish may soon **mutate** so that they can breathe air.

5. **fluctuate** (FLUK tyoo ate) Slightly different from the previous words, this verb means to change in a very specific way. When something fluctuates, it rises and falls irregularly, as if in waves. In fact, it comes from the Latin word meaning "to flow." It's not used to describe people.

- The mutable weather caused the price of corn to **fluctuate** wildly all spring.

- James stayed home from school because his temperature **fluctuated** from normal to 102.5 by morning.

6. **labile** (LAY bile) From the Middle English word meaning "forgetful," this adjective means "constantly changing" or "unstable." It is often used to describe a chemical reaction, but it can also be used to describe a person's character.

- The emotionally **labile** child would burst into tears at the drop of a hat and begin laughing only seconds later.

- Chili oil is a **labile** chemical compound which is destroyed by heat, so it doesn't taste spicy when you cook with it.

7. **erratic** (er RAT ik) This adjective is a bit different from the other words that mean changeable. From the Latin word that means "to wander," it connotes lacking consistency or regularity. There is a noun form— "erraticism"—but no one uses it.

- Joey's **erratic** behavior stymied his parents; they considered taking him to a psychologist.

- Martine's grades were so **erratic** that the teacher did not recommend her for the honors class.

8. **vacillate** (VASS ill ate) A good verb for a section on words about change, it means to swing indecisively from one idea or action to another. The noun form is "vacillation."

- Casey **vacillated** between going to school with a cold because she had a math test and staying home and getting some rest.

- After work, the busy mother **vacillated** between ordering in Chinese food and cooking a simple chicken dinner.

9. quicksilver (KWIK sil ver) As a noun, this word is a synonym for the chemical element mercury. More useful is its sense as an adjective meaning "changing its nature rapidly," a synonym for "mercurial" (see the "Down from Olympus" section).

- At the funeral of Julius Caesar, Marc Antony's oration causes the **quicksilver** crowd to withdraw its support from those who killed Caesar.

- Princess Melisande intrigues the reader with her **quicksilver** nature, cool and willful one moment, vulnerable and fragile the next.

10. equivocate (ee KWIV oh kate) Someone who is ambivalent often equivocates. This verb means to make a statement with one or more possible interpretations, often with the intention of misleading. The adjective form is "equivocal."

- When Sam finally got through to Lily and asked her to dinner, she answered with an **equivocal** "maybe."

- Macbeth felt betrayed by the **equivocating** witches when he realized that he had misinterpreted their ambiguous promises.

W hether you're rich or poor, you should know the words that help in conversations about money—having it, lacking it, earning it, or owing it.

1. **pecuniary** (pek KYUN ee err ee) From the Latin word for "property" or "wealth," this adjective simply means "having to do with money." One could say that all of the words on this list are "pecuniary words." A word with a similar meaning is "fiscal," which means "having to do with finances," which comes from the Latin word that means "treasury."

- After his wife died, Mr. Stevenson hired an accountant to deal with all of his **pecuniary** matters. He had left all of the household finances to her and had no idea how to pay all of the bills.

- The chief financial officer of the company was in charge of all **fiscal** matters, including salaries, bonuses, stock options, and budgetary issues.

2. **destitute** (DES tit toot) The Latin root of this word means "to abandon," and the adjective means "lacking all resources" or "completely impoverished." The noun form is "destitution."

- Utterly **destitute**, the family was forced to move into a homeless shelter in order to obtain food, clothing, and a place to sleep.

- "In cases of extreme **destitution**," said the social worker, "we call in all of the social services agencies to help pay for a family's basic expenses."

3. **fiduciary** (fih DOOSH ee err ee) This adjective means "holding in trust for another." As a noun, it is "a person who acts on behalf of another's interests and is required to fulfill those obligations with the utmost good faith." It comes from the Latin "fidere," which means "to trust." It is a word that is most often used for bank matters or legal documents.

- In failing to diversify the stock portfolio, the banker breached his **fiduciary** duty to his client's heirs.

- In this regard, the banker was acting as a **fiduciary**, but a bad one.

4. **stipend** (STY pend) The original Latin means "soldier's pay," but the word now means "any fixed payment (such as a salary) for services rendered." This is slightly different from an "honorarium," which is "a payment made for services rendered when a stipend is not traditionally required."

- The medical student received a year-long fellowship that included room and board and a **stipend** for his work on the research project.

- In gratitude for his speaking to the students about his experiences in Washington, the school agreed to pay the congressman a small **honorarium**.

5. **affluent** (AF floo ent) An adjective that means "rich, prosperous, wealthy," it comes from the Middle English word for "flowing." The money flows freely for affluent people. The noun form is "affluence."

- Gold River Estates is an **affluent** neighborhood. Every house has a swimming pool, a three-car garage, and a five-acre plot of land surrounding it.

- The psychologists are doing research on the impact of **affluence** on teen behavior. Their studies indicate that adolescents who come from upper middle class families may face different issues than teenagers from lower-income neighborhoods.

6. **solvent** (SOL vent) This adjective means "able to meet financial obligations." Someone who is solvent may not be rich but he or she can pay the bills. On the other hand, someone who is "*in*solvent" is not able to cover his or her debts. The noun form is "(in)solvency," but you can also refer to a bankrupt person as "an insolvent."

- Because they had no insurance, the Smith-Walcotts were **insolvent** when their house burned down in an accidental fire; they were forced to move in with relatives.

- "We're finally **solvent**!" exclaimed Horace to his new wife. "My new job will enable us to get a mortgage on a home and pay off our student debts."

7. **barter** (BAR ter) Although this verb means "to trade goods or services without the exchange of money," it has an interesting etymology. It comes from the Old French *barateour*, which means "swindler" or "cheat." The word no longer has the negative connotation. There's no reason why a barter arrangement can't be a fair trade.

- "Let's **barter**," said the hungry landscape gardener. "I'll plant a pretty garden in the front of your house if you cook me a steak dinner."

- Hoping to **barter** his prized Mickey Mantle baseball card for permission to use his older brother's new car, Amog began negotiations with his brother at the breakfast table.

8. **depreciation** (de preesh ee AY shun) This noun means "a decrease or loss in value due to age, wear, or market conditions." Its opposite is "appreciation."

- "I bought this car last year for $10,000," said Carlos, "but I'll sell it to you for $7,000. I drove it across the country and the extra mileage has certainly caused some **depreciation** in its value."

- Because of excellent climate conditions in California, the value of California wines **appreciated** considerably at the beginning of the century.

9. **remuneration** (re MYOON er ay shun) This is a noun that means "payment for goods or services provided." Salary is remuneration for work done, for example. A good synonym is "recompense." The verb form is "to remunerate."

- The hospital offered Caroline ample **remuneration** for her work in the intensive care unit because the hours were long and the schedule was very demanding.

- Carmen considered $20 per hour to be a fair **recompense** for babysitting the Harrison's four-year-old son, Irving, because he was very demanding and never went to bed when he was told.

10. **lucrative** (LOO kra tive) This adjective means "yielding money or profit." Another word for money is "lucre," however it generally has a negative connotation associated with money that comes from greed as in the mention of "filthy lucre" in the Bible (Titus 1:11). In fact, the word comes from the Latin root for "avarice."

- "Plastics is a very **lucrative** business, Benjamin," said Mr. Robinson. "You should consider a career in a field that will make you rich."

- The miser surveyed his **lucre** and rubbed his hands greedily. "I'm rich! Rich!" he exclaimed.

If you read the section titled "The Menagerie," then you know what a "herpetologist" does for a living, but there are lots of other vocations (from the Middle English word for "calling," it means a "regular occupation") and avocations (a word that means "hobbies") with names you might not easily recognize. There's even a word for someone who simply dabbles in an art or field of knowledge—a "dilettante" (from the Latin root for "delight"). Here is an assortment of words that connote fairly common professions or interests.

1. oenologist (ee NOL oh jist) From the Greek word for "wine," this noun means someone who appreciates, enjoys, or collects wine. It is also spelled "enologist."

- At my brother's birthday party, we asked Gerard, an **oenologist,** to recommend which wines to order for the table; he knew the best vineyards in France, Italy, and California as well as the best vintages.

2. taxidermist (TAX ih derm ist) A taxidermist is skillful at preparing, stuffing, and mounting the skins of dead animals for display in a lifelike state.

- The Museum of Natural History in New York has a team of **taxidermists** who prepare a variety of wildlife, from penguins to leopards to elephants, for exhibition in a series of dioramas. (A "diorama," by the way, is a three-dimensional scene in which figures, stuffed wildlife, or other objects are arranged in a naturalistic setting.)

3. husbandry (HUS band ree) The root of this noun comes from the Middle English word for "husband," but it means something different. Husbandry is an old-fashioned word for the field of agriculture, including breeding crops or raising livestock. Someone who performs husbandry is technically a "husbandman," but these days we say "farmer."

- John Deere makes all kinds of equipment that is used for **husbandry,** including a variety of tractors, hoes, and fertilizers.

4. balletomane (bal ET oh mane) This noun describes someone who is an ardent admirer of ballet, including both professional dance critics and zealous fans.

- Sidney is a real **balletomane**; she attends dance performances five times a week and is familiar with all of the season's new dance stars and their best roles.

5. **philatelist** (fil ATE a list) This is the noun for someone who collects and studies postage stamps, postmarks, and related materials. The word comes from the Greek word meaning "lover of things that are exempt from payment" because a postage stamp indicates prepayment of postage. Though it looks like an adverb, the noun for the collection of stamps is "philately."

- Billy is quite a dedicated **philatelist**. He has books of stamps from all around the world and from many different eras.

6. **legerdemain** (LEJ er deh MAIN) From the Old French word meaning "light of hand," this noun means "sleight of hand" or magic.

- Through a skillful act of **legerdemain**, Merlin the Great pulled a live rabbit out of his back pocket.

7. **lepidopterist** (lep id OPT er ist) This is the noun for someone who studies the branch of entomology (the study of insects) that focuses on butterflies and moths. The root of the word is the Greek for "winged creature."

- The **lepidopterist** carefully pinned the wings of the butterflies to the mat, hoping to get a better measure of their comparative sizes.

8. **numismatist** (noo MIZ ma tist) A numismatist is someone who collects or studies coins, money, and, often, medals. The field is called "numismatics," not "numismatism."

- A **numismatist** by avocation, Charlene loved to visit the Franklin Mint in Washington, D.C., because it had a famous collection of rare and antique coins.

9. **bibliophile** (BIB lee oh file) The Greek word "philos" means beloved or loving. Therefore, the suffix "phile" indicates a lover of the prefix that comes before it. So, an audiophile loves music; a Francophile loves French things, and a bibliophile is a lover of books. Interestingly, however, a lover of ballet is a "balletomane," not a "balletophile" (see #4).

- A passionate **bibliophile**, Jane spends hours rummaging through used book stores and libraries in search of first editions, original manuscripts, and unusual bindings.

10. **lapidary** (LAP id air ee) Although this word also means "marked by refinement or precision of expression" (see the "Talking about Talking" section) the noun form is also a vocation. A lapidary is someone who cuts, polishes, or engraves gems. It comes from the Latin word for "stone."

- The Italians were great **lapidaries**. One need only look at their Renaissance jewelry to see their skillful and unusual handling of gemstones and settings.

Sections 79–81

Match each word in the left-hand column with the phrase on the right that best suggests its meaning.

A.	affluent	1. _____	producing lots of money
B.	barter	2. _____	transformation
C.	bibliophile	3. _____	financially well-off
D.	capricious	4. _____	wavering between decisions
E.	destitute	5. _____	relating to money
F.	equivocate	6. _____	lover of books
G.	fluctuation	7. _____	sleight of hand
H.	legerdemain	8. _____	lacking financial support
I.	lucrative	9. _____	jumping around in mood
J.	metamorphosis	10. _____	trading goods or services
K.	oenologist	11. _____	payment
L.	pecuniary	12. _____	wine expert
M.	remuneration	13. _____	potentially explosive state
N.	vacillate	14. _____	up and down variation
O.	volatile	15. _____	deliberately mislead with words

PRACTICE, PRACTICE, PRACTICE #9

Sections 73–81

What word does each sentence need? Select the word that best fits the meaning of each of the sentences.

A.	ancillary	K.	meretricious
B.	apathetic	L.	pandemonium
C.	ebullient	M.	perambulate
D.	fluctuate	N.	pilfer
E.	galvanize	O.	pyrrhic
F.	jocular	P.	quicksilver
G.	lachrymose	Q.	quixotic
H.	legerdemain	R.	recidivism
I.	litigation	S.	solvent
J.	lurid	T.	strident

1. It seemed a very _____ plan for him to sell everything and move to Bora Bora "for inspiration," as he put it.

2. _____ broke out in the auditorium when the lights went out and the sound system failed; people were screaming and falling over each other trying to get to the exit.

3. I didn't want to listen to her _____ tale about the robbery and its aftermath because the details were too gruesome.

4. His _____ nature—serious one minute and joking the next—could be both delightful and disturbing.

5. That aspect of the scheme is not my primary focus; it's quite _____.

6. After her best friend moved to another town, she felt quite _____, and she tried to cheer herself up with watching cartoons.

7. If the public in general is _____, then the candidates representing the few who do care will have an easy time being elected.

8. They hope to solve the problem out of court because any kind of _____ is costly and time-consuming.

9. I'm so impressed with the way the new councilman cleared up the budget problem so quickly; it's practically a feat of _____!

10. Although he won the argument, he lost a good friend in the course of it, and his triumph must be feeling rather _____.

11. I cannot give my approval: that television show has only the most _____ type of appeal, and I don't want you to watch something so shabby.

12. I felt _____ all afternoon; I was practically floating on air after I learned I had won the short story contest.

13. The family was thrilled that it had finally become _____ and could pay off those pesky credit card bills.

14. Robert's _____ mood was annoying to his sister, who just didn't feel like engaging in laughing and teasing right then.

15. Hot one day, cold the next—I wonder how long the temperature will continue to _____ like this.

16. Although Hiram has his own apartment, he will still _____ from his parents' stock of groceries when he visits—how childish!

17. That prison has the lowest rate of _____ of any in the East; how do they have such success in helping released inmates not fall back into crime?

18. Shall we _____ the park for a while? I really feel like a stroll.

19. After seeing the documentary about world hunger Richard began to _____ other students into helping him raise funds for a charity that can help.

20. Although his words were kind, his tone of voice was _____ and left the hearer without the comfort he intended to give.

The Body and Beyond   82

M any words, such as "visual," related to the five senses are very common; a few, however, are less well known, such as #1–4 below.

1. **olfactory** (ole FAK tuh ree) Of or relating to a sense of smell.

- A person whose **olfactory** nerves are damaged not only has a lessened sense of smell but also a lessened sense of taste, since much delight in food comes from its smell.

- The narrator of F. Scott Fitzgerald's novel *The Great Gatsby* refers to "**non-olfactory** money," meaning, roughly, "Money doesn't smell."

2. **tactile** (TAK tul *or* TAK tile) Of or relating to a sense of touch. The meaning may be literal or figurative.

- Those who bake their own bread can enjoy the **tactile** pleasure of kneading and shaping the loaves.

- The critic Helen Vendler has commented on the "**tactile** language" used by the poet Seamus Heaney.

3. **audile** (aw DIAL) Of or relating to a sense of hearing, a word that, we guarantee, you will never encounter outside a technical context.
audible (AW dih bul) You'll often hear this word that means "able to be heard." If it's audible.

- The governor's words were barely **audible** to the large crowd at the rally, for the technician responsible for the correct functioning of the microphone could not be located.

- Peter Ustinov notes that if the world should blow itself up, the last **audible** voice would be that of an expert saying it couldn't be done.

4. **gustatory** (GUS ta tor ee) Of or relating to the sense of taste.
gusto (noun) This related word extends its meaning beyond "taste" to mean "an energetic sense of pleasure."

- When you have a bad cold, the keenness of your **gustatory** sense will be diminished.

- Shakespeare's character Falstaff brings a sense of **gusto** to all aspects of life, whether talking, joking, or falling in love; since we know he is fat, it is clear he has also overindulged in **gustatory** pleasures.

We now move beyond the senses to other parts of the body. In the sentences below, we'll see words in an increasingly indirect relationship to some part of the body.

5. **rhino-** (RYE no) (prefix) Words relating to the physical nose often use "rhino," which derives from the Greek word for "nose." Thus, a creature with a horn for a nose is a rhinoceros and rhinoplasty is an operation to reshape the nose. (Rhinestones, alas, are not gems in the nose but merely stones that originally were made in the region of the Rhine River.)

- Ms. Typaldos was grateful for her knowledge of Greek: when the doctor said her son was suffering from **rhinitis**, she knew he meant that the boy's nasal passages were swollen.
- After Melisande's cosmetic surgery, her teenage brother alluded to her recent "nose job." She reproved his crude phrasing and instructed him henceforth to refer to the procedure by its formal name, "**rhinoplasty**."

6. **hirsute** (HEER soot) Hairy, often unusually so. This unusual word derives directly from Latin.

- The **hirsute** face made it difficult to tell if the creature in the horror film was meant to be human or only partly human.
- The giggling girls at the swimming pool admitted that they were trying to decide which of the boys had the most **hirsute** back.

7. **visceral** (VISS er al) Descriptive of an emotional reaction that is deep, nearly instinctive, as if experienced in the intestines of the body, the *viscera*. In short, a (literally) "gut response."

- When an insensitive acquaintance parodied her favorite poem, Suellyn felt a **visceral** disgust.
- Should we act on our **visceral** responses or should we regard intellectual analysis as more important?

8. **genuflect** (JEN yoo flect) To kneel or to bend, touching one knee to the ground, primarily used in reference to an act of worship. This interesting verb comes into English from the Latin words for "knee" and "bend."

- The devout pilgrims making the long trip to Santiago de Compostela on foot **genuflected** whenever they passed an image of the cross, to them a sacred object.

- Sebastian's coworkers disliked his manner of flattering his employer; they half-seriously accused him of **genuflecting** whenever "the great man" crossed his path.

9. **epaulet** (EP uh let) This word, synonymous with the diminutive of the French word for "shoulder," refers in English to an ornament, frequently fringed, on the shoulder of a garment (most often a military uniform).

- Gregory looked unusually dashing in his regiment's dark blue uniform with its white **epaulets**.
- Although not a member of any branch of the military, Fiona delighted in her vintage clothing purchase—a dark plaid dress with silver braiding and gold **epaulets**.

10. **pedestrian** (ped EST ree un) Dull, ordinary. Everyone knows the noun "pedestrian" meaning a person who is walking. It derives directly from the Latin word for "foot." But much less common is the adjective "pedestrian," referring to language or to ideas. Here it is words or thinking that is figuratively "on foot" as opposed to words or ideas that have figuratively taken wing and soared.

- Hard work with a talented teacher of writing has made Alexi's prose much less **pedestrian**; her last essay immediately caught and held the reader's attention.
- Although Prof. Genet's work has been published in prestigious scholarly magazines, many find her thinking somewhat **pedestrian**.

Off and On

ff and on, now and then, every once in a while…the language has many words for the inconstant.

1. **sporadic** (spor AD ik) This adjective meaning "occurring irregularly" comes from the Greek word for "scattered like seed" (if you know plants, think of "spores").

- Mark's visits, though **sporadic**, were always welcome to his friends. "We'd rather have a little of him than a lot of someone else," they said generously.

- The teacher puzzled over Yvonne's end-of-term grade; when she was present she was brilliant, but her attendance had been highly **sporadic**.

2. **desultory** (DEZ ul tor ee) This adjective can be a synonym for sporadic, or it can mean "disconnected, jumping from one thing to another." The second meaning reflects the Latin root word "to leap."

- Dawn and Harry once carried on an intense online flirtation, but it has now dwindled to the **desultory** email.

- Gianna and Josie are both ardent readers but with differing styles: Gianna pursues one subject through several books while Josie prefers a more **desultory** manner, going from book to book.

3. **spasmodic** (spaz MOD ik) Another "off and on" adjective, this one coming from the word "spasm," with the suggestive idea of intense or abrupt occurrences at irregular intervals. (It is also still used in its medical sense of "relating to spasms.")

- If you really want to learn a foreign language, you'll benefit more from a little study every day than from longer bouts of study **spasmodically**.

- Luigi's **spasmodic** attempts to contact his old friend were prompted more by guilt than by a genuine desire to renew their acquaintance.

4. **paroxysm** (par OX is im) Speaking of "spasms" (see #3), we offer this noun meaning an irregular burst of emotion or action. (It too has its origins in medical usage.)

- Recovering from a bad cough, Inez gave away her tickets to *La Boheme*, fearing a **paroxysm** of coughing might interrupt a beautiful aria.

- Steve knew Naomi would be happy with the tickets to Hawaii he bought as a birthday gift, but he was not prepared for the **paroxysm** of happy tears the gift brought forth.

5. **quantum** (KWAN tum) You know already, don't you, that a "quantum leap" is a common phrase for a big change. But you may also enjoy knowing this is one of those intriguing linguistic incidences where popular use of a word changes its meaning. "Quantum," as a physics term, refers to the *smallest* possible change that can be measured. One scientist cleverly describes if as "such an infinitesimal level as to be infinite." Before it became wedded to "leap," it was simply the Latin word for "quantity," and you'll occasionally see it in older writing.

- Eighteenth-century writer Tobias Smollett describes himself as having "a respectable **quantum** of knowledge."

- What Shakespeare expressed as "a sea change" in his play *The Tempest* is now, in our scientific age, more often termed a **quantum** leap.

6. **fitful** (FIT ful) Here's another adjective meaning "occurring now and then"; think of the phrase "doing something by fits and starts." This word too (like #3 and #4) originates in a medical sense—"fits" was used for convulsions or seizures. (See second sentence below.)

- George made several **fitful** attempts to begin studying vocabulary for the Graduate Record Exam, but he decided to postpone the project until after his vacation.

- "After life's **fitful** fever, he sleeps well," says the insomniac Macbeth enviously of the king he recently murdered.

7. **intermittent** (in ter MIT ent) If you don't want to use sporadic, spasmodic, or fitful, you can use this adjective that also refers to the phenomenon of irregularity. "Intermission" is a related noun.

- "Shall we postpone the picnic?" asked Mrs. Assingham of her house guests. "They *are* predicting **intermittent** showers today, and I so hate it when the wicker basket is dampened."

- As a writer, Sally is improving, but she still displays only **intermittent** control over sentence structure.

8. **reiterate** (re IT er ate) A verb meaning to repeat what you've stated earlier. It comes from the Latin for "re-traveling."

- Ms. Pappas patiently **reiterated** the course requirements for careless students who had lost the original handout.

- Andy braced himself as his father began yet another **reiteration** of that anecdote about mowing lawns and raking leaves and never asking *his* dad for spending money.

9. **hiatus** (hie ATE us) It's a gap, a space, whether in time or continuity in general.

- There was a three-year **hiatus** in Valerie and Paul's friendship, but they picked right up where they had left off.

- The crudely lettered sign has a **hiatus** between the "o" and the "c," making "local corn" look like "lo-cal corn."

10. **lacuna** (la KOO na) This noun too refers to a gap or an empty space. From the Latin for "hollow or cavity" (and thus leading to both "lake" and "lagoon"), it forms its plural in the Latin way (see the first sentence below).

- "There are so many **lacunae** (la KOO nye) in my memories of the past," sighed Jennifer. "I remember my fifth birthday but almost nothing at all about being in the first grade."

- Greek scholars are comparing their educated guesses to fill in the **lacuna** in the third line of the newly discovered manuscript of a poem by Sappho.

A uthority is the subject of the list here—words for the people in charge and words for the orders they give.

1. imperious (im PEER ee us) From the Latin word for "empire," this adjective means "arrogantly domineering" or "dictatorial." It comes from the same root as "imperial," which has a more positive spin. Someone who is imperious is "bossy"; someone who is imperial is "regal" or "majestic."

- Josie thought her supervisor at the hospital was overbearing and **imperious**. She was always telling all of the other nurses how to do their jobs but rarely helping out when they were short-staffed.

- The **imperial** peacock proudly displayed his iridescent tail in the hopes of attracting the reluctant female hiding behind the juniper tree.

2. delegate (DELL uh gate) As a verb this word means "to authorize and send as one's representative" or "to commit or entrust to another person." It should not be confused with "relegate," which means "to assign to an obscure place" or "to classify" or "banish."

- If Stuart would only learn to **delegate** more of his responsibilities to his assistants, he would have more time to play golf and spend time with his kids.

- At the annual meeting of International Global Ltd., the members of the board and the top administration were seated around the huge mahogany table in the third floor conference room. All of the junior staffers were **relegated** to the folding chairs along the wall.

3. officious (oh FISH us) Someone who is officious is "too eager to offer unwanted advice or services to another." It suggests someone who is a know-it-all and is a bit bossy about it. It comes from the Latin word for "dutiful," but it has come to have a negative connotation.

- "If I were you, I'd line up all of my files neatly and keep my desk spotless," Prudence said, **officiously**. "An orderly desk represents an orderly mind."

- Chris's **officious** roommate consistently nagged him about keeping the floor swept and leaving his muddy shoes in the hallway.

4. **mandate** (MAN date) This noun means "an authoritative command" or "order." It can also be used as a verb. The adjective form is "mandatory," and it means "obligatory."

- The state's new legislation **mandated** that marijuana could not be used, even for medicinal purposes.

- "Attendance is **mandatory** at the graduation rehearsal," the principal announced to the senior class. "Anyone who does not show for rehearsal will not be allowed to attend the senior dinner in the dining hall this evening."

5. **patronize** (PAY tron ize) This verb has several meanings. The first is "to act as a patron or an active supporter." It also means "to be a regular, paying customer." It's in this section because it also means "to treat in a condescending manner."

- Dulcey felt **patronized** when Mr. Finch told her she did "a surprisingly good job." She didn't think it should have been surprising to her boss that she could actually file his papers in alphabetical order.

- For one week only, PCB, the huge drugstore chain, promised 50 percent off on all hair products to customers who regularly **patronized** their stores.

6. **fiat** (FEE aht) From the Latin for "let it be done," this noun means "an arbitrary order or decree," often authorized by the government.

- After the students practically destroyed the football field after the game, the school administration issued a **fiat** banning the consumption of alcoholic beverages at university sporting events.

- The **fiat** against abortion drove a significant number of women away from the Church.

7. **ordain** (or DANE) This verb has a religious meaning—"to invest with ministerial authority," but it also has a secular meaning. When something is "ordained," it is "ordered by virtue of a superior authority." It's meaning is quite close to "mandate."

- The Preamble to the Constitution states that "the people of the United States, in order to form a more perfect union…do **ordain** and establish this Constitution for the United States of America."

- Having completed his course work at seminary school, Joseph was **ordained** as a Protestant minister.

8. **pundit** (PUN dit) This word comes to us from the Hindi for "learned man" and it means "a person with an authoritative opinion." It is most often used to describe a source of political opinions. The noun form is "punditry."

- The cable news channel revealed its true politics when it brought in a conservative **pundit** to comment on the impact of the president's State of the Union address.
- "I'm tired of the **punditry** broadcast on all of the television news magazines," Mr. Cohen told his Media and Politics class. "It's easy to find a voice of authority on both sides of every issue but, in the final analysis, they don't tell us anything we don't already know."

9. **sovereignty** (SOV rin tee) Here's a noun that means "royal rank, authority, or power." It can also mean "complete independence" and "self-government." It is generally used to describe political situations. You wouldn't call your boss your "sovereign" unless you were being ironic about how she wields power.

- Emma Goldman, an early twentieth-century American writer and anarchist, defined "anarchy" as "the philosophy of the **sovereignty** of the individual."
- The United States declared its **sovereignty** from England in the Declaration of Independence.

10. **peremptory** (per REMP tore ee) From the Latin word for "to take away," this adjective means "putting an end to all debate or action, not allowing contradiction or refusal." It's no surprise then that a "peremptory" person is "offensively self-assured." Don't be confused if you sometimes spot a similar-looking adjective "preemptory." It occasionally sneaks into the language in place of the preferred form "preemptive" as in "Biggles made a preemptive bid for the property, an offer so good that would-be competitors retreated."

- The headmaster took a **peremptory** tone with the students who had missed too many classes. "Anyone who misses more than ten classes cannot graduate," he averred. "That's the rule and we're going to stick to it. There are no excuses."
- When Dara asked her mother whether she could stay out past her normal curfew on a school night, her mother replied with a **peremptory** "No!"

MAKE A MATCH #28

Sections 82–84

Match each word in the left-hand column with the phrase on the right that best suggests its meaning.

A. desultory   1. _____ hairy
B. fiat   2. _____ decree
C. genuflect   3. _____ wise person
D. hiatus   4. _____ boring, commonplace
E. hirsute   5. _____ state again
F. lacuna   6. _____ sense of smell
G. officious   7. _____ felt deep in the body
H. olfactory   8. _____ fit or outburst
I. paroxysm   9. _____ a gap in time
J. pedestrian   10. _____ kneel reverentially
K. peremptory   11. _____ in an unfocused manner
L. pundit   12. _____ an empty space
M. reiterate   13. _____ overly eager to advise
N. sovereignty   14. _____ in a commanding manner
O. visceral   15. _____ supreme power

T hat's what Greek philosopher Aristotle thought, and it's a belief confirmed by the many words in the language that deal with aspects of government and politics, a word that comes from the Greek word *polis* meaning "city."

1. **despot** (DES put) From the Greek word for "master," this noun implies just that—a ruler, generally an oppressive ruler. If you want a different sense, as in "a benevolent despot," you have to add the qualifying adjective.

- George Orwell's novel *1984* gives us the picture of complete **despotism**; citizens are controlled partly through force and partly through mind control.

- Perhaps the fact that Mr. Parnell reports to an overbearing boss helps make him a petty tyrant, a **despot** to his wife and children.

2. **demagogue** (DEM uh gog) It ought to be a good thing, for the root word is "a popular leader," but it isn't. Today the noun is always negative, naming a leader who gains power by manipulating the emotions of the people, who presumably don't detect the insincerity.

- Many consider Sen. Joseph McCarthy as a complete **demagogue**, one who played on citizens' fears about the Cold War to build his own career through obsessive "Communist hunting."

- Today we are so accustomed to seeing Josef Stalin as the embodiment of evil that it's hard to remember he was once a successful **demagogue**, a good speaker with a confidence-inspiring manner.

3. **edict** (EE dict) This noun refers to a declaration, a decree, an order that must be obeyed. The root word carries the same sense in "dictator."

- Mr. Cross runs his classroom like an amateur dictator: he doesn't give homework assignments but **edicts,** and woe to the student who doesn't listen carefully.

- Historically, the **Edict** of Nantes, a decree issued in 1598, gave some limited religious freedom to French Protestants.

4. **incumbent** (in CUM bent) In political terminology an incumbent is a person currently holding an office. The different but related use is of an adjective that expresses a duty or obligation, almost always expressed as in the second sentence below.

- Despite the attractive platform and energetic campaign that Ms. Yeshlovsky offered in her bid for office, the **incumbent** was still the favorite, perhaps because of the general inertia of most citizens.

- It is **incumbent** on all of us to participate in the political process, at least by voting on all elections.

5. **caucus** (KAW kus) Today, this noun refers to a political group that is part of a larger group. This small group may select delegates, pledge support for candidates, or recommend policy for the larger group. Let's hope everybody is sober while deliberating, for in Medieval Latin, a "caucus" was a drinking vessel!

- The Women's **Caucus** of the university faculty group has been instrumental over the past twenty-five years in making everyone more aware of gender inequities left over from the all-male years in the university's past.

- Because the Iowa Democratic **Caucus** is the first test of voter sentiment, it has assumed an importance that is out of proportion to the number of votes cast.

6. **coup** (KOO) In its most political sense, this is an abbreviated form of **coup d'etat** (KOO day TA), a sudden overthrow of government by a small group. In a more generalized sense, a coup (literally, in French, a stroke) is any successful, unexpected strategy.

- Jane Austen knew how to depict a **coup** in the world of courtship of two hundred years ago: wealthy young women and their scheming mothers never dreamed that Miss Elizabeth Bennet would end up winning the heart of Fitzwilliam Darcy and becoming the mistress of the elegant estate of Pemberley.

- Quite a **coup d'etat**! Milton Megabucks quietly bought up enough shares of stock to force his loathed uncle Matthias Megabucks out of his position as CEO of Megabucks Ltd.

7. **junta** (HOON ta) This Spanish word for a "small group" has come into English; it denotes either a small group of military officers seizing power in a country or a small legislative body, usually in Central or South America.

- Though not quite a **junta**, Lee's old prep-school ties with Greg and Eddie have been strong enough to switch some votes in their college fraternity.

- Some recall the multilingual *New Yorker* cartoon of some years past that depicts a small group of men entering a corporate office, saying, "We're a **junta** and this is a coup." (See #6)

8. **faction** (FAK shun) This noun refers to a conflicting element within a larger group. In a larger sense, it means the internal conflict itself.

- Shakespeare's *Julius Caesar* depicts the men who are plotting Caesar's assassination coming to visit Brutus, who solemnly notes "they are the **faction**" when he hears they are attempting to hide their faces.

- Unfortunately, the members of the church who used to enjoy frequent good fellowship with one another have become increasingly **factious**, not over religious issues but over small organizational concerns.

9. **gerrymander** (JER ree man der) This verb has to do with the lines drawn for voting districts in a way that favors one political party. The word came into existence in 1812 as a combination of the name of a little lizard—a "salamander"—and the last name of Elbridge Gerry, a former governor of Massachusetts. Gerry's party, allegedly, had redrawn district lines in a way that favored it and in a way roughly resembling the shape of the lizard.

- The original **gerrymandering** supposedly caught the artistic eye of Gilbert Stuart, noted portrait painter of George Washington, who detected the amphibious new shape.

- The pedant, one who just had to know more than everyone else, pointed out to his friend that "**gerrymander**" should "properly" be pronounced "gher-rymander," for Gerry himself used a "hard G" pronunciation for his name.

  (Extra knowledge for word lovers: that pedant could be called a "doryphore," a person who delights in pointing out the small mistakes of others.)

10. **constituent** (kon STIH tyoo ent) Politically speaking, a constituent is a resident of a region represented by a certain elected official. In a larger sense, it could be any person who authorizes a member of his or her group to speak for him or her.

- Representative O'Toole made a hasty pre-election flight from Washington to his home state so that he could meet with his **constituents**, learn their concerns, and impress upon them that he needed their votes.

- Students who were appointed to committees were told they would be practicing "non**constituency**-based" stewardship; in short, they'd be giving their own views, not necessarily views held by a majority of the student body.

86

Quarantine" refers, primarily, to keeping a person with a contagious disease away from contact with other humans. It literally refers to a period of forty days, a length of time that evokes an era without the power of modern-day medications.

1. **pestilence** (PES til enss) This scary noun refers to the kind of disease that causes a fatal widespread sickness. The first syllable gives you an understated memory clue. The word can also be used figuratively to describe something that brings annoyance or disapproval.

- The bubonic plague brought **pestilence** to Europe in the fourteenth century to a degree we can hardly imagine today; it's little wonder the phrase "the Black Death" came to be used as a synonym for this plague.

- The **pestilent** actions of the disgruntled employee were at first merely annoying, but when the "poison pen" letters turned into death threats, his boss knew he had to go to the police.

2. **murrain** (MUR in) Although this noun is still used for some diseases of cattle, you'll see it mostly in older literature or in poetic uses as a term for any dire disease.

- "May a **murrain** light upon you for the unhappiness you've brought upon my family," muttered the powerless cottager as his cruel landlord rode by.

3. **pandemic** (pan DEM ik) Yes, it sounds like "epidemic." Just as that word means a spreading of a disease, "pandemic" suggests an even wider spread of the contagion. "Pan" comes from Greek meaning "all." Like "epidemic," it can be used figuratively.

- Today we don't regard "flu" as a very serious condition, but **pandemic** influenza in the early twentieth century was fatal to a large number of people.

- "If the unemployment **epidemic** in this country is not to become a **pandemic**, we must act now to decrease the number of jobs being outsourced to other countries," said Dr. Mehta, who had made an extensive study of the situation.

4. **virulent** (VEER yoo lent) In a literal sense, this adjective refers to a very powerful form of a disease. By extension, it can be used to describe any negative but powerful force.

- "The strain of pneumonia afflicting patients this winter is a particularly **virulent** one," noted Dr. Siegel, adding that one Broadway play was forced to close its doors when both the star and his understudy were hospitalized from the disease.

- "Okay, you didn't like my book," wrote the author piteously to the reviewer, "but did your review have to be so **virulent**?"

5. **scourge** (rhymes with merge) As a noun, this word refers to a source of misery such as that caused by pestilence (see #1) or war. As a verb, it can mean to punish or, specifically, to whip (and the whip itself can be called a "scourge").

- Perhaps everything lies in the eye of the beholder: Europeans refer to Genghis Khan as "the **scourge** of Asia," while to his own people he was considered a great leader.

- Hamlet saw himself as sent to be both "**scourge** and minister"; in other words, he could both injure and heal.

6. **blight** (rhymes with light) Literally, it's a disease that afflicts plants. More commonly, you'll see it used for anything that has a strongly negative effect.

- The potato **blight** in Ireland in the nineteenth century ruined the potato crop and eventually stimulated a high degree of immigration to the United States.

- "Come now, young man," said Prof. McFyte to the student complaining about his final grade, "surely my giving you this grade of C+ hasn't **blighted** all of your prospects for the future."

7. **devastation** (de vas TAY shun) This noun refers to a widespread (see "vast" in the middle of the word) area of destruction from disease or some other destructive force. It can also be used metaphorically.

- The scene of **devastation** days after the tsunami was heartwrenching. Many who had survived the initial wave were dead or near death from the lack of uncontaminated water.

- "To protect yourself from this kind of emotional **devastation** in the future," said the counselor, not unkindly, "may I suggest you try to grow a thicker skin; you don't have to fall to pieces when someone frowns at you."

8. **bane** (rhymes with main) Literally, "bane" is a poison, as in certain plant names—wolf's bane, henbane. By extension, it's anything that causes ruin or great harm. If someone is the "bane of your existence," they figuratively poison your life.

- The poet John Milton calls gold "that precious **bane**," alluding to the fact that money can help bring happiness or misery, depending on its use.

- That country is just now beginning to see the long-term **baneful** effects of its foreign policy.

9. **baleful** (BAIL ful) You might, though it's unlikely, see "bale" used in older literature to mean "evil" or "emotional suffering." Most often today you'll see "baleful," meaning "sinister" or "harmful." Perhaps it's inevitable that there is some overlapping between the meanings of "baleful" and "baneful."

- Milton, who, in the entry above, calls gold "bane," describes the fallen angel Lucifer as rolling his "**baleful** eyes."

- The **baleful** stare of the security cop caused the boys to change their plans about daring each other to walk on the beams of the half-constructed building.

10. **pernicious** (per NISH us) Something deadly, dangerous, or destructive might be termed "pernicious." You may have heard it in the name of the disease "pernicious anemia," a particularly threatening form of the illness. "Deleterious" might be a good synonym.

- "This form of the bacteria is particularly **pernicious**," explained Dr. Epstein. "Just when we think we've developed a medicine to counteract it, it mutates into a newer, more deadly form."

- *Supersize Me* is a documentary vividly showing the **deleterious** effects of a diet made up primarily of meals from "fast-food joints."

87

J ust as eating gives the language several interesting words (see section 10, "What's Cookin'?"), drinking offers a liquid set of its own. Drink up!

1. **potable** (POTE uh bul) As "edible" is to eating, so "potable" is to drinking. In addition to this adjective form, it can also be used as a noun. "Potion" and "potation" are related nouns.

- Lavinia felt sure that water in all foreign countries, including Canada, was not **potable**, so only bottled water touched her lips while she was on the road.
- In addition to the huge platter of shrimp and crabs, Brenda and Bob offered their guests a wide array of **potables**, some adorned with tiny paper parasols.

2. **quaff** (KWAHF) If you sip daintily at your beverage, you're not quaffing. That action requires downing the drink with gusto. ("Swig" and "swill" are other verbs for hearty drinking.)

- The Viking warriors hoisted the flagons of mead into the air and then simultaneously **quaffed** them.
- The narrator of Edgar Allan Poe's poem "The Raven" longs to **quaff** a potion that will blot out his torturing memories.

3. **draft** (rhymes with laughed) This noun names the amount of liquid that can be taken in by one act of swallowing, one "pull" from the glass or bottle. ("Draft beer" is a related term in that it is beer that is "pulled" from a keg.) If you see the word in writing from England, it will be spelled "draught" but pronounced the same.

- Mr. Switters longed for a **draft** of some bracing potion, something that would give him strength and courage for his ordeal.
- When the speaker in John Keats's "Ode to a Nightingale" says, "O for a **draught** of vintage that hath been / Cooled a long age in the deep delved earth," he refers to the custom of cooling wine below ground.

4. **imbibe** (im BIBE) "To imbibe" is a formal way to say "to drink." It may also be used metaphorically. Its verbal relative "bibulous" (BIB u lus) refers to the consumption of alcoholic beverages.

- The neighborhood children spent long summer days sitting on the Milhorns' porch playing endless games of Monopoly and **imbibing** pitchers of lemonade.
- Even two months of **imbibing** gracious manners in Charleston, South Carolina, have not served to cure Barry's tendency to be rude.

5. **slake** (rhymes with snake) This verb is a formal way to refer to quenching or satisfying your thirst. It can also be used for the satisfying of other cravings. Its origin is related to the word "slack."

- Although the knight longed to pause and **slake** his thirst at the well, he pressed on, hoping to reach Daffydown Hall by nightfall.
- An hour of detailing his complaints against his boss served not to **slake** Ritchie's unhappiness with his job but to increase it.

6. **libation** (lie BAY shun) Historically, this noun describes the pouring out of a liquid, usually wine, as an offering as part of a religious ritual. It is now used informally, for any intoxicating beverage.

- "Hey, Jim, how's about heading for the club car and a cool **libation**?" said Al as they boarded the commuter train for home on a hot summer day.
- Aeschylus's Greek tragedy *The Libation Bearers* is named for the group of women who assist Electra in pouring out that **libation** onto the tomb of her father Agamemnon, killed by his wife.

7. **distill** (dis TILL) Distilling is a chemical process involving the condensation of a liquid in order to purify or concentrate it. You'll hear it in reference to water and to some alcoholic beverages. (And the "still" that Great-uncle Joe supposedly had in the basement or the backwoods derived from that word.) It can also be used figuratively.

- Since Max and Rebecca aren't really drinkers, their decision to organize their trip of Scotland and the Hebrides around visits to all the **distilleries** of single malt Scotch was a little surprising.
- When Regan, ready to enter the world of dating again, asked the more experienced Norm to **distill** all his wisdom about women into some advice, his pal unhelpfully said, "Just go for it, man."

8. **imbrue** (im BREW) This formal verb means "saturate" or "stain." It's easy to use "brew" as your memory device, and indeed that is the root word. A near-twin is "imbue," meaning "to permeate, to stain."

- A hilarious mock-suicide scene occurs near the end of Shakespeare's *A Midsummer Night's Dream* when the character of Pyramus stabs himself, saying, "Come, trusty sword, come, blade, my breast **imbrue**."
- **Imbued** with a strong sense of idealism from the reading of romanticized accounts of leaders' lives, Felix may have trouble adjusting to the day-to-day life of an aspiring political candidate.

9. **abstemious** (ab STEEM ee us) While its literal meaning can refer to moderate eating and drinking, it's often associated with not drinking alcoholic beverages—perhaps because its sound is similar to "abstinence" (from the verb "abstain"). (It once had a primary sense of abstaining from alcoholic beverages but may now be used more for abstaining from premarital sex.) A related word for one who partakes of no alcoholic beverages is teetotaler, coined by the nineteenth-century Temperance movement.

- Accustomed to what he termed "the good life," Smithers found prolonged visits with more **abstemious** relatives not only unpleasant but painful.
- Carrie Nation was not content with choosing a **teetotaling** life for herself; instead, she won her place in history with her habit of wielding her hatchet in public taverns.

10. **vintner** (VINT ner) Descriptions of main streets in old novels often have a reference to a "vintner's" shop—a store selling wine or possibly making wine. The root word is "vine," and you'll see it reflected in other words such as "vinous" (relating to wine) or "vintage" (the yield of grapes, often that of an especially good year. See #3, second sentence).

- In *A Tale of Two Cities*, Charles Dickens sets a powerful scene outside a **vintner**'s shop in Paris: a wine cask runs with red wine, symbolic of the blood soon to be shed in the French Revolution.
- Since we now associate him with the pasteurizing of milk, it's a little surprising to learn that Louis Pasteur wrote a book on **vinous** fermentation.

MAKE A MATCH #29

Sections 85–87

Match each word in the left-hand column with the phrase on the right that best suggests its meaning.

A.	abstemious	1. _____	oppressive ruler
B.	blight	2. _____	decree
C.	coup	3. _____	government overthrow
D.	despot	4. _____	conflicting element within a group
E.	edict	5. _____	plague
F.	faction	6. _____	cattle disease
G.	imbrue	7. _____	widespread contagion
H.	murrain	8. _____	strong negative effect
I.	pandemic	9. _____	deadly
J.	pernicious	10. _____	drinkable
K.	pestilence	11. _____	swig
L.	potable	12. _____	quench
M.	quaff	13. _____	saturate
N.	slake	14. _____	moderate in drinking
O.	vintner	15. _____	winemaker

Home Furnishings

88

R eaders of Harper Lee's *To Kill a Mockingbird* may remember that Tom Robinson gets into trouble when he's asked to "bust up a chiffarobe." But how many people today know that a "chiffarobe" is actually "a tall piece of furniture with drawers on one side and space for hanging clothes on the other?" Here are ten more lesser-known pieces of furniture.

1. **davenport** (DAV en port) Oddly enough, this noun can mean two entirely different pieces of furniture—both popular in the nineteenth century. It is either a large sofa, often convertible into a bed, or a small writing desk (which probably took its name from the manufacturer).

   • Fiona sat down on the **davenport**, hoping that Mr. Beebe would sit down next to her when tea was served.

2. **antimacassar** (AN tee mak ASS ar) This noun is a small piece of material placed on the backs of chairs and sofas that protects the upholstery from hair-oil stains. It comes from Macasar, which was a brand of hair oil, popular in the late nineteenth century.

   • The living room of Mrs. Carrington's country cottage was filled with knick-knacks and frilly decorations to protect her furnishings. There were doilies on the table, **antimacassars** on the sofa and chairs, and lacquer coasters scattered on the end tables.

3. **ottoman** (OT oh min) Originally, this noun meant a type of couch without arms or back, used for reclining. Its name came from its imitation of the kind of seating used in the Turkish or Ottoman Empire. Today, it is more commonly used to mean "a low, upholstered seat or cushioned footstool."

   • Harrison entered the drawing room, sat down in a brown, crushed velvet armchair, placed his feet up on the leather **ottoman**, and rang for the butler.

4. **credenza** (creh DEN zah) This noun comes from the Latin word for "trust," possibly from the practice of placing food or drink on a sideboard to be tasted by a servant to ensure that it contained no poison. It is a buffet or sideboard, usually without legs. It is also used to mean a piece of office

furniture with a long, flat top, containing file drawers and accessories for a computer.

- Millicent placed the large platter of turkey on the **credenza** in order to leave room on the table for the various side dishes and trimmings.

5. **chesterfield** (CHEST er field) Although this noun is known to mean "a single or double-breasted overcoat, usually with concealed buttons and a velvet collar," it is also a term for a large sofa with upholstered arms. This type of sofa was manufactured in Canada where it was commonly used at the turn of the twentieth century, but it was also popularly used in Northern California around the same time. Its name comes from the earl of Chesterfield.

- Since John Steinbeck's house in Salinas has opened as a museum and contains much of its original furniture, there is likely to be a large **chesterfield** in the front parlor that was originally used for seating visitors.

6. **hassock** (HASS ik) This noun comes from the Middle English word for "a large clump of grass," and it refers to a thick cushion used as a footstool or for kneeling.

- Dylan glanced around the room, looking for a comfortable place to sit. He settled for a rickety, wooden rocker and pulled over a small **hassock** upholstered in kilim on which to rest his feet.

7. **armoire** (ARM war) This word comes from the Latin word for "a chest for implements or tools." It evolved to mean a "large, often ornate cabinet, used for hanging clothes and often containing drawers." A good synonym is "wardrobe."

- Mr. Carnegie examined the **armoire** and wondered if it was large enough to contain all twenty of his suits and his rather extensive collection of dress shirts and ties.

8. **divan** (dih VAN) This noun has many obscure meanings, including "a counting room or public audience room used in Muslim countries," but it belongs in this section because it chiefly refers to a "a long, backless sofa, especially one set with pillows against a wall."

- In nineteenth-century paintings of odalisques, a harem girl is usually depicted reclining sensually on a **divan**, partially dressed and appearing to be awaiting her lover.

9. **highboy** (HIGH BOY) This noun means a tall, wooden chest of drawers, usually divided into two sections, one slightly wider, and standing on legs. The "boy" comes from "bois," the French word for "woods."

- Mrs. Walker kept most of her clothes in a mahogany **highboy**, her lingerie in the smaller drawers at the very top and her sweaters in the wider drawers below.

10. **commode** (cah MODE) This noun comes from the Middle English word for "convenient" and connotes several different types of furniture. It can mean "a low, elaborate chest of drawers," "a moveable stand or cupboard containing a washbowl," or "a chair enclosing a chamber pot." In some parts of the country, this word is a synonym for "toilet."

- The Roundthwaites' guest room was comfortably furnished with an oak, four-poster bed, a matching oak highboy and a **commode**, containing a delicately painted, porcelain pitcher and washbowl.

Country Yokel or City Slicker?

89

A s the title of this section suggests, slang offers words (many, like these, negative) that embody aspects of life in a rural area or in a city. But more formal English also has some fine words evoking these contrasting areas.

1. bucolic (bew KOLL ik) This adjective meaning "typical of the country-side" always has a connotation suggestive of leafy peace and quiet. Appropriately enough, the root is the Greek word for "cow."

- Selina likes the combination of rural and urban: when in a city she seeks out **bucolic** pockets such as small parks with trees and fountains, and in the country she can be found buying bandanas in the general store.
- **Bucolic** poetry has a long tradition, for both Greek and Roman poets depict shepherds philosophically discussing life, love, and art, everything but the care of sheep.

2. idyll (EYE dul) This noun can refer to a literary work depicting an idealized version of rural life or it can refer more generally to an pleasantly peaceful event or setting.

- Tom and Gina had an **idyllic** (eye DIL ik) summer in the northern part of Greece, living in a beautiful cottage on the edge of a forest and taking part in an international poetry seminar held in the village town hall.
- Alfred Lord Tennyson's long poem *Idylls of the King* tells many beautiful and fantastic tales of life at King Arthur's court.

3. pastoral (PAST or ul *or* pas TOR ul) This adjective may have either the literal sense, synonymous with "bucolic" (think "pasture"). In addition, it often has a metaphorical sense referring to the life of a minister, a pastor. (The link is the concept of the head of a religious congregation as the "shepherd" of a "flock" of followers.)

- The meadow made a perfect **pastoral** setting for the Philharmonic's performance of Beethoven's Sixth Symphony, nicknamed "the **Pastorale**" (pas tor AL).
- The Reverend James Martinson took his **pastoral** duties very seriously: he not only led inspiring services on Sunday but kept himself aware of the lives of all his parishioners, offering help when it was needed.

4. **rustic** (RUST ik) This is a frequently used adjective meaning "referring to the countryside." Its Latin root is the same word that gave rise to "rural."

- Bert likes the trappings of **rusticity** (rus TISS i ty), buying tables with twig-like legs and hanging a handmade wooden rake on his wall, but in reality he never wants to be more than ten minutes away from a shopping mall.

- It is easy to idealize a **rustic** existence; real-life farmers, whether in this era or an earlier time, can testify to the hard work essential to the endeavor.

5. **arable** (AIR uh bul) If you want to add an authentic farming term to your vocabulary, here's a good one. It describes land suitable for cultivation. Not related at all to "Arabs," it derives from the Latin word for "plow."

- Leyla's hopes of having a vegetable garden outside her kitchen door were not easily realized, for the hard-packed, sandy soil was not **arable,** and she is reluctant to spend the money required to replace it with topsoil.

- "Twenty acres of **arable** land will be auctioned off on Saturday morning to the highest bidder." Theola read the poster with growing interest. Could she persuade her city-born husband to join her in becoming a part-time farmer?

6. **urban** (URB un) and **urbane** (ur BANE) Plain old "urban" means "relating to a city," but "urbane" describes an elegance and refinement of manner that is by no means possessed by all who live in a city. Both derive from the Latin word for "city."

- Atlanta has recently been afflicted with "**urban** sprawl," the unplanned spreading of heavy population growth to areas on the edge of the city, a development that gives rise to major traffic congestion.

- The fictitious James Bond fits many people's definition of an **urbane** man: never at a loss, he always knows what to say, do, wear, drink.

7. **cosmopolitan** (KOS muh POL ih tun) If you're cosmopolitan, you're sophisticated enough to be at home anywhere in the world. Similarly, a cosmopolitan society has elements from many parts of the world. Not surprisingly, the two root words mean "world" and "city." (The related word "metropolitan," derives from "mother" and "city.") Opposites would be "provincial," "parochial," and "insular" (narrow in outlook, as if knowing only the world of a small province or parish or an isolated island).

- The poetry of Constantine Cavafy beautifully reflects the **cosmopolitan** nature of the ancient Egyptian city of Alexandria; there's nothing insular about his view of humanity.

- Despite the magazine's name, Christine found the periodical not **cosmopolitan** at all but rather quite provincial, having quite a limited perspective on the world.

8. **flaneur** (fla NUR) This French noun is coming to be more and more used in English. While it can have a negative sense of one who loafs or wastes time, it more often takes the positive sense of the name for a perceptive person who strolls about a city, unhurriedly noting and observing. (The feminine form in French is "flaneuse," but in English "flaneur" is unisex.)

- When asked her goals for the future, the prematurely sophisticated Julia promptly replied, "I think I'd like to be a **flaneur**."
- Janet Flanner, the Paris correspondent for *The New Yorker* from 1925 to 1975 wrote many columns dealing with her experiences as a **flaneur** in the streets of Paris; this pleasing verbal coincidence was, however, obscured by Flanner's use of the pseudonym "Genet."

9. **sophisticated** (so FIS ti kayt ed) This adjective, so positive in modern connotation as a synonym for "urbane," has a checkered past. It once carried the negative sense of "adulterated," "made unnatural." If you come across this use in older literature, you'll be one of the few to understand it. (See the second sentence below.)

- Tom Stoppard's play *Travesties* is written for a **sophisticated** audience, one that knows twentieth-century history and art and, especially, one that knows and knows well Oscar Wilde's play *The Importance of Being Earnest*.
- In the late seventeenth century John Dryden wrote, "I love not a **sophisticated** truth, with an alloy of lie in it."

10. **teem** (rhymes with beam) This verb meaning "abounding" or "swarming with" is often used of the crowds on city streets but can work equally well for nature's bounty in a rural setting.

- On Thanksgiving Day in New York the sidewalks are **teeming** with children and adults, clad in parkas and mufflers against the cold, patiently waiting for the bands and colorful floats of the annual parade.
- While Gary waited patiently with his family for the annual Thanksgiving Day parade, his mind wandered to thoughts of his childhood home in upstate New York where the vistas were endless and where the rivers and lakes, not yet frozen over, were **teeming** with fish.

How Interesting

Y ou can read the title of this section as "How interesting?" or "How interesting!" because all of the words below pertain to the range of expressions that mean either dull and ordinary or exciting and fascinating.

1. mundane (mun DANE) From the Old French word that means "world," this adjective means "of this world" or "secular" rather than "spiritual." It's in this section because it also means "ordinary" or "commonplace."

- On the first day of school, most of the teachers covered such necessary but **mundane** topics as school supplies, homework requirements, and grading policies.

- Because the minister at Christina's church feels it is important to engage in **mundane** matters as well as spiritual matters, many of the parishioners are actively engaged in political organizations and community service work.

2. prosaic (pro ZAY ik) Perhaps because this adjective comes from the Latin word for "prose" rather than "poetry," its meaning is "straightforward" or "matter-of-fact." More often, however, it has the more negative connotation of "unimaginative" or "dull."

- Winnie's description of her visit to Washington, D.C., was so **prosaic** that George couldn't decide if he had no desire to visit that city or no desire to go anywhere with Winnie.

- When Gideon asked Josh to give him a description of the girl he wanted to fix him up with, Josh replied rather **prosaically**: "She's got brown hair and brown eyes and a medium build."

3. quotidian (kwo TID ee en) This adjective, which comes from the Latin for "each day" means "occurring everyday." It's not just used to mean "daily"; it also describes something "commonly occurring" or "commonplace."

- Leopold decided to liven up his otherwise **quotidian** job by wearing silk pajamas to work and telling his colleagues they were the latest fashion in the workplace.

- Every weekday morning, Marybeth engages in a **quotidian** ritual that includes showering, brushing her hair and teeth, and having black coffee and a scone. Then, she walks her pet squirrel Zsa Zsa on its rhinestone-studded leash and drives to her job at the animal hospital.

4. **vacuous** (VAK yoo us) This adjective means "without substance or meaning," in short, "dull and stupid." It comes from the Latin word for "empty." Think "empty-headed."

- Knowing they'd rather be at the beach than sitting in a summer school classroom, the students stared **vacuously** at their teacher, clearly not listening to a word she said.
- At the cocktail party, the women sipped their drinks made **vacuous** conversation about the beauty of Michelangelo's art.

5. **inane** (in ANE) Like "vacuous," this adjective means "senseless" or "meaningless." The noun form is "inanity."

- The arguments made by the captain of the debating team were so **inane** that the team was forced to cut him before the next round of the championship.
- Tired of the **inanity** of Saturday morning children's programming, Jody and Paul decided to give away their television set and take their children on regular Saturday morning trips to the library.

6. **insipid** (in SIP id) From the Latin for "not savory" or "not tasty," this adjective means just that—"tasteless" or "dull." You can use it to describe the way a certain food tastes or just about anything else that's bland, including someone's personality. The noun forms are "insipidity" or "insipidness," but both are rarely used.

- "My chicken vindaloo was so **insipid** that I don't think I'll go back to Bombay Palace Cafe. I like my food to be spicier and more flavorful."
- Considering that he devoted himself to his job for over thirty years and was on such warm terms with his staff, Mr. Dobbs' goodbye speech at his retirement party was rather **insipid**.

7. **pique** (PEEK) This verb comes to us from the French and means "to prick" or "to provoke." It also can be used as a noun to mean "a feeling of wounded pride" or "indignation."

- "Your description of the restaurant really **piqued** my curiosity. I've never tasted Asian-Lithuanian cuisine before, and it sounds delicious," Patty said, patting her stomach.
- In a fit of **pique**, Lotta threw away her scale and said, "I'm tired of trying to look like the skinny models in all the fashion magazines. I'm chubby and I like myself just the way I am!"

8. **titillating** (TIT ill ate ing) From the Latin word for "tickle," this adjective means "to excite pleasurably," often erotically. The noun form is "titillation."

- In the 1950s, many love scenes were cut from popular films because Hollywood censors felt they would be too **titillating** to audiences.

- In last Sunday's book review, the plot description of James Harmon's new novel sounded so full of **titillation** that bookstores were sold out of the first printing by the end of the week.

9. **ponderous** (PON der us) This adjective means "having great weight." When a thought is "ponderous," however, it can be so heavy and unwieldy that it's actually "dull," another connotation of the word.

- The guest lecturer in Professor Zito's class, "Tupac Shakur and the Modern World," was so **ponderous** that most of the students could barely follow his thesis, and some even walked out in the middle.
- Nathaniel Hawthorne and Herman Melville often hiked on Monument Mountain near Arrowhead, Melville's home in Pittsfield, Massachusetts, and had heated and sometimes **ponderous** discussions about the state of contemporary literature.

10. **platitudinous** (PLAH tih TOO din us) A "platitude" is "a trite remark, often expressed as if it were something important." The adjective form describes any such expression. A good synonym is "banal" (bah NAL *or* BANE ul), which comes from the German for "summons to military service."

- "Spare me the **platitudes**, Pop," Ken retorted, when his father said, "Today is the first day of the rest of your life."
- The executives at the computer software and technology convention in Dallas found the keynote speaker's remarks on the future of high tech start-ups to be so **banal** that they booed him off the stage.

MAKE A MATCH #30

Sections 88–90

Match each word in the left-hand column with the phrase on the right that best suggests its meaning.

A.	arable	1. _____	large sofa
B.	armoire	2. _____	sideboard
C.	bucolic	3. _____	wardrobe
D.	cosmopolitan	4. _____	tall chest of drawers
E.	credenza	5. _____	pastoral
F.	davenport	6. _____	peaceful event or setting
G.	flaneur	7. _____	suitable for cultivation
H.	highboy	8. _____	relating to the city
I.	idyll	9. _____	perceptive city stroller
J.	inane	10. _____	sophisticated and worldly
K.	mundane	11. _____	swarming
L.	ponderous	12. _____	secular
M.	prosaic	13. _____	unimaginative
N.	quotidian	14. _____	occurring everyday
O.	teeming	15. _____	without substance
P.	urban	16. _____	weighty

PRACTICE, PRACTICE, PRACTICE #10

Sections 82–90

Directions: Select a word from the list below that best fits the blank in one of the sentences and place the letter in the blank.

A.	antimacassar	K.	mundane
B.	arable	L.	peremptory
C.	baleful	M.	quaff
D.	bucolic	N.	quotidian
E.	despot	O.	rustic
F.	desultory	P.	slake
G.	divan	Q.	sporadic
H.	faction	R.	teem
I.	imperious	S.	vintner
J.	inane	T.	virulent

1. Julie hated when her sister became _____ and ordered her to clean up her room and walk the dog.

2. John spends so much time with his _____ morning ritual of shaving, showering, and dressing that he never has time to read the newspaper.

3. After the team lost their third game in a row, the coach ordered them in a _____ voice to come to practice an hour earlier every day.

4. Mr. Swanson's secretaries thought that he was a _____ who demanded long hours at minimum pay.

5. Conflicted over their company's new hiring policies, the employees broke into different _____ and argued about the issues.

6. A _____ outbreak of the flu swept through the swim team, causing the best swimmers to miss the championship meet.

7. A _____ expression in his eyes, the rabid dog stumbled along the street toward Scout.

8. My uncle, a California _____, believes the particularly dry summer will prove disastrous for this year's grape harvest.

9. "You worry about the _____ matters of our Bible class such as where we're going to hold Saturday's picnic. I'll handle the spiritual work," Father Eccles told Mary.

10. A good _____ of ice-cold water is better than a soda on a really hot day.

11. No matter how much he drank, Joel could not _____ his thirst in the unbearable heat.

12. The new movie at the multiplex on Main Street was so _____ and so unoriginal that the boys left before it was over.

13. Gertrude always put an _____ on her armchair before Arthur arrived with his gelled hair.

14. Sandy lay back on the _____ in the parlor and listened contentedly to a Bach concerto.

15. The _____ view from my window included an open meadow filled with grazing sheep surrounded by a dense pine forest.

16. On parade days, the streets _____ with people lining up to see the band, the majorettes, and the homemade floats.

17. Because the land is so _____ in upstate New York, the local farmers grow everything from apples and pears to corn and alfalfa.

18. The Harrisons built a _____ log cabin and filled it with furniture crafted by local carpenters.

19. The head of the department made a _____ speech to his staff in September, moving from one topic to another without much coherence.

20. Tristan's interest in Renaissance painting inspired him to make _____ trips to Florence and the hilltowns of Tuscany.

C arpe diem—"seize the day"—the two Latin words that almost everybody knows. While not as widely used as "carpe diem," the words and phrases below have become part of the vocabulary of an educated English speaker.

1. **ad hominem** (ad HOM in em) Literally, it means "to the man," but the more precise meaning of "personal" can apply to a male or a female. It is most often (but not always) used to describe a kind of illogical personal attack.

- Rather than responding reasonably to his opponent's argument about international matters, the politician made an **ad hominem** attack, referring to the fact that she was overweight.

- Widget Inc. didn't really need an assistant associate director of internal affairs; the position was created **ad hominem** for the CEO's pampered nephew.

2. **alter ego** (ALL ter EE go) This phrase translates as "another me" or "another self." It refers to another aspect of one's identity.

- Although Neil works as a structural engineer, his **alter ego** is an expert on all things pertaining to ballet.

- Elena and Lila became such close friends that each regarded the other as her **alter ego**.

3. **bona fide** (BO na fied) Literally, this adjective phrase means "in good faith." In the plural, **bona fides** (BO na FEE dayz), however, is roughly a synonym for the noun "credentials."

- The real estate agent believed the most recent bid for the lush waterside property was not a **bona fide** offer, for the property was worth at least twice as much.

- At her first meeting of the International Spelunkers Association, Hanna offered several photographs of herself amid stalactites and stalagmites to establish her **bona fides** as a seasoned explorer of caves.

4. **caveat** (CAV ee aht) In English, this word functions as a noun meaning "a warning." In Latin, it's a verb in the subjunctive: "Let him—or her—beware." A Latin phrase or two retaining that verbal sense has come into English.

- Before closing the sale of the outsize canine, the breeder offered a **caveat** to Karl: "You probably don't want to make him angry."
- The phrase "trigger warning," which has recently sprung up on college campuses, carries the sense of an old Latin phrase **caveat lector**, "let the reader beware."

5. **compos mentis** (KOM pohs MEN tis) Originally a legal term for "a sound mind," this phrase and its opposite, **non compos mentis**, have drifted into more casual use, often with a humorous edge.

- The big blowout party for his graduation left Brandon feeling a tad **non compos mentis** the next day.
- When Jerome, who easily becomes seasick, was invited on a Caribbean cruise, he declined, saying, "Not so long as I'm **compos mentis**."

6. **de facto, de jure** (di FAK toh, di JUR ah) The first phrase means "in fact, in practice" while the second contrastingly means "as a matter of law." Even when this duet doesn't appear together, the use of one puts a reader in mind of the other.

- While racial segregation is, **de jure**, outlawed, civil rights advocates note many **de facto** examples.
- Terry and Chris have never gotten a license or had a wedding, but they consider themselves, **de facto**, married.

7. **erratum, errata** (er ROT um, er ROT ah) The singular and the plural mean, simply, "error" and "errors." Maybe the Latinate form adds a touch of scholarly class.

- A lone **erratum** marred the perfection of the title page, but printing "Meville" for "Melville" was a laughable mistake.
- The university press included an **errata** sheet with the volume, so that readers could, on publication, note incidental infelicities.

8. **minutiae** (min OO sha) Translating as "minutes," this word carries the sense of "trifles, unimportant details." Note the very English pronunciation.

- Only your very best friend can listen attentively as you recount the **minutiae** of your day—the way you couldn't find a pair of matching socks, the phone call that upset your coffee break, your random memory of an old boyfriend.
- The prize-winning biography included both the major themes of the Declaration of Independence as well as the **minutiae** of the lives of the Founding Fathers.

9. **pro bono** (pro BO no) In a nutshell, this phrase means "with no financial charge." Literally, it translates as "for the good."

- The Legal Aid program has lawyers who will work **pro bono** to help indigent clients prepare for a trial.
- Although Ian's summer job was **pro bono** work, he gained skills and experience that will enhance his resume.

10. **rara avis, sui generis** (RAIR ah AY vis *or* RAH rah AH vis, SOO ee JEN er iss) Two for one: both these phrases mean, in essence, "one of a kind." The first translates as "rare bird," the second as "of its own sort."

- A woman fluent in Japanese, English, and Anglo-Saxon? Haruko is indeed a **rara avis**.
- Col. McIntosh is **sui generis**—a Farsi-speaking career military man who plays the lute, teaches art history, and has a household shrine to Elvis Presley.

11. **sine qua non** (SIN ah kwa NOHN) An elliptical phrase referring to an absolutely essential thing or condition; it translates, roughly, as "that without which nothing is possible."

- Earning a PhD is a **sine qua non** if one wishes to become a tenured university professor.
- When Andrew Jackson received an honorary doctor of laws from Harvard University, he offered a toast entirely in Latlish: "E pluribus unum*—**sine qua non!**"

  * *e pluribus unum* (EE PLOOR ih bus OO num) "one out of many"; a common description of the USA—one country formed of many states.

92

W e all know that American cooking has borrowed many tips from French cuisine; similarly many French words have added a certain *je ne sais quois* (an indefinable quality) to English vocabulary.

1. **riposte** (rih POST) Used as either a verb or a noun, the word means "quick retort." In the sport of fencing, it means "a quick thrust given after parrying an opponent's lunge." It can be used to mean any clever, retaliatory reply—in words or actions.

- Insulted by his father's sarcastic remark about his poor table manners, James **riposted** with a flippant, "It must be in my genes." (The word "flippant" means "disrespectful levity.")

- The flirtatious banter between the countess and the duke was filled with ironic observations, teasing insults, and witty **ripostes**.

2. **risqué** (ris KAY) This adjective comes from the French word that means "to risk." It's no surprise that it means indelicate or bordering on the inappropriate.

- The plunging décolletage of her dress was a bit **risqué** for a Sunday church service. (Décolletage also comes from the French and means plunging neckline.)

- The professor's vulgar joke was a bit **risqué**, even for a class full of college students.

3. **fait accompli** (FAYT a com PLEE) This noun literally translates from the French as "accomplished fact." We use it to suggest a completed and therefore irreversible action. The plural, by the way, is faits accomplis.

- Her announcement to the press to run for mayor was a **fait accompli** and there was no turning back now.

- The CEO had second thoughts about the deal, but his signature on the contract made it a **fait accompli**.

4. **soignée** (swan YAY) Like so many of the words English has taken from the French, here's another word that evokes stylishness. This adjective comes from the Old French word that means "to take care of." We use it today to mean fashionable or elegantly sophisticated and well-groomed. It can, by the way, also be spelled with one "é."

- The **soignée** movie star arrived at the opening in a Chanel evening gown with matching accessories.
- The couple stopped for a nightcap at a **soignée** little club not far from the theater district.

5. **pastiche** (pah STEESH) This noun has two different but related meanings. The first is an artistic work that openly imitates, often satirically, the works of other artists. The other more simply means hodgepodge or collection of mismatched parts.

- The basilica in the Piazza San Marco in Venice is a **pastiche** of different architectural styles from several centuries.
- The musical was a **pastiche** of Broadway shows, gently mocking the overly romantic plots and melodramatic lyrics of the most popular productions.

6. **matinee** (ma tin AY) Although this noun comes from the French word "*matin,*" meaning morning, it actually means a performance that occurs in the daytime, usually in the afternoon. Although it's almost always used to describe a theater performance or a movie showing, it's also related to the Old French word "*matins,*" an ecclesiastical word that means morning prayer. It can also be used as an adjective:

- If we catch the **matinee** performance of the pastiche, we'll have plenty of time to go to the museum before it closes.

7. **insouciant** (in SOO see ont) Coming from the Old French word for "not troubled," this adjective means nonchalant (another French word that means "cooly unconcerned") or blithely indifferent. The noun form is "insouciance."

- Mrs. Winthrop walked her dog Bubbles with her usual **insouciance**, allowing him to jump on strangers and trample the gardens of her neighbors.
- I admired his **insouciant** expression after hearing the devastating news about his mother-in-law.

8. **faux** (FOH) Coming from the Old French word *fals*, meaning false, we use this adjective to mean fake or artificial. When we combine it with the French word *pas* or "step," as in *faux pas*, it's a noun that means social blunder.

- The hypocritical woman felt her moral edge because she was wearing a **faux** leopard coat.
- The **faux** sophistication of the King and the Duke was soon apparent to Huckleberry Finn.

9. **gauche** (GOASH) This adjective comes from the French word that means left or left-handed, but it also means awkward or clumsy, lacking social polish.

- The garrulous woman was considered **gauche** for talking during the funeral service. It was certainly considered a faux pas.

- The debonair urbanites were stunned by the **gauche** behavior of the country hostess who served apple juice with her *coq au vin*. ("Debonair" also comes from the French and means "carefree or jaunty.")

10. **anomie** (an oh MEE) The original French meaning of this noun is lawlessness, but it has taken on a more complex social and philosophical meaning. When one suffers anomie, one has a feeling of alienation and purposelessness caused by a lack of standards, values, and ideals.

- His silent friend wandered away in solitude and **anomie**.

- The dark, brooding student, lost in his thoughts, could not conceal his **anomie**.

93

All the words below have come to us from German. They are now commonly used in academic or intellectual discussions. They often have the ability to express in one compact word an idea that requires a longer English explanation.

1. **angst** (ONGST) This noun means "a feeling of neurotic fear or anxiety that often is accompanied by depression." It's related to the Old German word for "anger" and was considered a foreign word until the 1940s when Sigmund Freud's writings made it popular in English.

- Overwhelmed with **angst** over his impending graduation from college, Arthur stayed in bed all day and suffered insomnia at night.

- "You are not psychotic," said Dr. Melrose, Johanna's psychiatrist. "You are understandably feeling a bit of **angst** about your parents' divorce. Your anxiety attacks will subside if you continue to talk about your feelings."

2. **schadenfreude** (SHAWD en froid eh) This noun comes from the German words for "damage" and "joy" and means a pleasure derived from the misfortune of others.

- Revelling in a bit of **schadenfreude**, Oliver was happy to see his parents blame his brother for the Ming vase the boys broke while playing catch in the living room. He was tired of being the one who always got in trouble.

- Although she didn't want to admit to her **schadenfreude**, Abby was happy to hear that everyone but she failed the math final; she thought it would make her seem especially smart to her teacher.

3. **weltanshauung** (VELT an shung) From the German words for "world" and "view," this noun means a "perspective" or "world view."

- According to the Elizabethan **weltanshauung**, social, moral, and political values were determined by the principles of the Great Chain of Being.

- "If we all lived by the **weltanshauung** of today's teenagers," reflected the professor of pop culture at the midwestern college, "love, culture, and even religion could be determined by the internet."

4. weltschmerz (VELT shmertz) This noun comes from the German words for "world" and "pain" and means sadness over the evils of the world. The word was popularized by the nineteenth-century German poet Heinrich Heine.

- After watching the eleven o'clock news and seeing so many stories about violence, poverty, and war, Justin was overwhelmed by a sense of **weltschmerz**.
- Woody Allen's films are filled with **weltschmerz**, forcing audiences to ponder evil in the world, even as they laugh about it.

5. wunderkind (VUN der kinnd) From the German words "prodigy" and "child," this word is used to mean a person of remarkable talent or ability who achieves great success at a young age.

- A musical **wunderkind**, Sarita was playing violin at Carnegie Hall by the time she was nine.
- "The after-school math class is not just for **wunderkinds**," explained Ms. Ruddy. "Any child who is interested in math is welcome."

6. wanderlust (VON der lust) This noun means a very strong desire to travel and comes from the German words for "wander" and "desire." A related word is "wanderjahr," which is used to describe a year spent traveling, wandering, or taking an absence from one's work.

- Overcome by **wanderlust**, the Smith-Joneses both quit their jobs to travel around the world and take photographs of mountain ranges and oceans.
- Although Cliff was very happy at college, he decided to take a **wanderjahr** after his sophomore year and hike the Appalachian Trail.

7. bildungsroman (BIL dungs row MAHN) A popular word in the English classroom, this is a noun for a novel about the moral, psychological, and intellectual development of a youthful main character. It comes from the German words for "novel" (roman) and "formation."

- J. D. Salinger's *Catcher in the Rye* is a **bildungsroman** about the poignant experiences of Holden Caulfield after he drops out of prep school and tries to cope with what he calls the "phoneys" of New York City.
- *Adventures of Huckleberry Finn* is a **bildungsroman** that details the development of a boy who must confront his feelings about race, religion, and education in the pre-Civil War South.

8. gestalt (geh SHTALT) This noun comes from the German word for "shape," "form," or "appearance," but it is a bit more complicated than that. A gestalt is a physical, psychological, or symbolic pattern of elements so unified that its properties cannot be derived from the sum of its parts. In other words, the "gestalt" of something is its overall impression or sense, a whole that suggests more than the sum of its parts. It is also the name of a school of psychology founded in the early part of the twentieth century.

- The **gestalt** of the students in Mr. Ramirez's first period class was that they were bored; in fact, they were exhausted by yesterday's exam and not ready to absorb any new material.

- The **gestalt** created by the architect's plans for the contemporary art museum reflected the innovation, creativity, and originality of the work that would be displayed inside.

9. leitmotif (LITE mow teef) This is a noun that is used in discussing music or literature. In music, it is a melodic phrase, especially in Wagnerian opera, associated with a specific character, situation, or element. In a novel, it is a dominant or recurring theme.

- In his 1845 opera *Tannhauser*, Wagner uses an orchestral **leitmotif** to convey the theme of redemption through a woman's love.

- The idea of an individual's impotence in the face of oppressive bureaucracy is a **leitmotif** in the works of Franz Kafka.

10. zeitgeist (ZITE guyst) From the German words for "spirit" and "time," this word means "spirit of the age" or the taste and outlook that is characteristic of a particular time period or generation.

- Willy Loman's aspirations to be a successful salesman were typical of the post-World War II **zeitgeist**; his goals were to pay off the mortgage on his house, support his wife and family, and raise two ambitious sons.

- "Online dating is part of the **zeitgeist**," reflected Professor Brown. "We are a generation that believes that all of our needs can be met by the internet."

Sections 91–93

Match each word in the left-hand column with the phrase on the right that best suggests its meaning.

A.	alter ego	1. _____	spirit of the times
B.	angst	2. _____	world view
C.	anomie	3. _____	many small details
D.	faux	4. _____	unusual person
E.	gauche	5. _____	an essential part of
F.	insouciant	6. _____	awkward
G.	minutiae	7. _____	not of sound mind
H.	non compos mentis	8. _____	alternative personality
I.	pastiche	9. _____	retaliatory retort
J.	rara avis	10. _____	risky, inappropriate
K.	riposte	11. _____	elegantly sophisticated
L.	risqué	12. _____	collection of mismatched parts
M.	sine qua non	13. _____	nonchalant
N.	soignée	14. _____	neurotic anxiety
O.	weltanshauung	15. _____	fake
P.	zeitgeist	16. _____	alienation

T he words in this section all mean either "fat" or "skinny." Why use a harsh or blunt word when you can use one of the euphemisms listed below? (A "euphemism" [YOO fem iz im] is a gentle or indirect term that substitutes for a more offensive word.)

1. **rotund** (row TUND) Think of the shape of the rotunda on the Capitol in Washington. This adjective is used to describe a person, not a building, who is round or plump. It comes from the Latin word meaning "round." The noun form is "rotundity."

- The **rotund** professor disguised his weight with a well-fitted vest and a pair of crisply ironed slacks.

- Harold was so **rotund** that he took two seats on the airplane in order to fly comfortably.

2. **svelte** (SVELT) From the Italian word that means "to stretch out," this adjective means "slender" or "graceful in figure, thin."

- The **svelte** young woman had the figure of a fashion model and was able to wear the designer clothing, which was cut quite narrowly.

- Mario's ordinarily chubby body looked quite **svelte** in the Italian-cut suit.

3. **corpulent** (KOR pyoo lent) From the Latin word meaning "body," this adjective means "a lot of body" or "excessively fat." Someone who is corpulent is obese. The noun form is "corpulence."

- "A high-fat diet is almost guaranteed to cause **corpulence**," said Dr. Pritikin. "Stick with fruits and vegetables if you want to stay slim."

- Despite his **corpulence**, the actor Jackie Gleason was a graceful dancer. He carried himself like a man who was one hundred pounds lighter.

4. **emaciated** (ee MAYSH ee ate ed) The direct opposite of corpulent, someone who is emaciated is excessively skinny, usually as a result of starvation.

- After months of near starvation, the men and women in the concentration camps were pale and **emaciated**.

- Twiggy was a fashion model in the sixties whose **emaciated** frame provoked many teenagers to all but starve themselves.

5. **portly** (PORT lee) Although this adjective has the same meaning as corpulent, someone who is portly is generally more comfortable with his or her size. Although the word once meant "majestic" or "grand," it is now only used to connote "pleasingly plump."

- The **portly** woman waltzed gracefully onto the dance floor, obviously comfortable with her large size and slim dance partner.
- The **portly** gentleman tucked a napkin under his chin and dug into a heaping plate of spaghetti and meatballs, oblivious to the amused stares of the slimmer diners at the restaurant.

6. **ravenous** (RAV en us) Although this word doesn't exactly mean either skinny or fat it seems to belong here because it means "excessively hungry." From the Old French word that means "take by force," someone who is ravenous will do just about anything to get some food.

- **Ravenous** after running the marathon, Christina came home and devoured a huge steak, a plate of french fries, and a slice of apple pie.
- The **ravenous** hyenas devoured the remains of the wildebeest left by the lion.

7. **stout** (STOWT) Although this adjective also means "brave, determined, or resolute," it is more often used to mean "thickset or bulky in figure." It's also the word for a very dark beer or ale. Someone who drinks a lot of stout will probably become stout.

- Botero is famous for painting **stout** figures of men and women, often wearing bathing suits or scant clothing.
- The **stout** matron eyed the teenagers in tight jeans and cropped T-shirts disdainfully, knowing she could never wear such clothing.

8. **anorectic** (an or EK tic) Although this word is often associated with anorexia nervosa, a psychological disorder marked by a fear of becoming obese and a persistent unwillingness to eat, the adjective actually just means "marked by loss of appetite." It comes from the Greek word for "without appetite." The word is also often spelled and pronounced "anorexic."

- The **anorectic** girl took one look at the plate piled high with food and asked to be excused from the table.
- The heat and the malaria had an **anorectic** effect on the villagers; they were all thin as rails.

9. **buxom** (BUKS um) This adjective means "healthily plump" or "full-bosomed" and is reserved for describing females. It is quite similar to the Yiddish word "*zaftig*." A woman who is buxom is not fat; she is curvaceous.

- The **buxom** barmaid brought a tray of beer to the table, bending low as she distributed the glasses. All of the men grinned lasciviously (a word that means "lustily" or "lecherously").

- The actress Mae West was famous for her **buxom** figure, which was considered voluptuous (sensual) by both men and women.

10. **embonpoint** (OM bone pwan) The only noun in this list, this word comes from the French expression for "in good condition." In English, however, it means "rather plump."

- Accentuating her **embonpoint**, Margot wore a tight black dress to the cocktail party. Though her size was exaggerated, she looked quite alluring amongst the skinnier women.

- Notwithstanding her short stature and **embonpoint**, Selena made a wonderful fashion model because she wore her clothing with great style and élan (see "Do It in Style" section).

Although Shakespeare's character Juliet queried the importance of names in the phrase that gives this section its title, the playwright himself never undervalued them. And it's a pretty good bet he knew all the words in this list below.

1. nomenclature (NO men klay ture) The Romans had a special class of slaves called "nomenklators," whose function was to remind their masters of the names of those they met. The modern word "nomenclature" translates as "name call" and refers to a system or arrangement of words in particular discipline.

- When he began babbling about "xylem" and "phloem," I threw up my hands and said, "Please stop! I don't know the **nomenclature** of botany."

- When Callie graduated from law school, Will said, "Wow, you're an attorney now." She responded, "Get your **nomenclature** straight. I'm a lawyer. Attorneys have passed the bar exam."

2. taxonomy (tax OHN uh me) This noun refers to a method or system of arranging or classifying or, more loosely, a science of naming or labeling.

- The average high school cafeteria offers a study in informal **taxonomy**: your student guide is not slow to point out the "cool table" or the hallowed seats of the "jocks."

- Scientific **taxonomy** is very complex, for scientists must observe carefully in order to decide why, for example, opossums should not be grouped with porcupines.

3. pseudonym (SOO doh nim) The silent "p" at the start distinguishes this noun. It literally means "false name" and is most often used for the pen names chosen by some authors.

- Mark Twain is one of the best-known **pseudonyms**; Samuel Langhorne Clemens used it for all of his novels.

- Mary Ann Evans, a woman living in nineteenth-century England, chose a male **pseudonym**—George Eliot—for her novels.

4. **moniker** (MON ik er) Some see it as slang, some don't. Either way this noun is a name, a nickname, a pseudonym—what you're called. The origin puzzles linguists, who speculate that it may be a blend of "monogram" and "signature."

- "Put your **moniker** there on the dotted line," said the salesman, "and you've bought yourself a fine used car."
- If groups like Nine Inch Nails or the Dandy Warhols had less memorable **monikers**, would they be less known?

5. **epithet** (EP ih thet) In the world of names, this noun refers to a term used in addition to a person's name or as a substitution for the name. Out of the world of names, it can mean "an abusive or contemptuous word or phrase" such as profane or obscene language.

- The classical hero Achilles is characterized by the **epithet** "fleet-footed."
- As soon as the drivers in the two-car collision determined that no one was hurt, they jumped out of their vehicles and began angrily hurling **epithets** at each other.

6. **diminutive** (di MIN yoo tiv) Generally speaking, this word can be an adjective meaning "small," but in the category of names, it's a noun meaning "a form of a name expressing either affection" or—contrastingly—"contempt."

- When she was growing up, Susanna's father called her "Suzie-Q," a distinctive **diminutive** she loved to hear from him even after she turned twenty-one.
- The experienced politician raised his brow at opposition candidate Hiram Smith and said, "No, Smithy. We never went to war against Australia." The **diminutive** magnified his obvious contempt.

7. **sobriquet** (so bri KAY) This synonym for a nickname or an epithet comes straight from French where, patronizingly enough, it once meant "to chuck under the chin."

- Mr. Hanly's extensive vocabulary prompted his students to coin the admiring **sobriquet** "The Walking Dictionary."
- "The Great Cham" is a **sobriquet** used variously for the Khan of the Tartary region in Asia and for the eighteenth-century writer and dictionary maker Samuel Johnson.

8. **misnomer** (mis NO mer) This noun refers to an inappropriate or inaccurate name for a person or thing.

- To say I made eye contact with him would be a **misnomer**, for I found myself entranced by his bushy eyebrows and could not quit staring at them.
- When I asked Mr. Monaghan to name his best student, he replied, "It's Lucinda Poor—what a **misnomer**! She's anything but 'poor.'"

9. **appellation** (a pel AY shun) A name (usually one other than the proper name) or title given to someone or something. If you survived even a week in a French course, you'll remember Je m'appelle .... (My name is...)

- When I referred to the potter as an "artist," he modestly said, "I don't deserve so grand an **appellation**. I'm just a simple craftsman."
- The intricate rules of the Electoral College may cause the country to give the **appellation** of "president" to someone who was not the people's choice.

10. **shibboleth** (SHIB e leth) This noun refers to a password or a distinctive pronunciation that shows that a person is or is not an "insider," a person deserving the name of that group. (The word comes from a passage in the Hebrew scriptures: two tribes were distinguished by the inability of one to give the correct pronunciation of "shibboleth.") Today the word is also used in a looser sense for a distinctive trait of a certain group.

- The World War II film depicted the dazed Sgt. Pritchett desperately trying to recall the piece of baseball trivia that was the **shibboleth** of his unit. Without it, his comrades might think him a spy.
- The ease with which profane or obscene language is used in public may be the **shibboleth** of generational difference; older folk grew up with a taboo on so-called four-letter words.

Am I Timid? Or Are You Intimidating?

A m I scared because I'm temperamentally fearful? Or am I scared because you're so fearsome (scary)? This list offers some words for either possibility.

1. craven (KRAY ven) As adjective or as noun, it simply describes or refers to a coward or cowardly behavior. When the song from the classic Western film *High Noon* refers to a "craven coward," it's just doubling up the intensity of the word.

- Ms. Chapin pointed out to her students the line "thou... art sure no **craven**" in one of Poe's most famous poems: "The bird the speaker addresses wasn't cowardly, I agree, but also there aren't many words that rhyme with 'raven.'"

- While the corrupt but brave Don Giovanni, in Mozart's opera of the same name, boldly confronts the spirit of the departed Commendatore, his servant Leporello is **cravenly** hiding under the banquet table.

2. pusillanimous (PEW sil AN ih mus) If you're really angry at someone's cowardly behavior, this is the adjective to hiss at him or her—very satisfying in its sound! Even the word history is satisfying: it describes a spirit (Latin *animus*) like that of a weak, little animal such as a pullet, a young chicken!

- "There are times it is not only a duty but a pleasure to speak one's mind," said Ms. Cunningham sternly, "and expressing my disgust at your **pusillanimous** actions is one of those times."

- **Pusillanimity** can be found in the home as well as on the battlefield, for it may be emotional as well as physical.

3. timorous (TIM er us) To be timorous is to be full of apprehension, of fear. The same root word gives us "timid." Do NOT confuse this word with "temerity," which means the opposite—"daring"—and can be found in section 4.

- "Wee, **timorous**, cowering beastie," wrote poet Robert Burns to a field mouse, frightened because her nest has just been overturned by a plow.

- During the question and answer period after the talk, Walter wanted to address the speaker but was too **timorous** to speak up.

4. **tremulous** (TREM yoo lus) This adjective describes something physically trembling or quaking, particularly, though not exclusively, in response to fear.

- When the armed mugger demanded his wallet, Chuck **tremulously** brought it forth from his pocket.
- In a **tremulous** but clear voice, Rita spoke up to Mrs. Tipton, her second grade teacher, to protest the fact that her friend Ellie had been put into the dark cloakroom as a punishment.

5. **harrowing** (HAIR oh ing) If something really frightens you or distresses you, you might describe it with this adjective. A harrow is, literally, a farm implement that breaks up clods of earth, but these days the word is commonly used for an experience that gives you the figurative feeling of having your insides ripped out as if you'd been literally "harrowed."

- "It **harrows** me with fear and wonder," says Hamlet when, on the dark battlement of the castle, he first sees the ghost of his father.
- "What a **harrowing** experience for you," said Ms. Pitt sympathetically, "to have been stuck in that subway car for forty minutes."

6. **skittish** (SKIT ish) No, it doesn't mean you feel like putting on a skit. It means you're nervous or timid or you're undependably likely to change your mind.

- "I have a driver's license and all that," said Donna, "but I'm **skittish** about driving on anything more challenging than a quiet country road."
- "Yes, I know the Foxes said they'd buy the property, but don't count on it till the contract is signed because first-home buyers are notoriously **skittish**," counseled the real estate agent.

7. **rebarbative** (re BARB ih tiv) This adjective describes something repelling, something that irritates, such as, say, rubbing your cheek against the prickly stubble of a beard. Yes, the root word is the Latin for "beard" (as in "barber").

- In his later years, Nasby became increasingly **rebarbative**, often answering a friendly query such as, "How are you today?" with a sarcastic rebuff like, "Who wants to know?"
- While Edmund has his **rebarbative** moments, he can also be welcoming and friendly; the trick is to catch him in a good mood.

8. **impregnable** (im PREG nuh bul) If it's literally impregnable, it's something like a fort or a castle that cannot be taken by force. In the extended sense, a person is impregnable if he or she is likely to be right and is extremely firm in his or her convictions.

- "Of this, as of everything, I am certain," said Aunt Augusta confidently, reinforcing her nephew's sense of her **impregnability**.

- Ross was such an obnoxious person that I longed to refute his claims, but eventually I had to admit his facts were correct, his argument **impregnable**.

9. **redoubtable** (re DOWT uh bul) Don't try to guess the meaning of this adjective, for the person it describes arouses, depending on the context, either fear or respect. That kind of person isn't usually given to self-doubt!

- In the seventeenth century the English Parliament summoned the **redoubtable** Oliver Cromwell to lead their forces against the Royalist Army.
- Because Prof. Castillo was intolerant of error and demanded exacting precision of her students, they learned a lot, even though they found her personally **redoubtable,** not the type of teacher with whom they might have an informal chat.

10. **formidable** (FORM id ul bul *or* for MID uh bul) This adjective frequently describes a person or situation that arouses fear or dread, though in less personal contexts something formidable might inspire admiration (see the second sentence below).

- Ariel decided to live with the annoyances of her medical condition than to face the **formidable** prospect of the major surgery that could remedy them.
- Meg has excellent grades, high test scores, extracurricular activities she's devoted to, and a winning personality—a **formidable** combination for a college applicant.

MAKE A MATCH #32

Sections 94–96

Match each word in the left-hand column with the phrase on the right that best suggests its meaning.

A.	appellation	1. _____	system of classification
B.	buxom	2. _____	nickname often used for a child
C.	diminutive	3. _____	a literary alias
D.	epithet	4. _____	a curvaceous woman
E.	harrowing	5. _____	shaking, trembling
F.	impregnable	6. _____	somewhat overweight
G.	misnomer	7. _____	title for a person
H.	nomenclature	8. _____	really scary
I.	portly	9. _____	very cowardly
J.	pseudonym	10. _____	can't be defeated
K.	pusillanimous	11. _____	contemptuous word or phrase
L.	ravenous	12. _____	inappropriate name
M.	svelte	13. _____	very hungry
N.	taxonomy	14. _____	fashionably thin
O.	tremulous	15. _____	system of naming

I f you've read or seen Shakespeare's play *The Merchant of Venice*, you may recall a great speech by the female character Portia (disguised as a judge). It begins "The quality of mercy is not strained." On this page as well, "mercy" is not strained but is expanded to ten words, each of which has some connection with the concept of escaping punishment.

1. exonerate (eg ZAHN er ate) The root words have the idea of "laying down a burden." And, indeed, if you are exonerated, you are freed from a responsibility or blame, whether in a legal matter or something less official.

- Graham was accused of being the "redheaded boy" who threw an egg out the second floor of the school building onto a passerby in the street below, but he **exonerated** himself by having every student in his calculus class affirm that he was in the first floor calculus classroom at the time.

- "No officer worth his salt," said Major Rigsby-Radnor, "would *want* to be **exonerated** from his duty of fighting for Her Majesty Queen Griselda; in fact, I insist on leading the charge."

2. clemency (KLEM en see) An easy synonym for mercy, kindness, or even mildness (see second sentence below).

- The defense lawyer pleaded with Judge Hogarth to show **clemency** in sentencing in that his client was the sole support of two relatives and a former racing greyhound.

- "**Inclement** weather all weekend," said the weather reporter. "All picnics should be canceled."

3. indemnity (in DEM ni tee) This noun is defined as "security against hurt, loss, or damage," as in the financial form an insurance company might be able to provide.

- Slowly recovering from heartbreak, Ellen wistfully asked her mom, "Why isn't there some way to **indemnify** yourself against emotional distress? I'd rather lose money than hurt so much."

- Have you seen the old movie classic *Double Indemnity* about a wicked scheme to defraud an insurance company by attempting to stage an accidental death?

4. **amnesty** (AM nus tee) Talk about mercy! If you receive amnesty for a wrongdoing, you get a pardon, either literally or figuratively. The root words mean "absence of memory"—the bad thing you did is literally forgotten.

- The public library has declared an **amnesty** period of two weeks: anyone returning overdue books during this period will not be charged a fine.

- "Dad, I'm not asking for complete **amnesty** for violating my curfew by twenty minutes," wailed Ned to his stern father, who had grounded him for a month. "Couldn't you just give me some kind of community service?"

5. **forbear** (for BEAR) As a verb, this word expresses the idea of patiently enduring something unpleasant or refraining from something you might otherwise do. Don't confuse the verb with the noun forbear (or forebear), which is an ancestor, even if you're not a bear.

- "I am noted for the kindness of my disposition," said Gwendolyn, "but I have **forborne** as long as I can your insolence to me."

- **Forbear** the waving of your red handkerchief at that bull; he's said to be excitable.

6. **absolve** (ab ZOLV) There's often a religious connotation to this kind of forgiveness. Its root word means "to loosen" (think "dissolve").

- "I just can't read all of this thick Sunday newspaper. Will you **absolve** me of my moral duty to be thoroughly informed?" said Eugene to his wife.

- Author Frank McCourt states that he now, as an adult, has some understanding of his father but that he can still not grant him full **absolution** for abandoning a wife and young children.

7. **lenient** (LEEN ee unt) If you're lenient, you have a mild and tolerant outlook and forgo harsh punishment of someone even in a situation where you might have a moral right to such. "Indulgent" might be a rough synonym.

- "My parents were too harsh with me, so now I'm too **lenient** with my kids. They'll probably grow up and be too harsh with their kids," sighed Mr. McGoogle. "Is there any way to get it completely right?"

- Judge DiLucia was given to quirky judicial decisions. For example, he once exercised extreme **leniency** to a defendant who happened to have the same birthday.

8. **mitigate** (MIT uh gayt) This verb contains the idea of something being made less harsh, less severe. You'll often hear it in the phrase "mitigating circumstances," meaning that there are reasons for regarding the phenomenon in a softer light.

- Fernanda attempted to **mitigate** the degree of bitterness she felt toward her sister Roxanna, who had, she believed, wronged her but soon realized she needed the help and healing of time.

- "Dear Dragon," cried the maiden, "please **mitigate** your fiery wrath toward me. I promise to crochet a lovely mat for your lair, if you'll let me go."

9. **condone** (con DOAN) In its purest sense, this verb means "the overlooking or forgiving of wrongdoing." It is now being used in a somewhat stronger sense of meaning the giving of unspoken approval to something.

- The old saying from the '60s—"If you're not part of the solution, you're part of the problem"—implies that **condoning** wrongdoing is as bad as committing the action yourself.

- "I cannot **condone** the fact that you threw your lanyard at Skippy," said the group leader to the camper, "but since she has forgiven you, I will not administer a punishment."

10. **reprieve** (re PREEV) As a noun or a verb, this word refers to the granting of a temporary delay in a punishment or in the performance of a harsh duty. Sometimes you'll see the phrase "a temporary reprieve," but if it's permanent, it's not a reprieve.

- The prisoner received a thirty-day **reprieve** from the execution of his death sentence to enable his lawyer to investigate further the anonymous call that purported to offer new evidence.

- Entering the huge vaulted cathedral where a choir was singing Gregorian chants offered a welcome **reprieve** from both the hot July day and the noise of the plaza.

The Good, the Bad, and the Ugly

A moray is an eel, morale is spirit or confidence, morels are mushrooms, but morals are values, standards, principles of right and wrong, as defined in your society.

1. mores (MORE aze) This noun, always plural and spelled and pronounced exactly the same in English as in the Latin original, refers to customs, defining standards of behavior in any one culture. The Latin is the origin of the English word "morals" but not a synonym.

- "Is it okay to wear our shorts into this holy site?" queried Lindsay. "I don't know the local **mores**."

- **Mores** change gradually over time: these days even the best-mannered of women leave their white gloves at home when they head out for a day of shopping.

2. turpitude (TURP ih tude) This noun is a strong term for immoral, even shameful behavior. It is reserved for actions considered really "bad" in our society such as, for example, child molestation.

- Although the jury found Mr. Brown not guilty beyond a reasonable doubt, an accusation of a crime of such **turpitude** as his will follow him all his life.

- In Shakespeare's *Antony and Cleopatra*, the disappointed Enobarbus wonders how Antony would have rewarded his possible *good* acts "when my **turpitude** / Thou dost so crown with gold."

3. louche (LOOSH) This French adjective has come into English with the meaning of "possessing questionable taste or morality." Unlike the very serious "turpitude," it often is used with an air of slight amusement or mild amazement. Since it derives from the Latin word meaning "one-eyed," perhaps it is associated with slightly shady behavior at which one might wink, not shriek.

- "Algernon, you old scoundrel! I wouldn't have been startled to run into you in a **louche** bar in the wrong part of town but meeting you at a prayer breakfast is a surprise!"

- At seventeen, Charley is still a minor, but his parents give him complete freedom in choosing his friends, even tolerating the rather **louche** Ferdinand at their family dinner table.

4. **effete** (e FEET) Not immoral, "effete" denotes behavior or manner that is lacking in vital force or marked by self-indulgence. "Robust" might be given as an opposite. It has been often confused with "effeminate" (describing a man with traits deemed more appropriate to a woman), but the difference in meaning deserves preservation.

- In typical movies about the Wild West, the Eastern male new to the town is often shown as being **effete**—an overrefined creature who couldn't shoe a horse no matter how pressing the need.

- Hardy pioneer American women were far from **effete**, totally unlike the stereotype of females as delicate creatures requiring male protection.

5. **amoral** (AY mor uhl) This adjective means "completely lacking in any moral sense." The "a" represents the Latin prefix meaning "absence of." Don't confuse the word with "amorous," which means "relating to love."

- Prof. Demaris objects to journalists who describe hurricanes as being cruel or wicked. "Weather," he pronounced, "is strictly **amoral**."

- The criminal refused to make any statement of contrition about his act; in fact, viewers of the trial were bothered that he seemed so completely **amoral**.

6. **rank** (rhymes with bank) As an adjective, this word means "offensive." When it's not being used to describe behavior, it might describe a strong, unpleasant smell. Occasionally, it means "complete, total" with a sense of disapproval.

- "I'm not going to let some **rank** amateur come into my office and tell me how to run my business," snorted McGonigle.

- Shakespeare's Claudius was evil enough to kill his brother but was not amoral: he had enough conscience to lament, "O, my offense is **rank**. It smells to heaven."

7. **nefarious** (nuh FAIR ee us) If you're nefarious, you're wicked, stunningly wicked. The adjective derives from the Latin meaning "violation of divine law."

- "To call these terrorists '**nefarious**' would be redundant," noted Representative Hawkins.

- As the pilgrims enter the lowest circles of Dante's hell, they encounter the most **nefarious** of sinners—those who betrayed friends or relatives, including Ugolino, who may have eaten the bodies of his dead children.

8. **venal** (VEE nuhl) The venal person is corrupt, crooked, willing to sacrifice any principles if the price is right. Appropriately enough, it derives from the Latin word for "sale."

- "Throw the rascals out!" is a catchphrase used at election time in reference to **venal** politicians.
- One doesn't like to associate **venality** with the teaching profession, so it is all the more disturbing to learn that Mr. Whitt, the chemistry teacher, had been accepting bribes in exchange for high grades.

9. probity (PROBE ih tee) There are even a few words for *good* morals. A person of probity is a person of complete integrity.

- "The morals of a person of **probity** will never need probing," opined Bill, who could work a pun into almost anything.
- While his private life is not without rumors, no one has ever questioned Senator Choozme's financial **probity**.

10. rectitude (REK ti tude) This noun means moral uprightness; synonymous with probity, it comes from the Latin word for "straight."

- While Thomas Jefferson's morals are frequently examined and condemned, no one has made a dent in the **rectitude** of George Washington.
- "You should never hesitate to do good even if for the wrong reason; possessing **rectitude** of intention may be more common in angels than in humans," said Miss Dove to her students.

H ere is the last of our four "variety" offerings. As you're doubt-less guessing, "potpourri" means a mixture.

1. **aesthetic** (es THET ik) This adjective refers to the perception or appreciation of beauty.

- Those who want to be architects must have a very practical sense of how buildings function, but they must also have a strong sense of **aesthetics**; no one wants an ugly building, no matter how practical it might be.

- Bea is a complete **aesthete**: her kitchen toaster barely makes a piece of bread light tan, but she defends the appliance on the grounds that "the pink stripe across the middle makes it look really pretty."

2. **flaccid** (FLAS id *or* FLAK sid) It's from the Latin for "flabby" and that's what it means. It can be used in the literal or the figurative sense.

- The polio he suffered as a child left his leg muscles **flaccid**, but Wilfrid has not let wearing leg braces stop him from an active life and a successful career.

- Driving cross-country together, Grace and Emily kept up a nonstop, animated conversation about childhood, books, men, cats, careers, and life in general; the exchange became **flaccid** only when physical fatigue set in.

3. **trenchant** (TREN chunt) This word describes something forceful and effective, especially something quite sharp in its effective. Like the concrete noun "trench," it comes from a French word meaning "to cut," but this adjective is always used abstractly.

- Those who pride themselves on **trenchant** distinctions between good and bad, right and wrong, may oversimplify some of the most interesting and subtle questions about life.

- Luigi's analysis of the situation was both **trenchant** and witty; I don't think he's ever uttered a flaccid phrase in his life.

4. **milieu** (mil YUH *or* mil YOO) Another French friend firmly lodged in the English language, this noun means simply "place" or "environment" with a sense of being in the center or middle of it. It keeps its French plural form.

- Francine had a quiet, rural childhood, so when her college experience placed her in a **milieu** of fast-talking, sophisticated peers, she needed a year or so to adapt herself to this new way of living.

- Part of Gaspar's success as a journalist is that he has the knack of making himself at home with people from all varieties of social and cultural **milieux**, thus putting them at ease and making them willing to talk to him.

5. parvenu (PAR vuh noo) A newcomer to a "higher" level of social or economic status, one who doesn't yet know "how it's done"—this French noun brings with it into English a nondemocratic, judgmental perspective.

- "Hubert, that **parvenu**? I would never trust him to advise me on my finances. He doesn't even know how to place his silver at the end of the meal," Mrs. Hayes sniffily observed.

- Although his wealthy guests from the fashionable side of the bay were happy to attend Jay Gatsby's parties and drink his illegal alcohol, they continued to regard him as a **parvenu**, a man with a fancy automobile but without a horse.

6. ubiquitous (yoo BIK wit us) Literally, being everywhere at once. Obviously, it's used in a metaphoric or an exaggerated sense. It's from the Latin for "everywhere."

- To celebrate the publication of the new biography of Herman Melville, Andy and Dawn are starting a chain of teahouses called "Queequeg's Place." Here's betting those franchises will soon be as **ubiquitous** as Starbucks!

- Truman Capote was known for his **ubiquity** on the social circuit: this party one night, that one the next.

7. agog (a GOG) If you're eager, amazed, or excited, you may be agog.

- On his first trip to Asia, Henry revealed little in his words or on his face, but inside he was quietly **agog** with happiness at the new sights he had seen, the new experiences he was having.

- Spanish magician Juan Mayoral had the audience **agog** with wonder at the flame he transported to his buttonhole and at the red shoes that walked themselves to his door.

8. chicanery (shuh CAIN er ee) If someone uses chicanery on you, they're practicing dirty tricks, deceiving you.

- Miriam had trusted her financial adviser completely, so it was crushing, not only financially but personally, to learn that his **chicanery** had taken away half of her life savings.

- Ms. Bachelder had let the honor students have the key to her office "so we can have a quiet place to study," never realizing they hoped to find an advance copy of the AP Biology exam—she had never dreamed of such **chicanery** in the young!

9. desuetude (DEZ wuh tood) A fancy word for a state of disuse or inactivity.

- Mrs. Chasuble had a dislike of giving gifts that were "merely useful," as she termed it; her occasional exceptions were always antiques—an old magnifying glass, a wooden dish rack—as if their period of **desuetude** elevated them to a higher standard.

- While the law punishing those who walk of the western sidewalk in Fort Lulu remains on the books, its enforcement has, happily, fallen into **desuetude**.

10. palimpsest (PAL imp sest) This fascinating and complex word refers to either (a) a literal manuscript, possibly on hide or parchment, that has been written on, scraped, and written on again or (b) an object or place that similarly reflects layers of its history.

- We're accustomed to thinking of Rome as a **palimpsest** of classical, medieval, Renaissance, and modern life, but Prof. Limerick's lecture on Tucson, Arizona, has helped me see that southwestern city with its layerings of Indian, Hispanic, and Anglo life in a similar light.

- Dr. Ulanov was ecstatic when the vellum manuscript he purchased inexpensively in an Athens marketplace turned out to be a **palimpsest** with some recoverable diagrams by Archimedes on a lower layer: "Eureka!" he cried.

Whether it's a "ton of" something or just a "smidgen," a "chunk" or a "tidbit," the English language is filled with words that connote quantity. Here are some of the more colorful ways to mete out ("portion out" or "allot") the tinier portions.

1. snippet (SNIP it) Here's a noun to describe "a bit, scrap, or morsel." It is occasionally used informally to describe a small or mischievous person, usually a child.

- The Farthingtons had so many leftovers after Thanksgiving dinner that they filled a bowl with **snippets** of turkey and sweet potatoes and gave them to their dog, Manolo.

- "Listen, you young **snippets**," said Fagin, eyeing the boys playing a game of dice in the corner of the room. "I'm the boss here and you do as *I* say!"

2. scintilla (sin TILL ah) This noun means "a tiny amount," such as "a trace" or a "spark." In fact, it comes from the Latin word for "spark." It's also the root of the word "scintillating," which means "sparkling" or "fascinating."

- "I believe I taste a **scintilla** of nutmeg in this Sonoma Valley chardonnay," said the oenologist (see the "What's My Line" section).

- "There isn't a **scintilla** of kindness in my boss," whined Geoffrey. "He wouldn't let me have the day off, even though I told him it was the opening game of the World Series."

3. iota (eye OH tuh) This noun is not only the ninth and smallest letter of the Greek alphabet; it also connotes "a very small amount." The Latin spelling of the word is "jota" and gives us a different word with the same meaning: "jot."

- "There isn't an **iota** of truth in what you are telling me," Barney shouted at his son. "You were the last one to use the car and there was no dent in the fender when I drove it yesterday."

- Mrs. Rumple squeezed a **jot** of lemon into her tea and smeared a spoonful of marmalade on her scone.

4. **modicum** (MOD ih kum) From the Latin for "moderate" or "measure," this noun means "a small or modest amount." Of course that amount changes, depending upon what you are meting out.

- "I expect you to comport yourself with a **modicum** of manners," Mrs. Preston told the children. "That includes always saying 'please' and 'thank you' when it is appropriate."

- Because Lucy was on a diet, she allowed herself only a **modicum** of sugar each day, refusing a second helping of cake even though it was her own birthday.

5. **smidgen** (SMI jen) This noun comes from the Scottish for "small person" or "small amount" or, possibly, "small syllable." It, too, connotes an indeterminate but small amount.

- My mother is the kind of woman who cooks without recipes. Her cakes call for a "**smidgen**" of vanilla or a "**jot**" of lemon zest rather than "a quarter of a teaspoon" or "two pinches."

- Stuffed after the huge dinner, Cary asked for only a **smidgen** of pie for dessert.

6. **mite** (rhymes with tight) As a noun, this word can mean a lot of different tiny things— a small amount of money, a small insect, a child, or even a small particle. As an adjective it connotes "to a small degree."

- The sixteenth-century French essayist Michel de Montaigne once said, "Man is certainly crazy. He could not make a **mite**, and he makes gods by the dozen."

- "Aren't you being a **mite** ridiculous?" Tammy asked. "I can't believe you are so angry at me for being only two minutes late."

7. **soupçon** (SOOP sone) From the Old French word for "suspicion," this noun means a "tiny amount" or "just a trace or a hint."

- Brigitte bought a blue suit in Paris that was elegant but understated with just a **soupçon** of sexy mama in its design.

- Just as we can say, "I taste a suspicion of sugar in this iced tea," we can say, "there is a **soupçon** of cinnamon in this banana bread."

8. **dram** (rhymes with ham) Finally we have a noun for "a tiny amount" that has a specific weight. A "dram" is a unit of weight equal to $\frac{1}{16}$ of an ounce or 27.34 grains. As an apothecary weight, it is equal to $\frac{1}{8}$ of an ounce. It is often used to mean a small amount, however, without any reference to its actual weight value.

- In Act 5 of *Romeo and Juliet*, Romeo asks the apothecary for a **dram** of poison, hoping that a small quantity of the liquid will kill him quickly.

- The police officer listened to Fast Eddy's story without a **dram** of sympathy and then issued him a speeding ticket.

9. **shard** (rhymes with lard) This noun most often refers to a piece of broken pottery or a fragment of any brittle material, but it can also be used to mean "a small piece," usually larger than the tiny "mite," "iota," or "scintilla."

- The archaeologists working outside of the dig in the Sahara Desert found hundreds of **shards** of pottery piled in one area of the dig, leading them to believe that they had come upon an ancient wine cellar or food pantry.
- After he lost his job, his home, and his wife, Frank knew that he had no choice but to pick up the **shards** of his broken life, move to a new city, and start afresh.

10. **dollop** (DOLL up) This noun probably comes from the Norwegian word for "lump" and means "a small quantity" or "splash," usually of a liquid or soft solid.

- For dessert, Sybil served her famous homemade apple pie with a **dollop** of pralines-and-cream ice cream and a smattering of crushed macadamia nuts.
- Jad knew that he should take everything Tatiana said with a healthy **dollop** of suspicion; he knew she was prone to exaggeration and innuendo (see the "Oh, What a Tangled Web" section).

MAKE A MATCH #33

Sections 97–100

Match each word in the left-hand column with the phrase on the right that best suggests its meaning.

A.	abnegation	1. _____	trickery, deceit
B.	aesthetic	2. _____	environment
C.	agog	3. _____	accepted customs
D.	amoral	4. _____	sharply forceful
E.	chicanery	5. _____	temporary relief
F.	desuetude	6. _____	honesty
G.	effete	7. _____	without a conscience
H.	exonerate	8. _____	new arrival in world of society
I.	iota	9. _____	voluntary giving up of a right
J.	lenient	10. _____	really wicked
K.	milieu	11. _____	related to beauty
L.	mores	12. _____	period of disuse
M.	nefarious	13. _____	not harsh
N.	parvenu	14. _____	lack of vitality
O.	probity	15. _____	seemingly everywhere
P.	reprieve	16. _____	tiny bit of
Q.	shard	17. _____	small scraps
R.	snippets	18. _____	excited, amazed
S.	trenchant	19. _____	broken piece of pottery
T.	ubiquitous	20. _____	clear of blame

PRACTICE, PRACTICE, PRACTICE #11

Sections 91–100

Directions: Select a word from the list below that best fits the blank in one of the sentences and place the letter in the blank.

A.	absolve	K.	nefarious
B.	caveat	L.	pseudonym
C.	condone	M.	pusillanimous
D.	desuetude	N.	ravenous
E.	faux	O.	sobriquet
F.	flaccid	P.	soupçon
G.	formidable	Q.	stout
H.	harrowing	R.	svelte
I.	louche	S.	ubiquitous
J.	mitigate	T.	wanderlust

1. Physical therapy gradually began to strengthen the veteran's _____ muscles.

2. Abigail's _____ crocodile handbag looked genuine, even to her friends in the fashion business.

3. The weather bureau has just issued a stern _____ about driving during the nor'easter.

4. The soup needed a _____ of turmeric, decreed the chef.

5. Coco satisfied her _____ by spending her junior year in Vietnam.

6. The salesgirl told Alice that she was too _____ to wear a miniskirt and a shirt that exposed her midriff.

7. At 5'10" and 125 pounds, Rosa was _____ enough to be a fashion model.

8. After a full day of bike-riding, Michael was _____ enough to eat a five-course dinner.

9. George Orwell was the _____ for the British writer whose real name was Eric Blair.

10. My sister's given name is Greta, but her _____ is "Pickles" because she's always eating them.

11. Although he was afraid that he was _____, the lion in the *Wizard of Oz* was actually quite brave.

12. For someone who is claustrophobic, riding in an elevator to the top of a skyscraper can be a _____ experience.

13. Because of his speed and his strong serve, Stuart was a _____ opponent on the tennis court.

14. Ridden with guilt, Glenda went to confession in hopes that a priest might _____ her of her sins.

15. Betsy tried to _____ her anger at Frank by going out to dinner with her girlfriends.

16. "I cannot _____ your rude behavior," said Jerome's mother. "Wearing a hat at the dinner table is inexcusable."

17. Lonely and depressed, Tobias began frequenting _____ bars and hanging out with unsavory characters.

18. The _____ Jack the Ripper terrorized the women of London in the nineteenth century.

19. Cell phones are _____ on the streets of every major city in the world.

20. Jonas was so exhausted after his last week of work that he spent his weekend in a state of _____, barely getting out of bed.

On the Road

101

H ere's a list for the nomad (or "wanderer") in you. The list below offers words for journeys, for those who take them, and, in some cases, for how they take them.

1. **itinerant** (eye TIN er ant) As an adjective, this word means "traveling from place to place." It comes from the same route as "itinerary," which is "a proposed route or journey." It can also be used as a noun. Someone who travels around is "an itinerant."

- Following in his father's footsteps, Ethan moved to rural Pennsylvania and became an **itinerant** doctor, visiting the families of Appalachia and providing them with basic health-care services.

- In the 1960s, the Haight-Ashbury section of San Fransisco became an attractive area for **itinerants** from all over the country, who arrived there in search of sex, drugs, and rock and roll.

2. **vagrant** (VAY grint) This is a noun for "one who wanders from place to place without a permanent home or means of livelihood." It can also be used as an adjective. A more contemporary term, also used as a noun or an adjective, is "homeless."

- Since the Depression, many **vagrants** in Manhattan have built temporary shelters beneath the highway overpass leading to the Brooklyn Bridge.

- Despite the sign reading: "No **Vagrants**" on the door of the public restrooms, a homeless man was found sleeping on the tile floor beneath the sinks.

3. **sojourn** (SO jurn) From the Latin for "to spend the day," this noun means "temporary stay" or "brief period of residence." It may also be used as a verb.

- Last summer, the Sugarmans rented a villa overlooking a vineyard in central Tuscany and made regular **sojourns** to the surrounding hill towns of Montepulciano, Montalcino, Assisi, and Volterra.

- On their honeymoon, the Lesters **sojourned** to San Sebastián, Spain, before traveling to the French Riviera.

4. **transient** (TRAN zee ent *or* TRAN zhent) As an adjective, this word means "remaining in a place for only a brief time" or (like the related word "transitory") "passing with time." As a noun, it means "a person who stays somewhere for only a brief time, such as a hotel guest." It comes from the Latin for "to go over."

- The nineteenth-century American writer Henry David Thoreau walked the length of Cape Cod, Massachusetts, making **transient** visits to various beaches along the National Seashore.
- Mrs. Wallabee does not like to take **transients** into her rooming house, preferring long-term boarders whom she trusts.

5. **migrate** (MYE grayt) This verb means "to move from one country or region and settle in another" and is used to describe the behavior of both animals and people. Words that come from the same root—"emigrate" and "immigrate"—are used only to describe the activities of people. ("Emigrate" describes the movement *away* from the point of departure while "immigrate" describes the movement *to* a destination.)

- In the nineteenth century, a potato famine forced many Irish citizens to **migrate** to America in search of food and labor.
- The film *Winged **Migration*** beautifully details the precise choreography of the **migration** of various species of birds around the world.

6. **haj** (HAWJ) From the Arabic word for "pilgrimage," this noun literally means "a pilgrimage to Mecca," made during the religious life of a Muslim. It can be used, however, to signify any important journey. From the Arabic word for "flight," comes the word "hegira," which signifies the flight of Muhammad from Mecca to Medina in AD 622, marking the beginning of the Muslim era.

- Having exhausted all of the traditional forms of medicine, Karina decided to make a **haj** to Lourdes, France, with her daughter Katie to see if they could find a cure for Katie's cerebral palsy.
- A scholar of D. H. Lawrence, Professor Brentwhistle made a **haj** to Lawrence's home in Taos, New Mexico, to pay his respects at the author's gravesite.

7. **peripatetic** (PER ih pah TET ik) From the Greek word for "walk about" or "covered walk," where the philosopher Aristotle allegedly lectured, this adjective means "walking from place to place" or "traveling on foot." The word comes from the followers of Aristotle, who conducted his philosophical conversations while walking about in the Lyceum of ancient Athens.

- The **peripatetic** Anders Svensen made his living writing travel articles for various in-flight magazines.

- Easily bored and not yet willing to settle down with a wife and family, Theodore broke up with his fiancée and indulged his **peripatetic** impulses by hitchhiking from New York to California.

8. **peregrination** (PEH reg grin AY shun) This noun comes from the Latin word for "foreigner" and means to wander or travel abroad. The verb form is "to peregrinate."

- After her sophomore year in college, Kamisha planned a year of **peregrination**, starting in Africa and then traveling to Latin America and the Far East.

- Giving in to his wanderlust (see the "Achtung" section), Damian quit his job at One Hour Photo to **peregrinate** through Europe; he left Boston for Paris with an open-return ticket and no hotel reservations.

9. **circumvent** (sir cum VENT) This verb seems appropriate in a section about traveling since it means "to get around by artful maneuvering" or "to bypass."

- Clarissa **circumvented** her mother's anger at her for missing her curfew by avoiding the front door and climbing through an open window into her bedroom.

- In order to **circumvent** the rush hour traffic, the experienced taxi driver took a series of service roads to the airport.

10. **aberration** (AB ber AY shun) From the Latin word for "to go astray," this noun suggests a more figurative kind of travel. It means "a deviation from the expected course" and is more likely to connote not following expectations than physically traveling anywhere. The adjective form is "aberrant."

- "These poor grades are an **aberration** for Timmy," the principal told the Hammonds. "I've called you into my office to find out if there is some kind of problem at home since he is usually such a fine student."

- The psychologist could not account for Shamika's **aberrant** behavior. She was quite surprised to discover that her patient had disappeared on the day before her wedding without notifying anyone of her whereabouts.

T his is a book about words, and this is a section about the myriad (or "innumerable") ways to use them. All of the words below make up another batch that describe different speaking styles.

1. **encomium** (en KO mee um) A noun meaning "warm praise," often a formal tribute to a person or thing.

- In Erasmus' *In Praise of Folly*, the character of Folly composes an **encomium** to herself.

- After listening to each student's clever satirical piece inspired by *Gulliver's Travels*, the teacher launched an **encomium** of the students' imagination.

2. **expatiate** (ex PAY she ate) This verb comes from the Latin "to roam beyond one's usual boundaries." It means "to speak or write at great length about a subject."

- In Mark Kurlansky's book *Salt*, the author **expatiates** on the history, uses, and varieties of salt.

- Each time the teacher **expatiated** on her personal journey to self-fulfillment through literature, the students first began to yawn and then to ignore her altogether.

3. **verbiage** (VER bee ij) This noun comes from the Old French *verbier*, which means "to chatter." And it means just that—wordy, often pretentious, excessive language. It generally has negative connotations and is frequently misused in the expression "excessive verbiage," which is itself verbiage!

- There was so much **verbiage** in the eulogy delivered at Mr. Stilton's funeral that the mourners began to fidget instead of remembering his good qualities.

- Anyone could see that behind all the **verbiage**, the candidate's speech was full of lies and false promises.

4. **mawkish** (MAW kish) This adjective means excessively, even objectionably, sentimental.

- "I couldn't possibly watch another episode of that **mawkish** soap opera *Life Must Go On*," insisted Caroline, "without laughing out loud at what was supposed to be tragedy."

- The play relied on **mawkish** music to evoke tears in an audience that was unmoved by a sentimental script and amateurish acting.

5. **argot** (ARR go) This noun connotes the jargon, slang, or specialized vocabulary used by a particular group.

- Samantha expressed her shock at the behavior of her husband's family in the **argot** of the internet by exclaiming "OMG!"
- Jacob found that the **argot** of his teenaged daughter and her friends was as difficult to comprehend as their techno music or their passion for dirty, so-called vintage clothing.

6. **hortatory** (HOR tat or ee) This is an adjective that describes language marked by strong urging. A related verb, which means "to urge or encourage," is to exhort.

- After they lost to their rivals, the coach **exhorted** the students to buck up and prepare for the next game rather than dissolve in childish tears.
- The CEO's **hortatory** remarks about the future of e-banking was meant to inspire his sales team to work harder to represent small business clients online.

7. **dissimulate** (dis IM yoo late) This verb means "to disguise or conceal one's true feelings or intentions or to hide behind a false appearance." A good synonym is "dissemble." The noun form is "dissimulation."

- Even after dating him for six months, Patty never realized that her boyfriend had **dissimulated** and was, in fact, married with three children.
- The candidate's campaign speeches were filled with lies and **dissimulation**, yet he managed to convince his supporters that he was sincere.

8. **persiflage** (PER sif lozh) This noun comes from the Latin for "to whistle" and means "light, good-natured talk or banter."

- To set a playful tone at the first board meeting, the new director brought his guitar and made a welcome speech full of jokes and **persiflage**.
- David Ives is a favorite playwright among comic actors because his scripts are full of pratfalls and **persiflage**.

9. **palaver** (pal AV er) This word can be used either as a noun or a verb and means "idle—and usually prolonged and unnecessary—chatter, often intended to beguile or deceive the listener."

- Deborah **palavered** on about the weather in an attempt to avoid explaining to her boss why she was late for the meeting.
- When talking about the meaning of life or the purpose of existence, it's easy for someone to slip into **palaver** without ever providing any answers.

10. **perorate** (PER or ate) Here's a somewhat pretentious verb that means "to speak at length, often in a grandiloquent (or 'pretentious') manner." The noun form is "peroration."

- After the headmaster's dull and uninspired **peroration**, most of the parents squirmed in their seats during the awarding of diplomas to the 250 graduating seniors.

- Molly's ridiculous arguments during the debate caused her opponent to **perorate** with heated examples that would ensure her defeat.

Together/Apart

T he word "dichotomy" (dye KOT oh mee) comes to us from the Greek and means "the division into two contradictory parts." It belongs here because most of the words in this section make up a dichotomy between grouping things together or dividing them into distinct parts or dispersing them in many different directions.

1. **amalgamation** (ah MAL gam AY shun) This noun, which may have come to us from Arabic, means "to mix or combine into a unified whole." The verb form is "to amalgamate."

- The new poetry anthology in Ms. Van Meer's ninth grade English class contains an **amalgamation** of poets from Europe, Asia, Latin America, and the Caribbean.
- Tired of the disorganized array of papers on his desk, Mr. Candis asked his secretary to **amalgamate** them and put them in a file labeled "Desk Papers."

2. **admixture** (ad MIX chur) This noun means the same as "mixture" and comes from the Latin meaning "mix with." There is no verb form except "mix."

- Charlotte confronted the prospect of graduating from college and moving to New York with an **admixture** of anxiety, sadness, and excitement.
- The recipe for Leonore's chocolate cake involves adding sugar, eggs, and sour cream to an **admixture** of flour, baking powder, and cocoa.

3. **eclectic** (ek LEK tik) From the Greek word for "select," this adjective means "made up from a variety of sources." The noun form is "eclecticism."

- Global Crossings, the new shop on the corner of Maple and Elm Streets, sells an **eclectic** mix of Far Eastern home furnishings, Latin American folk art, and Native American jewelry.
- A musician known for his **eclecticism**, Smiling Lemon Hawkins has included jazz, pop, and folk tunes on his new CD.

4. **catholic** (KATH lik) With a lower case "c," this adjective has nothing to do with religion. It means "comprehensive" or "of broad scope" and comes from the Old French word for "universal."

- "We are hoping Carolyn Blink's new novel will have a **catholic** appeal since it is about finding love and doing meaningful work," said the publisher. "Everybody is interested in that."

- The topics for the school's weekly chapel talks are meant to be **catholic** in scope, covering any issues that are of interest to the student body, whether they are intellectual, spiritual, or emotional.

5. **motley** (MOT lee) Like eclectic, this adjective means "composed of a variety of sources." A good synonym is "heterogeneous." It comes from the Middle English word for "variegated cloth," which explains its other meaning— "having many colors."

- Seated at the bar in the newly gentrified neighborhood was a **motley** assortment of students, day laborers, and trendy urbanites in search of a hip, new hangout.

- Harlequins are famous for dressing in **motley** to amuse their audiences; their patchwork clothing is usually accompanied by oddly shaped hats and boots with bells on them.

6. **corroborate** (cor ROB or ate) This verb means "to bring in new evidence to strengthen or support an idea or argument." The noun form is "corroboration."

- Naomi's accusation of theft was given further credence after Leopold, who had witnessed the crime as well, **corroborated** her story.

- Urban legends are seldom accepted as truth because there is rarely a third party to **corroborate** these tales.

7. **asunder** (ah SUN der) We move to the "taking apart" portion of this section with this adverb, which literally means "apart" or "into separate pieces." It is only used to describe *how* something is done.

- Charlene was dismayed to find that her brother Nickolai had destroyed her Cabbage Patch doll, tearing **asunder** its arms and legs and scattering them in the yard.

- Part of the traditional wedding ceremony that comes from *The Book of Common Prayer* includes the words: "Those whom God hath joined together let no man put **asunder**."

8. **diaspora** (dye ASS por ah) This noun comes to us from the Greek word for "dispersion." With a capital "D," it refers to "the dispersion of the Jews from the sixth century BC, when they were exiled to Babylonia, to the present time." It may also be used, however, to refer to any "dispersion of a people from their original homeland" or any "dispersion of a language or culture."

- The persecution of the Jews before and during Word War II intensified the **Diaspora** that led many Jews to settle not only in the United States but in Latin America as well.

- There was a great **diaspora** of Europeans to New York's Lower East Side at the turn of the twentieth century; Italian, Polish, and Irish immigrants arrived in droves to seek opportunities for a better life.

9. **cleave** (KLEEV) Interestingly, this verb has two opposite meanings. On the one hand, it means "to split" or "to cut" or "penetrate." The noun form is "cleft," and the past tense is "clove." On the other hand, it means "to stick to" or "to be faithful to." In this case, the past tense is "cleaved."

- Iago put a **cleft** in Othello's relationship with Desdemona by convincing the jealous Moor that she was engaging in an extramarital affair.

- As the hurricane grew more forceful, blowing over trees and knocking down power lines, the children in the tall apartment building **cleaved** to their mother and cried out in terror.

10. **disseminate** (dis EM in ate) The verb comes from the Latin for "to sow." It means "to scatter widely" or "to disperse" as in "sowing seed."

- In her work *My Fight for Birth Control*, Margaret Sanger describes her struggle to provide birth control information, which was illegal to **disseminate** in the early part of the twentieth century.

- In order to discourage cigarette smoking, the American Cancer Society **disseminates** information on lung cancer and heart disease on their website and through printed pamphlets distributed in doctors' offices throughout the country.

T he title gives us a familiar contrasting or complementary pair of nouns. Some words here refer to the former, some to the latter.

1. eviscerate (ee VISS er ate) This verb can be used in two ways. It means "to disembowel or remove the entrails from a human or animal," or, more figuratively, removing the significant meaning of a speech or argument.

- Ancient Egyptians **eviscerated** their dead to prepare them for the process of mummification.

- Followers of Charles Darwin **eviscerated** the arguments proposed by Creationists with the theory of evolution.

2. iatrogenic (eye AT tro JEN ik) This adjective comes from the Greek for "brought forth by the healer." It's used to describe illness caused by medical intervention.

- Doctors say many cases of goiter are **iatrogenic**: they develop in response to medicine that has been prescribed for the patient.

- In the mid-twentieth century, some mental health professionals discovered that patients developed neuroses based on a doctor's comments to them: in short, their problems were **iatrogenic**.

3. androgyny (an DROJ in ee) From the Greek *andro* (male) and *gyne* (female), this noun means having both male and female characteristics. The adjective form—**androgynous**—is often used simply to mean characteristic of both sexes such as clothing or hairstyles.

- David Bowie's **androgynous** good looks appealed to both male and female fans.

- "Let's go to the hair salon on West 8th Street that specializes in **androgynous** styles," Astrid told Theo, "because then we can get matching Mohawks."

4. dorsal (DOR sul) This adjective comes from the Latin "dorsum" or "back," and describes something that is located on or near the back or upper surface of an organ or organism.

- It was easy to spot Caroline's horse in the paddock; the black **dorsal** stripe extending from her mane to her tail contrasted dramatically with her dun-colored body.

- Fearing a shark attack, the vigilant lifeguard demanded that the swimmers get out of the ocean when he spotted the silver wedge of a **dorsal** fin on an incoming wave.

5. **carapace** (CARE a pace) This noun means "the upper section of the shell that covers the back or part of the back of creatures like lobsters and crabs, spiders, and tortoises." (In turtles and tortoises, the underside of the carapace is called a "plastron.") It can also be used figuratively to mean "a protective outer layer."

- James developed a **carapace** of happy-go-lucky cheer to prevent his colleagues from recognizing his disgust with the dysfunction of the public relations department.
- The museum had a collection of rare objects including enameled Fabergé eggs, tiny gilt boxes, and the **carapaces** of turtles embedded with semiprecious stones.

6. **stigma** (STIG muh) This word comes from the Greek word for "mark" or "tattoo" and now means "a symbol of disgrace." The archaic plural "stigmata" is used by some Christians to describe the alleged body marks or sores in locations corresponding to the crucifixion wounds of Jesus.

- Jessica bears the **stigma** of having hired the sexist, racist efficiency expert who fired several talented staff members, so everyone ignored her suggestions for new hires.
- In 1224, St. Francis of Assisi is said to have revealed **stigmata** on his body— two marks on his palms, two on his feet where the nails were said to have fixed Christ to the cross, and one on his side, where the Bible says Jesus received a spear thrust from a Roman centurion.

7. **corporeal** (kor POR ee uhl) This adjective simply means "in bodily form." A close variant of it, **corporal** (KOR por ul), means "related to the body."

- The Thracian shepherds were astonished when the god Apollo appeared to them in **corporeal** form.
- Today **corporal** punishment in schools is outlawed in most countries, but it was very common in the nineteenth century.

8. **acolyte** (AK oh lite) This noun is used to denote a person who assists a priest or minister in services of some Christian denominations. It's also used as secular sarcastic slang for those who give overly attentive service to a powerful figure such as a boss.

- During the funeral mass at St. Gregory's, the young **acolytes** moved gracefully in their gold and white vestments in response to the needs of the Father Barnabas.

- Mr. Graves is both insecure and filled with a sense of self-importance: he always travels with two or three ambitious **acolytes** who fulfill his every wish.

9. **nephrology** (nef RAHL uh jee) This is the name of a medical specialty which focuses on the study and care of the kidneys. "Nephro-" comes from the Greek for "kidney."

- In his last year of medical school, Ben had to make the difficult decision of whether to become a pulmonologist and work with lung disease or a **nephrologist** and work with kidney disease.

- Acute **nephritis** occurs when a patient's kidneys suddenly become inflamed.

10. **expiate** (EX pee ate) This word can be used in a religious sense within Judaism, Christianity, and Greco-Roman paganism. It means "to get rid of any sense of estrangement between a Divine Power and an erring follower." (You can see a hint of the root word "pious" in this verb.) It can also be used figuratively within an all-human context.

- Odysseus sacrificed a spotless white bull to Hera in hopes of **expiating** any grudge that powerful goddess might be holding against him.

- Jeremy sent an extravagant bouquet of lilacs and lilies to his cousin Rachel; would these flowers **expiate** her annoyance at his forgetting her dinner party?

We're Outta Here

Get going! Later, Alligator! Catch ya on the flip side! Ciao! Have a good one! Toodle-oo! Twenty-three skidoo! Scram! The many ways of departing are not limited to slang. Here are ten ways of looking at a leaving.

1. usurp (yoo SURP) If you usurp someone's place (or power), you seize it unlawfully, you push them out.

- Modern day Christians disagree among themselves on whether the apostle Paul's statement that women ought not to **usurp** the authority of men should be taken literally today.

- Prince Hamlet knew his uncle had **usurped** his father's throne but heartbreak at the situation came sooner than the chance to speak up.

2. supplant (sup PLANT) This verb can be used as a synonym for "usurp," but it even more strongly suggests underhanded doings, trickery. How appropriate for a word whose origin means "to put one's foot under the sole of another's foot"; in short, "to trip up."

- Although Lisa was friendly enough to her, Sara Jane knew she was scheming to **supplant** her as division head.

- King Henry IV of England was himself a usurper, so when the old and ill man sees his son, Prince Hal, trying on his crown, he recognizes, unhappily, a young prince's desire to **supplant** an older ruler.

3. slough (SLUFF) When a snake sheds its skin, it is sloughing it off. So, more generally this verb refers to discarding something not regarded as desirable.

- "I know you're second semester seniors," said Mr. Krolik to his class, "but does that make it right to **slough** off your homework during these final weeks?"

- Mr. Crist-Jones was the picture of respectability as long as he was in his homeland, but the sunny climes of Spain and Portugal caused him to **slough** off his native primness and astonish even the "locals" with the vivacity of his flamenco technique.

4. secede (suh SEED) This verb refers to making a formal withdrawal of membership. Its most common use is to the secession (suh SESH un) of the Southern states from the Union at the time of the Civil War.

- Angered by his parents' refusal to let him attend Fabula's party, Dondre irrationally proclaimed, "If there were a way to **secede** from this family, I'd do it!"

- Who first said that if New York City tried to **secede** from New York State, Staten Island should **secede** from New York City?

5. **recede** (re SEED) If something recedes, it goes to a position or condition further back whether in time or in space.

- Denny has avoided "middle-aged spread," but his **receding** hairline makes it impossible for him to be mistaken for his twenty-year-old self.

- The real estate market has been flourishing for so long that experts predict a **recession** of values must be in the fairly near future.

6. **abdicate** (AB dik ate) One who abdicates chooses to give up power, especially that of a throne—no usurper need apply. A verb similar in sound and meaning is **abnegate** (AB neg ate)—the voluntary giving up of some right or pleasure.

- Some monarchy-watchers believe that Queen Elizabeth II should **abdicate** in favor of her son Charles.

- "I'm not into **self-abnegation**," avowed Mame, helping herself to more *foie gras*.

7. **wane** (rhymes with rain) This verb refers to the process of gradually growing smaller. It's often used in reference to the size of the visible moon along with its companion opposite "to wax," meaning to grow larger.

- Theo had once planned on majoring in math, but as his grades in the more advanced courses fell, his interest **waned**.

- Prof. Burke stated her belief that the power of the legislative branch was **waning** and thus the time-honored sense of checks and balances was threatened.

8. **valediction** (val uh DIK shun) A rather formal statement of farewell is called a valediction. Some schools still select a valedictorian, the student with the highest grades in the class who gets the official right to make a "goodbye speech" at graduation exercises.

- General Douglas MacArthur's **valedictory** speech to Congress in April 1951 is remembered chiefly for his moving quotation from an old barracks ballad: "Old soldiers never die; they just fade away."

- John Keats, knowing of his imminent death from tuberculosis, attempts, with sadness, to write, from Rome, a **valediction** to a friend in England, "I can scarcely bid you goodbye even in a letter. I always made an awkward bow."

9. **tergiversate** (ter JIV er sayt) Literally, to turn one's back (Latin *tergum*) on—to leave—a cause formerly supported. It can also be used to refer to speaking evasively, hoping to disguise one's meaning. One linguist puts it well in saying the word applies whether one is "ducking or weaving."

- In Dickens's *A Tale of Two Cities*, the unreliable character John Barsad fears he will be apprehended in France despite "his utmost **tergiversation**."
- Pres. George H. W. Bush is remembered for his clever phrase, "Read my lips. No new taxes," but not everyone remembers that he later **tergiversated** on that issue.

10. **ebb** (rhymes with web) In our end is our beginning: we close our presentation of one thousand and fifty-one words as we began, with a three-letter word: ebb. It means "to fall back, to recede, to go away."

- As the second millennium began to **ebb**, disputes arose as to whether the proper time to celebrate was the year 2000 or the year 2001. Although Stanley Kubrick had chosen the latter for his earlier film, the year 2000 won out for the many celebrations.
- No matter how many hours they spent in challenging each other or in perusing dictionaries, Margery's and Jane's pleasure in working together and their interest in words never **ebbed**.

MAKE A MATCH #34

Sections 101–105

Match each word in the left-hand column with the phrase on the right that best suggests its meaning.

A. androgyny
B. argot
C. carapace
D. circumvent
E. corroborate
F. diaspora
G. eclectic
H. encomium
I. eviscerate
J. haj
K. hortatory
L. itinerant
M. motley
N. secede
O. slough
P. sojourn
Q. stigma
R. usurp
S. verbiage
T. wane

1. _____ A noticeable sign of blame or fault
2. _____ A speech giving high praise
3. _____ A pilgrimage for religious purposes
4. _____ To take over the power or position belonging to another
5. _____ A scattering of the population of a nationality or ethnic group
6. _____ A hard shell or outer covering
7. _____ To grow smaller in size or in power
8. _____ Describing a speech of encouragement
9. _____ Defined by both male and female characteristics
10. _____ To withdraw voluntarily from a union
11. _____ Language or slang of a specialized group
12. _____ Excess of words
13. _____ To go around something
14. _____ To destroy the essential part of
15. _____ To give confirming evidence
16. _____ Having no fixed home
17. _____ A temporary stay in a place
18. _____ Drawing from many different sources
19. _____ Describing a jester's clothing
20. _____ To shed

Sections 101–105

Put the letter of the most appropriate word in the blank space of each sentence.

A.	abdicate	K.	iatrogenic
B.	aberration	L.	mawkish
C.	amalgamation	M.	palaver
D.	cleave	N.	peregrination
E.	corporeal	O.	peripatetic
F.	disseminate	P.	persiflage
G.	dissimulated	Q.	recede
H.	ebb	R.	stigma
I.	expatiate	S.	vagrant
J.	genuflected	T.	valediction

1. We go to doctors to be healed, not to acquire some _____ illness!

2. The store owner was sympathetic to the problem of homelessness, but he still didn't want a _____ sleeping in front of his door.

3. Some college professors stand stationary in front of a lectern; others are more _____ and walk around the room as they lecture.

4. We're here to take a quick vote on the issue, not to _____ about the pros and cons; it seems ridiculous to repeat what we said last week.

5. Joelle consulted the table of tides in the newspaper in order to find out when the water would begin to _____.

6. The Rev. Robert Parks will be giving the opening prayer, but who will be delivering the _____?

7. Some people believe that Queen Elizabeth II should _____ in favor of her son Prince Charles; others believe she should remain on the throne all her life.

8. It's one thing to be a little sentimental, but you don't want to go overboard and become _____.

9. Marriage is a serious matter; husband and wife should _____ to each other for a lifetime.

10. Ralph had a stay-at-home vacation with only one small _____ to visit his cousin on Long Island.

11. As the normally quiet Mrs. Coleman relaxed in front of the fire, she surprised her adult children by beginning to _____ on her childhood memories.

12. Helena is usually up at the crack of dawn; sleeping until 10:00 a.m., as she did today, was a real _____.

13. Most people I know are happy that being born to unwed parents no longer carries a _____.

14. As Susan entered the room for her audience with the Pope, she instinctively _____.

15. The poet John Milton saw God completely as a spirit; he never depicts Him in _____ form.

16. The block of the Senator's supporters was an _____ of Evangelicals and immigrants.

17. When Lola was asked to reveal her annual income, she _____ and spoke only in very general terms.

18. Planned Parenthood hopes to _____ information about their range of services at the Health Fair next week.

19. While the serious matters at the conference are important to Henry, he also enjoys the _____ among attendees during the breaks.

20. Clark wasn't particularly vain, but he was annoyed when he noticed his hairline was beginning to _____.

ENJOY YOUR NEW VOCABULARY!

SECTION A

Select the word in the left column that is most strongly suggested by each definition on the right and place its letter in the blank.

A.	admonish	1. _____	really poor
B.	banal	2. _____	enormous strength
C.	cacophonous	3. _____	scold
D.	dilatory	4. _____	dull, boring
E.	elixir	5. _____	unpleasant sounds
F.	fervent	6. _____	devoted to luxury
G.	goad	7. _____	shaky, quavering
H.	herculean	8. _____	delaying, tardy
I.	indigent	9. _____	evoking feeling
J.	noisome	10. _____	unpleasant smell
K.	pathos	11. _____	prod, urge
L.	recondite	12. _____	persuade by "sweet talk"
M.	sybarite	13. _____	obscure, little known
N.	tremulous	14. _____	magic potion
O.	wheedle	15. _____	intensity of emotion

SECTION B

Select a word from the list below that best fits the blank in one of the sentences and place the letter in the blank.

A.	antipathy	I.	jaded
B.	beseech	J.	nuance
C.	caustic	K.	panache
D.	cryptic	L.	restive
E.	destitute	M.	sedulous
F.	ebullient	N.	tenacity
G.	fulminate	O.	zealous
H.	garrulous		

1. A _____ fan of the Beatles since the sixties, Holly owns all of their records in their original vinyl format.

2. Jamie was so hurt by Andy's _____ remark about her sister that she refused to speak to him for the rest of the school year.

3. Although Sam was a _____ worker on the assembly line, he was fired for trying to unionize the plant.

4. Because the speaker was late for morning assembly, the students grew _____ and began to chatter noisily and stir in their seats.

5. Kate has so much _____ that she can wear her mother's old dresses, call them "retro," and look chic.

6. Ben knows Alexandra so well that he recognizes every small _____ in her moods.

7. Because the Bergmans had no homeowner's insurance, the fire that destroyed their house last weekend left them _____.

8. Chippy was _____ when he saw that he got an A in calculus after practically failing the midterm exam.

9. Since Marcella has such a strong _____ to Max, make sure you put them at different tables for the reception on the lawn.

10. "I _____ you, Winifred," said Harley, getting down on one knee. "Marry me. You won't regret it."

11. "I admire your _____," replied Winifred, "but I won't marry you no matter how many times you ask. I've already told you I am in love with your brother."

12. After traveling around the world with her rich uncle, Caroline was too _____ to get excited about a trip to the Jersey Shore.

13. In a _____ mood, Simon chattered about his love life, his favorite books, and his deepest fears, delighting Gwendolyn, who was tired of his brooding silences.

14. Bill began to _____ about Sandra's inability to control her children when he saw her two boys trample through his vegetable garden.

15. Mattie could not figure out what Helen meant by the _____ message she left on her answering machine.

SECTION C

Select the letter of the word that best fits the definition and place its letter in the blank.

_____ 1. to make impure by adding inferior ingredients
   a. conciliate   b. adulterate   c. dissent   d. satiate

_____ 2. vigor, vivacity
   a. brio   b. dollop   c. murrain   d. solace

_____ 3. whimsical or unpredictable.
   a. sonorous   b. myopic   c. smarmy   d. capricious

_____ 4. morally instructive
   a. didactic   b. spurious   c. compliant   d. deranged

_____ 5. calm and peaceful, golden
   a. abstemious   b. mercurial   c. halcyon   d. lubricious

_____ 6. to catch sight of
   a. abut   b. espy   c. entreat   d. quell

_____ 7. cranky or unruly
   a. evasive   b. ominous   c. obdurate   d. fractious

_____ 8. generous, courageously noble in mind and heart
   a. obsequious   b. magnanimous   c. officious   d. adventitious

_____ 9. lowest point
   a. apex   b. apogee   c. zenith   d. nadir

_____ 10. prone to outbursts of temper
   a. irascible   b. affable   c. acrid   d. racy

_____ 11. destructive, deadly
   a. acerbic   b. pernicious   c. adamant   d. otiose

_____ 12. formidable, arousing fear or awe
   a. redoubtable   b. lugubrious   c. querulous   d. recondite

_____ 13. foolish disregard of danger, recklessness
   a. succor   b. antipathy   c. temerity   d. alacrity

_____ 14. fearless, resolutely courageous
   a. amorphous   b. indefatigable   c. indolent   d. undaunted

_____ 15. predominant influence—as of a state, region or group—over another
   a. hegemony   b. oligarchy   c. fiat   d. nepotism

SECTION D

Match each word in the left-hand column with the phrase on the right that best suggests its meaning.

A.	autocrat	1. _____	overly sentimental
B.	bellicose	2. _____	bear-like
C.	clemency	3. _____	not harmonious
D.	dissonant	4. _____	peevish, complaining
E.	eke	5. _____	willingness to show mercy
F.	fastidious	6. _____	very hot
G.	harridan	7. _____	to get with great effort
H.	labyrinthine	8. _____	warlike
I.	lugubrious	9. _____	meticulous
J.	maudlin	10. _____	gloomy
K.	obsequious	11. _____	servile
L.	querulous	12. _____	to displace, usurp
M.	supplant	13. _____	intricately structured
N.	torrid	14. _____	vicious woman
O.	ursine	15. _____	despot

SECTION E

Select the word from the list below that best fits each of the sentences and place the letter in the blank.

A.	acoustics	I.	jocular
B.	affluent	J.	minion
C.	blandishment	K.	otiose
D.	clandestine	L.	recapitulate
E.	duplicitous	M.	senescence
F.	exacerbate	N.	tyro
G.	formidable	O.	vermilion
H.	indefatigable		

1. The lecturer offered to _____ her main points for any audience member who had arrived late and thus missed the presentation of the three themes.

2. Although I am accustomed to dressing in grays and blacks, my fashion consultant suggested I try a warmer tone such as _____.

3. Sylvia was tired of _____ meetings with her lover; she wanted the world to know of their romance.

4. Mr. and Mrs. Garten, both around sixty years old, are moving to Florida soon, saying wittily they want to act in their _____, not their senility.

5. The family was _____ enough to send Ruby to summer camp but lacked the means for her to go to private school.

6. The _____ was assigned a mentor who could help him learn the customs at his new job.

7. Ellen had enormous energy but was not _____; after five miles of brisk walking she requested a brief pause.

8. While he has been known to be _____ to the extent of telling a few social untruths, he would never lie under oath.

9. Ms. Biscotti was in a _____ frame of mind, kidding around before class with all her students.

10. Withers was a _____ presence in the board room; junior associates had been known to down antianxiety medication before meetings.

11. The _____ in the new auditorium are far from ideal; music played there sounds harsh and tinny.

12. It's hard to resist William's _____; he knows just what to say to make you feel good.

13. Wouldn't you like to be a top executive and be able to ask a _____ to get coffee for you?

14. Don't let Sarah pull you into a fight; remember you want to lessen the tension in your relationship, not _____ it.

15. When have I ever been so _____? June and July have gone by without my accomplishing any of the projects I'd planed.

SECTION F

Select the letter of the word that best fits each definition and place its letter in the blank.

_____ 1. rather boring, perhaps because of its regular occurrence
    a. quiescent   b. acerbic   c. quotidian   d. rancid

_____ 2. a skilled teller of anecdotes, stories
    a. raconteur   b. pundit   c. toady   d. scion

_____ 3. to show not guilty, to remove blame
    a. exonerate   b. abnegate   c. fulminate   d. vacillate

_____ 4. a confusing entanglement
    a. folio   b. farrago   c. bravado   d. imbroglio

_____ 5. native to a region
a. adventitious   b. treacly   c. vacuous   d. indigenous

_____ 6. to say again, to repeat
a. implore   b. reiterate   c. gad   d. fluctuate

_____ 7. friendly, easy to get along with
a. dissolute   b. affable   c. draconian   d. euphonious

_____ 8. relating to the concept of beauty
a. flaneur   b. ribaldry   c. aesthetics   d. tenebrous

_____ 9. excited, amazed
a. agog   b. athwart   c. venial   d. unctuous

_____ 10. energy, life
a. caucus   b. catharsis   c. riposte   d. verve

_____ 11. to bully or force into action
a. leaven   b. barter   c. hector   d. indict

_____ 12. a bad start, bad omen for the future
a. inexorable   b. unremitting   c. propitious   d. inauspicious

_____ 13. to make a very specific condition
a. vie   b. stipulate   c. adjure   d. absolve

_____ 14. sly, indirect critical remark
a. innuendo   b. jeremiad   c. hiatus   d. incubus

_____ 15. a trial, a hardship
a. gloaming   b. gorgon   c. tribulation   d. invective

SECTION G

Now for something a little different. These questions require not just rote memory but a little thinking. As you'll see from the answer key, some of these have several possible answers. The important point is that you've been able to apply your knowledge of the vocabulary words.

EXAMPLE: The book may represent the zeitgeist of the 1930s, but you have to admit it's rather soporific. Explain the meaning of this sentence to someone who lacks your skill with words.

Answer to example: The book gets the feeling of the times in the 1930s, but it's also pretty boring since it tends to make you fall asleep.

1. Mary asked an oenologist to recommend something potable for those who are frugal. In simple terms, what has Mary done?

2. Jim's hat is askew and people on the street are looking askance at him. Explain.

3. Prof. Norris told Eileen not to change one iota of her poem before submitting it for publication. What does he think of her poem?

4. What might a lepidopterist put in his highboy?

5. Jocelyn sits down at the table with a libation and a libretto. Where might she be?

6. (a) For those attracted to women: Do you think you'd like to keep company with a frenetic fishwife?

   (b) For those attracted to men: I'd like to fix you up for a date with a rotund roué—okay?

7. The henchman contemplated his diurnal tasks. What's he doing?

8. Van regarded it as a filial duty not to be disheveled at dinner. What can we deduce about Van's parents? Or about Van?

9. If your sibling started in on a harangue, how might you respond?

10. The docent was delivering a panegyric about the current exhibit. Who's doing what?

More Practice

You saw this format before. You are asked to form a mental response that uses your knowledge of your new words. As the Key indicates, varying answers are possible for many questions.

Set #1

1. If you asked a laconic herpetologist why he or she chose that line of work, what might the person reply?

2. Do you find ribaldry risible? Why or why not?

3. A pedagogue is planning an evening with the divan and the ottoman. Can you picture him?

4. Give an example of someone aping an eminent person.

5. Do you consider vituperating a relative a venial offense?

6. Mr. Hatcher was often captious in his comments on student papers, but his tone was never virulent. Describe his style of grading essays.

7. Which of the following is a canonical work? *Macbeth, How to Retire Early*, or *One Hundred Amazing Buffoons*.

8. Is a munificent person likely to become a pariah? Why or why not?

9. A character in a Poe story has a family motto: "No one challenges me with impunity." What is his probable response to an insult?

10. Can you name a story or novel with a pubescent protagonist?

Set #2

1. Which of the following superheroes might be seen as a virago? Explain. Spider-Man Wonder Woman Batman

2. If a lupine creature were an interloper in your backyard, what might be your response?

3. Would you rather hang around an autodidact or a demagogue? Why?

4. What kind of gaffe might a voracious person commit?

5. Would you prefer to be spoken to in a stentorian tone or a sonorous tone? Explain.

6. Is there any situation in which you could imagine yourself being obsequious to your nemesis?

7. Is a caryatid likely to be amorous?

8. Everything on the table in front of you is palatable or potable. What are you most likely getting ready to do?

9. Jenny says her grandmother is fervent about protocol. What does she mean by that?

10. Your new neighbors are raucous on the first night they are in the house. Do you consider this propitious?

Set #3

1. If your younger sibling is embarrassing you by being fractious at a social gathering, which of the following will probably be most helpful to you in dealing with the situation? Herculean strength? Manic temerity? Savoir faire?

2. Would you engage in half an hour of angst or half an hour of repartee?

3. Bathos or pathos? Which do you prefer in literature?

4. You're painting a scene of carnage. What color of paint will you need a lot of?

5. Your family has undergone quite a diaspora since the first ancestor came to these shores. How hard will it be to arrange a family reunion?

6. Would you rather have a boon or a boor come into your existence soon?

7. You can have a cup of coffee this afternoon with a slatternly person or a smarmy person. Which do you choose and why?

8. Does anyone have a sobriquet for you? If so, what? If not, would you like to have one?

9. Do you enjoy it when friends are inscrutable? Why or why not?

10. Frank Vesser is an itinerant numismatist. What might we find Mr. Vesser doing?

Set #4

1. What might an epicurean be sedulous about?

2. Would you consider me gauche if I offered you an honorarium for what you did yesterday?

3. Describe a time when you have felt beleaguered.

4. You dream that you have encountered a dolorous doppelgänger. What kind of person have you met?

5. In what season might a woman be most likely to wear something diaphanous?

6. The atmosphere at a meeting with some acquaintances is tense. What might leaven it? What might exacerbate it?

7. Is an iconoclast more likely to have audacity or meticulousness?

8. Does your name have an easily formed diminutive? Explain.

9. Can you think of any kinds of situations that usually make you skittish? Explain.

10. Do bovine creatures play a central or tangential role in your life? Might anyone declare such creatures to be nugatory in his or her existence?

Answer Key

INTRO MAKE A MATCH
1. C
2. A
3. B
4. B
5. C
6. D
7. D
8. C
9. C
10. A
11. A
12. C
13. D
14. B
15. B
16. D
17. B
18. C
19. C
20. A
21. B
22. A
23. D
24. B

MAKE A MATCH #1
1. D
2. A
3. B
4. R
5. N
6. S
7. E
8. K
9. P
10. I
11. O
12. C
13. Q
14. T
15. H
16. M
17. F
18. J
19. G
20. L

MAKE A MATCH #2
1. K
2. A
3. I
4. M
5. G
6. O
7. N
8. L
9. E
10. J
11. C
12. F
13. H
14. B
15. D

MAKE A MATCH #3
1. Q
2. O
3. K
4. A
5. G
6. B
7. M
8. N
9. H
10. S
11. D
12. F
13. P
14. I
15. R
16. E
17. L
18. J
19. T
20. C

PRACTICE, PRACTICE, PRACTICE #1
1. K
2. A
3. T
4. H
5. F
6. P
7. G
8. C
9. E
10. R
11. S
12. L
13. K

14. Q
15. J
16. O
17. B
18. D
19. N
20. M

MAKE A MATCH #4
1. M
2. Q
3. O
4. J
5. P
6. C
7. G
8. B
9. I
10. H
11. E
12. K
13. A
14. D
15. N
16. L
17. F

MAKE A MATCH #5
1. D
2. G
3. B
4. L
5. P
6. O
7. I
8. E
9. H
10. K
11. J
12. Q
13. C
14. N
15. M
16. A
17. F

MAKE A MATCH #6
1. K
2. B
3. C
4. D

5. J
6. O
7. N
8. R
9. M
10. E
11. G
12. Q
13. I
14. L
15. A
16. P
17. H
18. F

PRACTICE, PRACTICE, PRACTICE #2
1. Q
2. G
3. A
4. S
5. M
6. N
7. K
8. L
9. R
10. T
11. D
12. F
13. H
14. B
15. J
16. P
17. E
18. O
19. C
20. I

MAKE A MATCH #7
1. O
2. G
3. F
4. A
5. K
6. B
7. J
8. C
9. H
10. M
11. D
12. E

13. N
14. P
15. I
16. L

MAKE A MATCH #8

1. F
2. A
3. O
4. D
5. Q
6. G
7. J
8. C
9. S
10. R
11. N
12. M
13. E
14. B
15. P
16. H
17. L
18. I
19. K

MAKE A MATCH #9

1. G
2. N
3. L
4. K
5. C
6. O
7. B
8. J
9. P
10. E
11. D
12. A
13. I
14. F
15. H
16. M

PRACTICE, PRACTICE, PRACTICE #3

1. S
2. C
3. F
4. K
5. P
6. A
7. H
8. L
9. M
10. D
11. N
12. R
13. T
14. J
15. B

16. G
17. O
18. Q
19. I
20. E

MAKE A MATCH #10

1. K
2. P
3. I
4. B
5. N
6. M
7. C
8. E
9. L
10. A
11. D
12. F
13. G
14. O
15. H
16. J

MAKE A MATCH #11

1. H
2. I
3. E
4. P
5. K
6. M
7. D
8. N
9. A
10. G
11. C
12. B
13. O
14. J
15. L
16. F

MAKE A MATCH #12

1. J
2. N
3. M
4. P
5. C
6. A
7. L
8. G
9. H
10. K
11. F
12. B
13. I
14. E
15. Q
16. D
17. O

PRACTICE, PRACTICE, PRACTICE #4

1. D
2. J
3. M
4. B
5. P
6. K
7. R
8. Q
9. T
10. G
11. I
12. E
13. A
14. N
15. L
16. O
17. F
18. S
19. C
20. H

MAKE A MATCH #13

1. M
2. O
3. K
4. A
5. B
6. N
7. J
8. G
9. I
10. L
11. E
12. F
13. C
14. D
15. H

MAKE A MATCH #14

1. F
2. M
3. K
4. E
5. B
6. J
7. N
8. C
9. G
10. D
11. P
12. H
13. A
14. O
15. I
16. L

MAKE A MATCH #15

1. F
2. E

3. G
4. A
5. P
6. L
7. O
8. I
9. H
10. M
11. B
12. K
13. N
14. D
15. J
16. C

PRACTICE, PRACTICE, PRACTICE #5

1. R
2. I
3. K
4. G
5. Q
6. A
7. N
8. M
9. E
10. P
11. J
12. D
13. S
14. C
15. O
16. F
17. H
18. B
19. L
20. T

MAKE A MATCH #16

1. F
2. E
3. D
4. B
5. I
6. A
7. C
8. O
9. J
10. H
11. N
12. M
13. L
14. K
15. G

MAKE A MATCH #17

1. J
2. O
3. I
4. G
5. A

6. E
7. N
8. P
9. M
10. D
11. C
12. H
13. F
14. K
15. B
16. L

MAKE A MATCH #18

1. L
2. C
3. G
4. O
5. I
6. K
7. P
8. J
9. A
10. N
11. H
12. F
13. B
14. E
15. M
16. D

PRACTICE, PRACTICE, PRACTICE #6

1. I
2. L
3. M
4. C
5. O
6. S
7. H
8. T
9. G
10. N
11. D
12. F
13. P
14. A
15. K
16. E
17. B
18. J
19. R
20. Q

MAKE A MATCH #19

1. N
2. G
3. E
4. L
5. B
6. H
7. C

8. D
9. O
10. K
11. M
12. I
13. R
14. Q
15. P
16. F
17. J
18. A

MAKE A MATCH #20

1. K
2. A
3. D
4. M
5. C
6. O
7. L
8. H
9. F
10. B
11. G
12. N
13. I
14. E
15. J

MAKE A MATCH #21

1. K
2. L
3. J
4. F
5. D
6. E
7. O
8. P
9. C
10. B
11. G
12. I
13. M
14. Q
15. H
16. A
17. N

PRACTICE, PRACTICE, PRACTICE #7

1. J
2. I
3. E
4. A
5. D
6. O
7. K
8. B
9. L
10. S
11. H

12. R
13. Q
14. P
15. C
16. F
17. T
18. N
19 G
20. M

MAKE A MATCH #22

1. C
2. H
3. P
4. L
5. D
6. B
7. N
8. O
9. F
10. I
11. G
12. A
13. E
14. K
15. J
16. Q
17. M

MAKE A MATCH #23

1. G
2. J
3. L
4. M
5. A
6. C
7. K
8. D
9. E
10. O
11. H
12. N
13. I
14. B
15. F

MAKE A MATCH #24

1. M
2. G
3. H
4. K
5. P
6. A
7. B
8. L
9. F
10. Q
11. R
12. I
13. E
14. O

15. C
16. D
17. J
18. N

PRACTICE, PRACTICE, PRACTICE #8

1. L
2. M
3. B
4. S
5. R
6. A
7. H
8. G
9. P
10. I
11. J
12. C
13. Q
14. K
15. E
16. F
17. O
18. T
19. N
20. D

MAKE A MATCH #25

1. H
2. I
3. K
4. A
5. O
6. Q
7. L
8. D
9. N
10. B
11. E
12. P
13. J
14. M
15. C
16. G
17. F

MAKE A MATCH #26

1. L
2. G
3. P
4. Q
5. I
6. A
7. M
8. B
9. N
10. F
11. H
12. O
13. R

14. K
15. E
16. D
17. C
18. J

MAKE A MATCH #27

1. I
2. J
3. A
4. N
5. L
6. C
7. H
8. E
9. D
10. B
11. M
12. K
13. O
14. G
15. F

PRACTICE, PRACTICE, PRACTICE #9

1. Q
2. L
3. J
4. P
5. A
6. G
7. B
8. I
9. H
10. O
11. K
12. C
13. S
14. F
15. D
16. N
17. R
18. M
19. E
20. T

MAKE A MATCH #28

1. E
2. B
3. L
4. J
5. M
6. H
7. O
8. I
9. D
10. C
11. A
12. F
13. G

14. K
15. N

MAKE A MATCH #29

1. D
2. E
3. C
4. F
5. K
6. H
7. I
8. B
9. J
10. L
11. M
12. N
13. G
14. A
15. O

MAKE A MATCH #30

1. F
2. E
3. B
4. H
5. C
6. I
7. A
8. P
9. G
10. D
11. O
12. K
13. M
14. N
15. J
16. L

PRACTICE, PRACTICE, PRACTICE #10

1. I
2. N
3. L
4. E
5. H
6. T
7. C
8. S
9. K
10. M
11. P
12. J
13. A
14. G
15. D
16. R
17. B
18. O
19. F
20. Q

MAKE A MATCH #31

1. P
2. O
3. G
4. J
5. M
6. E
7. H
8. A
9. K
10. L
11. N
12. I
13. F
14. B
15. D
16. C

MAKE A MATCH #32

1. N
2. C
3. J
4. B
5. O
6. I
7. A
8. E
9. K
10. F
11. D
12. G
13. L
14. M
15. H

MAKE A MATCH #33

1. E
2. K
3. L
4. S
5. P
6. O
7. D
8. N
9. A
10. M
11. B
12. F
13. J
14. G
15. T
16. I
17. R
18. C
19. Q
20. H

PRACTICE, PRACTICE, PRACTICE #11

1. F
2. E

3. B
4. P
5. T
6. Q
7. R
8. N
9. L
10. O
11. M
12. H
13. G
14. A
15. J
16. C
17. I
18. K
19. S
20. D

MAKE A MATCH #34

1. Q
2. H
3. J
4. R
5. F
6. C
7. T
8. K
9. A
10. N
11. B
12. S
13. D
14. I
15. E
16. L
17. P
18. G
19. M
20. O

PRACTICE, PRACTICE, PRACTICE #12

1. K
2. S
3. O
4. M
5. H
6. T
7. A
8. L
9. D
10. N
11. I
12. B
13. R
14. J
15. E
16. C
17. G
18. F

19. P
20. Q

1. I
2. H
3. A
4. B
5. C
6. M
7. N
8. D
9. K
10. J
11. G
12. O
13. L
14. E
15. F

1. O
2 C
3. M
4. L

5. K
6. J
7. E
8. F
9. A
10. B
11. N
12. I
13. H
14. G
15. D

1. B
2. A
3. D
4. A
5. C
6. B
7. D
8. B
9. D
10. A
11. B
12. A
13. C
14. D
15. A

1. J
2. O
3. D
4. L
5. C
6. N
7. E
8. B
9. F
10. I
11. K
12. M
13. H
14. G
15. A

1. L
2. O
3. D
4. M
5. B
6. N
7. H
8. E

9. I
10. G
11. A
12. C
13. J
14. F
15. K

1. C
2. A
3. A
4. D
5. D
6. B
7. B
8. C
9. A
10. D
11. C
12. D
13. B
14. A
15. C

ENJOY YOUR NEW VOCAB: SECTION G

1. In simple terms, Mary has asked a wine expert (oenologist) to recommend an inexpensive but drinkable wine.

2. Jim's hat is on at a funny angle and people are giving him slightly funny looks.

3. Professor Norris must really like Eileen's poem. An iota is the tiniest little detail, and he doesn't want her to change even that.

4. A lepidopterist is an expert on butterflies and a highboy is a tall chest of drawers, so maybe he's placing his butterfly net in a drawer or possibly some mounted specimens of butterflies.

5. Jocelyn has a drink (a libation) and the text of an opera (libretto) in front of her. So maybe it's intermission at an opera performance. Or maybe she's having a drink while listening to an opera at home.

6. a. It's a rare taste that would like a woman who's not only frenzied but also coarse and abusive.

   b. Similarly, few people seek out an overweight lecher.

7. Here we have some kind of person in a subordinate position to a powerful person (henchman) looking at his daily (diurnal) tasks. You can write the script of what kinds of things his boss asks him to do on a daily basis.

8. Obviously, Van's parents like for him to have a neat and orderly appearance (not disheveled) at dinner, and Van is respectful enough to follow their wishes.

9. A harangue is a speech characterized by strong emotion, often anger or annoyance. Depending on you and your relationship with your sibling, you might get angry that you have to listen to this or you might feel sympathetic (if you haven't heard it too often before).

10. Since a docent is a speaker or tour guide in an institution such as a museum and a panegyric is a speech of enormous praise, we can assume this person is raving with delight about the current exhibit.

POSTSCRIPT KEY

Set #1

1. A herpetologist is an expert on reptiles and amphibians and a laconic person speaks in few words, so a laconic herpetologist might say, "Snakes are interesting" or "I like snakes"—something very brief.

2. Ribaldry refers to humor that is at least mildly sexual in its nature. If you're offended by this kind of joking, your answer would be "no," but if you usually laugh at it, then you do find it risible because that word means "worth laughing at."

3. A pedagogue is a teacher, a divan is a sort of sofa, and an ottoman is a footstool. So we picture this person slouched on the couch with his feet on a footstool...maybe grading papers or preparing a lesson?

4. "Aping" refers to imitating and "eminent" means famous, so if you're aping Eminem, you're trying to be a hip-hop artist; if you're aping Jimmy Carter, you're volunteering for Habitat for Humanity. Et cetera.

5. If you're vituperating someone, you're harshly rebuking them. A "venial" offense is a small, easily forgivable one. So your answer would vary, depending on how you get along with your relatives, whether they easily forgive you, and the like.

6. Mr. Hatcher has exacting, maybe even "picky," standards because "captious" means "pointing out even trivial faults." But since his tone is never bitterly hostile ("virulent"), maybe his students don't mind.

7. A no-brainer here. Macbeth is the only one of these three that is completely accepted by those who set the standards for literature.

8. Since a munificent person is a very generous one, he or she is not likely to become a pariah, an outcast.

9. If he lives up to his family motto (and he does), he doesn't let people challenge him without being punished, so he would do something to get revenge on the person who harmed him. (In the case of this story "The Cask of Amontillado," he walls the offender up into a niche in the basement.)

10. Here you're looking for a tale with a main character on the verge of adolescence. Holden Caulfield of *The Catcher in the Rye* is just a little too old, and Scout in *To Kill a Mockingbird* is just a little too young, but you get the idea.

Set #2

1. Wonder Woman is the only candidate because a virago, by definition, is female.

2. Maybe you'd try to lure it into a cage or maybe you'd scream to frighten it or maybe you'd call animal control: you know best how you'd respond to a wolf as an unwanted visitor in the yard.

3. Most people would pick an autodidact (one who has done much of his or her learning without formal teaching) over a demagogue (one who seeks power through manipulation of the people), but you may have your own reasons for making the opposite choice.

4. A voracious person is really really hungry, so the social error (gaffe) he or she might make would probably have to do with food—maybe grabbing a sandwich out of someone else's hand or trying to talk while gobbling away.

5. Unless you have a special reason for preferring a loud, commanding tone of voice to a pleasing one, you're likely to pick "sonorous."

6. Your nemesis is your perpetual enemy. You might be obsequious (exaggerated in your agreement to follow that person's wishes) only if he or she had you cornered. But maybe not even then!

7. A caryatid is a stone statue (the figure of a maiden as a column), so she's unlikely to have any warm, romantic feelings.

8. If it's palatable, you can eat it; if it's potable, you can drink it, so you're probably at the dinner table.

9. Jenny's grandmother really believes in following accepted social standards, so she might get upset when Jenny sends a thank-you note by email rather than on "proper" stationery.

10. I wouldn't consider it a good sign for the future ("propitious") if my neighbors were raucous (noisy) on their first night in my neighborhood.

Set #3

1. Savoir faire is definitely what you need here; you need some suave way to control your cranky sibling, and physical force or frenzied boldness probably aren't going to do the trick.

2. For us, a half an hour of lively back-and-forth conversation (repartee) sounds infinitely preferable to half an hour of anxiety.

3. Pathos, hands down. It refers to the quality of evoking feeling in a reader whereas bathos suggests triteness or sentimentality.

4. Red, you'll need red. "Carnage" is slaughter, bloodshed.

5. A "diaspora" is a scattering, so your family reunion will need lots of organization to locate and contact relatives in many states.

6. We think everyone would prefer a timely benefit (boon) to an unmannerly oaf (boor), no?

7. This one is a tougher call. A slatternly person is dirty and untidy, and a smarmy person is hypocritical, maybe possessing phony charm. Unless you're desperate to be flattered, hope that the messy person is a great conversationalist.

8. A sobriquet is a nickname, so you know if you have one and if you see it as affectionate and chummy or, as in some cases, rude and insulting.

9. "Inscrutable" means "hard to figure out," not a highly desirable quality in a friend, unless you enjoy the complexity and challenge of it.

10. Mr. Vesser is an expert in coins (numismatist) and since he's itinerant, he's on the road a lot. Perhaps he visits coin shops and museums.

Set #4

1. An epicurean cares a lot about food and drink, so he or she might be sedulous (attentive, hard-working) about tracking down some special ingredients or preparing a dish a certain way.

2. Only you know what you did yesterday, but an honorarium is a sum of money, so you probably wouldn't consider me tacky and inappropriate if I offered it to you.

3. You have just described a time when you felt besieged, surrounded, by problems, possibly by overwork.

4. Your dream featured a sad, grieving "double" of yourself.

5. A diaphanous garment is a flimsy, lightweight one, so "summer" would be the most obvious answer.

6. Telling a joke might leaven ("lighten") a tense atmosphere while insulting one of your acquaintances (or doing something similar) would exacerbate it—make it worse.

7. An iconoclast, by definition, needs daring (audacity), since he or she likes to smash things held dear by society. Some iconoclasts may also be meticulous (tending carefully to small details), and some not.

8. If you're named "Will," you could easily be "Willie," and if you're "Rose," you can easily be "Rosie" or "Rosetta." But "Clark" and "Gretchen" may be less likely to have an affectionate (or contemptuous) alternative form of their names.

9. If you're skittish, you're nervous, eager to get away from the stimulus that makes you feel that way. It might be a certain type of family gathering, a challenging situation behind the steering wheel, or many other kinds of things.

10. Bovine creatures are cows and relatives such as oxen and buffalo. If you live on a dairy farm, they're central to your life. For others who drink milk, eat ice cream, wear leather shoes, they're certainly tangential—touching your existence in an indirect way. Only the lactose intolerant who always choose synthetics for shoes and belts could call them of absolutely no value (nugatory) in their lives.

ABOUT THE AUTHORS

Edward B. Fiske served for seventeen years as education editor of the *New York Times*, where he realized that college-bound students and their families needed better information on which to base their educational choices. He is also the author of *The Fiske Guide to Colleges*.

Jane Mallison has more than twenty years of experience teaching English and has been a member of the College Board SAT committee.

Margery Mandell has an MA in English from Columbia and is the coauthor of *Million Dollar Words*.

NOTES

OFF TO COLLEGE WITH THE COMPLETE LINE OF FISKE BOOKS!

Get the Fiske college-prep advantage
for all four years of high school!

Visit collegecountdown.com to purchase and for
access to more essential college planning resources.

Completely updated every year

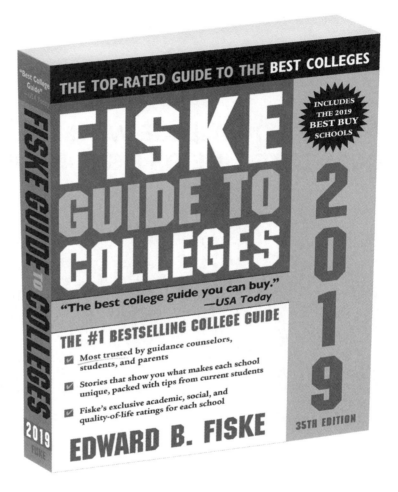

FISKE GUIDE TO COLLEGES 2019
978-1-4926-6209-9 • $24.99

The bestselling and most trusted college guide used by students, parents, and counselors across the country! The guide includes an in-depth look at more than 300 colleges and universities in the United States and abroad. It rates each school on a scale of 1 to 5 on academics, social life, and quality of life. It also describes campus culture, lists each school's best programs, and provides average SAT and ACT scores. *Fiske Guide to Colleges* is unequaled at capturing the true essence of each school while providing all the necessary statistics.

Understand the admission process and where you fit in best

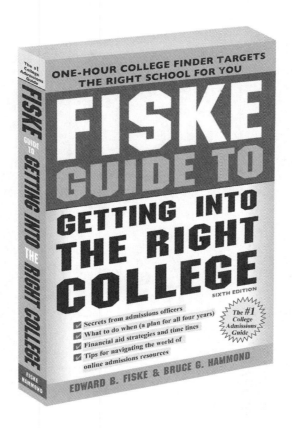

FISKE GUIDE TO GETTING INTO THE RIGHT COLLEGE
978-1-4926-3330-3 • $16.99

Fiske Guide to Getting Into the Right College takes students and parents step-by-step through the college admission process, including selecting your top choices, interviewing, getting letters of recommendation, understanding how admission offices work, and getting the most financial aid you can. The expert advice and tips will help you get accepted at a challenging school that fits your personality and learning style.

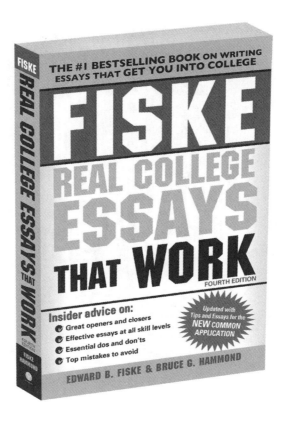

Matriculate with confidence

FISKE 250 WORDS EVERY HIGH SCHOOL GRADUATE NEEDS TO KNOW
978-1-4022-6081-0 • $12.99

Here are the 250 most important words students need to know to be successful in college and beyond, from the former Education Editor of the *New York Times* and a leading authority on college admission. Each entry contains information on the word origin, a complete definition, and example sentences, making it both the perfect gift for high school graduation and an effective tool for expanding students' vocabulary, increasing word comprehension, and honing their writing skills.

Discover the words
you need to succeed

FISKE 250 WORDS EVERY HIGH SCHOOL FRESHMAN NEEDS TO KNOW
978-1-4022-6078-0 • $12.99

Starting off with a powerful vocabulary is the best way to prepare for a successful, stress-free time in high school. *Fiske 250 Words Every High School Freshman Needs to Know* will give you the tools to sharpen your writing skills and use language evocatively. Nail your English essays, the SAT and ACT writing tests, and all of your college and scholarship applications.